Two week loan

Please return on or before the last date stamped below.
Charges are made for late return.

−8 NOV 1996		
CANCELLED		
10 DEC 1996 CANCELLED		
14 MAR 1997		
CANCELLED		
−9 DEC 1999		
CANCELLED		
CANCELLED		

An Introduction
to Political Sociology

This introduction to an increasingly important
area of the study of politics will find a wide
readership among undergraduate students of
politics and of sociology in colleges and
universities. The authors have assumed no
previous knowledge of either politics or
sociology, and the terms used in the book are
all defined in easily understandable terms

An Introduction
to Political Sociology

MICHAEL RUSH and PHILIP ALTHOFF

NELSON

THOMAS NELSON AND SONS LTD
36 Park Street London WIY 4DE
PO Box 18123 Nairobi Kenya
Thomas Nelson (Australia) Ltd
597 Little Collins Street Melbourne 3000
Thomas Nelson and Sons (Canada) Ltd
81 Curlew Drive Don Mills Ontario
Thomas Nelson (Nigeria) Ltd
PO Box 336 Apapa Lagos
Thomas Nelson and Sons (South Africa) (Proprietary) Ltd
51 Commissioner Street Johannesburg

© Michael Rush and Phillip Althoff 1971
Diagrams © Thomas Nelson and Sons Ltd 1971
First published in Nelson's Political Science Series
and in Nelson's University Paperbacks 1971
ISBN (hardback) 0 17 138035 5
ISBN (paperback) 0 17 170005 8

Printed in Great Britain by
Western Printing Services Ltd, Bristol

To Jean and Barbara

Acknowledgments

The authors gratefully acknowledge the permission of the undermentioned to reprint material as indicated in the text:

The American Academy of Political and Social Science, Philadelphia, Pennsylvania for material from *The Annals*; the American Institute of Public Opinion, Princeton, New Jersey; the American Political Science Association and Professor V. Subramaniam for material from the *American Political Science Review*; Attwood Statistics (Nederland) N.V., Rotterdam; the Editors of the *British Journal of Sociology* and Dr Mark Abrams; Doubleday & Co Inc, New York, Heinemann Educational Books Ltd, London and Professor Seymour M. Lipset for material from *Political Man*, New York, 1959 and London, 1960; the DOXA Istituto per le Ricerche Statische e l'Analisi dell'Opinione Pubblica, Milan; the European Co-ordination Centre for Research and Documentation in Social Sciences, Vienna for material from a comparative three-nation study on 'Images of a Disarmed World', 1964–5; Eyre & Spottiswoode Ltd, London and Essential Books Inc, Fair Lawn, New Jersey for material from J. F. S. Ross, *Elections and Electors*, London, 1955; Gallup, London and Gallup International; Granada Publishing Ltd (MacGibbon & Kee Ltd), London for material from W. L. Guttsman, *The British Political Elite*, London, 1963; the Controller of Her Majesty's Stationery Office and Dr A. H. Halsey and Mr I. M. Crewe for material from *The Civil Service (Fulton Report)*, Vol. 3 (I), Cmnd. 3683, 1968; the Indian Institute of Public Opinion Private Ltd, New Delhi; Institut Français d'Opinion Publique, Paris; Institut für angewandte Sozialwissenschaft, Bonn–Bad Godesberg; Institut für Demoskopie Allensbach GmbH, Allensbach am Bodensee; Instituto de la Opinión Pública, Madrid; the Journal Press, Provincetown, Mass. and Dr Holger Iisager for material from the *Journal of Social Psychology*; Little, Brown & Company Inc, Boston, Mass., Faber & Faber Ltd, London and Professor Richard Rose for material from *Politics in England*, Boston, 1964 and London, 1965; Little, Brown & Company Inc, Boston, Mass. for material from Richard R. Fagen, *Politics and Communication*, Boston, 1966; McGraw-Hill Book Co, New York and Professor David Easton and Professor Jack Dennis for material from *Children in the Political System*, New York, 1969; Professor Dwaine Marvick of the University of California, Los Angeles; METRA DIVO Beratungen GmbH, Frankfurt am Main; the *Minneapolis Tribune* for material from the Minnesota Poll; National Opinion Polls Ltd, London; Professor Marvin E. Olsen of the University of Chicago; Mr Roger Pethybridge of the University College of Swansea; Princeton University Press, Princeton, New Jersey, Professor Gabriel A. Almond and Professor Sidney Verba for material from *The Civic Culture*, Princeton, New Jersey, 1963 (Little, Brown edition, Boston, 1965); Princeton University Press and Professor Gabriel A. Almond and Professor James S. Coleman for material from *The Politics of the Developing Areas*, Princeton, New Jersey, 1960; the Editor of the *Public Opinion Quarterly*; the Public Opinion Survey Unit, University of Missouri, Columbia, Missouri; Random House Inc and Professor Donald R. Matthews for material from *The Social Background of Political Decision-Makers*, New York, 1954; the Society for the Psychological Study of Social Issues and Professor Alex Inkeles for material from the *Journal of Social Issues*; UNESCO and Professor Robert D. Hess for material from the *International Social Science Journal*; and Yale University Press and Professor Bruce M. Russett, Professor Hayward R. Alker Jr, Professor Karl W. Deutsch and Professor Harold D. Lasswell for material from the *World Handbook of Political and Social Indicators*, New Haven, Conn., 1964.

Contents

List of Abbreviations

AIOP	American Institute of Public Opinion, Princeton, New Jersey
ALP	Australian Labour Party
APOP	Australian Public Opinion Polls
ATTS	Attwood Statistics (Netherlands)
CAL	California Poll, San Francisco
CHP	Republican People's Party (Turkey)
CPSU	Communist Party of the Soviet Union
DIVO	METRA DIVO Beratungen GmbH, Frankfurt am Main
DMS	Institut für Demoskopie Allensbach GmbH, Allensbach am Bodensee
DOXA	DOXA Istituto per le Ricerche Statische e l'Analisi dell'Opinione Pubblica, Milan
EGA	Encuestas Gallup de la Argentina
EMNID	EMNID Institut, Bielefeld
ENA	École Nationale d'Administration
GMA	Gallup Markedanalyse, Denmark
IFOP	Institut Français d'Opinion Publique
IIPO	Indian Institute of Public Opinion
INFAS	Institut für angewandte Sozialwissenschaft, Bonn–Bad Godesberg
IOP	Instituto de la Opinión Pública, Madrid
MINN	Minnesota Poll of the *Minneapolis Tribune*
NDP	New Democratic Party (Canada)
NIP	National Institute of Psychology, Teheran
NOP	National Opinion Polls, Great Britain
POSU	Public Opinion Survey Unit, University of Missouri
PRIO	International Peace Research Institute, Oslo
SOC	Gallop (Social Surveys), Great Britain
VC	European Co-ordination Centre for Research and Documentation in Social Sciences, Vienna

Note: the opinion poll designations are those used in the periodical *Polls*.

Preface

This book was originally conceived when we were both teaching at the University of Western Ontario in 1967–8. It was during this time that the conceptual framework which forms the basis of the book was evolved, and the preliminary work of gathering the material begun. Since then a complex – and we hope fruitful – trans-Atlantic collaboration has continued, resulting in the present volume.

We have attempted to draw together into this one volume the many strands of social and political behaviour which constitute political sociology and to offer a unified concept of its many facets. In so doing we have sought to contribute to the increasing attention being paid to political sociology and to demonstrate its crucial importance in the study of politics.

We would like to express our grateful thanks to our colleagues who helped and encouraged us at various stages in the writing of this book, and to Mrs Susan Ridler, who typed the final manuscript under considerable pressure of time. A special debt is due to Dr K. W. Watkins, the editor of the series in which this book appears, without whose continuing encouragement, unlimited patience and unfailing advice this book would not have been written. A similar but much deeper debt, however, is due to our respective wives, to whom this book is dedicated.

Finally, we gratefully acknowledge permission to make use of already-published material. Although this book draws on material from many sources, we, of course, remain responsible for its contents.

M.D.R.
Department of Politics
University of Exeter

P.A.
Department of Political Science
Kansas State University
Manhattan

1 · Introductory

The term 'sociology' was coined by Auguste Comte (1798–1857), one of the founding fathers of the discipline. Simply defined, the term means the study of society, but in practice it is the study of society from a particular point of view. Both Comte and Herbert Spencer (1820–1903), another of the founding fathers, stressed that the *society* was the basic unit of sociological analysis, the various social institutions (such as the family and political, economic and religious institutions) and the interrelationship between these institutions being the sub-units of analysis. Thus, in endeavouring to emphasize this societal context, modern sociologists have variously defined sociology as, 'the science that deals with social groups',[1] and 'the study of human interactions and interrelations'.[2] The focus of sociology is therefore upon human behaviour, but it is concentrated on neither individual nor collective behaviour as such – these may be regarded as the province of psychiatry and psychology. What sociology is concerned with is human behaviour – both individual and collective, but more often collective – and its relation to society; sociology is therefore the study of human behaviour within a societal context.

Political science is less easy to define, however. Whereas sociology is concerned with human behaviour from the point of view of society and is in this respect all-embracing, politics is clearly concerned only with certain aspects of society. Thus, as W. G. Runciman has argued, 'such separate disciplines as economics, or demography, or criminology, or politics should be regarded as

[1] Harry M. Johnson, *Sociology: A Systematic Introduction*, London, 1961, p. 2.
[2] Morris Ginsburg, *Sociology*, London, 1934, p. 7.

co-ordinate but distinctive branches of sociology (or social science)'.[1] It is not difficult to suggest those aspects of society which are of central concern to the study of politics: particular social institutions, such as legislatures and executives, political parties and interest groups, immediately spring to mind, as do particular areas of human behaviour, such as the electoral or legislative processes; but it is more difficult to delimit the boundaries of political science and hence to define it. In an effort to circumvent this problem most definitions have sought to delineate the essence of politics. Thus we are told that the central concern of politics is the resolution of human conflict, or the process by which society makes decisions or evolves policies, or authoritatively allocates resources and values, or that it is the exercise of power and influence in society. Whether any of these is the essence of politics is a matter of opinion, but few would dispute that each of these concepts is of great concern to the political scientist.

It is in many respects helpful to regard power as the focal point of political studies, but, just as we have defined sociology as the study of human behaviour within a societal context, so it is important to stress that we are looking at power within the same societal context. This still avoids the question of a definition, however, and all these attempts to suggest the essence of politics point to a particular area of study – the means by which man solves his problems with his fellow-men. Looked at this way, political science involves the study of the problems themselves, of the machinery that may be evolved to deal with them, of the factors which influence men in their solution, and, by no means least, of the ideas which influence men in dealing with them.

In this sense, 'political science is a subject matter, not an autonomous discipline. . . . The subject is defined by a problem.' For the author of these words, Bernard Crick, that problem is government, which is 'the activity of maintaining order'.[2] Here, of course order means the regulation of relations between men in the very widest sense and not simply that suggested in the phrase law and order. Political science is not synonymous with the study of

[1] W. G. Runciman, *Social Science and Political Theory*, London, 1965, p. 1. See also W. J. M. Mackenzie, *Politics and Social Science*, London, 1967.

[2] Bernard Crick, 'The Tendency of Political Studies', *New Society*, 3 November 1966, p. 683. See also his *In Defence of Politics*, London, 1962.

government, but it encompasses it in that it examines, in Crick's phrase, 'the function of government in society'.

Whatever the rationale for regarding political science as an integral part of sociology, it has, academically, developed as a separate discipline. This was probably inevitable, given its original links with historical and legal studies and the efforts of many early sociologists to link their subject with the natural sciences. This is true of each of the social sciences: each has different origins and development, often accidental in nature, so that the practitioners of each 'subject' have come to regard them as separate disciplines and tended to ignore related 'subjects':

> Whatever is a 'problem' for one discipline becomes a 'given', an external factor, for the neighbouring discipline. For instance, economists assume political structures to be given. Likewise, sociologists assume economic structures to be given. In a similar vein, political scientists assume social structures to be given. Each discipline throws light on a set of variables precisely because other factors are assumed to be external, distal and equal.[1]

At the same time, political scientists have long recognized the importance of sociology to the study of politics, and the theories of men like Marx, Weber, Mosca, Pareto and Michels have had a profound effect on political studies. It has been recognized that no political system, no political institution, no politician works in a vacuum, and sociological studies have provided valuable insights into the societal environment within which politics function. This has become increasingly apparent as more attention has been paid by political scientists to comparative studies in general and developing societies in particular. In this process there has developed a considerable body of work which may legitimately be regarded as the realm of *political sociology* – the examination of the links between politics and society, between social structures and political structures, and between social behaviour and political behaviour.

THE ORIGINS AND DEVELOPMENT OF POLITICAL SOCIOLOGY

The origins of a discipline, subject or area of study are often obscure, and to suggest particular individuals as 'the founding fathers' of a particular body of knowledge is a perilous process.

[1] G. Sartori, 'From the Sociology of Politics to Political Sociology', *Government and Opposition*, 4, 1969, p. 196.

Thus some of our readers may object either to our citing of Comte and Spencer as founding fathers of sociology or to the omission of Marx or Durkheim or Weber. Nevertheless, certain figures stand out as individuals whose contributions have been of fundamental importance. In the case of political sociology two such figures stand out: Karl Marx (1818–83) and Max Weber (1864–1920).

Marx's contribution was both massive and varied, and not, of course, limited to political sociology. His contribution falls into three areas: general theory, specific theory and methodology. Following Hegel, Marx developed a theory of historical inevitability based on the dialectic of thesis, antithesis and synthesis, but unlike Hegel he based his theory on the material conflict of opposing economic forces, resulting in the ultimate overthrowal of capitalism and the creation of a classless society. Marx's interpretation of history was based on the twin pillars of economic and sociological theory. He developed David Hume's labour-value theory into the theories of surplus value and the exploitation of labour, and these formed the basis of his major sociological theory, the class struggle. He also developed a theory of alienation which argued that the working class or proletariat became increasingly alienated from the rest of society as their work became a means of avoiding starvation rather than a means of self-expression. Closely involved with the theories of the class struggle and alienation is the concept of class consciousness – the recognition by individuals in society that they belong to economically based groups – which formed an essential prerequisite of class conflict.

Many criticisms have been levelled at Marx's theories, some based on their general validity, others on their predictive value. For example, although he did not ignore the importance of ideas as sociological factors, Marx regarded them as dependent rather than independent variables, thus subordinating them to his economic interpretation of history. The role of Marxism as an *ideology* in many parts of the world would suggest that Marx over-emphasized the economic subordination of ideas. Similarly, the failure of a number of his predictions and his failure to anticipate the adaptive capacity of capitalism, have cast doubt on his theories. These criticisms, however, do little to diminish his contribution to political sociology. Both his general theories of economic determinism and dialectical materialism and his specific theories of the class struggle, class consciousness and alienation have stimulated an enormous amount of work, some of it seeking to support Marx's ideas, some of it seeking to disprove them. The result has been a vast contribution to knowledge, which has in turn often stimulated yet further work.

Quite apart from this, however, Marx made a further vital contribution in the field of methodology. His development of 'scientific socialism' laid down standards of scholarship and methods which were an example to subsequent social scientists. Marx endeavoured to give his theories a firm basis in fact by amassing a vast amount of evidence which he sought to examine in a systematic and rigorous fashion. How successful he was in this remains a matter of dispute, but the very fact that he claimed this for his theories meant that both his followers and critics had to make similar endeavours.

Perhaps inevitably, the second founding father of political sociology, Max Weber, was one of Marx's leading critics. Weber's contribution consisted not only of a major critique of Marx, but of a considerable number of specific studies and concepts of importance to political sociology. In his work *The Protestant Ethic and the Spirit of Capitalism*,[1] and in his studies of India, China and the Jewish people, Weber sought to demonstrate that non-economic factors, especially ideas, were important sociological factors. Moreover, in examining social stratification in various societies he argued that social strata could be based not only on an individual's 'class' or economic position in society, as Marx asserted, but also upon his status or social position in society, or upon an individual's position in the societal power structure. These could, Weber acknowledged, be overlapping, but not necessarily identical.

Weber also contributed several important conceptual and methodological ideas to political sociology. 'Politics', Weber declared, '. . . means striving to share power or striving to influence the distribution of power, either among states or among groups within a state', the state being defined as, ' a human community that (successfully) claims the *monopoly of the legitimate use of physical force* within a given territory.'[2]

---

[1] Originally published in 1904–5, English translation, London, 1930.
[2] Max Weber, 'Politics as a Vocation', in *From Max Weber: Essays in Sociology*, translated and edited by H. H. Gerth and C. Wright Mills, London, 1948, p. 78. (Original italics.)

Weber was thus very much concerned with the exercise of power and with the justification or legitimacy of its exercise. Weber's concept of *legitimacy* – the grounds on which the exercise of power is accepted – was one of his most important contributions to political sociology. There were, Weber believed, three major types of legitimacy:

> First, the authority of the 'eternal yesterday', i.e. of the mores sanctified through the unimaginably ancient recognition and habitual orientation to conform. This is 'traditional' domination. . . .
>
> Second, there is the authority of the extraordinary and personal *gift of grace* (charisma), the absolutely personal devotion and personal confidence in revelation, heroism, or other qualities of individual leadership. This is 'charismatic' domination. . . .
>
> Finally, there is domination by virtue of 'legality', by virtue of the belief in the validity of legal statute and functional 'competence' based on rationally created *rules*.[1]

These three types of legitimacy are an example of another of Weber's important contributions. Traditional, charismatic and legal domination were 'pure' or *ideal types* and were not therefore mutually exclusive. Weber's concept of the ideal type is simply the construction of historically observable facts into a model or bench mark against which other, similar phenomena could be measured. In using the term 'ideal' he is not passing any judgement on the models he constructed, merely plotting points on a sociological graph. The construction of ideal types has been and remains a fruitful tool in the hands of the political sociologist.

Weber's other major methodological legacy was the concept of sympathetic (or subjective) understanding, or *Verstehen*, as applied to sociology. Weber felt that human behaviour could be better understood if account were taken of the motives and intentions of those directly involved in that behaviour. It was natural that Weber should stress such a concept, given the importance he attributed to the force of ideas as sociological factors. None the less, it has led to criticism of Weber's work on the grounds that, regardless of his claims that it was value-free, the examination of men's motives involved an interpretive element which could not be ultimately objective. Inevitably, Weber's work has been criticized on other grounds, such as historical accuracy, but his work and ideas have, like those of Marx, proved a stimulus to subsequent generations of sociologists and political scientists.

[1] ibid., pp. 78–9. (Original italics.)

Although Marx and Weber may properly be regarded as the founding fathers of political sociology, there are, of course, others whose contribution, whilst less fundamental and stimulating, remains nevertheless important. Furthermore, a brief examination of some of these contributors illustrates the development of political sociology. The work of Alexis de Tocqueville (1805–59) is a case in point. In his *L'Ancien Régime et la Révolution* (1856) he argued that the Revolution of 1789 did not mark a complete break with the past and that some measure of continuity was inevitable, thus anticipating many later ideas on the process and nature of social change. One of Marx's contemporaries, Walter Bagehot (1826–77), editor of *The Economist* from 1860 to 1877 and an influential observer of the political scene during this period, also deserves mention. Bagehot examined the links between culture and personality, and between political institutions and behaviour. He argued that it was possible to delineate a national character for various countries, expounding this theme to great effect in *The English Constitution* (1867), in which he asserted that English political institutions were derived from the deferential nature of the English people. Bagehot also distinguished between constitutional theory and practice, speaking of the 'dignified' and the 'efficient' parts of the constitution, and this book remains a classic contemporary account of and commentary upon Cabinet and parliamentary government. Bagehot's other major work in the field of political sociology was *Physics and Politics* (1872), in which he applied the concept of evolution to the origins and development of societies, placing particular emphasis on the part played in this process by imitation.

It was the process of imitation as a social phenomenon that characterized the work of a French sociologist, Gabriel Tarde (1843–1904), who may also claim to have contributed to the development of political sociology. Not only did Tarde in general claim that the political system of any society was inextricably linked with the social structures of that society, but he also stressed the importance of two other areas which have become of prime concern to political sociologists. Tarde examined and stressed the social impact of modern communications in the form of the telegraph, telephone, and mass-produced books and newspapers, and sought to formulate links between the mass media and the individual. In so doing he anticipated such theories as the role of the individual 'opinion leader' and the 'two-step flow of communication'. In addition to this, Tarde emphasized the role of élites, particularly as means of diffusing ideas through society, pointing the way not only to the major counter-attack against Marxism but to the next major development in political sociology.

The élite theorists, Vilfredo Pareto (1848–1923) in *The Mind and Society*[1] and Gaetano Mosca (1858–1941) in *The Ruling Class*,[2] sought to refute Marxism by acknowledging the existence of a ruling class or élite, but arguing that this élite did not necessarily owe its position to economic supremacy and that political and social change came about by a circulation of élites which was not necessarily attributable to economic factors. We shall be examining their ideas in Chapter 4, but it should be noted that the concept of the élite has been of major importance to political sociology, not only in stimulating such later élite theorists as James Burnham and C. Wright Mills, but in concentrating the attention of sociologists and political scientists upon such phenomena as political parties and interest groups.

Two of the earliest contributors to the study of political parties were M. Ostrogorski (1854–1919) and Roberto Michels (1876–1936), the former in *Democracy and the Organization of Political Parties*[3] and the latter in *Political Parties: A Sociological Study of the Oligarchical Tendencies of Modern Democracy*.[4] Both authors examined the organizational development of political parties and came to similar conclusions: that such organizations were inevitably dominated by small groups of activists and that popular control was both a sham and an impossibility – for Ostrogorski party politics was inevitably 'caucus politics', for Michels all political organizations were subject to an 'iron law of oligarchy'.

As increasing attention was paid to the organization of political parties, so other observers began to look at the sources of their electoral support. In the United States, for example, Stuart Rice

[1] Originally published in 1916 and translated into English as *The Mind and Society*, London, 1935.

[2] Originally published in 1896, revised in 1923, and translated into English as *The Ruling Class*, London, 1939.

[3] London, 1902.

[4] Originally published in 1911, English translation 1915. See also his *First Lectures in Political Sociology*, translated by Alfred de Grazia, Minneapolis, 1949.

in his *Quantitative Methods in Politics*[1] published a study of the voting behaviour of a sample of respondents over a period of time (this was the first known panel study), a trend analysis of electoral statistics and the results of ecological research he had conducted. Another example is the work of Rudolf Herbele on the sources of Nazi support prior to their accession to power in 1933.[2]

At the same time trends in social science generally led some political scientists to examine the role of personality in politics. The most prominent of these was Harold Lasswell, whose *Psychopathology and Politics* and *Politics: Who Gets What, When and How?*[3] are classics of the period. This concentration on the individual as the unit of analysis produced an inevitable reaction in the form of increasing attention being paid to the links between culture and politics, and between economic development and political systems. Important examples of work in these fields are *The Civic Culture*[4] by Gabriel Almond and Sidney Verba, *Politics in the Developing Areas*,[5] edited by Gabriel Almond and James Coleman, and Seymour Martin Lipset's *Political Man* and *The First New Nation*.[6]

The circle has almost taken a full turn: the earliest work in political sociology was concerned with explaining the totality of political behaviour within a societal context – with what we now call macro-research; this was followed by criticism of this work and concentration of the details of political behaviour within their context – a concern with micro-research; finally, there have now been attempts to link the results of these efforts together. Whether these efforts have been successful or are likely to be in the future is, as we suggest in our final chapter, a matter of opinion, but this is in no way a criticism of those who make the effort.

APPROACHES AND METHODS

It should already be apparent from our discussion of those who have contributed to our knowledge of political sociology that a number of approaches and methods are appropriate to its study.

[1] New York, 1928.

[2] Rudolf Herbele, *From Democracy to Nazism: A Regional Case-Study on Political Parties in Germany*, Baton Rouge, Louisiana, 1945.

[3] Chicago, 1930, and New York, 1936, respectively.

[4] Princeton, N.J., 1963.   [5] Princeton, N.J., 1960.

[6] Garden City, New York, 1960, and London, 1963, respectively.

But, as Sartori has pointed out, approaches and 'research methods are largely decided by the kind of evidence which is available for the units and the kind of problems with which one deals.'[1]

In using the term 'approach' we mean a particular orientation or point of view. For instance, one such orientation is the historical approach, which, as we have already seen, was of particular importance to both Marx and Weber. Quite apart from this, however, such an approach provided a necessary perspective to such studies, both in a temporal and a contextual sense.

Another approach involves the use of comparative data by which studies of political phenomena in one society are used to throw light on similar or contrasting phenomena in another. This approach was used, for example, by both Ostrogorski and Michels in their studies of political parties, and in the environmental studies of Almond and his colleagues and Lipset, cited above.

The value of these two approaches is not normally questioned, but other orientations are subject to criticism. The traditional institutional approach, for instance, has long been cited as inadequate and unrealistic because it ignores the realities of political behaviour by concentrating on legalistic and constitutional factors. This is, however, to overstate the case: political behaviour takes place within an institutional framework and neither the behaviour nor the institutions can be adequately explained without an understanding of both. This is implicit in most studies of political parties and legislative behaviour.

In contrast to the institutional approach, the behavioural approach endeavours to avoid what are regarded as the faults of other approaches. It is characterized by stressing the individual as the basic unit of analysis, and the need to separate facts from values and to make verifiable generalizations. Behaviouralism has undoubtedly led to considerably greater rigour in social and political analysis by laying down high standards, but it has also been criticized for neglecting the advantages of other approaches. In practice, like the other approaches we have mentioned, behaviouralism is best seen as one of several possible orientations, all of which may be fruitful according to the nature of the problems being studied.

This particular observation is even more applicable to the methods used in the study of political sociology. Obviously con-

[1] Sartori, 'From the Sociology of Politics to Political Sociology', p. 198.

siderable reliance is placed upon quantitative methods, including the use of statistical surveys and aggregative data, such as that used in studies of political ecology. Much of the work based on these methods involves the use of sophisticated statistical techniques, in particular correlation and significance tests. It is important to appreciate, however, that statistical evidence based on such tests, however positive, is an indication of some relationship which may or may not be casual. What such evidence does do is to provide a basis for further work as well as an indication, often a very strong indication, of what are likely to be the key variables in a particular problem.

In addition to gathering quantitative material, the political sociologist also relies upon gaining considerable insight through the use of intensive interview surveys (including the use of panel studies involving the periodic interviewing of the same respondents), of case-studies, and of direct or indirect participation in the political process. The use of interviews is of particular importance in investigating the motives of those involved in the political process and as a means of testing theory against practice. Similarly, case-studies allow resources to be used intensively, whilst participation in the political process, either directly as an 'actor' or indirectly as an observer, has often been an effective method.

Finally, considerable use is made of theories and models both to provide guidelines for research and to offer explanations of the phenomena studied. A theory may be defined as 'a heuristic device for organizing what we know, or think we know, at any particular time about some more or less explicitly posed question or issue'; and a model as, 'a rather general image of the main outline of some major phenomenon, including certain leading ideas about the nature of the units involved and the pattern of their relations.'[1]

One of the major types of theory of interest to the political sociologist is that known as systems theory, which argues that all social phenomena are part of discernible, regular and internally consistent patterns of behaviour. We may therefore speak of, say, a social system and a number of interdependent sub-systems, such as those concerning economics or politics. Each of these sub-systems may be further subdivided, so that it is common when dealing with particular sub-systems to speak of the economic system or the political system and so on. One of the leading

[1] Alex Inkeles, *What is Sociology?*, Englewood Cliffs, N.J., 1964, p. 28.

proponents of systems theory is Talcott Parsons, whose book *The Social System*[1] and other work has been the basis of much academic controversy and stimulus. Parsons and a number of other sociologists, notably Marion Levy and Robert Merton, have become identified with what is known as the functional approach to systems theory. The term function is defined as 'the objective consequence of a pattern of action for the system'.[2] Functionalism depends ultimately on the Parsonian view that a system seeks to achieve particular goals and that all behaviour and phenomena are related to this end. This has led to the development of structural-functionalism, which argues that all social behaviour and phenomena (constituted as patterns of action or structures) fulfil (or fail to fulfil) particular functions for the system. There is no doubt that the structural-functional approach has thrown light on areas which have been previously overlooked or neglected and, in particular, has offered significant explanations of phenomena as fulfilling a particular need or function. None the less, as Runciman has pointed out, there has been a tendency to confuse *purpose* with *results* through the use of the term *goal*, while the fundamental precept that a system necessarily has goals in this sense may be questioned. In addition, structural-functionalism has been criticized for being unable to account adequately for systemic change and being ideologically biased in a conservative or static direction. These last two criticisms are, of course, closely connected, and we will be dealing with the problem of societal change in Chapter 2.

In the field of political studies, David Easton's *The Political System, A Framework for Political Analysis* and *A Systems Analysis of Political Life*[3] suggest an alternative to the functional approach. This is known as input-output analysis. Easton is especially concerned with how a political system continues to exist and what causes it to change. He therefore suggests that certain contributions are made to the political system in the form of 'inputs'. These may be *demands* for action or *support* for the system. Following a conversion process, 'outputs' in the form of *authoritative decisions* are produced. There is also a process of reaction to these

[1] Glencoe, Illinois, 1951.
[2] Oran R. Young, *Systems of Political Science*, Englewood Cliffs, N.J., 1968, p. 29.
[3] New York, 1953, Englewood Cliffs, N.J., 1965, and New York, 1965, respectively.

decisions which Easton terms 'feedback'. Easton's theory has been adapted to a structural-functional framework by Gabriel Almond, who has constructed what he terms a developmental approach to politics.[1] Just as Easton and Almond sought to provide theoretical frameworks which would incorporate those areas of study which they felt had been previously neglected, so their critics have complained that they, in turn, have neglected the 'traditional' area of institutions. In fact Almond was seeking to link institutions and processes and his main problems stem from his use of a structural-functional approach.

Most of these theories use models of various sorts to illustrate and clarify the arguments on which they are based. It is our intention to use a number of models which seem appropriate to the concepts which we regard as central to political sociology. In so doing we would stress that these models are intended to help explain these concepts and not act as substitutes for them.

A CONCEPTUAL SCHEME

We have defined political sociology as being a subject area (some would say discipline) which examines the links between politics and society, between social structures and political structures, and between social behaviour and political behaviour. In so doing we regard political sociology as a theoretical and methodological bridge between sociology and political science, or what Sartori has called 'an inter-disciplinary hybrid'.[2]

Our conceptual scheme is based upon four concepts: political socialization, political participation, political recruitment and political communication. These concepts are interdependent and interlocking, and we have defined them as follows:

Political socialization is the process by which an individual becomes acquainted with the political system and which determines his perceptions of politics and his reactions to political phenomena. It involves the examination of the social, economic and cultural environment of society upon the individual and upon his political attitudes and values. Political socialization is the most important

---

[1] See Gabriel Almond and G. Bingham Powell, *Comparative Politics: A Developmental Approach*, Boston, Mass., 1966.

[2] Sartori, 'From the Sociology of Politics to Political Sociology', p. 197.

link between the social and political systems, but may vary considerably from one system to another. From a political point of view, political socialization is extremely important as the process by which individuals may become involved, to varying degrees, in the political system – in political participation.

Political participation is the involvement of the individual at various levels in the political system. Political activity may range from non-involvement to office-holding. Because political participation varies from one society to another, and because it varies within particular societies, it is important to examine the concepts of political apathy and alienation and their role in non-involvement and limited involvement. It is also important to stress that participation may also result in motivation for increased participation, including the highest level – that of holding various types of office – which involves the process of political recruitment.

Political recruitment is the process by which individuals secure or are enlisted in the roles of office-holders. Recruitment is a two-way process and may be formal or informal. It is a two-way process in that individuals may themselves seek the opportunity or may be approached by others to become holders of such positions. Similarly, recruitment may be formal in that individuals may be recruited openly by means of institutional machinery of selection or election, and informal in that individuals may be recruited privately with little or no recourse to such machinery. This also involves some consideration of whether those who hold these offices can be said to constitute a clearly defined political group or élite.

Political communication is the process by which politically relevant information is transmitted from one part of the political system to another, and between the social and political systems. It is a continuous process involving the exchange of information between individuals and groups of individuals at all levels of society, and includes not only the expression of the views and wishes of members of society, but also the means by which the views and proposals of those in power are transmitted to society and the latter's reaction to those views and proposals. Political communication plays a crucial role in the political system: it constitutes its dynamic element and is a vital part of political socialization, participation and recruitment.

We have deliberately concentrated on political processes in formulating our four concepts, but not to the exclusion of political and social institutions: these we regard as an integral part of the processes we describe and as an essential part of any attempt to explain the connection between social and political phenomena, which is the task of political sociology.

2 · Political Socialization

Political socialization was described in Chapter 1 as the process by which an individual becomes acquainted with the political system and which determines his perceptions of politics and his reactions to political phenomena. It is determined by the social, economic and cultural environment of the society in which the individual lives and by the interaction of the experiences and personality of the individual. Political socialization is therefore the key concept of political sociology in several respects. First, the three other concepts of participation, recruitment and communication are inextricably linked with it – participation and recruitment because they are partially dependent variables of socialization and communication because it provides the dynamic element in socialization. Second, political socialization demonstrates the interaction and interdependence of social and political behaviour. And finally, as a necessary corrollary of that interaction and interdependence, it demonstrates the interdependence of the social sciences in general and of sociology and political science in particular.

In a sense, the importance of political socialization has long been recognized, though this has, until fairly recently, been implicit rather than explicit. For example, once some sort of association between the personal characteristics of individuals and voting behaviour had been established through various types of electoral studies, many of the explanations offered implied some form of socialization. In other words the experiences of and values held by, say, a British manual worker are such that he is more likely than a non-manual worker (who will have had different experiences and hold different values) to vote for the Labour party. Until the publication in 1959, however, of Herbert Hyman's *Political Socialization*,[1] political scientists' treatment of the concept had been fragmentary rather than systematic.

This relative neglect on the part of political scientists is in many respects curious, since political philosophers have long stressed the importance of what amounted to political socialization, or at least to particular manifestations of it, while many a politician has been aware of the value of political education. Both Plato and Aristotle placed importance on the training of members of society for various types of political activity; Rousseau recognized the role of education in inculcating values; and the liberal philosophers of the nineteenth century placed great stress on what Robert Lowe described as the need 'to educate our masters'. Similarly, throughout history great use has been made of formal education for political purposes: this is as apparent in the medieval church's monopoly of education as it is in the totalitarian states of the twentieth century.

If political scientists paid little attention to socialization, however, or at least took it for granted, to the anthropologist, the social psychologist and the sociologist it has long been an important concept, and it is from these disciplines that we draw our three initial definitions of socialization:

[1.] ... those patterns of social action, or aspects of action, which inculcate in individuals the skills (including knowledge), motives, and attitudes necessary for the performance of present or anticipated roles ... [and which continue] throughout normal human life, in so far as new roles must be learned;[2]

[2.] ... the whole process by which an individual, born with behavioural potentialities of immense range, is led to develop actual behaviour which is confined within a much narrower range – the range of what is customary and acceptable for him according to the standards of his group;[3]

[3.] ... communication with and learning from other human beings with whom [the individual] gradually enters some sort of generalized relationship.[4]

[1] *Political Socialization: A Study in the Psychology of Political Behaviour*, Glencoe, Ill., 1959.
[2] David F. Aberle, 'Culture and Socialization', in Francis L. K. Hsu (ed.), *Psychological Anthropology: Approaches to Culture and Personality*, Homewood, Ill., 1961, p. 387.
[3] Irvin L. Child, 'Socialization', in G. Lindzey (ed.), *Handbook of Social Psychology*, Cambridge, Mass., 1954, Vol. 2, p. 655.
[4] S. N. Eisenstadt, *From Generation to Generation*, London, 1956, p. 26.

Quite clearly these definitions have a great deal in common, and they effectively introduce several important facets of socialization. First, socialization is fundamentally a process of learning, learning from experience, or what Aberle calls 'patterns of action'. Secondly, a general indication is given of what is learned in that the broad limits of the individual's behaviour are laid down and, more specifically, in terms of knowledge (or information), motives (or values) and attitudes (or opinions). Furthermore, it is stressed that we are concerned not only with the behaviour of the individual but also with the behaviour of the groups to which the individual may belong. Thirdly, socialization is not necessarily confined to childhood and adolescence (even though these may be the most significant periods), but may continue throughout adult life. Finally, it is suggested that socialization is a necessary pre-condition of societal activity, and, both implicitly and explicitly, provides an explanation of social behaviour.

There are, however, two problems associated with these definitions. First, to what extent is socialization a process of systemic perpetuation? This is of considerable importance in examining the relationship between socialization and societal change, or, in functionalist terms, system maintenance. It is important to consider this problem from a functionalist point of view for a moment because one of the major criticisms of functionalism, as we have already seen, has been its alleged inability to account satisfactorily for systemic change, and, while the concept of socialization is not exclusively the prerogative of functionalist theorists, it is none the less an integral part of functional theory. To the functionalist, the process of socialization effectively explains how a system may persist over time: the system, if it is to persist, demands that certain functions must be fulfilled by means of the roles carried out by individuals or groups of individuals, and that the performance of these roles cannot be assumed but need to be learned. In other words, a society perpetuates itself by teaching its new members those values and modes of behaviour which that society regards as appropriate and acceptable. Thus a child may acquire from his parents a number of firmly held beliefs, such as a belief in the freedom of speech, the sanctity of marriage, particular religious beliefs, a belief in the rule of law and so on, and, assuming that these beliefs are widely held in the society concerned, it is reasonable to suggest that it is unlikely that there will be fundamental changes in the attitudes towards free speech, marriage, religion or the rule of law within the forseeable future. This is not, of course, to suggest that change will never occur, but merely to posit circumstances in which change is less rather than more likely. The fault, therefore, of functionalist theory, with its emphasis on system maintenance, is that it offers an explanation of why change does not occur or is minimized without offering an explanation of why change does occur, especially when such change is fundamental.

There is, in fact, no reason at all why a theory of political socialization should not be able to account for both the absence and the existence of systemic and societal change, provided such a theory allows for the inclusion of two important variables and does not confine itself to what is learned, who is taught, who teaches it and what the results are. These two variables are *experience* and *personality* and it will later be argued that both the experience and the personality of an individual (and more particularly of groups of individuals) are fundamental to the process of socialization and to the process of change.

The second problem arising out of these definitions of socialization concerns the extent to which it is an overt or covert process, conscious or unconscious, comprising not only learning but instruction. That instruction may be an important part of socialization cannot be doubted: parents may teach their children certain modes of social behaviour; societal education systems may include a provision for civic education; the state may carefully propagate its official ideology; but it cannot be stressed too much that a great deal of socialization, perhaps the greater part of it, is experiential and as such is largely covert, unconscious, unrecognized and unacknowledged. Thus terms like 'inculcate' and, to a lesser extent, 'led to develop' tend to obscure this important facet of socialization. 'Political education . . . begins', as Michael Oakeshott has pointed out, 'in the enjoyment of a tradition, in the observation and imitation of the behaviour of our elders, and there is little or nothing in the world which comes before our eyes which does not contribute to it. . . . We are aware of a past and a future as soon as we are aware of a present.'[1] Thus, in spite

[1] Michael Oakeshott, 'Political Education', in P. Laslett (ed.), *Philosophy, Politics and Society*, Oxford, 1956, p. 17.

of the fact that socialization may be partially open, systematic and deliberate, it is totally unrealistic to assume that the significance of every experience is recognized by the agent (and, perhaps to a lesser extent, the subject) of the action or actions involved in that experience. Similarly, the contribution of the subject's personality to the experience may go equally unrecognized.

These two problems of systemic persistence or change and the deliberate inculcation of particular beliefs are, as it has been shown, of considerable importance to socialization in general, but they are of crucial importance to *political* socialization since they inevitably involve the question of the persistence or change of particular régimes as well as the deliberate inculcation of particular political beliefs. In short, political socialization becomes involved in the realm of political controversy. It is but a short step in the eyes of some critics from the academic 'neutrality' of system maintenance, equilibrium and stability to the political partisanship of conservatism, preservation of the status quo and reaction. Political socialization ceases to be a concept seeking to explain how particular beliefs and orientations are acquired in *any* political system and becomes associated with explanations of why system A is in various ways superior to system B. Such views, however, result from a tendency to confuse the concept with particular results that may stem from its use. If a study of political socialization in one country shows that through a variety of agents individuals acquire beliefs and orientations which tend to perpetuate the political system of that country, it does not follow that this is necessarily true for all other countries. What it does suggest is that the various socializing agents are working in the same direction and that any countervailing agents are weak; but this does not preclude the existence of *conflicting* agents of socialization which, far from perpetuating a particular political system, may affect radical change.

In formulating a definition of political socialization, therefore, it is important to allow for both systemic persistence and change and for both the deliberate and unplanned learning of political behaviour, and the following two definitions should be seen in this light:

[1.] . . . [the individual's] learning of social patterns corresponding to his societal positions as mediated through various agencies of society.[1]

[1] Hyman, *Political Socialization*, p. 25.

[2.] . . . the process whereby political attitudes and values are inculcated as children become adults and as adults are recruited into roles.[1]

Both these definitions suffer, however, from the problems already mentioned, in that they do not offer a means of accounting for systemic change (concentrating as they do on socialization for existing 'societal positions' and roles to the apparent exclusion of the creation of new ones); nor do they distinguish sufficiently between deliberate and unplanned learning. Fred I. Greenstein, in an article on political socialization in the *International Encyclopedia of the Social Sciences*, has sought to clarify the difference between what he has termed the narrow and broad definitions of political socialization:

> . . . the deliberate inculcation of political information, values and practices by instructional agents who have been formally charged with this responsibility;

and,

> . . . all political learning, formal and informal, deliberate and unplanned, at every stage of the life cycle, including not only explicitly political learning but also nominally non-political learning of politically relevant personality characteristics.[2]

The last definition does allow for both persistence and change (at least by implication) inasmuch as no specific purpose is attributed to the socialization process. Moreover, it emphasizes that socialization is a continuing process involving all kinds of learning. David Easton and Jack Dennis, in pleading for a neutral definition of political socialization, have provided an effective, but short definition which, because it is deliberately broad, is able to encompass the various facets of Greenstein's second definition. They define political socialization simply as:

> . . . those developmental processes through which persons acquire political orientations and patterns of behaviour.[3]

The manner in which political orientations and behaviour are acquired and the results of their acquisition remain a matter for investigation.

It is now possible to posit a model of political socialization and

[1] Almond and Powell, *Comparative Politics*, p. 24.

[2] Fred I. Greenstein, 'Political Socialization', in *International Encyclopedia of the Social Sciences*, Vol. 14, New York, 1968, p. 551.

[3] David Easton and Jack Dennis, *Children in the Political System: Origins of Political Legitimacy*, New York, 1969, p. 7.

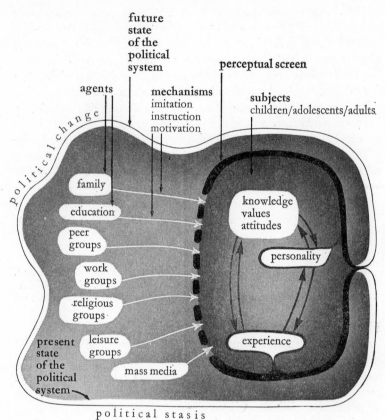

Figure 1. *A model of political socialization*

this is illustrated in Figure 1. The model seeks to trace the socialization process through its various stages from its beginnings in childhood to its ultimate significance in adulthood. As a model it does not suggest an absolute and arbitrary process of socialization that does not admit variation from one political system to another. Socialization is conceived as a process which continues throughout life, affecting child, adolescent and adult. At the same time, it is not suggested that each is affected equally, either within a particular system or between systems. Its temporal development, moreover, is not continuous in the sense that the individual regularly and systematically undergoes experiences which are significant and relevant to his subsequent political behaviour, even in those political systems in which regular and systematic political instruction is an important part of political socialization. Even in such systems there will be experiences which are irregular, possibly infrequent, but which are none the less of political importance in the development of an individual's political behaviour.

Similarly, although it is possible to posit the elements of political socialization, it is not suggested that these are acquired in a particular order, nor that they are of equal significance. Thus it is possible to distinguish between the acquisition of knowledge or information, values or basic beliefs, and attitudes or opinions on specific matters. While knowledge, which is basically though not exclusively factual, may precede the formation of values and attitudes, the reverse may also occur and knowledge may be used to support a particular value or attitude after its formation. At the same time, knowledge is affected by values and attitudes and cannot therefore be totally objective, if only because of the inevitable selectivity exercised by the individual. Moreover, it is also clear that attitudes are closely related to values in that an individual's basic beliefs will play a crucial part in determining his reaction to particular stimuli and to the formation of particular attitudes or opinions, but attitudes may precede values, especially on an imitative basis. It is also likely that there will be a 'feedback' process by which attitudes, or more particularly the consequences of attitudes, will affect an individual's values. Attitudes may or may not be borne out by experience, and this may serve to confirm or possibly undermine particular beliefs. Finally, values and attitudes will affect the individual's acquisition of knowledge by influencing his selection of information. Thus the three elements are analytically distinguishable but closely inter-related.

The model further suggests that the various elements of political socialization are transmitted through a variety of agents, but once again primacy is not given to any one agent or group of agents. Quite apart from the fact that some of these agents are more applicable to some of the subjects of socialization than others, they may also vary in importance from one political system to another, and sometimes within a political system. Thus children will be more likely to be affected by the influences of family and education, adults by work groups and the mass media. In communities such as the Israeli kibbutz or the Chinese commune, the role of the family may be minimized, compared with its influence in Europe or North America. Education will obviously vary in its impact, especially between those countries in which it does not go beyond the primary stage for the majority of the population and those in which there is extensive higher education. Or again, work situations differ considerably from one country to another, creating important environmental differences, quite apart from specific organizational differences, such as the degree to which the work force is unionized.

The way in which these various agents transmit the elements of political socialization also varies, and the model suggests three such ways or mechanisms: imitation, instruction and motivation. Robert Le Vine suggests that these are the mechanisms of political socialization in childhood,[1] but there is no reason why they should not be applicable to the whole socialization process. Imitation is the copying of the behaviour of other individuals and is obviously of great importance in childhood socialization, yet it need not be confined to childhood behaviour. What seems more likely is that pure imitation will be found among children, but as an adolescent and adult mechanism it becomes increasingly mixed with the other two mechanisms, so that a degree of imitation will be found in both instruction and motivation. Instruction is more or less self-explanatory, although it should be stressed that it is not confined to formal learning. An individual may be deliberately placed in a situation which is instructive in nature – this is clearly the case, for example, in various types of vocational training 'on the job', some of which may be relevant to political behaviour; while the practice of some organizations or groups of individuals to form discussion groups is an explicit but informal type of instruction. Although both imitation and instruction are specific types of experience, the third mechanism, motivation, is most closely identified with experience in general. Motivation is the learning of what Le Vine has called 'appropriate behaviour' through a process of trial and error: the individual learns directly from his experience what actions are most congruent with his attitudes and opinions. The term 'appropriate' refers not to the extent to which the individual is led to conform to some norm of group behaviour (though this may well be the result), but to the process by which

[1] Robert Le Vine, 'Political Socialization and Culture Change', in Clifford Geertz (ed.), *Old Societies and New States*, New York, 1963, pp. 280–303.

the individual relates action to attitudes and opinions to his *experience*.

Experience is one of the key variables of the model in that an individual's political behaviour is partially determined by the sum of his experience. His knowledge, values and attitudes are contributory to his experience and are in due course affected by it. In the same way the transmission of knowledge, values and attitudes through the various agents of socialization are both experiences in themselves and in time become affected by other experiences. Thus an individual's politically relevant experience arises out of and is contributory to the process of political socialization. As a result of his interviews in depth with fifteen American working men, for example, Robert Lane concludes that the individual's conception of political problems is seen through the variety of his experiences. Furthermore, his conception may be irrational in the sense that it is unplanned and unsystematic, but not necessarily within the context of his own experience. Thus the individual may ignore factors which seem to an outside observer to be important, because they fall outside his experience. It is also important to stress that where experiences are shared by a number of individuals they may acquire much greater significance in the formation of values and attitudes.[1] Group experiences are likely to reinforce commonly held values and attitudes, while the general nature of widely shared experiences often assumes considerable political significance. Widespread economic prosperity or deprivation, the rapidity of social change, frequent violence or prolonged peace, the existence or absence of social tension and so on, may provide an experiential environment which contributes to the individual's political orientations and pattern of political behaviour.

The other key variable in political socialization is the individual's personality. This too is related to his experience, but remains distinguishable from it. Political observers have long posited various types of political temperament or personality. Bluntschli, for example, linked the Hippocratic theories of temperament with various broad types of political philosophy: the reactionary was melancholic, the conservative phlegmatic, the progressive sanguine and the radical choleric. Similarly, Macaulay speaks of two classes – the conservative and the liberal.

[1] Robert E. Lane, *Political Ideology: Why the American Common Man Believes What He Does*, New York, 1962, Chapter 24.

Modern observers have sought types of political character or personality based on psychological phenomena. J. P. Guilford defines personality as an individual's 'unique pattern of traits'. Traits are defined as 'any distinguishable, relatively enduring way in which one individual differs from others', and, from the point of view of political behaviour, particular attention is paid to those traits which are 'shared' in varying degrees, by large segments of the population'.[1] Many political personality types have been posited, but there is little agreement on any range of types. Some writers have concerned themselves with a particular type, others with a general typology. Erich Fromm, for instance, describes one type as the *automaton* – a person who loses his sense of individuality by conforming to popular values.[2] Harold Lasswell suggests a range of types: the *political agitator*, who is skilled in the area of personal contact and the rousing of political emotions; the *political administrator*, who is skilled in the manipulation of organizations and situations; the *political theorist*, who is skilled in the manipulation of ideas; and the *bureaucrat*, who over-emphasizes formal rules and organization and responds habitually to given situations.[3] Similarly, David Riesman has devised a threefold grouping: the *tradition-directed* person, who lacks any conception of politics and who reacts to a limited, parochial environment; the *inner-directed* person, whose orientations stem from childhood and who is unresponsive to contemporary influences; and the *other-directed* person, who is oriented to contemporary influences.[4]

Probably the best-known attempt to posit a particular type of political personality, however, is that of T. W. Adorno *et al.*, in *The Authoritarian Personality*. By means of various attitude scales the authors posit a series of behavioural characteristics which, they suggest, comprise the authoritarian personality. These may be summarized as follows:

Attitude of dominance towards subordinates.
Attitude of deference to superiors.

[1] J. P. Guilford, *Personality*, New York, 1959, pp. 5–6, quoted in L. A. Froman, 'Personality and Political Socialization', *Journal of Politics*, 23, 1961, p. 344.
[2] Erich Fromm, *Escape from Freedom*, New York, 1941, pp. 153–83.
[3] Harold D. Lasswell, *Power and Personality*, New York, 1948, Chapter 4.
[4] David Riesman, *The Lonely Crowd*, New Haven, Conn., 1950, Chapter 1.

A sensitivity to power relationships.

A tendency to perceive the world in a highly structured fashion.

An excessive use of stereotyped images.

An adherence to whatever values are conventional within the individual's immediate environment.

A tendency to be superstitious.

A preoccupation with virility.

A pessimistic view of human nature.

Strong moral views.

A tendency to be impatient with and generally intolerant of opposition.[1]

Earlier studies during the Second World War and in the immediate postwar period linked authoritarian (and often Fascist) attitudes with particular personality traits,[2] but the methodology used in *The Authoritarian Personality* was criticized on such grounds as its failure to take account of left-wing authoritarianism and the alleged inaccuracy and subjectivity of the most well-known of the scales used, the Fascism or F-Scale. Greenstein asserts that Adorno and his colleagues deal 'more with prejudice than with . . . psychological dispositions toward authority'.[3] In spite of the criticism of *The Authoritarian Personality*, the work is a landmark in the attempts to delineate various types of political personality and it has stimulated much of the subsequent work in the field.

There have also been attempts to delineate a 'democratic personality', but most of these have been theoretical rather than research-based. Inkeles and Lasswell, for example, offer similar, but slightly different traits:

[1] T. W. Adorno, Else Frenkel-Brunswik, Daniel J. Levinson and R. N. Sandford, *The Authoritarian Personality*, New York, 1950, pp. 242–62.

[2] e.g. Fromm, *Escape from Freedom*; H. V. Dicks, 'Personality Traits and National Socialist Ideology', *Human Relations*, **3**, 1950; and Ruth Benedict, *The Chrysanthemum and the Sword*, Boston, Mass., 1946.

[3] Fred I. Greenstein, 'Personality and Political Socialization: the Theories of the Authoritarian and Democratic Character', *Annals of the American Academy of Political and Social Science* (henceforth cited as *Annals*), **361**, September 1965, p. 83.

Inkeles[1]	**Lasswell**[2]
Accepting of other people	Warm attitude towards other people
Open to new experiences and ideas	Share values with other people
Responsible but watchful attitude towards authority	Wide range of values
Tolerant of differences	Confidence in environment
Controlled emotions	Relative freedom from anxiety

H. J. Eysenck has attempted a two-dimensional approach to the problem of political personality by the use of two attitude scales: (1) a *Radicalism-Conservatism* syndrome (the R-factor) and (2) a *Tough-minded-Tender-minded* syndrome (the T-factor). The R-factor is virtually self-explanatory, consisting merely of assessing the degree to which an individual holds radical or conservative views. The T-factor involves the following pairs of traits:

Tender minded	**Tough minded**[3]
Rationalistic (going by 'principles')	Empiricist (going by 'facts')
Intellectualistic	Sensationalistic
Idealistic	Materialistic
Optimistic	Pessimistic
Religious	Irreligious
Free-willist	Fatalistic
Monistic	Pluralistic
Dogmatical	Sceptical

According to Eysenck, both factors are psychologically based: the R-factor is based on *learning*, i.e. by a process of rewards and punishment derived from hedonistic theories of learning; and the T-factor is based on conditioning, i.e. the influence of association or continuity, and is thus a series of involuntary, emotional

---

[1] Alex Inkeles, 'National Character and Modern Political Systems', in Hsu (ed.), *Psychological Anthropology*, pp. 172–208.

[2] Harold D. Lasswell, 'Power and Personality', in *The Writings of Harold D. Lasswell*, Glencoe, Ill., 1951, pp. 495 ff.

[3] H. J. Eysenck, *The Psychology of Politics*, London, 1954, p. 131.

responses. Furthermore, tough-mindedness is associated with *extraversion* and tender-mindedness with *introversion*. Tough-mindedness is also closely associated with aggression, dominance and, to a lesser extent, with rigidity and narrow-mindedness.

The connection between the two factors, using British ideological positions, is as follows:

Fascism: tough-minded conservatism
Communism: tough-minded radicalism
Conservatism: intermediate tender-minded conservatism
Labourism: intermediate tender-minded radicalism
Liberalism: tender-minded intermediate radicalism-conservatism

The problem with most of these attempts to evolve a typology of political personality is that, while the various traits ascribed to particular personality types are often recognizable, they tend to remain isolated syndromes or points on a continuum. There is often the further problem of relating the particular traits to specific political behaviour. Probably the greatest problem, however, is that of linking these concepts with particular political systems. Eysenck has had some success in this, and he reports that his two-dimensional analysis has been successfully applied in a number of countries, including the United States, West Germany and Sweden, as well as Britain. How applicable it is to, say, totalitarian societies or developing societies remains an unanswered question. Even within similar political systems, there may be important differences, especially in the significance of such scales as the R-factor, and it is therefore important to take into account the particular environment concerned. For example, the extent to which violence is regarded as a legitimate means of political expression is likely to vary not only according to the personality of the individual, but also in relation to norms of the political system concerned. Any attempt, therefore, to delineate various types of 'national character' is fraught with problems. None the less, it is important to bear in mind that personality remains an important factor in the process of political socialization.

*

Political socialization is the process that results from the elaborate interplay between an individual's personality and his politically relevant experiences. These experiences are not necessarily specifically political, of course, but they are relevant because they shape his political behaviour. Experiences which are primarily social or economic may have political significance: thus movement from one neighbourhood to another may influence an individual's party identity or a period of unemployment may result in an individual becoming politically alienated. Political socialization is therefore characterized by an intricate network of knowledge, values and attitudes transmitted between individuals and groups of individuals within a political system resulting from and contributing to a set of experiences interwoven around the personality of the individual to form a syndrome of political behaviour. The knowledge, values and attitudes acquired by the individual form a *perceptual screen* through which the individual perceives political stimuli. Since the individual's knowledge, values and attitudes are subject to change, this perceptual screen is not necessarily immutable. Furthermore, some stimuli will be accepted and others rejected, so that the political behaviour, especially in respect of political participation, inevitably varies from one individual to another.[1] An individual's political behaviour, however, like his behaviour in general, develops only gradually. Clearly not all individuals develop in the same way or at the same pace, but it is possible to suggest the main lines of that development within particular political systems, and it is to this question that we now turn.

THE DEVELOPMENT OF POLITICAL SOCIALIZATION
Childhood and Adolescence   Frank and Elizabeth Estvan have shown in their book, *The Child's World*, how children gradually become aware of a wider environment, how they become increasingly perceptive in response to particular situations, and how their whole outlook becomes increasingly coherent and total, where before it was fragmented and limited.[2] The children in this study were asked to identify and comment on a series of pictures depicting

[1] See Lester W. Milbrath, *Political Participation*, Chicago, 1965, Chapter 1.
[2] New York, 1959, Chapters 3–8.

various scenes in American life, including a picture of the Capitol in Washington, D.C. Just over half of the children (51 per cent) recognized the picture as a governmental (or political) scene in whole or part. Not surprisingly, older children recognized the picture as a governmental scene more frequently and made much more sophisticated comments on the scene than younger children, so that the Estvans concluded:

> Boys and girls enter school with little conception of government, only one-fourth managing to achieve a partial or structural recognition of this scene. By the time they are in sixth grade, the proportion has about trebled . . . [but] ideas and attitudes about government are slow to appear and to mature.[1]

Furthermore, the Estvans' general conclusions also have some relevance to political socialization. They found that environment was an important factor in socialization: urban children, for example, were more likely than rural children to recognize the picture of the Capitol, and this was attributed to a more local orientation on the part of children in rural areas. Children's perceptions of situations were found to be highly individual: in commenting on the picture of the Capitol, children varied considerably on the particular aspect which aroused their interest, and a number of them identified the picture as the Capitol in Madison, Wisconsin (the state in which the survey was conducted). In identifying particular points of interest, moreover, younger children were far more likely to comment on the people in the picture, whereas older children usually commented on both the people and the building, thus suggesting a progression from the merely human element to the recognition of a material element as well. The authors also found that the attitudes of the children became increasingly consistent as they got older and increasingly consistent with the various social backgrounds from which they were drawn.

As a result of survey research into political socialization, David Easton and Robert Hess suggest that in the United States political learning begins at the age of three and is well-established by the age of seven. The early stages of political learning involve the development of environmental ties, such as 'attachment to their schools' and the recognition that they live in a particular country. A simple sense of patriotism appears to be one of the earliest

[1] ibid., p. 204.

manifestations of political learning: Easton and Hess found that young children had a belief in the 'beauty of their country' and the 'goodliness and cleanliness of its people'. These early manifestations are followed by the recognition of the visible symbols of public authority, such as the policeman, the president and the national flag, but by the age of nine or ten there is increasing awareness of more abstract concepts, such as voting, democracy, civil liberty and of the role of citizens in the political system. By the age of seven or eight, moreover, the majority of American children have identified themselves with one or other of the country's two major parties.[1]

In an earlier article, Easton and Hess suggest that the child's earliest views of the President of the United States are as an authority figure and that the child's image of his father and of the President are similar during early school years. As they become older, children become increasingly aware of the President as part of a more complex governmental hierarchy:

> First, this initial socialization is to an image viewed in personal terms – that is, to someone whom the child sees as a person, rather than an impersonal group or institution; second, early in the process of political socialization, the President represents for the child a focus for an emerging sense of identification with a political community at the national level; third, to the child the President stands as a symbol of undifferentiated government that includes all levels and holds essentially all governmental authority; and fourth, the President serves as a central orientation point for an increasing awareness of the other elements of the political system . . . the Vice-President is seen as someone who helps the President; Congress is viewed as a group that takes orders from the President and performs certain tasks at his command.[2]

This progression from the simple to the complex, from the personal to the institutional, is seen clearly in the data presented by David Easton and Jack Dennis in their book *Children in the Political System*.[3] Their data was based on a national sample survey of American school-children from Grade 2 to Grade 8 (i.e. from the ages of seven or eight to thirteen or fourteen). The children were first asked which of a number of symbols they associated with government (Table 1).

[1] David Easton and Robert D. Hess, 'The Child's Political World', *Midwest Journal of Political Science*, 6, 1962.

[2] David Easton and Robert D. Hess, 'The Child's Changing Image of the President', *Public Opinion Quarterly*, 24, 1960, pp. 634–5.

[3] New York, 1969.

Table 1. *Symbols associated with government among U.S. schoolchildren*[1]

	Police-man	George Wash-ington	Uncle Sam	Voting	Supreme Court	Capitol (%)
Grade 2	8	39	16	4	5	14
Grade 8	2	2	16	47	16	7
Teachers	1	1	5	72	13	5

	Congress	Flag	Statue of Liberty	President Kennedy	Don't know (%)
Grade 2	6	16	12	46	16
Grade 8	49	12	20	23	2
Teachers	71	6	8	15	—

Grade 2 pupils were far more likely to associate government with persons, such as the President, or George Washington, or the policeman, and with visible symbols, such as the national flag or the Capitol building in Washington, whereas by Grade 8 government presented a much more complex picture to the children, which involved the recognition of institutions, such as Congress and the Supreme Court, and processes, such as voting. At the same time, the number who failed to identify government with any of the symbols suggested fell from 16 to 2 per cent between Grades 2 and 8 while the recognition of a more complex symbol like the Statue of Liberty increased from 12 to 20 per cent.

It is also clear from the data presented by Easton and Dennis that children's understanding of government is much more than a vague association with particular symbols: they also become increasingly aware of the different roles of the various governmental institutions, as Table 2 shows.

Table 2. *Understanding of the roles of governmental institutions among U.S. schoolchildren*[2]

A. Who does MOST to make the laws?

	Congress	President	Supreme Court	Don't know	Total (%)
Grade 2	5	76	11	8	100
Grade 8	85	5	8	1	99
Teachers	96	1	3	0	100

[1] Adapted from Easton and Dennis, *Children in the Political System*, Table 6–2, p. 116.

[2] Adapted from Easton and Dennis, *Children in the Political System*, Tables 6–3 and 6–4, pp. 119 and 120.

B. Who does the MOST to run the country?

	Congress	President	Supreme Court	Don't know	Total
Grade 2	4	86	3	7	100
Grade 8	35	58	4	3	100
Teachers	61	36	3	0	100

The saliency of the president in the minds of the younger children is very clear in the responses to these two questions: in both cases the president is the only figure or institution of real importance. By the time they reach Grade 8, however, children are aware that government is more complex, and although a majority still believe that the president does most to run the country, more than a third attribute this role to Congress; while the overwhelming importance of Congress as a lawmaking body is recognized by more than four-fifths of the pupils in Grade 8. It should also be noted that whereas the law-making function was largely transferred from the president to Congress between Grades 2 and 8, the question who does most to run the country is a more complicated notion and there is no comparable transfer: instead opinion is divided.

A further example of the widening political horizons of the children interviewed in the Easton and Dennis survey is shown by the extent to which they associated particular individuals with government:

Table 3. *The association of particular individuals with government among U.S. schoolchildren*[1]

Which of these people works for the government? (percentage replying 'yes')

	Milkman	Policeman	Soldier	Judge	Postman	Teacher
Grade 2	29	86	68	86	57	48
Grade 8	8	81	98	94	93	59
Teachers	1	77	100	91	99	45

Pupils in Grade 2 clearly associated both the policeman and the judge with government and, to a lesser extent, the soldier, but there was also evidence of some confusion and uncertainty. Thus

[1] Adapted from Easton and Dennis, *Children in the Political System*, Table 6–5, p. 122.

29 per cent said that the milkman was employed by the government and there was considerable uncertainty about the teacher and the postman. Pupils in Grade 8 had a clearer idea of which individuals did work for the government, and their political horizon had widened considerably. The overwhelming majority linked the soldier, judge and postman with government and only 8 per cent thought the milkman worked for the government. The altered positions of the policeman and the teacher are probably a reflection of an increasing awareness of the various levels of government and possibly some understandable difficulty in distinguishing between the 'government' and various other public authorities. Thus slightly fewer of the Grade 8 children said that the policeman was employed by the government, and it is as well to remember that in the United States police are employed by federal, state and city authorities. Similarly, the position of the teacher is probably a confusing one: although the survey was conducted in public (state) and not private schools, there is no immediate reason why the teacher should be associated with government employment any more than the school boards should be regarded as government agencies.

Although their data suggests a progression from the simple to the complex, from limited to broad conceptions, Easton and Dennis stress that there was no evidence to support a theory of political socialization involving a gradual and systematic linear progression or widening series of concentric circles in the development of the child's political awareness. They stress that, on the contrary, political learning appears to be fragmented and variable, so that a child may become aware simultaneously of familial authority, the role of the policeman and the existence of the President, while awareness of the three main levels of government – national, state and local – develops in a similar fashion, with the child having some knowledge of each, but far from a complete picture.[1]

As they grow older children also become aware that various individuals and groups play a role in the political process, and Easton and Dennis suggest that by Grade 4 (nine to ten years) children have some knowledge of the part played by trade unions, big business, newspapers and the churches, an awareness, in other words, of the informal areas of politics. This awareness is accom-

[1] Easton and Dennis. *Children in the Political System*, Part 2.

panied by the development of attitudes about government and politics, including party identity, and an increasing distinction between institutions and people, between political offices and the persons holding those offices.

Easton and Dennis posit four stages in childhood political socialization:

1 The recognition of authority through particular individuals, such as the child's parents, the president and the policeman;
2 The development of a distinction between internal and external authority, i.e. between private and public authority;
3 The recognition of impersonal political institutions, such as Congress, the Supreme Court, and voting;
4 The development of a distinction between political institutions and the persons engaged in the activities associated with those institutions, so that idealized images of particular persons such as the president or a Congressman are transferred to the presidency and Congress.[1]

Some differences in the rate of development were found in relation to sex, I.Q., religion and socio-economic status, but these were generally small and unsystematic, although Easton and Dennis suggest that the higher rate of development among those of higher socio-economic status might result in more deeply rooted beliefs.[2]

Easton and Dennis have also investigated the acquisition by children of political efficacy or political competence: that is, the feeling on the part of the individual that he can exert some influence in the political system. Easton and Dennis found that the feeling of political competence increased from 16 per cent in Grade 3 to 58 per cent in Grade 8, but they stress that this does not depend either on the ability to understand government or on the amount of information the respondents possessed. The feeling of competence did tend to increase, however, in relation to I.Q. and socio-economic status.[3]

[1] ibid., Part 3.
[2] ibid., Part 4.
[3] Easton and Dennis, 'The Child's Acquisition of Regime Norms: Political Efficacy', *American Political Science Review*, 61, 1967, pp. 25–38.

The picture that Easton and Dennis draw of political socialization during childhood is clear enough, even though, as they themselves point out, it is an incomplete picture and leaves many gaps. At a fairly early age children do have some idea of what government is, even if their earliest conceptions are concentrated heavily on the figure of the president. Gradually their horizon widens and they become increasingly aware of the complexity of the political system, including some understanding of the importance of the informal facets of the political process. The child's picture becomes more complete, more coherent; his political knowledge increases, values are formed and attitudes develop; and, finally, some feeling of political competence may also arise. The whole theme of this picture, however, revolves around a single concept, for the main conclusion of *Children in the Political System* is, 'that the child is learning to orient himself to the structure of authority.'[1]

Roberta Sigel has provided more specific evidence of how important authority is to the young child: in a study of the reactions of children to the assassination of President Kennedy, she found that the greatest emotional shock at the sudden removal of the central figure of authority was suffered by the younger children in her sample.[2] If the view that attitudes towards authority are both the earliest manifestations of, and central to, political socialization is correct, then it is of immense importance to theories of legitimacy: the acceptance of a given authority – a matter which will be considered later in this chapter.

The emphasis laid on the importance of authority is closely related to theories concerning the role of the family in political socialization. We have already seen that Easton and Hess found that children had similar images of their fathers and of the president during their early school years, and that both were regarded as authority figures.[3] Such a view is in many respects crucial to the main hypothesis of Easton and Dennis. On a much wider front, however, the family has long been regarded as one of the earliest and most important agents of political socialization.

[1] Easton and Dennis, *Children in the Political System*, p. 399.
[2] Roberta S. Sigel, 'Some Explorations into Political Sociology: Schoolchildren's Reactions to the Death of a President', in Martha Wolfenstein and Gilbert Kliman (eds.), *Children and the Death of a President*, New York, 1965.
[3] See p. 32 above.

Robert Lane has suggested that there are three ways in which the foundations of political belief may be laid through the family:

1 By overt and covert indoctrination;
2 By placing the child in a particular social context;
3 By moulding the child's personality;

and together they constitute what Lane has called 'the Mendelian law of politics'.[1] Similarly, James C. Davies has argued that role of the family in political socialization is based on its broader task of providing for the needs of the child. Thus, by having its physical needs and its need for love and affection provided for, the child gradually acquires an identity of its own and, subsequently, is able to identify itself with others – the family serving as its earliest reference group to which the child looks for guidance as well as sustenance. This leads Davies to conclude '. . . most of the individual's political personality – his tendencies to think and act politically in particular ways – have been determined at home, several years before he can take part in politics as an ordinary adult'.[2] The evidence to support such assertions tends to be fragmentary in nature, and the exact role of the family in political socialization requires further research.

There is, however, extensive evidence linking the family with party preference. A study of the 1952 presidential election found a strong tendency for voters to support the same party as their parents, and not surprisingly, the strength of this tendency increased where both parents voted for the same party. Thus of those voters, both of whose parents were Democrats, 82 per cent were also Democrats, and of those with Republican parents, 73 per cent were Republicans.[3] Furthermore, Philip Converse and Georges Dupeux found that there was a strong correlation between an individual *knowing* his father's political identity and his

[1] Robert E. Lane, 'Fathers and Sons: The Foundations of Political Belief', *American Sociological Review*, 24, 1959, pp. 502–11. See also *Political Ideology*, Chapter 17.

[2] James C. Davies, 'The Family's Role in Political Socialization', *Annals*, 361, September 1965, p. 11.

[3] Angus Campbell, G. Gurin and Warren E. Miller, *The Voter Decides*, New York, 1954, p. 99.

own political identity.[1] Similarly, among a sample of college students interviewed by Philip Nogee and Murray Levin, 74 per cent had the same party preference as their parents, and this congruent identification was higher where both parents agreed and lower where there was only one parent or where the parents disagreed.[2]

What is not clear, however, is whether the influence of the family extends beyond party preference, and, even in the case of party preference, exactly how political values are transmitted from parent to child. Indeed, some doubt has been cast of the whole question of the importance of the family as an agent of political socialization by Kent Jennings and R. G. Niemi. Using a sample of Grade 12 pupils (i.e. senior high-school students), they confirmed the findings of earlier studies that the degree of party identification between parents and children is strong – only 7 per cent of their sample had a *totally different* party preference from their parents. When they investigated the transmission of attitudes on particular issues, however, and the values underlying such attitudes, they found a much lower incidence of parent–child congruence. Unfortunately, they did not take into account the fact that their sample was drawn from senior high-school students and that this in itself might account, in part at least, for differences between the attitudes of parents and children, since as seventeen- or eighteen-year-olds these students would have been subjected to other agents of socialization for a number of years, including some eleven or more years of full-time education. Even so, allowing for such considerations, this study does suggest that it is erroneous to assume that parents transmit to their children a complete set of values, let alone attitudes on particular issues.[3]

Evidence on the nature of parental transmission – *how* political values are transmitted from parent to child – is almost non-existent. One study, however, does throw some light on the matter: Karen Orren and Paul Peterson asked a sample of American

[1] Philip Converse and Georges Dupeux, 'Politicization of the Electorate in France and the United States', *Public Opinion Quarterly*, **26**, 1962, pp. 1–23.

[2] Philip Nogee and Murray B. Levin, 'Some Determinants of Political Attitudes among College Voters', *Public Opinion Quarterly*, **22**, 1958, pp. 449–63.

[3] M. Kent Jennings and R. G. Niemi, 'The Transmission of Political Values from Parent to Child', *American Political Science Review*, **62**, 1968, pp. 169–84.

parents whether they explained the assassination of President Kennedy to their children, and, if so, how. A majority (65 per cent) did *not* explain the event to their children at all. Those who did were more emotionally affected by the assassination, tended to be better informed politically, and of higher social status. This last finding was independent of the degree of political information, even though those of higher social status are normally better informed politically. The explanations offered to younger children naturally tended to be simpler in form and often involved a religious element, whereas those offered to older children tended to be broader, more historical and more political in form. In general, however, parents avoided giving negative explanations and refrained from mentioning some of the more unpleasant aspects of the event.[1]

The fact that nearly two thirds of the parents offered no explanation at all is itself significant, of course. Does this mean that they had no impact on their children's views of the assassination of the president? The study reports on the deliberate actions of those parents who *did* explain the event to their children, but this does not preclude the possibility of children being affected by the actions of their parents short of deliberate explanation – the impact of parental emotion (or even of parental silence) could be more significant than overt explanation.

If this study is any guide of the extent to which parents are overtly involved in political socialization, then we must assume that the majority of parents are covertly rather than overtly involved in transmitting knowledge, values and attitudes to their children. This is, in fact, implicit in all theories of the role of the family in political socialization: the evidence that children are likely to adopt the party preferences of their parents is overwhelming, and Jennings and Niemi probably go too far in more or less limiting the political role of the family to this. Even the evidence available on the congruence of parent–child party preference offers no specific explanation of how this preference is transmitted. Children whose parents are actively involved in politics, or strongly committed to a particular party, may be subjected to a greater degree of direct or indirect indoctrination

[1] Karen Orren and Paul Peterson, 'Presidential Assassination: A Case-Study in the Dynamics of Political Socialization', *Journal of Politics*, 29, 1967, pp. 388–404.

than children whose parents are less interested in political activity. In the latter case, unconscious influences may be more important, and as Lane suggests, the social milieu created may be an important means of political socialization. If this is so, then it is likely to be the case for the majority of individuals, since only a fairly small minority of people are actively involved in political activity. The significance of the findings of Converse and Dupeux may be simply that the majority of American children know their fathers' political identities and that the initial reaction is to assume the same identity. As an initial reaction it may be a question of blind faith or implicit trust, but subsequent experience may well confirm, to a greater or lesser degree, the correctness of that initial reaction.

It is perhaps important to distinguish between party preference and the various values that an individual comes to adopt. Party preference is something specific in the sense that the individual identifies himself with a political party, with a party *label* – and that label is specifically contextual. An individual thinks of himself as, say, a Democrat, and this becomes a point of reference: the more closely he identifies an issue as a party matter, the more likely he is to react as a Democrat – at elections for the president, or Congress, or the state governor or legislature he will probably vote Democrat; similarly, on issues on which the party has clearly defined views, he will probably support the party line; but in an election at local level for the district attorney or sheriff he may well vote on personal rather than party grounds if he happens to know one or more of the candidates; while he may also ignore the party line in a local referendum where he feels well-informed on the issue concerned. The personnel and the issues change, but the party remains.

Compare this with the much less specific sense of identification as, say, a 'liberal'. Obviously it is possible to posit certain basic values associated with a liberal point of view, such as a belief in freedom of speech, equality before the law, and so on, but, quite apart from securing agreement as to what such beliefs mean in *practice*, their meaning may also differ over time. Can it be said with confidence that the term 'liberal' means the same from one generation to another? Even assuming a measure of agreement within a generation, the application of 'liberal' views will vary considerably in practice in response both to the situation and the individual concerned. To be a 'liberal' is a diffuse commitment; to be a Democrat is a specific commitment. The majority of Democrats may regard themselves as 'liberals', but not all 'liberals' are necessarily Democrats.

The available evidence on the role of the family in political socialization suggests that children are, on the whole, influenced environmentally rather than directly. The family provides and is part of an environment which is conducive to the acquisition of certain knowledge, values and attitudes which are commonly held by that family. At the same time, the child becomes increasingly subject to other influences which may or may not reinforce the effect of early socialization, and one of the most important of these is education.

Education has long been regarded as an important variable in the explanation of political behaviour, and there is considerable circumstantial evidence to suggest that it is important as an agent of political socialization. In their five-nation study, for example, Almond and Verba found that the more extensive an individual's education the more likely he was to be aware of the impact of government, to follow politics, to have more political information, to possess a wider range of opinions on political matters, to engage in political discussion with a wider range of people, to feel a greater ability to influence political affairs, to be a member of and to be active in a voluntary organization, and express confidence in his social environment and exhibit feelings of trust.[1] Similarly, innumerable studies have shown a correlation between electoral behaviour and education, while other studies have found significant correlations between education and subjective class identification. Moreover, many of the studies cited earlier traced the development of political knowledge, values and attitudes through the various school grades, and the figures already given in Tables 1, 2 and 3 show a convergence between the attitudes of the children and the attitudes of their teachers.

Although, in a number of instances, marked differences remain, the attitudes of Grade 8 pupils are, for the most part, closer to those of the teachers than they are to those of the Grade 2 pupils. For Grade 2 pupils the two most important symbols associated with government were President Kennedy and George Washing-

[1] Almond and Verba, *The Civic Culture* (Little, Brown, Boston, Mass., 1966), pp. 315–24.

ton; but for Grade 8 pupils they were Congress and voting, and for teachers voting and Congress (Table 1). Grade 2 pupils felt that the president did most to make the laws, but Grade 8 pupils and teachers attributed this role to Congress (Table 2). On the more difficult question of who did most to run the country, a majority of pupils in both grades nominated the president, but whereas this was the view of 86 per cent of those in Grade 2, the proportion dropped to 58 per cent in Grade 8, compared with 36 per cent of the teachers. Conversely, only 4 per cent of the pupils in Grade 2 but 35 per cent in Grade 8 nominated Congress, compared with 61 per cent of the teachers (Table 2). The association of various individuals with the government showed a less clear-cut dichotomy, but a general convergence between the views of pupils and teachers remains (Table 3).

In spite of the evidence offered above, the influence of education as an agent of political socialization remains implicit rather than explicit. The evidence is, in fact, almost entirely circumstantial – persons with differing levels of education tend to possess differing levels of political knowledge, hold differing values and attitudes, and exhibit different political behaviour. There is no reason to believe that the connection is spurious, but the problem of ascertaining the exact relationship is a difficult one. For example, what is the relationship between education and class or status? If members of a particular social class or group are more likely to receive higher education, then some relationship will exist between the two. Conversely, the same will be true if those who do receive higher education come, as a result of that education, to regard themselves as members of a particular class or group. Education may therefore be a dependent or an independent variable. The position is complicated, as the findings of the study by Raymond Murphy and Richard Morris of the relationship between occupation, subjective class identification and party affiliations show: when they controlled their statistics for education the relationship between subjective class identification and occupation persisted for those with an elementary or high-school education, but disappeared for those with a college education. They also found a strong correlation between party affiliation, income and occupation, but these income and occupational differences tended to disappear among those with higher education, so that the latter were more likely to identify themselves as middle class and Republican regardless of income and occupation.[1]

A number of studies have endeavoured to establish what effect various aspects of education have on children and adolescents. Kenneth Langton and Kent Jennings examined the impact of the civics curriculum in American schools and came to the conclusion that it was in no way 'significantly associated with students' political orientations'.[2] Another study found no direct relationship between attitudes towards politics and participation in extracurricular high-school activities;[3] while a survey of freshmen and senior college students in California found no differences in their levels of political knowledge nor in the values they held.[4]

Once again, the evidence available suggests general rather than specific influence, environmental rather than direct socialization. As children emerge from the early influence of the family into the wider world of school and peer groups,[5] they become subject to other influences which may reinforce or conflict with early politicization. Thus Hyman has shown that political discussion not only tends to increase in the family between the ninth and twelfth grades, but among friends within the child's own grade.[6] Furthermore, Martin Levin found a tendency for individuals to adopt the majority view within peer groups, so that in a school in a predominantly Republican area the children of Democratic parents tended to become Republican and vice versa.[7]

As far as political socialization during childhood and adolescence is concerned, we can say with some confidence *what* is

[1] Raymond J. Murphy and Richard J. Morris, 'Occupational Situations, Subjective Class Identification and Political Affiliation', *American Sociological Review*, 26, 1961, pp. 383–92.

[2] Kenneth P. Langton and M. Kent Jennings, 'Political Socialization and the High School Civics Curriculum in the United States', *American Political Science Review*, 62, 1968, p. 866.

[3] D. Ziblatt, 'High School Extra-Curricular Activities and Political Socialization', *Annals*, 361, September 1965, pp. 20–31.

[4] Charles G. McClintock and Henry A. Turner, 'The Impact of College upon Political Knowledge, Participation and Values', *Human Relations*, 15, 1962, pp. 163–75.

[5] Peer groups are properly defined as groups of equals, but are commonly regarded as synonymous with age-groups.

[6] Hyman, *Political Socialization*, p. 101.

[7] Martin L. Levin, 'Social Climates and Political Socialization', *Public Opinion Quarterly*, 25, 1961, pp. 596–606.

learned and *when* it is learned, but it is with less confidence that we can say *how* it is learned. The acquisition of political orientations and patterns of behaviour seems to owe far more to the influence of environment and experience than to specific learning or indoctrination.

Adult Socialization If the emphasis already laid upon environmental and experiential influences is correct, then it is reasonable to assume that these influences will continue to be of importance during adult life and that the process of socialization continues beyond childhood and adolescence. The main outlines of future political behaviour may well be determined in the earlier period, but this is more likely to create a situation in which there is interaction between early political socialization and the environmental and experiential influences of later life than to preclude adult socialization. A limited example will illustrate our point: there is evidence to suggest that members of legislatures undergo a process of socialization following their election, and that their subsequent legislative behaviour is determined partly by their knowledge, values and attitudes as these existed prior to election, and partly by their experiences within and reactions to their new environment in the legislature.[1] In such circumstances some degree of socialization is inevitable, but probably no more inevitable than the day-to-day experiences of ordinary men and women.

Political socialization during adult life has not been the subject of much study, although there is some evidence arising from studies of electoral behaviour, class consciousness, the influence of work situations and the development of ideology. Even so, it is at least possible to suggest those areas in which adult socialization may be important. Just as the child is gradually brought into contact with more and more of the world around him, so also is the adolescent, and the change from adolescent to adult life marks

[1] See Kenneth Prewitt, Heinz Eulau and Betty H. Zisk, 'Political Socialization and Political Roles', *Public Opinion Quarterly*, **30**, 1966, pp. 569–82; Duncan Macrae Jr and Edith K. Macrae, 'Legislators' Social Status and their Votes', *American Journal of Sociology*, **66**, 1960–1, pp. 599–603; Donald R. Matthews, *U.S. Senators and their World*, Chapel Hill, North Carolina, 1960; Allan Kornberg, *Canadian Legislative Behaviour*, New York, 1967; and Anthony Barker and Michael Rush, *The Member of Parliament and His Information*, London, 1970.

another important stage in political socialization. Some of the contacts made during childhood and adolescence may continue in a somewhat similar form through friendship and acquaintance; others may continue or be renewed through other mediums, such as work, leisure, religion or the mass media; but some, and the experiences they bring, will be new. For some, these new experiences will simply reinforce early socialization, but for others varying degrees of conflict will occur which may result in important changes in political behaviour. Movement from a rural to an urban area, change of employment or experience of unemployment, membership of voluntary organizations, the development of leisure interests, religious conversion, the absorption of fact and opinion via the mass media – these may all have some significant effect on an individual's political behaviour.

Electoral studies have again and again found correlations between party preferences and characterics of the voters which are related to environment and experience.[1] The study by Murphy and Morris already cited found that respondents who worked in commerce, finance and records were more likely to identify themselves as middle class and vote Republican, whereas those who worked in manufacturing, building and maintenance were more likely to identify themselves as working class and vote Democrat. Lewis Lipsitz, in a study of auto-workers in Detroit, found greater work dissatisfaction among unskilled workers, and these workers tended to be more pessimistic about the future, both individually and generally, more radical politically and less tolerant than skilled workers.[2] Robert Lane's study, *Political Ideology*, suggests that for the American 'common man' his experience of democracy through small voluntary groups and 'a *general* sense of satisfaction . . . leads him to accept and endorse the political system of his society'.[3] In addition, Lane's 'democrats' had a belief in at least the partial control of their own existence; they accepted the realities of politics in that they recognized that politicians are human and that delays, contradictions and confusion are, to some extent, part of the process; and this tended to be part of their

[1] See R. R. Alford, *Party and Society*, Chicago, 1963, and S. M. Lipset and Stein Rokkan (eds.), *Party Systems and Voter Alignments*, New York, 1967.

[2] Lewis Lipsitz, 'Work Life and Political Attitudes: A Study of Manual Workers', *American Political Science Review*, **58**, 1964, pp. 951–62.

[3] Lane, *Political Ideology*, p. 91. (Original italics.)

general attitude to life rather than a specifically *political* attitude. Lane argues that the individuals he interviewed saw political problems, whether local, national or international, through the variety of their experiences. These experiences were not necessarily political, however: their total experience provided one perspective and those experiences which seemed especially relevant to the situation provided others. Moreover, their attitudes on particular situations were closely identified with the various groups to which they belonged, and these *reference* groups, acting as guides or touchstones in the individual's reaction to his experiences, provide further evidence of a continuing process of socialization during adult life.

The knowledge, values and attitudes acquired during childhood and adolescence will be measured against the experience of adult life: they may be reinforced, undermined or modified by that experience; to suggest otherwise is to suggest a static political behaviour. If the processes of adult socialization tend to reinforce those of childhood and adolescence, the degree of change may be limited to that of increasing conservatism with age, but where conflict occurs, then radical changes in political behaviour may result: such conflict may have its roots in early political socialization, but it may also be attributable to the experiences of later socialization. Bernard Berelson and his co-authors found that among their sample of voters the agreement in party preference between the voter and his three closest friends increased markedly with age between twenty-one and forty-five. Of those in the twenty-one to twenty-five age group, 53 per cent voted the same as their three closest friends; in the twenty-six to thirty-four group this had increased to 69 per cent; and in the thirty-five to forty-four group to 75 per cent; but thereafter it levelled out to 77 per cent for those of forty-five or over.[1] Similarly, the tendency for husband and wife to agree on party preference is very strong and the impact of adult socialization in general may be one of increasing social homogeneity. Conversely, the impact of social mobility introduces an element of conflict: one study suggests that upward mobility often results in the individual adopting the party of the social group he has joined, without, however, fully adopting the values and attitudes of that party; while downward mobility

[1] Bernard Berelson, Paul F. Lazarsfeld and William N. McPhee, *Voting*, Chicago, 1954, p. 97.

often results in the retention of party preference, but the partial acceptance of the values and attitudes of the lower social group.[1] In the United States the evidence on adult socialization points largely to a tendency to reinforce early socialization, but there is also evidence to link adult socialization with changes in political behaviour.

Almond and Verba have effectively summarized the results of political socialization in the United States in their study *The Civic Culture*. They found that 85 per cent of their American respondents cited their governmental and political institutions when asked what they were proud of in the United States – far behind came those who cited the economic system (23 per cent) and social legislation (13 per cent).[2] This widespread pride in the country's political system was matched by an identical proportion who felt that the national government had some effect on their daily life; while 76 per cent felt that the effect of the national government was beneficial.[3] Similarly, the overwhelming majority felt that they received equality of treatment from the government officials (83 per cent) and from the police (85 per cent), although much lower proportions (48 and 56 per cent) expected serious consideration of their point of view in encounters with officials and the police.[4] While only 27 per cent said that they regularly followed accounts of political and governmental affairs, a further 53 per cent said that they did so from 'time to time', a total of 80 per cent thus taking some interest in political matters; while 76 per cent said that they sometimes discuss politics with other people.[5] Finally, 75 per cent felt that they could do something about an unjust national regulation.[6]

A picture of considerable political homogeneity is thus presented, in which the political system of the United States is accepted by the vast majority of Americans. This does not, of

---

[1] Eleanor E. Maccoby, Richard E. Matthews and Anton S. Morton, 'Youth and Political Change', *Public Opinion Quarterly*, 18, 1954, pp. 33–6. See also Fred I. Greenstein and Raymond E. Wolfinger, 'The Suburbs and Shifting Party Loyalties', *Public Opinion Quarterly*, 22, 1958, pp. 473–82.

[2] Almond and Verba, *The Civic Culture*, p. 64.

[3] ibid., pp. 46 and 48. The proportion for local government was 88 per cent.

[4] ibid., pp. 70 and 72.

[5] ibid., pp. 54 and 79.

[6] ibid., p. 142; the proportion for a local regulation was 77 per cent.

course, preclude conflict *within* the political system, but what Oakeshott has called 'the arrangements of society' are broadly accepted. Even among those who accept these arrangements, conflict occurs over the policies to be pursued and who is to pursue them. While recognizing this general homogeneity it is, nevertheless, important not to overlook variations in the process of political socialization. This is important in two senses: first, there may be variations within the general homogeneity; and, second, there may be variations (or deviations) from it.

Almond and Verba's data support the view that the political system is broadly accepted in the United States, but within that acceptance there are likely to be many gradations, ranging from total acceptance to near rejection. It is also likely that the paths to that acceptance have varied – the agents of socialization, the relevant experiences and the significant environmental influences may differ from individual to individual. Thus a study of political socialization in one area of the United States led its authors to conclude:

> Children in the relatively poor, rural Appalachian region . . . are dramatically less favourably inclined toward political objects than their counterparts in other parts of the nation.[1]

Similarly, in investigating political socialization among American Negroes, Dwaine Marvick found that not only could a meaningful distinction be made between the socialization of white persons and Negroes, but between various sub-groups:

Table 4. *Proportions of various sub-groups in the U.S. who
have never tried to influence a local decision*

SUB-GROUP	%
Southern Negroes	95
Young Negroes	89
All Negroes	86
Old Negroes	83
Northern Negroes	76
'Poor whites'	73
National white cross-section	70

SOURCE: Dwaine Marvick, 'The Political Socialization of the American Negro', *Annals of the American Academy of Political and Social Science*, **361**, September 1965, p. 120.

[1] D. Jaros, H. Hirsch and F. J. Fleron Jr, 'The Malevolent Leader: Political Socialization in an American Sub-Culture', *American Political Science Review*, **62**, 1968, pp. 574–5.

Apart from variations of this sort, however, there are those who may not accept the political system or who have considerable reservations about it. Just as those who accept the system come to do so through the process of political socialization, so also do those who totally or partially reject it – those who are totally or partially *alienated*; and these individuals will form an important part of our discussion of political participation in Chapter 3.

*

The data available on political socialization in other parts of the world is much less extensive and more fragmentary than that available on the United States. None the less, it is possible to make some comparisons which illustrate some of the similarities and differences, while a good deal may be inferred from our knowledge of the political systems of these other countries in general. Furthermore, some of the research conducted in other countries not only throws light on the process of political socialization in general, but deals with areas which have, as yet, received little or no attention in the United States.

Some useful comparative material is available on the subject of party identification. Converse and Dupeux, for instance, found that whereas 75 per cent of the respondents of a national survey in the United States identified themselves with one or other of the two major parties, less than 45 per cent of their French respondents identified themselves with political parties and a further 10 to 15 per cent with broad categories, such as 'left' and 'right'. As we have already noted, however, they also found a strong correlation between an individual *knowing* his father's political identity and his own political identity, and whereas 82 per cent of the Americans could recall the political identities of their fathers, this was the case with only 28 per cent of the Frenchmen.[1] There is also evidence that the age at which the individual adopts a party preference varies from one country to another. It was noted earlier that by the age of seven or eight most American children have adopted a party preference, but Hyman points out that in Sweden a survey showed that 66 per cent of the thirteen- to fifteen-year-olds were undecided, and that it was not until the

---

[1] Converse and Dupeux, 'Politicization of the Elecorate in France and the United States', p. 9.

age of nineteen that a majority expressed a party preference.[1] Opinion polls in other countries have also shown substantial minorities of adolescents who have shown no party preference: in a survey of the fifteen to twenty age-group in Australia, 33 per cent said they were undecided when asked which party they supported (APOP, March 1967); while 34 per cent in a poll of eighteen- to twenty-year-olds in Britain were undecided (SOC, August 1967). Similarly, a study of Danish students in the period 1946–8 found that the great majority had formed political *attitudes* by the time they had reached the age of eighteen, but nearly a quarter did not do so until they were nineteen years of age or over.[2] It is in fact instructive to compare the respective ages at which these Danish students said they first formed political and religious attitudes (Table 5).

Table 5. *Date of the formation of political and religious attitudes among Danish students*

Date of formation of attitude	ATTITUDE	Political %	Religious %
School years: 7–14		21	74
Adolescence: 15–18		55	19
Adult: 19 or over		24	7
	Total	100	100

SOURCE: Iisager, 'Factors Influencing the Formation of and Change of Political and Religious Attitudes', Table 5, p. 257.

The contrast between the ages at which the students formed political and religious attitudes is marked: approximately three-quarters had formed religious attitudes by the age of fourteen, whereas by the same age little more than a fifth had formed political attitudes. Conversely, nearly a quarter, as we have already noted, did not form political attitudes until they were nineteen or more, compared with only 7 per cent in the forming of religious attitudes.

The study undertaken by Iisager also provides some information on another aspect of political socialization which awaits fuller

[1] Hyman, *Political Socialization*, p. 62.
[2] Holger Iisager, 'Factors Influencing the Formation of and Change of 'Political and Religious Attitudes', *Journal of Social Psychology*, **29**, 1949, pp. 253–65.

investigation. A good deal has been said about the distinction between overt and covert socialization, but little work has been undertaken on what factors the *subjects* of socialization feel influenced their values and attitudes. The students in Iisager's sample were asked what factors had contributed to the formation of their political and religious attitudes. The factors which contributed to the formation of their political attitudes showed considerable variety and included reading, friends, parents, discussions, reasoning and dramatic incidents, but those influencing religious attitudes were heavily concentrated on the home and the school. Moreover, when they were asked which of these factors had been the most important for politics, the first three were reasoning, dramatic incidents and discussions, with parents coming sixth; whereas those for religion were reading and parents (first equal), and school.[1] The results of another study which illustrates the same point are shown in Table 6.

Table 6. *Agents of socialization among children in Chile: who teaches you all you know about the President?*

CLASS	Father or Mother	School	Other	Total (%)
Working class	6	56	38	100
Middle class	42	22	36	100

SOURCE: Robert D. Hess, 'The Socialization of Attitudes Toward Political Authority: Some Cross-National Comparisons', *International Social Science Journal*, 15, 1963, Table 2, p. 554.

It is possible in both the Danish and the Chilean studies that the perceptions of the respondents coincide with the actual agents of socialization, but it is also possible that they have underestimated or overestimated some of the factors involved – the influence of their parents in the formation of their political attitudes may have been greater than the Danish students and working class Chilean children realized, for example. There may, in other words, have been a degree of covert socialization of which they were unaware. If these respondents are accurate in their perceptions, however, then the data suggests that not only does the timing of particular aspects of political socialization vary from one political system to

[1] ibid., Table 3, p. 256.

another, but that the agents of socialization may also vary. The evidence available on socialization in the United States suggests that the family is an important agent of socialization, but this may not be true for all countries, as research on Japan suggests. In a survey of Japanese law students in 1960, Yasumasa Kuroda found that although the overwhelming majority of his respondents were supporters of the Socialist party, most of their parents supported other parties or no party at all. Kuroda concludes that the family is not a major agent of political socialization in post-war Japan and suggests that in a country like Japan, which has undergone considerable and rapid change in a short period of time, the major agencies of political socialization are likely to be more diffuse.[1] It may well be that party preferences of these Japanese students is, among other things, a reaction *against* the political values and attitudes of their parents, and it may therefore be possible to speak of *negative* socialization on the part of the family in this case. Whichever is the case, however, Kuroda produces strong evidence to suggest that in Japan the family plays a different role in political socialization.

A greater contrast may be seen in the Israeli kibbutz, where the traditional role of the family has been reduced and socialization is much more the concern of the whole community. Children are separated from their parents in the kibbutz: they sleep, eat and study in groups in special houses, although they do spend time with their parents during the latter's periods of leisure. The principles and framework of the education they receive is decided by the kibbutz community and embodies formal education (including ideological instruction), periods of manual work (normally agriculture), and instruction in the social and cultural life of the kibbutz. The children not only learn about the political organization of the kibbutz, but actually experience the working of that organization through their own parallel political institutions. The highest authority in the kibbutz is the general assembly, comprising all adult members of the community, and this body elects a management committee, which is subject to a fairly frequent rotation of membership. Similarly, the children have their own general assembly and elected committee, which serve both as a mark of

[1] Yasumasa Kuroda, 'Agencies of Political Socialization and Political Change: the Political Orientations of Japanese Law Students', *Human Organization*, **24**, 1965, pp. 328–31.

their separation from adult life and as a preparation for their assumption of adult roles.[1]

Some evidence has been offered on the differences in political socialization both within a particular political system and between political systems of a broadly similar nature – that is, those which may be termed modern democracies. It is, however, obvious that, compared with the United States and those other countries of which brief mention has been made, countries which have very different political systems from those of modern democracies are likely to have important differences in political socialization, and it is to these that we now turn.

POLITICAL SOCIALIZATION IN TOTALITARIAN SOCIETIES

Only by radically remoulding the teaching, organization, and training of the young shall we be able to ensure that the results of the efforts of the younger generation will be the creation of a society that will be unlike the old society, that is a Communist Society – v. I. LENIN, 'The Tasks of the Youth Leagues', speech delivered to the Third All-Russian Congress of the Russian Young Communist League, 2 October 1920 (Lenin, *Selected Works*, II, Moscow, 1947, p. 661).

. . . we have set before ourselves the task of inoculating our youth with the spirit of this community of the people at a very early age . . . And this new Reich will give its youth to no one, but itself take youth and give to youth its own education and its own upbringing – ADOLF HITLER, 1 May 1937 (*Speeches of Adolf Hitler, April 1922–August 1939*, London, 1942, p. 549).

By definition, the totalitarian state seeks to control all aspects of society, and as these speeches by Lenin and Hitler show, great stress is inevitably laid on socialization in general and political socialization in particular. The ideology of the state becomes the official basis of all action and pervades all activities. Political socialization is not and cannot be left to find its own channels; nor to purvey uncontrolled knowledge, values and attitudes which may contradict or undermine that ideology. The minds of men must be captured, guided and harnessed to the needs of the state

[1] See Eisenstadt, *From Generation to Generation*, pp. 104–7, and Rivkak Bar-Yoseph, 'The Pattern of Early Socialization in the Collective Settlements of Israel', *Human Relations*, **12**, 1959, pp. 345–60.

through the vehicle of its ideology. Thus totalitarian societies differ from modern democracies in the degree of control they exercise over the political socialization of their members. All governments seek, directly or indirectly, to socialize members of society to varying degrees by the control of information, but in the totalitarian society that control is all-pervasive. None the less, the basic process of political socialization as the acquisition of political orientations and patterns of behaviour is as applicable to totalitarian societies as it is to modern democracies, but the emphasis placed on particular subjects, agents and mechanisms may vary both in kind and effectiveness.

The transition from the non-totalitarian to the totalitarian illustrates the differences that are likely to be found in political socialization. The pre-totalitarian generation of individuals will probably have been subjected to a process of political socialization markedly different from that of subsequent totalitarian generations. It is likely that their knowledge, values and attitudes will be markedly different and that these will be carried over into the new régime. It is likely, of course, that the new régime will subject them to a substantial degree of adult socialization through its control of the mass media. The first totalitarian generation may find itself in an ambiguous position since it will be subjected to extensive socialization by the régime, but it may also find that their parents and other members of the older generation represent a counter-force to that socialization. Later generations, however, will be subject almost exclusively to socialization by the state. Thus in the early stages of its rule the totalitarian régime must undermine the process of pre-totalitarian socialization, 're-educate' the pre-totalitarian generation, and prepare for the socialization of the 'new' generation. This was abundantly clear in Nazi Germany and in the U.S.S.R.

Adolf Hitler was, as his speech quoted above makes clear, fully aware of the contribution that political education or socialization could make to the entrenchment and continuance of the régime he had established. He was also aware that the control by the Nazi régime of the mass media was a necessary but insufficient condition for the inculcation of National Socialist ideology among the German people: the political experiences of Imperial Germany and the Weimar Republic were no guarantee of support for Hitler. The political socialization resulting from those experiences could be reinforced and undermined where appropriate, and Hitler made every effort to see that they were, but of much greater importance was the political education of German youth. It was necessary, however, to minimize any anti-Nazi influence that the older generation brought up under the Imperial and Republican régimes might have over the generation growing up under the Nazi régime. Hitler therefore paid not only considerable attention to formal education but also sought to control and limit the role of the family in political socialization.

Children in Nazi Germany were taught that their first loyalty was to the state, personified by the *Führer*, and that any evidence of disloyalty should be reported to the authorities. Children were encouraged to watch, indoctrinate and, if necessary, report their parents and other relatives: the privacy of the family was breached and its influence undermined. Even where the family unit resisted infiltration by its own members, it was vulnerable through the activities of 'friends' – fellow pupils of the children, fellow workers and neighbours of the parents: the establishment of a system of denunciation rendered all vulnerable.

Of greater importance, however, especially for the future, were the twin pillars of political socialization in Nazi Germany – formal education and the youth movements. Inevitably all teachers had to be trained in National Socialist ideology and to be politically reliable. Education was centralized and an order of priorities laid down:

> Hereditary tendencies; general racial picture.
> The character (degree of adherence of National Socialism).
> The physical make-up or 'body' (degree of usefulness in the event of a future war).
> (And last) Knowledge (Here the knowledge of objective reality, regarded as a last offshoot of liberalism, is often punishable where it is not merely regarded as absurd and reprehensible).[1]

All lessons revolved around the official ideology and the learning of 'useful' knowledge. All subjects were redefined in the light of National Socialist ideology and all textbooks were rewritten. History became 'the essence of political education' and 'the crown of all teaching of history consists only of following the *Führer*'.[2]

---

[1] Erika Mann, *School for Barbarians: Education under the Nazis*, London, 1939, p. 48.

[2] ibid., p. 51, quoted from official textbooks.

Mathematics became 'an expression of the Nordic fighting spirit', while the textbooks in mathematics were essentially 'practical'. For example, one textbook, entitled *National Political Practice in Arithmetic Lessons*, contained problems based on Germany's former colonies, such as the total loss in area and population, their proportional distribution between the mandatory powers, and comparisons with the area and population of Germany; other problems dealt with the capacity and performance of military aircraft and other military problems. Another textbook was called *Aerial Defence by Numbers* and contained problems on the effectiveness of air-raid shelters and defence against gas attacks. Nor did the Jewish 'problem' escape mathematical treatment: another textbook, *Germany's Fall and Rise – Illustrations Taken from Arithmetic Instruction in Higher Grades of Elementary School*, contained problems based on the number and proportion of Jews in Germany.[1] All subjects were subordinated to the supreme discipline of racial science, to which even the natural sciences had to conform.

Socialization through formal education was paralleled and strengthened through the Nazi youth movements. There had been strong youth movements in Germany prior to Hitler's accession to power and before the First World War. These were taken over by the new régime, and in 1936 all non-Nazi youth organizations were declared illegal:

> . . . All of the German Youth in the Reich is organized within the Hitler Youth.
> . . . The German Youth, besides being reared within the family and schools, shall be educated physically, intellectually and morally in the spirit of National Socialism . . . through the Hitler Youth.[2]

In 1939 membership of the Hitler Youth became compulsory, and any parents who resisted the indoctrination of their children were liable to have them taken out of their care. Between the ages of six and ten German children received preliminary training in history, camping, athletics and ideology. At the age of ten they were tested and, if suitable, the boys graduated to the *Jungvolk*, the girls to the *Jungmädel*, at which point they swore an oath of allegiance to the *Führer*. At the age of fourteen boys entered the Hitler

[1] ibid., pp. 61–2.
[2] Decree outlawing all non-Nazi youth organizations, quoted in William L. Shirer, *The Rise and Fall of the Third Reich*, New York, 1959, p. 253.

Youth proper and received systematic instruction in ideology and physical and military training. At the age of eighteen they joined the Labour Service, followed by military service. The pattern for girls was similar, but they had their own organizations, the *Jungmädel* (from ten to fourteen) and the *Bund Deutscher Mädel* (from the age of fourteen to twenty-one), followed by a year's service in agriculture.

The whole apparatus of the state was geared to the socialization of German youth, and this was, as Hitler declared in 1933, to be the foundation of the Third Reich:

> When an opponent declares, 'I will not come over to your side', I calmly say, 'Your child belongs to us already . . . What are you? You will pass on. Your descendants, however, now stand in the new camp. In a short time they will know nothing else but this new community.'[1]

A similar pattern of socialization is found in the Soviet Union, with emphasis on both formal education and youth movements. All teaching must conform to Communist ideology, and textbooks are similarly used as a means of political instruction. The Communist youth movement is similar in many respects to that found in Nazi Germany, but differs in that it is increasingly selective as children become older. Thus while all children are subject to early political learning through play, singing, story-telling and so forth, and membership of the Young Pioneers between the age of nine and fourteen is virtually universal, membership of the principal youth organization, the Komsomol, is much more selective. The recommendation of a Communist party member or two Komsomol members is necessary and the Komsomol is an important channel of recruitment into the Communist party itself. Komsomol members receive direct political instruction and military and para-military training.[2]

A further parallel with Nazi Germany is found in the attempts made to undermine the influence of pre-totalitarian experiences in general and family influence in particular.[3] A number of studies

[1] Speech of 6 November 1933, quoted in Shirer, *The Rise and Fall of the Third Reich*, p. 249.

[2] Merle Fainsod, *How Russia is Ruled*, Cambridge, Mass., 1963 (revised edition), Chapter 9.

[3] See also James R. Townsend, *Political Participation in Communist China*, Los Angeles, 1967, who reports that the Communist régime in China 'has tried, albeit with mixed success, to replace loyalties to the family and other particularistic units with loyalty to the political community' (p. 221).

of refugees from the U.S.S.R. carried out at Harvard University
in the early 1950s found evidence of conflict between different
generations in Russia. Those with parents whose political experience stretched back well into the Tsarist period found that their
parents often contradicted what they had learned at school and in
the various youth organizations: although some were confused
as a result of this, it is some indication of the effectiveness of
political socialization in Russia after the Revolution that many
simply did not believe what their parents said. One study in particular examined the child-rearing values held by various generations of Russian parents. The values were as follows:

1 Tradition: mainly religion, but also including family ties and
   tradition generally.
2 Achievement: industriousness, attainment, material rewards,
   social mobility.
3 Personal: honesty, sincerity, justice, mercy.
4 Adjustment: 'getting along', 'staying out of trouble', 'security
   and safeness'.
5 Intellectual: learning and knowledge as ends.
6 Political: attitudes, values and beliefs dealing with the government.

Table 7. *The child-rearing values of the two generations of Russian
          parents.*

VALUES	Tsarist generation	Revolutionary generation
	%	%
Tradition	75	44
Achievement	60	52
Personal	32	44
Adjustment	16	21
Intellectual	12	22
Political	12	20

SOURCE: Alex Inkeles, 'Social Change and Social Character: the Role of
Parental Mediation', *Journal of Social Issues*, **11**, 1955, pp. 12–23.

The Tsarist or pre-revolutionary generation placed overwhelming
stress on tradition, followed by achievement as child-rearing
values, whereas the revolutionary generation placed achievement

first, with tradition, although second, much reduced in importance, while increased emphasis was placed on personal values, on adjustment, and intellectual and political values. Inkeles suggests that these changes may be attributed to the impact of change upon the values of the respondents, to a process of socialization following the 1917 Revolution. He further tested this hypothesis by asking his respondents what values they held in respect of occupation, but this time he used three generations – Tsarist, revolutionary and Soviet, the latter having been brought up by parents of the revolutionary generation. The Tsarist generation stressed rewards and tradition as the most important values, but the two subsequent generations overwhelmingly stressed self-expression, although there was a significant increase in political values as well. It may be surmised that both self-expression, in the form of the individual's contribution to the welfare of society, and a greater stress on political fulfilment may be regarded as in accordance with Communist ideology, together with a reduction in the value of tradition, and that these may be attributable to a process of socialization.

The Soviet case is particularly interesting because, unlike the National Socialists in Germany, the Communists have been in power long enough to see generations born and growing up which have no direct contact with pre-Soviet Russia through personal experience and whose parents were born under the Soviet régime. Furthermore, generations are now growing up who have little or no contact with those who grew up in the earliest years of the régime, the years of the New Economic Plan, the Five-Year Plans, of collectivization, and of industrialization; similarly Stalin's Russia and the Second World War are to them history, not experience. These and future generations will have experienced the full process of political socialization under a totalitarian régime, a fact which may have important implications for the continuance of that régime.

Evidence from East European countries tends to support the data presented on the Soviet Union. Opinion polls among young people in Yugoslavia, for example, found that although 57 per cent of high school pupils said that their parents were the most important factor influencing their views, only 37 per cent said that their views were the same as their parents and 25 per cent said they were completely different. A poll of university students found that 63 per cent accepted Marxism as a 'true revolutionary theory'.[1] Another study of Polish respondents in 1964 found a relationship between knowledge of Communist doctrine and whether or not the respondents had been educated under the Communist régime (Table 8).

Table 8. *Knowledge of Communist doctrine and education under the Communist régime in Poland, 1964*

	Educated before 1946–8	Educated since 1946–8
Knew of the theory of the withering away of the state	7	22
Total respondents	34	36

SOURCE: Roger Pethybridge, 'The Assessment of Ideological Influence on East Europeans', *Public Opinion Quarterly*, **21**, 1967, pp. 38–50.

The implication of the data in the table is clear as far as *knowledge* of the theory of the withering away of the state is concerned, but Pethybridge presents additional data which casts some doubt on the effectiveness of formal instruction in Marxism-Leninism in Poland. He found that whereas five of those educated before 1946–8 believed that the state would wither away, this was still the case with only eight of those educated under the Communist régime. It is important to note, however, that most of the former were either self-taught in Marxism-Leninism or else were militant Communist party members. Poland, with a substantial Catholic population, may, of course, be a special case, but the relatively recent accession to power of the Communist régime may also be an important factor in political socialization.

The evidence available on political socialization in totalitarian societies is inevitably limited and fragmentary, but the evidence and data presented does give some idea of the nature of the process in such societies. Political socialization is not left to run its course, but becomes an integral part of a totalitarian system, a means by which the régime overtly seeks to perpetuate itself and the ideology on which it is based. Thus close attention is paid to socialization throughout adult life in the Soviet Union: the general population receives carefully controlled information through a

[1] Stanislaw Skrzypek, 'The Political, Cultural and Social Views of Yugoslav Youth', *Public Opinion Quarterly*, **29**, 1965, pp. 87–106.

vast network of face-to-face contacts with 'agitators'; Communist party members and candidates for party membership receive ideological instruction in political schools – more general instruction is achieved through discussion groups or seminars, through public lectures organized by the All-Union Society for the Dissemination of Political and Scientific Information; and by making standard works in Communist and Marxist-Leninist literature available at low cost; while more general socialization is sought through the strict control of the mass media.[1] Indeed, the term '*political* socialization' is almost a misnomer: given the nature of totalitarian societies, in which all is legitimately 'political', the process becomes one of socialization in general. The orientations and patterns of behaviour acquired are not specifically political but societal in nature. In this sense, at least, there is a parallel between socialization in totalitarian societies and in primitive societies, in that the distinction between the social and the political is minimal. Moreover, a number of totalitarian societies place considerable emphasis on ritual in the socialization process, and this is also a feature of the process in primitive societies. The comparison must not, of course, be taken too far; none the less, the similarities are noticeable and possibly significant.

POLITICAL SOCIALIZATION IN PRIMITIVE SOCIETIES

It is in primitive societies that the role of socialization in general is seen most vividly, especially in those societies which have or had existed long enough to establish strong societal traditions which define the structure and roles of society. Although differences in socialization exist between various primitive societies, such societies lack the differentiation found in complex modern societies, and the process of socialization is characterized by an intrinsic unity emphasizing ritual, the legitimization of societal roles and, often, the achievement of status. Political socialization is an integral part of learning societal roles in general rather than political roles in particular. The Buganda people of East Africa, for example, lived in a highly-centralized monarchical system with a hierarchy based not on classes or groups but upon the status of

[1] See Alex Inkeles, *Public Opinion in Russia: A Study in Mass Persuasion*, Cambridge, Mass., 1958.

the individual. This allowed considerable social mobility within the hierarchy, but did not prevent the principle theme of socialization being respect for parents and deference to superiors, a theme which was of great importance in maintaining the hierarchical system.[1]

Primitive societies may differ considerably, however, in their socialization processes, even though they may have certain common characteristics, as Robert Le Vine has shown.[2] Le Vine examined socialization among two tribes in south-west Kenya, both of which were uncentralized and patriarchical groups, had a similar subsistence base and were characterized by blood feuds. The Nuer, however, were basically egalitarian and passive in attitude, whereas the Gusii were authoritarian and aggressive, and the children of each tribe were encouraged in their respective traditions. The importance of tradition, the emphasis on such socialization techniques as ritual, initiation, and the frequent stress on hierarchy and status found in primitive societies form an important link between them and modern societies. We have already seen that similar emphases are to be found in totalitarian societies, and this may be the result of the degree to which the social and the political are integrated, though these characteristics are also important in the socialization processes of developing societies in Asia, Africa and Latin America. In these societies we find the conjunction of the old and the new, the traditional and the modern.

POLITICAL SOCIALIZATION IN DEVELOPING SOCIETIES

The conjunction of the old and the new can be seen most clearly in those parts of the world which were formerly colonized by European powers. To varying degrees the colonial powers introduced Western political institutions, bureaucracy, culture and education. In the majority of cases these various manifestations of modern Western societies remained, if not intact, at least in

---

[1] See L. A. Fallers, 'Despotism, Status Culture and Social Mobility in an African Kingdom', in *Comparative Studies in Society and History*, **2**, 1959, pp. 11–32, and A. I. Richards, *East African Chiefs*, London, 1960, Chapter 2.

[2] Robert Le Vine, 'The Internalization of Political Values in Stateless Societies', *Human Organization*, **19**, 1960, pp. 51–8.

existence, invariably forming the vehicles of modernization in these societies. In juxtaposition to them, however, there remained the many manifestations of the traditional societies which had existed before colonization. During the struggle for independence, these traditional attitudes and influences tended to be submerged in the unity maintained by the common goal of national independence. Once independence was achieved the traditional pressures reasserted themselves, usually becoming the basis for interest groups and political parties. The result is a complex mixture of the traditional and the modern, consisting of a series of modern institutions resting (often precariously) on a traditional base which is continually under the impact of the increasing pressure of industrialization and urbanization. The traditional processes of socialization continue to shape the orientations and patterns of behaviour of the majority of the people, while the political leaders endeavour to break down those traditions which appear to be obstacles to 'progress'. Socialization becomes fragmented, however, partly because many developing countries consist of the amalgamation of several (often many) traditional societies, which often become competing power groups in new nations; and partly because the distinction between the social and the political becomes sharper. Specifically political institutions – executives, legislatures, judiciaries, political parties, interest groups – which are not integral parts of the traditional societies are created. These institutions have not evolved out of the traditional societies and the socialization processes of the latter may be ill-equipped for dealing with such institutions. The institutions are not, in other words, integrated into the social system and such legitimacy as they may possess is often precarious. Furthermore, the distinction between the institutions and those who hold office in them is blurred, and any failure of the individual office-holder, real or perceived, reflects on the institution.

This is clear from a study of political socialization in Colombia in which a questionnaire used in similar studies in the United States was replicated for comparative purposes. This study showed that whereas American children had increasingly favourable attitudes towards government and the political system as they proceeded through the various grades in school, Colombian children became increasingly critical. By the highest grade half of the Colombian children agreed with the statement, 'in the government there are some big, powerful men who run everything and don't care about the opinions of ordinary people', compared with only 6 per cent of U.S. children. Similarly, the *highest* proportion of U.S. children who said that they had no chance to express their opinions was 18 per cent, and this proportion fell steadily with grade, but among the Colombian children the *lowest* was 17 per cent and the highest 28 per cent, though the proportion fluctuated between grades.[1]

At the same time important similarities in socialization between developing countries and modern democracies may be found. Research on political socialization in Jamaica found strong party identity among school-children, especially among those who came from politically motivated families, and tendencies for children to conform to the dominant partisan pattern in their schools. Thus it is possible to detect patterns of reinforcement and cross-pressures of a type found in countries like Britain and the United States.[2] There is also evidence of class differences of the sort similar to those found in the latter countries. Upper class students in Panama, for example, were shown to be more anti-Communist than middle-class students, who showed greater concern with economic problems, were more likely to regard politics as dishonest and were more critical of the president and the National Assembly.[3] Similarly, Kenneth Langton, in the research cited above, found that working class Jamaican students were less committed to democracy, gave less support to civil liberties for minority groups, were less inclined to vote and generally less politically motivated than middle and upper class students.

Many new states have attempted to meet the problems created by the conflict of the traditional and the modern by means of political education. In 1964, for instance, the Kenyan government published an Education Commission Report describing the type of citizens that schools are expected to produce. Pupils are expected to have a commitment to national unity, tolerance of

[1] R. Reading, 'Political Socialization in Colombia and the United States', *Midwest Journal of Political Science*, **12**, 1968, pp. 352–81.

[2] Kenneth P. Langton, 'Political Partisanship and Political Socialization in Jamaica', *British Journal of Sociology*, **17**, 1966, pp. 419–29, and 'Peer Group and School and the Socialization Process', *American Political Science Review*, **61**, 1967, pp. 751–8.

[3] Daniel Goldrich and Edward W. Scott, 'Developing Political Orientations of Panamanian Students', *Journal of Politics*, **23**, 1961, pp. 84–105.

tribal, racial and religious differences, acceptance of social change and social equality. Similar aims may be found in Tanzania, and a survey of schoolchildren in these two countries found that majorities regarded the most important purpose of their schools as being to teach them to be 'good citizens'. The problem of the conflict between the traditional and the modern is illustrated, however, by the fact that the respondents in both Kenya and Tanzania exhibited overwhelming trust of their fathers, teachers and religious leaders (with no significant difference between primary and secondary levels), but trust of political leaders declined between these two levels from 72 per cent to 57 per cent in Kenya and from 89 per cent to 63 per cent in Tanzania. A similar result was found in Uganda.[1]

David Apter effectively summarises the problem of political socialization in developing societies when he suggests that the ideologies of many new nations take the form of a religion, not in a specifically spiritual sense but in that they are theocratic in practice. Leaders become deified and the state ideology is given the rank of a religion. Apter further suggests that although this process may assist the process of modernization and industrialization, it renders political change difficult – a change in politics may require a change of 'religion'.[2] The central problem of political socialization in developing societies is that of coping with change. This is well illustrated by the example of Turkey, where a systematic attempt was made both to effect and accommodate change following the First World War. Mustapha Kemal (Kemal Atatürk) sought to modernize Turkey not only materially but through the processes of socialization. Considerable stress was laid on the symbols of nationhood – the national flag and anthem, national holidays, monuments, military parades and the encouragement of Turkish language and history. Educational opportunities were increased and teachers were trained in methods of teaching the ideology of the Republican People's party (C.H.P.), the only official party. Adult socialization was achieved through 'People's Houses' in which political ideas stressing modernization,

[1] David Koff and George van der Muhl, 'Political Socialization in Kenya and Tanzania: A Comparative Analysis', *Journal of Modern African Studies*, 5, 1967, pp. 13–51.
[2] David E. Apter, 'Political Religion in the New Nations', in Geertz (ed.), *Old Societies and New States*, pp. 57–104.

secularism and nationalism were discussed and disseminated. Considerable changes were effected, and in 1945 Atatürk's successor, Ismet Inönu, called for the formation of other parties. These were formed and Turkey entered a period of competitive party politics. The system broke down, however, because the two main parties represented the main divisions in the nation – the traditional and the modern, the rural and the urban – while no agreement could be reached on an electoral system acceptable to both sides. The period ended with the military *coup* of 1960, and this has been followed by a further attempt to introduce a competitive party system based on free elections.[1]

Ghana provides a similar example, where, following a period of military rule which brought an end to the régime of Kwame Nkrumah in 1966, new elections were held in 1969 as a prelude to the resumption of civilian rule. The severe problems which face a developing country comprising a variety of groups and traditions can also be seen vividly in the history of Nigeria since its independence in 1960. Robert Le Vine has argued that political socialization in developing countries tends to be related more to local, tribal, ethnic and regional rather than national political systems. There are, he suggests, three important factors in the political socialization in such societies:

1. The growth of population in developing countries may outstrip their capacity to 'modernize' traditional family life through industrialization and education.
2. There is often an important disparity in education and traditional values between the sexes so that women may be more firmly attached to the latter, yet the mother may play an important role in the early socialization of the child.
3. It is likely that the influence of urbanization, which is invariably regarded as a powerful force in breaking down traditional values, is at least partially offset by the transference of traditional values into urban areas, especially by the establishment of tribal and ethnic communities in these areas.

Le Vine therefore concludes that it is misleading to regard traditional values as something which must be destroyed or replaced:

[1] Joseph S. Szyliowicz, 'Political Participation and Modernization in Turkey', *Western Political Quarterly*, **19**, 1966, pp. 266–84.

they need to be combined with the new institutions and patterns of behaviour.[1] The evidence available on political socialization suggests that some such process is necessary, possibly inevitable. No break with the past can be complete, and even though far-reaching and fundamental changes may be effected, an element of continuity remains. In the very act of seeking a break with its past a society is influenced by that past, however different the future may be. Political socialization is therefore closely involved in the process of change.

POLITICAL SOCIALIZATION AND CHANGE

It is clear that the nature of political socialization varies over time and according to the environment of which it is part and to which it contributes. Political socialization is therefore related to the nature of the polity and the degree and nature of change:

> The more stable the polity the more specified the major agencies of political socialization will be.
>
> Conversely, the greater the degree of change in a non-totalitarian polity, the more diffused the major agencies of political socialization will be. The more basic the degree of revolution in a polity, the more specified the major agencies of political socialization will be. (No revolutions are complete without setting up some specific agencies of political socialization in order to cut off the continuation of traditional values which are detrimental to the new régime.)
>
> The more totalitarian the nature of political change, the smaller and more specific the number of major agencies of political socialization will be.[2]

The more homogeneous a society and the longer it has persisted over time, the more likely it is that the process of socialization will become clearly defined and relatively unified, and a similar effect is likely in societies in which there is an overt attempt to control the process of socialization. Conversely, in heterogeneous societies and those subject to frequent and radical change, the process of socialization is likely to be fragmented and applicable to various groups in society rather than to society as a whole. At any given period in time, it is possible to posit for any given society a *political culture* which may be defined as the politically relevant

[1] Le Vine, 'Political Socialization and Culture Change', pp. 284–5.
[2] Kuroda, 'Agencies of Political Socialization and Political Change', p. 331.

values and attitudes of a society. The relationship between political culture and political socialization is crucial, since it is by means of the latter process that these politically relevant values and attitudes are transmitted from one generation to another. This does not mean, of course, that these values and attitudes are immutable, since the process of socialization is continuous and may effectively contribute to their change as well as their persistence.

In *The Civic Culture*, Almond and Verba presents the results of a cross-national survey of political culture. In their conclusions they suggest that each of the five nations they studied – the United States, Britain, West Germany, Italy and Mexico – has its own distinctive political culture. The United States and Britain were characterized by a general acceptance of the political system, by a fairly high degree of political participation and by a widespread feeling among respondents that they could influence affairs to some degree. Greater stress was laid on participation by Americans, whereas British respondents exhibited a greater deference towards their government. The political culture of West Germany was marked by a degree of detachment from the political system and a more passive attitude towards participation, but respondents nevertheless felt able to influence affairs. In contrast to these three countries, Italy showed widespread political alienation, involving low political interest, low participation and a feeling of an inability to influence affairs; while Mexico was a mixture of acceptance of the theory of politics and alienation from its substance.

A key factor in the concept of political culture is that of *legitimacy* – the extent to which a political system is accepted by society. As Weber pointed out, the basis of that legitimacy may vary. Furthermore, it is important to understand, as Lipset points out in *Political Man*, the basic legitimacy of a political system does not preclude conflict. Agreement may exist over the basic political framework, but within that framework conflict may continue over both means and ends. At the same time, if the conflict over means and ends becomes extensive, it may undermine any agreement over the political framework. Lipset argues that it is the existence of conflict within consensus that forms the basis of modern democracies. The concept of legitimacy is not, of course, limited to modern democracies – the political system in a totalitarian society may enjoy widespread legitimacy as a result of political socialization, just as the political system of a non-totalitarian society may be denied legitimacy. In another of the studies of Soviet refugees by Harvard University, Raymond Bauer found that younger respondents (i.e. those who grew up under the Soviet régime) had normally accepted the Soviet system initially and had seldom always been opposed to the régime. Moreover, these respondents generally retained important ideological commitments, such as support of the Welfare State and for the state ownership of various industries, and tended to blame the Soviet *leadership* rather than the *political system* for their disillusionment.[1] This evidence would suggest that Soviet political *system* enjoys (or enjoyed) a widespread degree of legitimacy. Conversely, the problems of the German Weimar Republic and the French Fourth Republic have been attributed in part to a loss of (or even a failure to acquire) legitimacy.

It is also important to understand that legitimacy may extend to many aspects of the political system or may be limited to a few. There is, for example, widespread evidence that most Americans accept their major political institutions – the presidency, Congress and the Supreme Court – but a distinction is drawn between the political institutions and the persons who wield power through them for a given period of time. At the end of that period of time they, or the party they represent, may win a further period of power or else their opponents may secure office. In either case, both those who seek power and those who choose between the rivals for office are normally prepared to abide by the results of electoral decision. Similarly, the right of the president or Congress to exercise their powers is not normally questioned, but the use to which those powers are put is subject to frequent criticism. Criticism of the political system in other countries may be much more fundamental, however, possibly to the extent of denying the system's legitimacy or subjecting it to severe strain. The expectation of violent change, for example, may differ substantially from one country to another: only 9 per cent of the respondents in an American opinion poll said that at some future date 'military leaders in the United States would try to take over the White House and rule the country (MINN, July 1966); whereas 46 per cent of respondents in an Argentine poll in 1966 expected the

[1] Raymond A. Bauer, 'Some Trends in Sources of Alienation from the Soviet System', *Public Opinion Quarterly*, **19**, 1955, pp. 279–91.

government to fall as a result of a *coup d'état* (EGA, Buenos Aires, March 1966).

The case of West Germany illustrates not only the extent to which a political system may be regarded as legitimate, but how this legitimacy may change over a period of time. Germany has suffered a series of drastic changes in its political system in the present century – changes which have been twice associated with military defeat and national humiliation, thus presenting severe problems of legitimacy. This would certainly appear to be true of the Weimar Republic, the impact of which on present-day West Germans appears to be limited: in 1966 no less than 53 per cent of the respondents said that they 'had no idea of the Weimar Republic' (EMNID, January 1966). It is not surprising, therefore, to find that the present Federal Republic lacked widespread legitimacy for a considerable period after its establishment in 1949, nor that the attitudes of West Germans towards Hitler, towards the first Chancellor of the Federal Republic and towards various ideas held strongly in other Western European countries, and towards the Federal Parliament, should have changed only slowly in the post-war period.

In 1951 only 32 per cent of the respondents in a West German poll were prepared to say that Germany was to blame for the outbreak of war in 1939; by 1956 this proportion had risen by 47 per cent; by 1964 to 51 per cent; and by 1967 to 62 per cent. (DMS, May 1967). Similarly and not surprisingly, no one was prepared in 1950 to say that Konrad Adenauer merited the accolade of the German who had 'made the most valuable achievement for Germany', compared with 10 per cent who nominated Hitler for this role; but by 1966 Adenauer's standing had risen to 44 per cent, Hitler's falling to 2 per cent (DMS, December 1966). In the same way, in 1953, 12 per cent of the respondents in a survey said they would vote for Hitler if he were still alive, compared with 67 per cent who said they would vote against him. Although a year later Hitler's opponents had swelled to 81 per cent, his supporters had actually risen to 15 per cent, though by 1967 this had dwindled to 4 per cent (EMNID, February 1967). Attitudes towards the basic ideology of the political system and the principal political institution of the Federal Republic tended to change equally slowly.

Table 9. *West German attitudes towards their political system*

(A) What are the most important 'freedoms'?

FREEDOM	1949	1954	1958	1962	1963	1964	1965	1967
Of religion	12	16	16	13	14	11	14	15
Of speech	26	32	44	47	56	48	54	52
From fear	17	17	10	8	10	10	8	10
From want	35	35	28	17	15	25	19	24
Don't know	10	–	2	15	5	6	5	5
	100	100	100	100	100	100	100	106*

SOURCE: EMNID, November 1967.   * Multiple response.

(B) What is your opinion of the Bonn Parliament?

OPINION	1951	1952	1953	1958	1963	1965	1967
Definitely good	7	3	9	6	4	3	5
Basically good	28	27	37	31	42	49	53
Moderate	31	35	31	41	36	34	28
Poor	9	13	10	16	7	4	4
No answer	25	22	13	6	11	11	10
Total	100	100	100	100	100	101	100

SOURCE: EMNID, August 1967.

The data presented in Table 9 suggests that the Federal German Republic and the political system of which it is part gained legitimacy only gradually in the postwar period. This same period was, of course, marked by Germany's reconstruction and economic recovery, and the figures in Section A of the table are consistent with the view that, as Germany again found her place among the Western nations (especially as part of the NATO alliance) and as economic prosperity increased, so the emphasis placed on 'freedom from fear' and 'freedom from want' tended to decrease, while the stress placed on the less material value of 'freedom of speech' increased. A number of writers, notably S. M. Lipset and James Coleman, have suggested that there are significant correlations between modernization and democracy,[1] but it is likely that the significance lies in delineating the conditions in which democracy is able to flourish, and this concept may be extended to posit the conditions under which legitimacy is likely to exist. It is possible, for example, that opinions of the Bonn Parliament in West Germany improved because the country became more

[1] Lipset, *Political Man*, pp. 45ff., and Almond and Coleman (eds.), *Politics of the Developing Areas*, pp. 538ff.

prosperous – the political system became more widely accepted as people became more satisfied with primarily non-political matters. The legitimacy of the political system becomes related to societal satisfaction.

Over a period of time, however, the situation may become complicated. It is likely that the various institutions which comprise the political system will become increasingly distinct from those who, at any given time, exercise power through them. The political institutions may thus acquire a legitimacy which was lacking in the early stages of their existence and it becomes increasingly possible for the members of a society to subject those who wield power to criticism without criticizing the political system itself. Ultimately, the political system may acquire a degree of legitimacy which enables it to withstand considerable strain caused by societal dissatisfaction. In the period following the 1966 election, for example, the British government found itself subject to increasing criticism and experienced growing unpopularity, and opinion poll evidence suggests that this was paralleled by widespread dissatisfaction with various aspects of the political system: 68 per cent of those interviewed said that they did not have 'enough say in the way the government runs the country'; 69 per cent agreed that important issues should be decided by referendum rather than left for the government to decide; 46 per cent favoured a coalition rather than government by either of the major parties; and 44 per cent said they were dissatisfied with the parliamentary system (SOC, May, June and September 1968). How far is this evidence of a loss of legitimacy by the British political system?

The various proposed remedies which received widespread support from respondents – fixed terms of office for the government (63 per cent), the appointment of industrialists and businessmen as Ministers (61 per cent), committees of M.P.s to run government departments (56 per cent), the provision of offices and secretarial help for M.P.s (51 per cent), a reduction in the number of M.P.s (48 per cent), and the establishment of regional parliaments (47 per cent) – hardly suggest fundamental changes in the political system. This would suggest that where the system enjoys widespread legitimacy, the degree of dissatisfaction within society has to be considerable before a change of political system is likely or before the political system is seriously undermined.

Legitimacy may also be somewhat fragmentary – extended more fully to some aspects of the system than to others. The existence of a republic in France, for instance, probably enjoys very considerable legitimacy, so that a restoration of the monarchy has found little support there since the last serious attempt towards the end of the nineteenth century. Other French political institutions are less firmly established and no French constitution has achieved the inviolability of the American. Thus, in any given society, there may be overwhelming agreement on certain fundamentals, such as the holding of periodic elections, the maintenance of a particular form of executive, legislature and judiciary, the creation of a neutral bureaucracy, and so on, but other aspects of the political system may be the subject of conflict. An agreement to hold periodic elections does not constitute agreement on the actual electoral machinery; agreement on a particular form of executive, legislature and judiciary does not constitute agreement on the use to which these institutions are to be put; and agreement on the desirability of creating a neutral bureaucracy does not constitute agreement that the bureaucracy is neutral.

Political socialization is the process by which individuals acquire knowledge, values and attitudes about the political system of their society. It does not assure that society legitimacy for its political system, though that may be the result. It may equally result in the denial of legitimacy, but whether this leads to stasis or change will depend on the circumstances of that denial. Where lack of legitimacy is accompanied by active hostility to the political system, then change is likely, but where it is accompanied by apathy towards the political system, the result is stasis. Through his experiences the individual acquires political orientations and patterns of behaviour which 'may contribute to the maintenance or replication of a given system, to its transformation or to its total destruction.'[1]

---

[1] Easton and Dennis, *Children in the Political System*, p. 66.

3 · Political Participation

We have already seen how the process of political socialization provides the individual with a perceptual screen through which he receives political stimuli. We now have to deal with the effects of these stimuli as they are seen in the process of political participation, the extent to which individuals are involved at various levels in the political system. Political participation may be considered from four points of view:

1   What are the types or forms of political participation?
2   What is the extent of political participation?
3   Who participates?
4   Why do they participate?

FORMS OF POLITICAL PARTICIPATION
There is little difficulty in suggesting the various forms of political participation, regardless of the type of political system concerned: the roles of the professional politician, the voter, the party activists, and the demonstrator immediately spring to mind. It is important, however, to posit the full range of political activities and to see whether there is some sort of hierarchical relationship between them. The simplest and most meaningful hierarchy is probably one based on the degree or extent of participation.

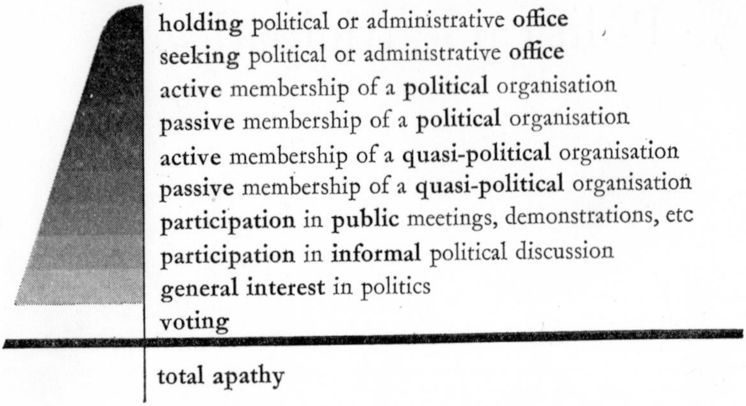

holding political or administrative office
seeking political or administrative office
active membership of a political organisation
passive membership of a political organisation
active membership of a quasi-political organisation
passive membership of a quasi-political organisation
participation in public meetings, demonstrations, etc
participation in informal political discussion
general interest in politics
voting

total apathy

Figure 2. A hierarchy of political participation

The hierarchy suggested in Figure 2 is intended to cover the whole range of political participation and to be applicable to all types of political systems. The significance of the various levels is, of course, likely to vary from one political system to another, and particular levels may be of great consequence in one system and of little or no consequence in another.

It is also important to appreciate that participation at one level of the hierarchy is not necessarily a precondition of participation at a higher level, though this may be true for certain types of participation.

At the top of the hierarchy there are those who hold various types of office within the political system, including both holders of political office and members of the bureaucracy at various levels. They are distinguished from other political participants in that, to varying degrees, they are concerned with the exercise of formal political power. This does not exclude the actual exercise of power, nor the exercise of influence, by other individuals or groups in the political system. Power may or may not reside among the office-holders, but they remain important because normally they are the formal repositories of power. Any consideration of the office-holders must also include some consideration of those who aspire to and seek the offices concerned. The roles of office-holders and potential office-holders, however, will be dealt with in Chapter 4, where political recruitment is considered.

Below those who hold or seek office in the political system, there are those who are members of various types of political or quasi-political organizations. These include all types of political parties and interest (or pressure) groups. From the point of view of the political system, political parties and interest groups may be defined as *agents of political mobilization*. They are organizations through which individual members of society may participate in certain types of political activity involving the defence or promotion of particular ideas, positions, situations, persons or groups through the political system.

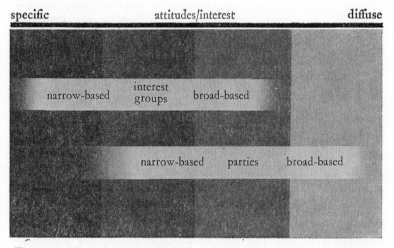

Figure 3. The relationship between political parties and interest groups

Figure 3 looks at the relationship between political parties and interest groups. The basic distinction between the two lies in their attitudes. Interest groups are those organizations which seek to promote, defend or represent limited or specific attitudes, whereas political parties seek to promote, defend or represent a broader spectrum of attitudes. The support that interest groups and political parties receive, however, may be specific or diffuse, stemming, that is, from only a few individuals or groups in society, or from a diverse and large number of individuals or groups. Thus an interest group has limited objectives, such as the introduction, repeal or modification of certain laws or regulations, the protection of the interests of a particular group in society, or the promotion of particular ideologies, beliefs, principles or ideas. In some cases the objective is especially limited – the abolition of capital punishment or opposition to the siting of an airport, for instance – and the interest group ceases to operate once its objective has been achieved (or defeated). In other cases the objective is of a continuing nature – the protection or extension of civil rights and liberties or the defence of various economic interests, for example – in which case the interest group concerned has an indefinite existence. The range of matters which may give rise to interest groups is obviously legion, but it is clear that some of these groups will attract only limited, others widespread, support. Trade unions, for instance, may fall into either category according to the size and nature of the industry in which they operate. Similarly, the extent to which groups are involved in *political* activity varies considerably, from the group operating entirely within the political sphere to the group which does so only occasionally. A group like the Campaign for Nuclear Disarmament, for example, operates for the most part as a specifically political interest group, whereas groups like the Automobile Association are not concerned solely with providing motorists with a political voice. In Figure 2, therefore, the term 'political organization' is intended to include both political parties and those interest groups whose *raison d'être* is primarily political, and the term 'quasi-political organization' to include those interest groups whose function is only partly political.

Political parties, like interest groups, may enjoy diffuse or specific support, but differ from interest groups in that they have diffuse rather than specific attitudes. Their objectives range over the whole spectrum of problems with which society is faced, although a particular party may place greater emphasis on some problems or aspects of problems than others. Some political parties, however, have a broad support base, others a narrow support base. The pragmatic, bargaining mass parties of modern democracies and the totalitarian mass parties of Nazi Germany and various Communist states are examples of broad-based parties, while the regional, religious, ethnic and élitist parties found in many parts of the world are examples of narrow-based parties.

Participation in political parties and interest groups may take an active or passive form, ranging from holding office in such an organization to the provision of financial support through the payment of subscriptions or membership dues. No sharp distinction between active and passive membership is intended and the individual may move from one to the other as circumstances vary. There remains, nevertheless, a basic commitment to the organization through membership, which may have some political significance, both for the organization and the individual, by strengthening the bargaining position of the organization and influencing the political behaviour of the individual.

For various reasons individuals may not belong to any political or quasi-political organizations, but they may be persuaded to participate in some form of public meeting or demonstration. This form of participation may be spontaneous, but it is far more likely to have been organized by political parties or interest groups as part of their political activity. Many, perhaps in some cases all, of the participants will be members of the organizing bodies, but not necessarily, and non-members may be persuaded to support the objects of the meeting or demonstration. Such activity is, however, intermittent and does not have the continuous nature of even the minimal commitment of membership of a political or quasi-political organization.

Another intermittent form of political participation is that of informal political discussion by individuals in their families, at work or among friends. Obviously the incidence of such discussions varies both among individuals and in relation to events. More discussion is likely during election campaigns or at times of political crisis, while discussion may be inhibited or encouraged by the attitudes of the family, fellow-workers or friends.

Some people may not discuss politics with anyone, however, but may, none the less, have some interest in political matters and maintain that interest through the mass media. They will be able to keep themselves informed about what is happening and form opinions about the course of events, but they will tend to limit their participation to this and, possibly, to voting.

The act of voting may be regarded as the least active form of political participation since it requires a minimal commitment which may cease once the vote is cast. Furthermore, regardless of other restrictions which may exist, the act of voting is inevitably restricted by the frequency of elections.

In considering political participation, however limited it may be, some attention should be paid to those who do not participate at all in the political process. Whether this is by choice or because of factors beyond the control of the individual remains to be seen, but whichever it is, such individuals may be described as totally apathetic.

Two matters have deliberately been excluded from the hierarchy in Figure 2: alienation and violence. This is because neither can be properly considered in a hierarchical sense. It will later be argued that alienation may result in participation or non-participation: an individual who feels hostile towards society in general or the political system in particular may withdraw from all types of participation and join the ranks of the totally apathetic, or he may become active at various levels of participation. Participation does not necessarily involve acceptance of the political system and alienation may be expressed by political activity as well as inactivity.

Similarly, violence may manifest itself at various levels in the hierarchy, not only in the form of demonstrations or riots, but also through various political and quasi-political organizations, some of which may regard violence as an effective means of achieving their ends.

THE EXTENT OF POLITICAL PARTICIPATION

Having outlined the various forms of political participation it is obvious that their importance will vary from one political system to another. Moreover, they will vary within a system over time. Various limitations on political participation will therefore exist. Some of these limitations will be formal in nature, others will be informal.

In primitive societies, where politics tends to be closely integrated with societal activity in general, participation is likely to be high and may be difficult to distinguish from other activities. In developing societies, however, with their combination of modern and traditional institutions and influences, participation may be limited by such factors as the level of literacy and the general problem of communication. Contrasting with this, political participation in totalitarian societies may, for some forms of participation, be very high and for others very low, while by definition one of the most important characteristics of totalitarian societies is

any one party

that they seek to control participation in the political process at all levels. The greatest degree of variation is likely to be found in modern democracies, which, while usually encouraging participation by various means, generally leave it to find its own level. *many p. competing for any*

It is useful to consider political participation in a hierarchical sense, but it should also be borne in mind that some levels of participation may be absent from some political systems. Not all political systems have elections or any form of voting; some systems severely restrict or ban public meetings and demonstrations, while others forbid the formation of political parties and other types of political or quasi-political organizations, and so on. Furthermore, apathy, alienation and the use of violence clearly *repressive* vary considerably from system to system, but remain important factors in any examination of political participation. Even where participation occurs at the same level in different political systems, however, its nature and significance may vary. This is clearly shown by a brief perusal of voting in different political systems.

The purpose of voting, for example, may be to elect (directly or indirectly) a government, or various officials, or members of a legislature, or to approve or disapprove of certain proposals by means of a referendum or plebiscite, or to enforce legislative responsibility through the device of 'recall' (which enables an electorate to call its representative to account). The voter in the United States is faced with as many as forty choices at some election times: he is called upon to choose a president, a senator, and a member of the House of Representatives (all at federal level), a governor, members of the state legislature and various officials (all at state level), various local government officials (at county and, possibly, municipal level), members of bodies like school boards, and, not infrequently, to participate in a referendum and, more rarely, in a 'recall'. Even in those years when no federal offices and fewer state offices are at stake, the choice remains formidable, and it is as well to remember that presidential elections occur every four years and congressional elections every two. Compared with this the demands made upon the British voter are mild: general elections must take place at least once every five years, but in practice occur on average about once every three years; there is also the occasional by-election, but these are infrequent for any particular constituency; at local level elections may occur annually or at three-year intervals, and some electors are called upon to elect representatives to more than one local government body, and again by-elections may occur from time to time; and finally, but very rarely, a referendum may be used at local level to decide a particular issue. At the very most, therefore, the British voter could be faced with seven choices (assuming the occurrence of a general election, national and local by-elections, and a referendum) in one *year*, though not at one time, while his American counterpart is faced with nearly six times this number.

The significance of voting also differs according to the purpose of the elections: national elections are usually regarded as more important than local elections, while the election of a chief executive is normally more important than the election of a member of a legislature. Other factors, such as the extent of the franchise, may also affect the significance of voting. In some political systems voting may play a very important role, such as deciding which party or persons will hold political power for a certain period, but in other systems voting may be little more than a ritual by which those in power seek to confer legitimacy on their rule. Whatever the purpose of voting, however, there is little doubt that it varies considerably from one political system to another, and, moreover, that the number of people who vote also varies considerably.

Table 10. *Comparison of voting turnout in different types of societies*

STAGE OF ECONOMIC AND SOCIAL DEVELOPMENT	Votes as to % of voting age population
(1) 'Traditional primitive' societies	30
(2) 'Traditional civilizations'	49
(3) 'Transitional 'societies	41
(4) 'Industrial revolution' societies	69
(5) 'High mass consumption' societies	78

SOURCE: Bruce M. Russett, Hayward R. Alker Jr, Karl W. Deutsch and Harold D. Lasswell, *World Handbook of Political and Social Indicators*, New Haven, Conn., 1964, p. 294. For definitions of each type of society, see ibid., pp. 293–303.

The figures in Table 10 illustrate vividly the extent to which voting turnout differs from one type of society to another. The possible reasons for these variations do not concern us for the moment, but it is important to appreciate how variable the lowest form of political participation can be. The percentages shown in the table are the means for each category, and these have a range of 30 to 78 per cent, but the lowest voting turnout found by Russett and his colleagues was 1·9 per cent (Rhodesia and Nyasaland), and the highest 99·6 per cent (Soviet Union), so that the actual range is very large indeed. It does not, of course, follow that, because there is a high voting turnout, other types of participation will also be relatively high. Much depends on the reasons for a high or low turnout. Thus there is a considerable contrast between voting turnout and the extent to which people are interested in politics, some idea of which can be seen from the results of opinion polls in various countries (Table 11).

Table 11. *Levels of interest in politics in the United States, Britain and West Germany*

(A) United States and Britain

LEVEL OF INTEREST	United States	Britain
	%	%
Great deal of interest/Very interested	19	15
Some interest/Interested	47	37
Not very much/Not really interested	29	33
None/Not at all interested	5	15
Total	100	100

(B) West Germany

LEVEL OF INTEREST	
	%
Very deeply/Deeply interested	11
Rather interested	20
Somewhat interested	25
Hardly interested	19
Not at all interested	25
Total	100

SOURCES: United States: MINN, February 1966.
Britain: Mark Abrams, 'Social Trends and Electoral Behaviour', *British Journal of Sociology*, **13**, 1962, p. 233.
West Germany: DIVO, March 1966.

Although the terms used in these surveys are not identical, they are sufficiently similar to allow comparison. It is clear from the table that interest in political affairs is highest in the United States and lowest in West Germany. Nevertheless, the differences are not great, especially among those who claim the most interest.

It is also interesting to compare voting turnout with interest in politics. In spite of the fact that the United States respondents showed the greatest interest in politics, turnout is normally higher in Britain, though lower in West Germany. It is therefore misleading to expect the relationship between voting turnout and other forms of participation to have any exact relationship or ratio, although it is possible to speak of political systems as having a high or low rate of political participation in general. What is clear is that a basic hierarchical pattern remains, and it is to be expected that fewer people say that they are very interested in politics than actually vote, and that fewer people *discuss* politics than say they are at all interested in it.

Table 12. *Frequency of discussing politics with other people in the United States, Britain and West Germany*

FREQUENCY	United States	Britain	West Germany
	%	%	%
Sometimes	76	70	60
Never	24	29	39
Other and don't know	–	–	1
Totals	100	99	100

SOURCE: Almond and Verba, *The Civic Culture*, p. 79.

If the figures in Tables 11 and 12 are compared, it is clear that this is in fact the case: in each country more people say they are to some degree interested in politics than actually discuss it, and the proportion who discuss politics frequently is, of course, much smaller, as another West German survey shows. The respondents were asked how often they discussed politics with their fellow-workers: 16 per cent replied 'often', 52 per cent replied 'sometimes', 22 per cent replied 'never', with the remaining 10 per cent giving no answer (INFAS, October–November 1967).

There is very little data available on the extent to which people participate in demonstrations, public meetings and other intermittent forms of participation, but a fragmentary picture does emerge. A Danish poll suggests that the number of people who participate in any sort of demonstration is fairly small: only 8 per cent of the respondents said that they had *ever* done so (GMA, February 1968). Compared with this, 57 per cent of the respondents in a Norwegian poll said that they had spoken at a meeting, but only 18 per cent had ever written to a newspaper to promote a point of view (PRIO, November-December 1964). Similarly, in the United States a survey found that 13 per cent of the respondents had written to their Congressman or some other public official, and 15 per cent had spoken to a public official 'within the past year' (POSU, June–July 1965). Another poll in the United States found that only 11 per cent of the respondents said that it was likely that they would attend a forthcoming precinct caucus meeting (MINN, February 1966).

With the exception of the fairly high proportion of Norwegian respondents who said that they had spoken at a meeting (although they, too, were asked whether they had *ever* done so), these are not especially high levels of participation. It is possible, however, that the specifically political nature of an election campaign might produce increased levels of participation.

Table 13. *Levels of participation in election campaigns in the United States and Britain*

(A) United States (recent election campaigns)

ACTIVITY	Proportion participating %
Talked to someone and tried to show them why they should vote for a particular party or candidate	30
Attended party meetings, rallies, or dinners, etc.	13
Gave money to help the campaign of one of the parties or candidates	14
Distributed campaign literature, etc.	7

(B) Britain (1966)

ACTIVITY	Proportion participating %
Watched a Conservative broadcast on TV	78
Watched a Labour broadcast on TV	78
Watched a Liberal broadcast on TV	69
Listened to any party broadcast on the radio	21
Read an election address	49
Heard a local candidate at a meeting	10
Canvassed for a candidate	2
Other work for a candidate	2

SOURCES: United States: POSU, June–July 1965.
Britain: SOC, April 1966.

As with levels of interest in politics, there are problems of comparability between the figures in the two sections of Table 13, but this has little significance since they are sufficient to demonstrate that there is little increase in participation during election campaigns, apart from that which can be associated with increased political communication in Section B.

Much more data is available on the membership of voluntary organizations, which include both political and quasi-political organizations, although the majority probably fall into the second category.

Table 14. *Membership of voluntary organizations in various countries*

NUMBER OF ORGANIZATIONS	United States	Britain	Germany	Italy	France	Mexico
	%	%	%	%	%	%
At least one	57	47	44	29	20	25
More than one	32	16	12	6	6	2

SOURCES: United States, Britain, West Germany, Italy and Mexico: Almond and Verba, *The Civic Culture*, pp. 246 and 264. France: IFOP, March–April 1966.

Membership of voluntary organizations varies considerably from one country to another, as the figures in Table 14 show. Furthermore, the extent to which these organizations may be regarded as 'political' varies. With the exception of the Italian respondents, Almond and Verba found that approximately two-fifths of those who were members of voluntary organizations believed that one or more of the organizations to which they belonged were involved in political affairs; the proportion for the Italian repondents was one-fifth.[1] It none the less remains difficult to assess the significance of membership of voluntary organizations on a comparative basis, partly because the nature of membership varies considerably from one country to another, and partly because of the problem of assessing the respective levels of active and passive membership.

The membership of political parties provides a useful example of the first problem. Maurice Duverger has shown clearly how political parties may be based on various types of membership. He posits three types: (1) 'cadre' parties, where membership is based on a limited élite group of important individuals (typified by the

[1] Almond and Verba, *The Civic Culture*, p. 251.

British Conservative and Liberal parties prior to the rise of the Labour party); (2) 'cell' and 'militia' parties, where membership is based on a centralized hierarchy directly responsible to the leadership (typified by Communist and Fascist parties respectively); and (3) mass-membership parties, based on a dues-paying membership to which the leadership is to varying degrees constitutionally responsible (typified by many European Socialist parties).[1] There is often, as Duverger points out, a further complication in some mass-membership parties in that a number have indirect or affiliated members, that is, members who belong to the party by virtue of their membership of some other organization (in most cases a trade union) which is affiliated to the party. Since the number of members that these organizations choose to affiiliate often represents what they are prepared or can afford to pay to the party in dues rather than the actual number of members who wish to be associated with it, the affiliation of an organization to the party is of greater significance than the association of the individual members. Thus the British Labour party has some six million affiliated members, but rather less than a million individual members. The British Conservative party, on the other hand, has no affiliated members and an individual membership of more than two million. This presents the problem of comparing like with like. Until 1965, for example, members of the ruling bodies of constituency Labour parties did not have to be *individual* members of the Labour party, while membership of the Conservative party is not necessarily a prerequisite of selection as a Conservative candidate.[2] A more difficult comparison exists between American and British parties, since, as Leon Epstein notes:

> Dues-paying is still unusual in major American political parties – so much so that a recent text was not far wrong in asserting that 'there are no card-carrying Republicans or Democrats'. For the national parties, as such, the statement is entirely correct. And in state parties little is known of regular dues-paying by members outside of California and Wisconsin. Locally, however, there are dues-paying clubs – like those in New York and Chicago.[3]

[1] Maurice Duverger, *Political Parties*, translated by Barbara and Robert North, London, 1954, Book I.

[2] Michael Rush, *The Selection of Parliamentary Candidates*, London, 1969, pp. 56 and 153n.

[3] Leon Epstein, *Political Parties in Western Democracies*, New York, 1967, p. 123.

It is clearly important to take into account the particular environment in which various political organizations have to work. It is also important, however, to take account of the second problem mentioned above – the extent to which membership of voluntary organizations is active or passive. Almond and Verba found that the proportion of their respondents who were members of voluntary organizations and had held office tended to vary (Table 15).

Table 15. *Holding office in voluntary organizations*

COUNTRY	Proportion of members who have held office
	%
United States	46
Britain	29
West Germany	16
Italy	23
Mexico	34

SOURCE: Almond and Verba, *The Civic Culture*, p. 257.

As might be expected, the majority of people (in four of the five countries listed in Table 15) the overwhelming majority are passive rather than active members of the voluntary organizations to which they belong. If these proportions are expressed as percentages of the total number of respondents in the five-nation study, they are, of course, much lower: 26 per cent for the United States, 13 per cent for Britain, 7 per cent for Germany and Italy and 8 per cent for Mexico. In most voluntary organizations, however, the *most* active individuals – those who exercise the most influence and take the crucial decisions – constitute a much smaller proportion of the membership than those who hold some sort of office. It is doubtful, for example, whether more than 5 per cent of the individual and affiliated members of Constituency Labour parties and only 1 per cent of the members of local Conservative associations in Britain (largely because Conservative associations tend to have larger memberships) are in any way associated with the selection of their parliamentary candidates, yet this is one of the most important roles of local parties.[1]

Once again, we can see that the higher we ascend up the hierarchy the fewer the number of people who participate. Lester Milbrath has summed up the situation in the United States as follows:

[1] Rush, *The Selection of Parliamentary Candidates*, pp. 35, 164, 276 and 279.

Probably less than 1 per cent of the American adult population engage in the top two or three behaviours [i.e. holding public and party office, being a candidate for office and soliciting political funds]. Only about 4 or 5 per cent are active in a party campaign, and attend meetings. About 10 per cent make monetary contributions, about 13 per cent contact public officials, and about 15 per cent display a button or sticker. Around 25 or 30 per cent try to proselyte others to vote a certain way, and from 40 to 70 per cent perceive political messages and vote in any given election.[1]

Similarly, Richard Rose has summarized the position in Britain:

Table 16. *Hierarchy of political participation in Britain*

ACTIVITY	Proportion of electorate involved
	%
M.P.s, senior civil servants	0·01
Local party activists	0·4
Individual party members	10
Organization officers (past and present)	14
Very interested in politics	15
Informed (name six major politicians)	16
Party members (all categories)	25
Organization members	47
Voters (1964)	77

SOURCE: Richard Rose, *Politics in England*, London, 1965, p. 94.

The evidence on the extent of political participation is clear enough, even if it is somewhat fragmentary, nor is it difficult to discover *who* participates. What *is* difficult, however, is finding out *why* they participate, and since the problem of who participates may throw light on why they do so, it is to these two questions that we now turn.

WHO PARTICIPATES AND WHY

Thus far we have only touched upon the question of apathy, but in examining the reasons for participation it is inevitable that we should ask why some people shun all forms of political participation, or participate only at the lowest level. This is all the more important in view of the fact that those who do participate in most forms of political activity constitute a minority (often a very small minority) of the members of any society.

[1] Milbrath, *Political Participation*, p. 19.

A variety of terms are assigned to these non-participants, and they are variously described as *apathetic, cynical, alienated* or *anomic*. Quite obviously these terms are by no means synonymous, although they may be related to one another and possibly have some characteristics in common. It is therefore important to distinguish between the four terms and examine how they have been applied to studies of political participation.

Apathy may be defined very simply as a lack of interest in or lack of concern for persons, situations or phenomena in general or particular. From a sociological point of view, it may apply to society in general or merely to certain aspects of society. Like many behaviour patterns it is often linked to a particular personality syndrome:

> The apathetic's characteristics – inability to recognize personal responsibility or to examine – or even to accept – his own emotions and feelings; vague, incomprehensible feelings of worry, insecurity, and threat; complete, unchallenging acceptance of constituted authority (social codes, parents, religion) and conventional values – form a self-consistent pattern which, in a clinical situation, would be labelled *passivity*.[1]

These characteristics are contrasted by the same authors with those of the active individual, which comprise:

> an emphasis on strivings for ego-satisfaction, independence, maturity, and personal happiness . . . active attempts to achieve self-understanding . . . sensitivity to others' feelings, emotions and conflicts . . . great social consciousness and emphasis on social contribution and love-giving.[2]

As far as political participation is concerned, therefore, the most important trait of the apathetic individual is his passivity or abstention from political activity. It is nevertheless important to consider whether the term apathy should be limited to those who refrain from all types of political participation (including voting), or whether it should be used more widely to apply to those who refrain from more active participation, especially those who shun activity through political or quasi-political organizations. The hierarchy shown in Figure 2 referred only to the totally apathetic, to those who refrain from all types of participation, but to assume that apathy is in no sense applicable to other levels in the hier-

[1] Paul H. Mussen and Anne B. Wyszynski, 'Personality and Political Participation', *Human Relations*, 5, 1952, pp. 78–9. (Original italics.)
[2] ibid.

archy is to be less than realistic. Thus, while apathy may be total, it should be recognized that there may be degrees of apathy. In other words, one explanation of non-participation at various levels of the hierarchy may simply be that of apathy.

Morris Rosenberg[1] has suggested three major reasons for political apathy. His conclusions were based on a series of unstructured interviews in depth. The first reason is the perceived consequence of political activity. This may take several forms: the individual may feel that political activity is a threat to various aspects of his life. He may, for example, believe that it will alienate his friends and neighbours, or even members of his family – his social position may, he feels, be disturbed or undermined; or political activity may threaten his occupational position by identifying him too closely with a particular party or point of view; or he may feel that political activity would threaten or undermine his self-esteem by exposing what he regards as his own ignorance, inadequacies and incompetence. In general, therefore, where the individual is faced with controversy or cross-pressures, he may find political inactivity more congenial than activity.

Rosenberg's second reason is that the individual may regard political activity as futile. As a single individual, he may feel that he is totally unable to influence the course of events and that the political forces he perceives are in any case beyond the control of the individual. Moreover, he may regard the results of political activity as a foregone conclusion and feel that even combining with others to achieve some political aim is useless. Finally, he may perceive a gulf between his ideals and political reality, a gulf of such proportions that no amount of political activity seems likely to bridge it.

Third, like Milbrath,[2] Rosenberg regards 'spurs to action' or political stimuli as important factors in encouraging political activity, and the absence of such stimuli may contribute to feelings of apathy. The individual may feel that the subject-matter of politics is not very interesting and may even divorce many actions from the political sphere because he perceived them as personal rather than political. Furthermore, he may feel that political

[1] Morris Rosenberg, 'Some Determinants of Political Apathy', *Public Opinion Quarterly*, **18**, 1954, pp. 34–66.
[2] *Political Participation*, Chapter 2.

activity provides little or no immediate satisfaction and few direct results. In sum, political participation is perceived as utterly inappropriate to the personal and material needs of the individual.

Cynicism, as against apathy, which involves relative passivity and inactivity, is an attitude applicable to either activity or inactivity. Robert Agger and his colleagues define cynicism as being 'contemptuously distrustful of human nature', and by means of an attitude scale designed to measure the degree to which their respondents were cynical, both personally and politically, they sought to relate cynicism to various aspects of political behaviour.[1] They found that Democratic party supporters tended to be slightly more cynical than Republicans, and that the latter were considerably more trusting, although this may have been linked with Republican control of the White House at the time the survey was conducted. This did not, however, appear to constitute a complete explanation, since Agger and his colleagues found clear links between cynicism and other variables. They found, for instance, that political cynicism tended to decrease with higher education and, to a lesser extent, with higher income. Of greater significance for political participation, however, was their finding that the more cynical their respondents the less they felt able to influence events, and that in general political participation decreased with cynicism.

Cynicism, then, is a feeling that the actions and motives of others are to be regarded with suspicion, that pessimism is more realistic than optimism, and that the individual must look after his own interests because society is basically self-centred. Politically cynicism manifests itself in a variety of ways: the feeling that politics is 'a dirty business', that politicians are not to be trusted, that the individual is at the mercy of manipulating groups, that the 'real' power is exercised by 'faceless men', and so on. It should be recognized, however, that cynicism may be extensive, even where a political system is generally regarded as enjoying widespread legitimacy (Table 17).

---

[1] Robert E. Agger, Marshal N. Goldstein and Stanley A. Pearl, 'Political Cynicism: Measurement and Meaning', *Journal of Politics*, **23**, 1961, pp. 477–506. See also Edgar Litt, 'Political Cynicism and Political Futility', *Journal of Politics*, **25**, 1963, pp. 312–23.

Table 17. *Evidence of cynical political attitudes in Britain*

ATTITUDE	Proportion agreeing
	%
Most politicians will promise anything to get votes	78
Most politicians care more about their party than the country	66
Politicians are all talk and no action	59
Most politicians are in it for what they can get	57
Once they become M.P.s they forget about the voters	55

SOURCE: NOP, February 1968.

Each of the cynical attitudes about British politics and politicians shown in Table 17 had the support of a majority of the respondents, in several cases very substantial support. Much depends, of course, on how strongly opinions are held, but it is significant that they are widely held and suggests that, like apathy, cynicism should be regarded as a matter of degree. A person who is extremely cynical may well feel that political participation in any form is futile and thus join the ranks of the totally apathetic, but for others their cynicism may simply limit their participation or merely be regarded as 'the only realistic way of looking at things'. Cynicism may not, therefore, preclude participation at any level of the hierarchy, although it may provide an explanation of non-participation by particular individuals at particular levels.

Alienation suggests actual hostility, where cynicism suggests a certain distaste for politics and politicians. Robert Lane defines political alienation as 'a person's sense of estrangement from the politics and government of his society . . . (and) . . . the tendency to think of the government and politics of the nation as run *by* others *for* others according to an unfair set of rules'.[1] Clearly such an attitude goes far beyond cynicism, and Lane suggests that, as far as the United States is concerned, it is misleading to speak of widespread alienation and more meaningful to think in terms of those who are 'politically divorced'.[2] The latter are those who regard the government as being of little or no consequence for them. Such an attitude may be quite widely held, as Almond and Verba found in their five-nation study (Table 18).

[1] Lane, *Political Ideology*, pp. 161 and 177.
[2] ibid., p. 173.

Table 18. *Proportion of 'politically divorced' individuals in the United States, Britain, West Germany, Italy and Mexico*

COUNTRY	National government		Local government	
	No effect	Don't know	No effect	Don't know
	%	%	%	%
United States	11	4	10	2
Britain	23	4	23	3
West Germany	17	12	18	8
Italy	19	24	22	18
Mexico	66	3	67	3

SOURCE: Almond and Verba, *The Civic Culture*, pp. 46 and 47.

As the table shows, only a small proportion of respondents in the United States felt that neither national nor local government had an effect on their daily lives, but in the other four countries higher proportions expressed this view – as many as two-thirds in the case of the Mexican respondents. With Germany and Italy, especially the latter, the proportion who replied 'don't know' is higher than in the other three countries, and the sense of being politically divorced may be somewhat higher than Almond and Verba's actual figures suggest. If account is taken of the 'don't knows' (though in what proportion remains a matter of judgement), then the proportion of British and German respondents believing that the government is of little or no consequence to them personally would probably be similar, while the proportion of Italian respondents would be substantially higher.

Anomie: whether those who adopt an attitude of alienation should be described as 'politically divorced' or 'alienated' is a matter of opinion, but the attitude is also consistent with the fourth term mentioned above – 'anomie'. This was devised by Durkheim in his famous study of suicide,[1] and is described by Lane as 'a sense of value loss and lack of direction' in which the individual experiences a feeling of ineffectiveness and that authority 'doesn't care', resulting in the devaluation of his goals and the loss of urgency to act.[2] Leo Srole has developed an anomie scale which has been used in a number of studies. Using this attitude scale, Srole found

[1] Emil Durkheim, *Suicide*, translated by John A. Spaulding and George Simpson, and edited by George Simpson, London, 1952.
[2] Lane, *Political Life: Why People Get Involved in Politics*, Glencoe, Illinois, 1959, pp. 166–9.

a close relationship between anomie (which he regards as syony-mous with alienation) and the authoritarian personality.[1] Other studies, however, have sought to use the Srole scale to measure degrees of anomie (alienation) among various groups in society. Using a sample of respondents from Detroit in 1958, for instance, Marvin Olsen found considerable variation in levels of anomie according to race, income and education (Table 19).

Table 19. *Levels of anomie in the United States (Detroit)*

CHARACTERISTIC	Proportion with a high score on the Srole Scale
	%
Negroes	53
Whites	30
High-income white collar ⎫ Low-income white collar ⎬	22
High-income blue collar	30
Low-income blue collar	47
Unemployed	54
Some college education	18
High school education	35
Less education	45

SOURCE: Marvin E. Olsen, 'Alienation and Political Opinions', *Public Opinion Quarterly*, 29, 1965, pp. 200–12.

With the exception of the difference between white persons and Negroes, Olsen found that levels of anomie were closely associated with occupation, a finding supported by Lipsitz's study of skilled and unskilled auto-workers in Detroit and the relationship between job satisfaction and political attitudes.[2] Olsen's study suggests that anomie not only varies between groups, as might be expected, but that it is a fairly widespread, at least in Detroit. In addition to measuring levels of anomie, he also found that respondents with high scores on the Srole scale favoured more government action in domestic affairs and a decrease in foreign aid, and that they were more likely to favour limits on the freedom of speech. These findings are important for our purposes in so far as they provide evidence of the political opinions held by those whom Olsen regards as 'alienated'. Further evidence of this is

[1] Leo Srole, 'Social Integration and Certain Corrollaries: An Exploratory Study', *American Sociological Review*, 21, 1956, pp. 709–16.
[2] See Chapter 2, p. 46 above.

provided by Frederic Templeton, who, using the Srole Scale on a sample of respondents in California, tested the relationship between anomie and political interest and knowledge, and political participation as measured by voting (Table 20).

Table 20. *Relationship between anomie (Srole Scale) and political interest, knowledge and participation*

LEVELS OF INTEREST, KNOWLEDGE AND PARTICIPATION	Manual workers (anomie score)		Non-manual workers (anomie score)	
	Low	High	Low	High
	%	%	%	%
High political interest	44	29	52	39
High political knowledge	44	12	52	18
Constant party voter	75	54	66	45

SOURCE: Frederic Templeton, 'Alienation and Political Participation: Some Research Findings', *Public Opinion Quarterly*, 30, 1966, pp. 249–61.

In each case, Templeton found that those respondents who had a high anomie score had lower levels of political interest, knowledge and participation than those with a low anomie score. He also found that those with a high anomie score were more likely to alter their voting behaviour from one election to another.

There is little doubt that apathy may be explained by cynicism, alienation or anomie, yet it is doubtful whether single or collectively they provide a complete explanation. What does seem clear is that political apathy is closely linked to general apathy: Lane, for instance, found that those of his respondents who were politically alienated were also alienated to varying degrees from society;[1] while Agger and his colleagues found that political cynicism was linked to personal cynicism. Moreover, the concept of anomie and the anomie scale evolved by Srole are based on social rather than political attitudes. Political behaviour is, as the process of political socialization suggests, an integral part of social behaviour. The more an individual is involved in social activities generally, the more likely he is to participate in the political sphere. William Erbe, for example, in a replication of various studies of political participation, found that organizational involvement was a major antecedent of political participa-

[1] Lane, *Political Ideology*, Chapter 11.

tion, at all levels.[1] Similarly, a comparison of group leaders with a sample of the general population in the United States found that the group leaders were more socially integrated than the general population.[2]

It is important, however, to make the distinction between apathy, cynicism, alienation and anomie clear. Defined simply, apathy is a lack of interest, cynicism is an attitude of distaste and disenchantment, while alienation and anomie both involve a feeling of estrangement or divorce from society, but where alienation is characterized by hostility, anomie is characterized by bewilderment. The available evidence suggests that the totally apathetic are, at the very least, cynical and more often alienated or anomic. Apathy, cynicism, alienation and anomie, however, are all matters of degree and may therefore affect not only those who shun all forms of participation, but those who are involved in political activity. Relative degrees of apathy, cynicism, alienation and anomie may account for non-participation at the higher levels of political participation while not precluding activity at lower levels of the hierarchy. Moreover, alienation, far from taking a passive form, may result in considerable political activity, particularly that involving violent political action.

For example, following its establishment in 1948, the Communist régime in Hungary systematically sought to undermine the social and economic position of the upper and middle classes, and this was combined with a programme of 'Russification', all of which resulted in social, economic, cultural and political alienation among members of these classes. A study based on intensive interviews with refugees from Hungary, following the revolt of 1956, found that those who had suffered a loss of socio-economic status were more hostile and more uncompromising in their attitudes towards the Communist régime than those who had suffered no such loss. Furthermore, these respondents were also more active in the revolt *before* the Russian intervention than those who had suffered no loss of status.[3] It would appear that

[1] William Erbe, 'Social Involvement and Political Activity', *American Sociological Review*, 29, 1964, pp. 198–215.

[2] Arnold M. Rose, 'Alienation and Participation: A Comparison of Group Leaders and the "Mass",' *American Sociological Review*, 27, 1962, pp. 834–8.

[3] Henry Gleitman and Joseph T. Greenbaum, 'Hungarian Socio-Political Attitudes and Revolutionary Action', *Public Opinion Quarterly*, 24, 1960, pp. 62–76.

the more alienated sections of Hungarian society were, under certain conditions, not only more likely to express their hostility in an active rather than passive form, but that under those conditions violence was an acceptable form of political participation. The less alienated sections of society tended to participate in the revolt only *after* the Russian forces had invaded the country and thus provided them with a stimulus to action.

It is therefore important to link alienation with the expression of extreme hostility, including the use of violence. In those societies in which alienation is widespread and in which the political system has only limited legitimacy, various forms of hostility to the political system in particular and the social system in general are likely to be manifested. The extent to which such hostility will include the use of violence depends on a variety of factors, some practical, some material, some traditional, some ideological. The use of violence may, for example, depend on the extent to which it is regarded as a viable means of securing particular ends – if it is thought that the assassination of a public figure, or a *coup d'état*, or armed insurrection, or mob violence is likely to effect the changes desired, then violence is more likely, but its use also depends on other factors. Thus while violence is often the last resort of those whose situation is desperate, the more sophisticated forms of violence depend upon the availability of material means. The availability of arms, efficient means of communication and effective leadership are, for instance, usually found in the successful *coup d'état* or armed insurrection. The availability of the means to effect violence may be offset, however, by traditions or ideologies which militate against the use of violence as an instrument of political policy.

In the United States, for instance, the traditional right to bear arms, legally recognized in the Second Amendment to the Constitution, has been associated with the levels of social violence in America and with the fact that four presidents have been assassinated, yet, as we have already seen, the expectation of a military *coup d'état* is very low and ideological norms militate against this form of political violence. In many countries the armed forces have the means of political violence at their disposal, but lack the will to use them for political ends. In other countries it is widely expected, though not necessarily accepted, that the armed forces will intervene with force in political affairs from time to time, and such traditions are often difficult to break down, as the United States found in Nicaragua in the 1920s and 1930s. During a period of military intervention in Nicaraguan affairs, the United States government sought to establish and train a National Guard which would remain politically neutral once independence had been restored to the country, but this did not prevent the National Guard from being involved in the assassination of a prominent guerrilla leader, Augusto Sandino, in 1934, nor did it prevent the guard's commander, General Anastasio Somoza, from assuming the presidency in 1937 and effectively establishing a dynasty whose power depended on its control of the National Guard.

Similarly, the widespread use of assassination and terror may stem from the ideological acceptance of violence as a legitimate political instrument. The ideological acceptance of violence is thus characteristic of various groups (such as the nineteenth-century Russian Anarchists, Lenin's Bolsheviks, the Resistance groups in German-occupied countries during the Second World War, the E.O.K.A. organization in Cyprus, the Mau-Mau in Kenya, or the Vietcong in Vietnam) which seek to overthrow existing political régimes. Russett and his colleagues devised an index of violence (although it should be noted that the index referred to social violence generally rather than exclusively political violence) based on the number of violent deaths per million population. They found that a low level of violence was associated with those countries that had either high or low levels of income, whereas a higher level of violence was found in those countries in the middle-income range. They associated violence with development and suggested that countries undergoing extensive social, economic and political change were more likely to experience violence.[1] Certainly it is reasonable to suggest, as in the case of political socialization, that the conflict between the traditional and modernizing influences is an important factor; and in the case of political participation such conflict may take the form of violence.

The use of violence for political ends may be regarded as one, but only one, manifestation of political alienation. Obviously, hostility to a particular régime or even to a particular social system need not take a violent form. Socialist groups in many countries have, for example, sought fundamental changes in the

[1] Russett *et al.*, *World Handbook of Political and Social Indicators*, pp. 306–7.

social system and yet have shunned violence as a means of effecting those changes. Alienation may therefore stimulate a variety of forms of political participation or result in abstention from such activity.

Since the use of violence for political ends may be regarded as a manifestation of political alienation, it is misleading to associate the latter solely with political inactivity. Furthermore, it is also clear that many of those politically active at some levels may, none the less, be cynical about political phenomena and apathetic about other types of participation. Whether individuals are described as apathetic, cynical, alienated or anomic, they remain in effect part of a *satisfaction-dissatisfaction* syndrome. It is also possible, of course, that those who are politically apathetic are satisfied rather than dissatisfied, but this is a subject on which little or no research has been done. As already noted, the available evidence on those who are totally apathetic suggests that they are, to varying degrees cynical, alienated or anomic, but it may well be that those who are apathetic about the higher levels of political participation are satisfied rather than dissatisfied. Conversely, apart from those who are alienated in a way that encourages them to be politically active rather than inactive, there is evidence to link satisfaction rather than dissatisfaction with increased political participation.

Using a national sample survey in the United States, Frank Lindenfeld found that those respondents who expressed *financial satisfaction* were more involved in political life.[1] Levels of involvement was measured in terms of interest in politics, feelings of political competence or efficacy, and actual participation in political activities. Lindenfeld also found that among respondents of low socio-economic status, financial dissatisfaction was related to feelings of political alienation and apathy, but this is not the case between medium- and high-status respondents who were financially dissatisfied. We have already seen in Table 19 that scores on the Srole anomie scale vary considerably from one demographic group to another, and it is instructive to compare two of these groups on levels of satisfaction (Table 21). While it should be noted that the figures in Tables 19 and 21 are based on different surveys at different times, and therefore too much stress should not be laid on the actual details, it is notable that Negro

[1] Frank Lindenfeld, 'Economic Interest and Political Involvement', *Public Opinion Quarterly*, **28**, 1964, pp. 104–11.

Table 21. *Levels of dissatisfaction among whites and Negroes in the United States*

	Proportion dissatisfied	
AREA	Whites	Negroes
	%	%
Work	8	18
Education	16	23
Housing	19	44
Income	29	49

SOURCE: AIPO, November 1966.

respondents showed a much higher proportion with a high score on the anomie scale and much higher levels of dissatisfaction than white respondents, especially over housing and income. All the various studies of cynicism, alienation and anomie that have been cited in this chapter have found that the levels of these phenomena have varied according to such factors as education, income, occupation and from country to country, and this is common to all levels of political participation. Although there is insufficient data available on every level of participation to demonstrate the importance of all these factors, there is enough to show that it is likely that their importance is widespread.

A number of electoral studies in various countries have shown that voting turnout varies considerably from one group of voters to another, and these studies have been summarized by S. M. Lipset (Table 22). He also suggests that a number of environmental factors influence turnout: whether the election is taking place at a time of crisis; the extent to which the policies of the government are relevant to the individual; the extent to which the individual has access to relevant information; the extent to which the individual is subjected to group pressures to vote; and the extent to which the individual is subjected to cross-pressures.[1]

A similar pattern is found with levels of political interest (Table 23). The West German survey (Section B) also showed that political interest increased with age, income and occupational status, and was higher in urban areas and certain regions. Another West German survey found that women discuss politics less than

[1] Lipset, *Political Man*, pp. 185–216.

Table 22. *Social characteristics correlated with voting turnout*

HIGHER TURNOUT	LOWER TURNOUT
High income	Low income
High education	Low education
Occupational groups:	Occupational groups:
Businessmen	Unskilled workers
White-collar employees	Servants
Government employees	Service workers
Commercial crop farmers	Peasants, subsistence farmers
Miners	
Whites	Negroes
Men	Women
Middle-aged people (35–55)	Young people (under 35)
Older people (over 55)	
Old residents in the community	Newcomers in the community
Workers in Western Europe	Workers in the United States
Married people	Single people
Members of organizations	Isolated individuals

SOURCE: Lipset, *Political Man*, p. 184.

Table 23. *Social characteristics correlated with political interest in Britain and West Germany*

(A) Britain

LEVEL OF INTEREST	Men	Women	Working class	Middle class	Left school Under 16	Left school 16 or over
	%	%	%	%	%	%
Very interested	21	8	14	17	14	19
Interested	39	35	30	52	32	53
Not really interested	29	38	38	22	37	22
Not at all interested	11	19	18	9	17	6

(B) West Germany

LEVEL OF INTEREST	Men	Women	Primary education No vocational training	Primary education Vocational training	Secondary education Lower grade	Secondary education Completed higher grade
	%	%	%	%	%	%
Very deeply/deeply	16	8	6	13	19	26
Rather interested	28	14	11	23	29	43
Somewhat interested	28	21	22	27	25	12
Hardly interested	17	20	21	20	13	14
Not at all interested	11	37	40	17	14	5

SOURCES: Britain: Abrams, 'Social Trends and Electoral Behaviour', p. 233.
West Germany: DIVO, March 1966.

men: only 6 per cent of the women respondents said that they *often* discuss politics, compared with 19 per cent of the men, while 37 per cent said they *never* discuss politics compared with 17 per cent of the men (INFAS, October-November 1967). Almond and Verba found that

> talking politics . . . [is] closely related to educational attainment. The frequency of talking politics rises sharply from primary to secondary to the university levels in all five countries. But the difference between educational levels are not as sharp in the United States and Britain as in the other three countries.[1]

Although the information on participation in demonstrations is very limited, the Danish poll cited earlier (p. 84) found differences in participation between men and women, and between members of different parties. Only 5 per cent of the women respondents had ever taken part in a demonstration, compared with 11 per cent of the men; and members of left-wing parties were far more likely to have taken part in demonstrations than members of other parties (GMA, February 1968).

The likelihood of members of the public writing to M.P.s, Congressmen or other legislative representatives also increases with education and occupational status,[2] while a survey in Minnesota found that participation in party meetings increased markedly among those with a college education: of those respondents who had been to grade school or high school, 16 per cent said it was likely that they would attend a forthcoming precinct caucus meeting, compared with 30 per cent of those with a college education (MINN, February 1966).

A similar pattern was found by Almond and Verba in participation in voluntary organizations. The data in Table 24 confirm the pattern that is characteristic of other forms of participation: men are more likely to be members of voluntary organizations than women, and participation increases with education. Almond and Verba also note that 'higher occupational status generally involves more frequent voluntary association membership, though the relationship is not as close as that between education and

[1] Almond and Verba, *The Civic Culture*, p. 83.
[2] See Hedley Cantril (ed.), *Public Opinion 1935–46*, Princeton, N.J., 1951, p. 703.

Table 24. *Membership of voluntary organizations by sex and education*

CHARACTERISTIC	United States	Britain	Germany	Italy	Mexico
	%	%	%	%	%
Men	68	66	66	41	43
Women	47	30	24	19	15
Primary education, or less	46	41	41	25	21
Some secondary education	55	55	63	37	39
Some university education	80	92	62	46	68

SOURCE: Almond and Verba, *The Civic Culture*, pp. 247 and 249. In assessing membership of voluntary organizations Almond and Verba have excluded *church* membership and confined religious organizations to 'church-related organizations' rather than recording church affiliation. If the latter were included, female membership of voluntary organizations would be higher, especially in such Catholic countries as Italy and Mexico.

affiliation'.[1] Moreover, the five-nation study also found that activity *within* voluntary organizations, as measured by having held office, was greater among men than women and again increased with education. The major exception to this was that more women than men (52 per cent compared with 41 per cent) had been officers of voluntary organizations in the United States, and the authors suggest that this may be because women's organizations tend to be smaller, thus providing a greater opportunity for their members to hold office.

Although the data presented on the variations in political participation is both fragmentary and not always directly comparable, it is sufficient to demonstrate that participation does vary in relation to a number of important social characteristics and that these variations are not confined to particular countries, but are found in different countries with varying social and political systems. There are, of course, differences between various countries, but the basic patterns are similar. Milbrath suggests that political participation varies in relation to four major factors: (1) the extent to which the individual receives political stimuli; (2) the individual's personal characteristics; (3) the individual's social characteristics; and (4) the political setting or environment in which the individual finds himself.[2]

[1] Almond and Verba, *The Civic Culture*, p. 249n.
[2] See Milbrath, *Political Participation*, passim.

The more the individual is exposed to political stimuli through personal and organizational contacts and through the mass media, the more is he likely to engage in political activity. Obviously this exposure is likely to vary from individual to individual, and it is after all part of the process of political socialization. Someone who belongs to a family which frequently discusses politics, or to an organization which encourages political activity, is likely to be stimulated into political activity. Similarly, exposure to the mass media may stimulate and maintain the individual's interest in political affairs and increase the likelihood of his participation in those affairs. At the same time, the individual has a measure of control over his exposure to political stimuli and may choose to avoid personal and organizational contacts, either generally or merely those which are specifically political. Thus those who are interested in politics are likely to welcome the opportunity to participate in the political process or may feel that they have some obligation, moral or otherwise, to do so. By means of the perceptual screen outlined in Chapter 2 (p. 30), the individual limits the stimuli which surround him, some consciously, others subconsciously. His knowledge, values and attitudes, his experience and his personality, affect his response to these stimuli and thus the extent to which he engages in political activity. An individual who lacks knowledge or information about a political problem or situation is less likely to feel competent to participate in any effort to resolve that problem or change that situation; political competence or efficacy increases with knowledge. Similarly, the individual's values and attitudes may militate against participation to the extent that he is cynical, alienated or anomic, or they may encourage political activity because they fulfil feelings of duty, obligation or achievement. Or again, experience of political participation, or lack of it, is likely to influence the individual's attitude towards future participation, while the nature of his personality is likely to be important. Sociable, dominant and extravert personalities, for instance, would be more likely to engage in political activity, whereas less sociable, submissive and introvert personalities would not.

A person's social characteristics, such as his socio-economic status, his racial or ethnic group, his age, sex and religion, whether he lives in a rural or urban area, whether he belongs to voluntary organizations, and so on, are all likely to influence his political participation, as we have already seen in a number of instances.

Although the receiving of political stimuli and the nature of the individual's personal and social characteristics are crucial in influencing the extent to which he is politically active, it is important to take into account the political environment or setting. This applies as much to the constitutional and institutional arrangements found in a particular political system as it does to its less formal aspects, such as the nature of the party system, or regional differences, or factors affecting particular events, such as elections. The separation of powers in the United States, for instance, affects political participation in important areas like interest group activity. Thus American interest groups pay a great deal of attention to Congress because it has considerable independence in the exercise of its legislative powers. Conversely, in Britain, the attention of interest groups tends to be concentrated more upon ministers and upon the bureaucracy because Parliament does not normally act independently of the executive.

In the same way, the legal requirements of an electoral system may influence political participation. An obvious example is that of compulsory voting: Russett and his colleagues report that seven countries require members of their electorates to vote, and with one exception the level of voting is higher than the mean for countries at a similar stage of development.[1]

Other factors, such as the nature of the party system, are also important. For example, societies characterized by fairly rigid class divisions are more likely to give rise to class-based parties, and the existence of such parties usually increases participation among the lower classes. This is the case in Britain and a number of other Western European countries, which, compared with the United States, where there is no party based on the working class, have powerful Socialist parties to provide vehicles for working-class participation. A variation of this theme may be seen in Canada, where the presence of the New Democratic party (and its predecessor, the Co-operative Commonwealth Federation) marks a departure from the broadly-based, loosely-organized pragmatic parties common to North America by seeking an electoral base of working-class support.[2]

[1] Russett et al., *World Handbook of Political and Social Indicators*, pp. 84–6 and 294.
[2] See Gad Horowitz, *Canadian Labour in Politics*, Toronto, 1968.

Regional differences provide yet another type of environmental factor, often forming the basis of variations in electoral behaviour and other forms of political participation. For instance, the long association between the Democratic party and the American South, the presence of Quebec within the Canadian federal system, the tribal divisions in Nigeria, the physical separateness of the component parts of Indonesia, all contribute to the patterns of political participation in their respective countries.

Beyond specific examples, however, by far the most significant differences in political environment are those which mark off a political system as belonging to a particular 'type' or 'group'. Clearly there are differences in political environment between countries like Britain and the United States, or Ghana and Nigeria, or the Soviet Union and Hungary, but more fundamental differences are found between, say Britain, Nigeria and the Soviet Union, between modern democracies, developing countries and totalitarian states.

There is every reason to believe that the personal and social characteristics of the individual are important in all types of political systems, although the particular characteristics which are important will vary from system to system. Socio-economic status is undoubtedly important in Britain, for instance, as are tribal groupings in Nigeria and ethnic differences in the Soviet Union. The U.S.S.R., in fact, provides an excellent example of how social characteristics are just as important in a totalitarian society as they are in other types of political system in the field of political participation.

This is especially clear from the data available on the membership of the Communist Party of the Soviet Union (C.P.S.U.), which has been subject to important changes in its social composition since the Revolution of 1917.[1] We have already seen that in countries like the United States, Britain and West Germany, women tend to be less active in politics than men, and the same is true of the Soviet Union: in 1924, 8 per cent of the members of the C.P.S.U. were women, and by 1961 this figure had risen to approximately 20 per cent. Similarly, 7 per cent of the voting delegates at the Seventeenth Party Congress in 1934 were women, compared with 22 per cent at the Twenty-Second Congress in

[1] The data that follows is taken from Fainsod, *How Russia is Ruled*, Chapter 8.

1961, while it was not until 1957 that Madame Furtseva became the first woman to be elected a full member of the party Presidium. The proportion of party members with a higher education has also increased from less than 1 per cent in 1922 to more than 6 per cent in 1947, but of much greater significance is the increase among delegates to the party congresses from approximately 10 per cent in 1934 to 52 per cent in 1961, although the proportion was as high as 59 per cent in 1952. Changes have also taken place in the occupational backgrounds and social origins of party members. Prior to the Revolution, three-fifths of the party members were workers by social origin, a third were middle class (or non-manual) and less than 5 per cent of peasant origin. By 1929 the proportion of party members of peasant origin had risen to a fifth, those of non-manual origin had fallen to a sixth, while those of worker origin remained at three-fifths – although in the intervening period the proportion of peasants had risen to more than a quarter and the proportion of workers to two-fifths. What was of greater significance, however, as Fainsod points out in commenting on the party at the end of this period, was the fact that,

> In terms of social origin, its membership was predominantly working class. In terms of occupation, workers at the bench only slightly exceeded those performing administrative or other non-manual work.[1]

Furthermore, as the data on the proportion of party members of peasant origin suggests, the membership of the C.P.S.U. is predominantly urban rather than rural in character. In 1927 the ratio of party members within the population was 319 : 10,000 in cities and 25 : 10,000 in villages, and by 1947 approximately 27 per cent of party members lived in rural areas. Yet, according to the official census data in 1926, the rural population of the Soviet Union constituted 82 per cent of the total population and, in 1939, 67 per cent. Similarly, the distribution of national-ethnic groups in the C.P.S.U. does not entirely reflect their distribution within the population generally. Russians, Georgians and Armenians, for instance, are over-represented, while a number of other groups are under-represented.

In the field of party membership, the party seeks to control the composition of that membership to a much greater extent than any non-totalitarian political party. Entry to the party is carefully

[1] ibid., p. 259.

controlled: would-be members must first serve a probationary period as candidates for membership, and their applications must provide detailed information about their backgrounds and qualifications and be supported by three party members. The C.P.S.U. is not intended to be a mass organization to which all supporters of the régime and party belong, but a body which provides political leadership and acts as a focal point of political power. The membership of the C.P.S.U. has never been more than a small proportion of the population of the U.S.S.R. – in 1961 the total number of party members and candidates constituted less than 5 per cent of the Russian population.[1] Furthermore, from time to time the party leadership has sought to exclude certain groups from party membership and to encourage other groups to join the party. The various purges that have occurred since the inception of the Communist régime in Russia have usually resulted in a reduction of the number of party members, and these have often affected particular social groups. Similarly, the qualifications for party membership have varied, often excluding specific groups as a matter of policy. Conversely, strenuous efforts have been made at various times to recruit particular groups, but these efforts have hardly, as Fainsod points out, resulted in a party which is a microcosm of the Russian population:

> In enlisting the new technical and administrative intelligentsia as its primary cadre beginning in the late thirties, the party's position among rank-and-file workers tended to weaken, and it risked increasing isolation from the production line. The recent emphasis on the recruitment of leading workers and collective farmers represents an effort to redress the balance. . . . Party membership among rank-and-file workers and farmers remains thin, and the ordinary collective farmer, even more than the factory worker falls outside the circle of the party élite. Although the party has strengthened its position among women . . . they continue to be largely inactive in party affairs. The nationality weaknesses of the party offset its great Russian, Georgian and Armenian strength . . . [and reflect] the slowness of Communist penetration in the rural sections of the areas acquired since World War II.[2]

It is clear from the data presented above that social characteristics are significant factors in determining the membership of the C.P.S.U., although it is difficult to judge how far its composition is a reflection of supply and how far it is a reflection of demand. None the less, political participation in the Soviet Union is subject

---

[1] ibid., pp. 232 and 280. [2] ibid., pp. 281–2.

to conditions not present in non-totalitarian societies. In the
latter, participation through such organizations as political parties
is invariably encouraged, but the state does not normally seek to
control the whole process of political participation in the way it
does in totalitarian societies. Elections in the U.S.S.R., for
example, are not a means of choosing between alternative sets of
leaders, but, in the words of a former Soviet politician:

> '... a mighty instrument for further educating and organizing the masses
> politically, for further strengthening the bond between the state mechan-
> ism and the masses, and for improving the state mechanism and grubbing
> out the remnants of bureaucratism . . . [Elections show] that the entire
> population of the land of the Soviets are completely united in spirit.'[1]

or, as Fainsod himself describes them, 'Soviet elections serve as
a form of national mobilization.'[2] Thus elections in which over
99 per cent of the electorate actually votes, and in which a similar
proportion supports candidates of the 'Communist and non-Party
bloc', are intended to serve as demonstrations of political mobilization and are probably the C.P.S.U.'s least important role in the
process of political participation.

The various party organizations in the Soviet Union are the
major vehicles of political participation. The role of the primary
party units, for instance, is to recruit and admit new party members, to organize ideological instruction and maintain the ideological commitment of party members, to implement the policies
and achieve the aims of the state, to act as a check on administrative efficiency, and to conduct mass agitation and propaganda.
Obviously, several of these functions are performed by political
parties in modern democracies, but two characteristics distinguish
the C.P.S.U. from the latter: first, it is the only party which is
allowed to exist in the U.S.S.R., and secondly, the informal power
links between party and governmental officials and the parallel
organizations of the party and the government place the C.P.S.U.
in a position of political dominance unequalled by any party in
a competitive party system. Furthermore, the C.P.S.U. is not
simply one means of political mobilization, nor is it one of
several vehicles of political recruitment, nor one of many channels of political communication: in each case it is either by far

---

[1] A. Vyshinsky, quoted in ibid., p. 238.
[2] ibid., p. 382.

the most important or the sole instrument by which these political processes are effected.[1]

A very similar situation is found in Communist China, although there are some differences resulting from the Chinese social and political environment. For instance, turnout at elections is not as high in China: in local elections in 1953-4 and 1956 the turnout was 86 per cent, which, according to one observer, 'represents a substantial achievement in view of the traditional political and cultural obstacles to political participation in China.'[2] Nevertheless, elections serve a similar purpose to those in the Soviet Union. According to the party press, elections are a means of raising mass political consciousness, of stimulating increases in production, of strengthening unity, of democratic education for the masses and of teaching the party cadres about the structure of the state and making them aware of their political rights and duties, as well as being a means for securing demographic and political information.[3] Moreover,

> In the Chinese political system, popular political activities constitute one of the primary structures through which the C.C.P. [Chinese Communist Party] executes its policies. The party also relies on mass political participation for the political education of the people, the recruitment of new party members and other activists, the creation and maintenance of popular identification with the present régime, and informing the party about popular moods and demands.[4]

The form and nature of political participation clearly varies from one type of political system to another, even where ostensibly similar political institutions, such as elections or political parties, exist. In spite of such differences, however, all political systems appear to exhibit some sort of relationship between political participation and the personal and social characteristics of those who are politically active. The nature of this relationship depends upon the social and political environment of each political system. Most modern democracies have a social environment characterized by an extensive but relatively flexible system of social stratification, and a political environment which ideologically seeks to encourage political participation. Primitive societies provide an integrated social and political environment in which

---

[1] See ibid., Chapter 7.
[2] Townsend, *Political Participation in Communist China*, p. 119.
[3] ibid., pp. 135-6. [4] ibid., p. 211.

the differentiation between political and other sorts of activity is less marked than in more developed societies. Totalitarian societies are also characterized by the integration of social and political activity, but, unlike primitive societies, the political environment takes ideological precedence over the social environment. Developing societies tend to have fragmented social and political environments: the social environment is frequently based on a relatively rigid system of traditional social stratification which modernizing forces are trying to break down, and this forms the basis of a political environment in which largely modern institutions co-exist, political behaviour being determined by essentially traditional forces.

Explanations of the political behaviour of individuals in general, and political participation, in particular, are not especially difficult to suggest. S. M. Lipset, for example, drawing upon a wide range of studies and data, has offered explanations of various aspects of electoral behaviour, including turnout, the direction of voting and support for extremist movements.[1] Similarly, exhaustive voting studies in a number of countries offer strong evidence to support a wide range of hypotheses.[2] In particular, the association between socio-economic status and electoral behaviour has been widely documented,[3] and a great deal of attention has been paid to those individuals who 'deviate' from the norm of 'class voting'.[4] These studies suggest that the political behaviour of the individual is determined by the interaction of the individual's

[1] Lipset, *Political Man*, Chapters 4–9.

[2] See, for example, the various studies of American presidential elections: Paul F. Lazarsfeld, Bernard R. Berelson and Hazel Gaudet, *The People's Choice*, New York, 1948; Bernard R. Berelson, Paul F. Lazarsfeld and William N. McPhee, *Voting: A Study of Opinion Formation in a Presidential Campaign*, Chicago, 1954; Angus Campbell, Gerald Gurin and Warren E. Miller, *The Voter Decides*, Evanston, Ill., 1954; and Angus Campbell, Philip E. Converse, Warren E. Miller and Donald E. Stokes, *The American Voter*, New York, 1960. See also, S. M. Lipset, Paul F. Lazarsfeld, Allen H. Barton and Juan Linz, 'The Psychology of Voting: An Analysis of Political Behaviour', in G. Lindzey (ed.), *Handbook of Social Psychology*, Vol. 2, pp. 1124–75.

[3] For useful comparative material, see Robert R. Alford, *Party and Society*, Chicago, 1963, and S. M. Lipset and Stein Rokkan, *Party Systems and Voter Alignments*, New York, 1967.

[4] For a discussion of working-class support for the British Conservative party, see Robert T. McKenzie and Allan Silver, *Angels in Marble*, London, 1968, and Eric Nordlinger, *Working Class Tories*, London, 1967.

basic social and political attitudes and the specific situations with which he is faced. The association between various personal and social characteristics (such as socio-economic status) and political behaviour may be the result of conscious or unconscious motivation, or, what is more likely, some combination of the two. This association does not, however, constitute an explanation, nor does it establish a causal relationship, even though the association of, say, those of lower socio-economic status with parties of the left and those of higher status with parties of the right surprises no one.

Rudolf Herbele suggests that there are four problems which make studying the motives for social and political behaviour difficult. Firstly, the real motives may be deliberately concealed by the individual and the observer is consequently misled by what appears to be accurate information. Secondly, the real motives may not, in fact, be apparent to the individual and he may have rationalized his action before, after or during the event. Thirdly, the real motives may be unapparent not only to the individual whose action is being investigated, but to others who have influenced his action. Finally, motives are invariably complex and difficult to measure accurately.[1]

The difficulties of studying motivation do not, of course, preclude attempts to analyse the range of possible motives for action. Weber, for example, suggested that there are four types of motives:

1 The *value-rational*, based on the rational acceptance of the values of a group or movement.

2 The *emotional-affectual*, based on resentment of or enthusiasm for an idea, organization or individual.

3 The *traditional*, based on the acceptance of the behavioural norms of a social group to which the individual belongs.

4 The *purposive-rational*, based on personal advantage.[2]

Similarly, Robert Lane in his study of political involvement, argues that political participation fulfils four functions. First, as

[1] Rudolf Herbele, *Social Movements: An Introduction to Political Sociology* New York, 1951, pp. 94–5.

[2] See Max Weber, *Theory of Social and Economic Organization*, translated and edited by A. M. Henderson and Talcott Parsons, New York, 1947, pp. 115–18.

a means of pursuing economic needs; secondly, as a means of satisfying a need for social adjustment; thirdly, as a means of pursuing particular values; and fourthly, as a means of meeting subconscious and psychological needs.[1] There is, in fact, a basic similarity between Weber's typology of motivation and Lane's functions of political participation. If Weber and Lane are correct, then political participation is determined by the basic social and political attitudes of the individual, which are closely associated with his personal and social characteristics as well as with the social and political environment which forms the context of his political behaviour. Because this social and political environment varies from one society to another, political participation varies from one political system to another.

The individual acquires his political orientations and pattern of political behaviour through the process of political socialization, and his experience of social and political phenomena, through various levels and types of political participation (or through abstention from such participation), is part of a continuing process of socialization and a crucial factor in influencing his future participation. Furthermore, the individual is not faced with unchanging social and political phenomena, since these are subject to changes of problems, personnel and time – to the *uniqueness* of any given political event. It is likely, moreover, that the higher the level of political participation the more crucial these factors become, so that the process of political recruitment becomes an area of particular interest to the political sociologist.

[1] Lane, *Political Life*, pp. 102 and 114, and Chapters 9 and 10.

4 · Political Recruitment

The proportion of individuals in any given society who are active at the highest level of political participation – those who hold political and administrative offices – constitute only a tiny minority of the total population. Moreover, this proportion is scarcely increased to any significant extent if those who *seek* political and administrative office are included, as indeed they must be if effective assessment of political recruitment is to be made. The fact that those who are most active politically constitute a minority in society is of significance for two reasons: firstly, because it is a major feature of all political systems, with the possible exception of those in some primitive societies; and secondly, because it forms the basis of a number of important theories which seek to explain the working of political systems in terms of oligarchies, élites and classes.

Whatever the validity of these theories, however, one of the major concerns of political sociology is to examine and account for the recruitment of those who exercise political power, whether this is through the holding of political offices, such as prime minister or president, cabinet member or state governor, local councillor or mayor, or through being a member of the national or local bureaucracy and being a civil servant, state administrator or local government officer. Similarly, this concern extends to the personnel of the ruling party and governmental hierarchy in totalitarian societies.

It is important to examine recruitment to the bureaucracy, not only because the distinction between the *politician* and the *administrator* is inevitably blurred in the totalitarian societies of the Soviet Union, Eastern Europe and Communist China, but also because the distinction between *policy* and *administration* becomes increasingly meaningless as one moves from the periphery to the centre of the political system. The relationship between politicians and senior members of the administrative machine is such that the impact of politicians on administration and of administrators on policy is invariably profound. This is not to say that the impact of one is always greater than the impact of the other, nor to suggest some sort of equilibrium or counter-balancing forces: the relationship between the two will, of course, vary from one political system to another, and in some instances they will constitute opposing forces, in others complementary forces, and often a mixture of the two.

For example, a number of political systems endeavour to separate political and bureaucratic offices by instituting a doctrine of political neutrality for administrators. This is the case in Britain, for example, where civil servants are recruited through politically neutral machinery and, once appointed, are expected to maintain their political neutrality by refraining from the higher levels of political activity and by serving impartially each government no matter what its political complexion may be. Thus governments may come and go, different parties may hold political power, but the civil servant remains in office. Such a system may be contrasted with that found in the United States, where the party in power institutes extensive changes of personnel in the higher echelons of the civil service on assuming office. This system involving the extension of direct party control from political to administrative offices stems partly from the belief that direct control of these administrative offices is necessary, partly from the historical belief that such a turnover of personnel is administratively beneficial and partly from the long-established tradition that administrative office is a legitimate means of rewarding the party faithful, hence the term 'spoils' system. This close relationship between the ruling party and the holders of administrative office is, however, most clearly seen in totalitarian political systems, where the doctrine of a political neutral bureaucracy is not only anathema, but a contradiction in terms. This does not exclude the possibility of a turnover of personnel, particularly as a result of purges, but in a totalitarian system there are no alternative groups waiting to assume office.

The institutional arrangements of each political system are

another relevant factor in political recruitment. Whether a political system has unitary or federal institutional arrangements, or the extent to which there is a fusion or separation of powers, for instance, will provide important environmental variations. Furthermore, the working characteristics of the political system are also important. Canada provides another example of a political system in which the doctrine of a politically neutral civil service is accepted, but also illustrates a deviation from this doctrine to the extent that a number of prominent politicians, among them Mackenzie King and Lester Pearson, have entered politics through the civil service, so that there exists a certain amount of cross-recruitment between politicians and administrators, although it is mainly a matter of administrators becoming politicians rather than vice versa. Or again, as Alfred Diament has argued in the case of France under the Fourth Republic, where there is

> a weak political consensus the administrative machinery necessary for a modern style will develop its own rules and procedures. It will create a system of internal controls to supplement, or even take the place of, the external control mechanisms. Ultimately the system will develop procedures for operating without any political direction whatsoever.[1]

THE MACHINERY OF POLITICAL RECRUITMENT

The machinery of political recruitment is naturally subject to infinite variation, although two particular devices – those of elections and formal examinations and training – may be regarded as the most important. Even these two devices are, of course, subject to considerable variations, many of which have important implications for political recruitment. Before considering the most important devices, however, some mention should be made of other methods that have been used from time to time and which, in some cases, are still important in various political systems. One of the oldest methods used to secure political leaders was that of sortition, or the drawing of lots: this method was used in ancient Greece. A similar method, which is designed to prevent the domination of office and positions of power by a particular individual or group of individuals, is that of rotation.

[1] Alfred Diament, 'A Case-Study of Administrative Autonomy: Controls and Tensions in French Administration', *Political Studies*, 6, 1958, p. 147.

The 'spoils' system of the United States is, in effect, a rotational system of recruitment, while a number of countries have constitutional provisions which are designed to ensure some degree of rotation of executive personnel. The president and vice-president of the Swiss Federal Council, for example, serve only for a year and may not be immediately re-elected for a further term of office. Similarly, the 24th Amendment to the United States Constitution stipulates that no president may be elected for more than two terms of office; in seventeen Latin American states, no incumbent president may immediately succeed himself, while in Mexico no president may *ever* be re-elected to office.

Another long-standing method of recruitment, common to many political systems, is that of seizing office by the use or threat of force. The violent overthrowal of a political régime, whether by *coup d'état*, revolution, military intervention from outside, assassination or mob violence, is often, though not necessarily, instrumental in effecting radical changes of personnel at the higher levels of political participation. The most immediate and obvious result of such methods is the replacement of political office-holders, but changes in bureaucratic personnel are usually brought about more slowly, especially in complex and highly-developed societies.

Just as there are recruiting devices which are normally associated with extensive changes of personnel, so there are others which are associated more often with the continued recruitment of the same type of personnel. One such device is that of patronage, a system which was very common in earlier times in the United States and Britain, and which remains important in many developing countries. Prior to the reforms of the nineteenth century, for instance, patronage was part of an elaborate system of bribery and corruption which pervaded many areas of public life in Britain. This system was partly a well-established method of influencing the exercise of political power by varying degrees of control over the results of general elections and of support in Parliament *between* elections, and partly a means of political recruitment, since entry to Parliament and the embryonic civil service was secured almost totally through the patronage system. It is, however, misleading to regard patronage as specifically designed to secure and maintain political control, since the system as it existed in the eighteenth century was merely a development of long-standing practices whose purposes varied considerably from patron to patron, while it was far from a guarantee of a subservient House of Commons.[1] It was, moreover, a system in which preferment could be *purchased* by an individual seeking office, as well as one in which individuals could be persuaded to act in a particular way in return for 'favours'. As a system of political recruitment, therefore, it did not necessarily secure office-holders who were 'suitable', either politically or in terms of ability.

Differing from the system of patronage, but also tending towards the perpetuation of particular types of personnel, is a device which may best be described as 'the emergence of natural leaders'. In the past this has served as a rather crude justification for aristocratic rule, and it remains in most political systems as a vital contextual factor. Thus even though it can now be argued that the leader of the Conservative party in Britain no longer 'emerges', since he is elected by a ballot of Conservative M.P.s, the political system imposes a number of contextual limitations which severely reduces the number of potential Conservative leaders from which the choice is made. In other words, quite apart from the convention that he must normally be an M.P., a Conservative leader must also exhibit various abilities which enable him to fulfil the demands of a parliamentary and cabinet system of government: the ability to conduct an effective election campaign, the ability to meet the demands of parliamentary debate, the ability to shoulder the responsibilities of high office, and so on.

Clearly, such demands are made of all party leaders who aspire to high political office in Britain, although their parties are likely to make further specific demands related to the exigencies of the time and the nature of the party concerned. It can thus be argued that the environmental or contextual conditions that a particular political system imposes tend to favour the emergence of particular types of leader and to exclude or limit the emergence of other types. Such individuals may or may not be 'natural leaders' in the sense that they command the loyalty and support of followers who regard them as inherently superior, but they may be regarded as 'natural leaders' in the sense that they represent the types of

[1] See Basil Williams, *Oxford History of England: The Whig Supremacy, 1714-60* (2nd edition, revised by C. H. Stuart), Oxford, 1962, pp. 28-30.

leader most likely to emerge in a particular political system. The prominence of members of the legal profession in many legislatures has been attributed to a variety of factors arising out of the political environment: the tendency for legislative representatives to be drawn from groups with relatively high social status; the extent to which legal skills, such as the public presentation of arguments, mediation and the ability to assimilate the principle points of a situation quickly, are useful in a legislative setting; the relative ease with which lawyers adjust their legal careers to the demands of political activity (both in maintaining a legal career whilst politically active and returning to it should such activity lessen or cease); and the extent, especially in countries like the United States, to which lawyers are used as advisers by people generally, and by politicians in particular, on a range of matters which go far beyond mere legal advice. In the case of the United States, a further factor may be added: the fact that the majority of legal and judicial offices are filled by election provides lawyers with an additional incentive to be politically active.[1]

A more limited method by which existing leaders may contribute towards the recruitment of particular types of leaders is by means of co-option. Strictly speaking, co-option involves the election into a body of an individual by existing members, and though this is fairly common in such political institutions as local councils in England and Wales (both through the election of aldermen and as means of augmenting committees), it is less common in this strict sense at higher levels of office-holding. None the less, a process which is basically similar forms the basis of recruitment to the United States Cabinet, and occasionally, to the British Cabinet. Unlike the latter, the President's Cabinet is not chosen from members of the legislature – the separation of powers expounded in the Constitution forbids this – but from wherever he can secure suitable personnel. Thus a president may recruit prominent businessmen and industrialists, members of the academic and legal professions, as well as appointing recognized politicians to his Cabinet. More rarely, a British prime minister may appoint an 'outsider' to his Cabinet or to some post outside

[1] For a discussion of the political role of lawyers in the United States, see Heinz Eulau and John Sprague, *Lawyers in Politics: A Study of Professional Convergence*, Indianapolis, 1964, and Donald R. Matthews, *The Social Backgrounds of Political Decision-Makers*, New York, 1954, pp. 30–2.

the latter. In 1964, for example, Harold Wilson appointed Frank Cousins, general secretary of the powerful Transport and General Workers' Union, as Minister of Technology (with a seat in the Cabinet) and several other non-parliamentarians as ministers outside the Cabinet. In each case, however, steps had to be taken to bring these appointees into Parliament, either by securing them a seat in the House of Commons (as in the case of Cousins) or by making them life peers, so enabling them to sit in the House of Lords. Any attempt on the part of the prime minister to make more than the occasional appointment from outside Parliament, however, would be regarded, if not unconstitutional, at least in contravention of the norms of the British political system.

The methods by which members of the judiciary are appointed is usually subject to less variation than is the case with political and administrative office-holders. Judicial office-holders have normally received legal training, although they are not necessarily practising members of the legal profession at the time of their appointment. In countries like France, members of the legal profession are trained as advocates or for judicial office and the two sections of the profession are separated from the outset. Appointment to judicial office lies in the hands of a special council representing the executive, legislature and judiciary. In Britain, however, no special provision is made for training future members of the judiciary, and these are drawn from the ranks of the legal profession, in practice from barristers. The latter need not be engaged in full-time practice, and it is not unusual for M.P.s who are also barristers to become judges. It is also customary for holders of legal portfolios in any government (such as the Lord Chancellor, the Attorney-General and the Solicitor-General) to hold legal qualifications. These last appointments lapse, of course, with a change of government, but appointments to the judiciary are made by the executive and held during good behaviour, although age-limits have been applied in practice. A different system exists again in the United States, although here some distinction needs to be drawn between members of the federal and state judiciaries. Federal judges, including members of the Supreme Court, are nominated by the president and their appointment is confirmed by the Senate. At state level, however, this method of nomination by the executive and ratification by the legislature is used in only a minority of cases, and in the majority of the states judges are elected by the populace. Even so, judges are drawn from the legal profession, but the use of election illustrates both how methods of selecting the judiciary may vary and, in particular, the extent to which election is used in the United States as a means of recruiting public officials.

For the most part, however, elections are used in political systems as a means of choosing politicians rather than holders of administrative or judicial office, and it is to their use in this respect that we now turn.

An election may be defined as a means of choosing between two or more alternatives by the casting of votes, but this having been said it is important to recognize the infinite variety of electoral systems. They may vary, as far as the election of office-holders is concerned, according to who is elected, by whom and how. Thus elections may be used to choose members of the executive, the legislature or the judiciary. The right to participate in elections may be restricted to varying degrees, and the particular method by which the votes are cast and counted is subject to considerable variation. Some elections may be described as indirect in that the electors cast their votes for a group of individuals who subsequently constitute an electoral college, which proceeds to conduct a second election to decide who shall hold the office at stake. This, technically, is the method by which the President of the United States is chosen – not by direct popular vote, but by an electoral college comprising representatives of the states of the union. In practice, however, the electoral votes of each state are normally cast in favour of the candidate securing the largest popular vote in the state. None the less, this still means that it is possible for a presidential candidate to secure a majority of the electoral college votes but a minority of the nation-wide popular vote.

Most elections, however, involve the *direct* choice of office-holders by the electors, although the choice of the voters is likely to be restricted by the legal qualifications laid down for the holders of political office and by the methods by which political parties select their candidates. In some cases the legal qualifications for office-holders are minimal, demanding merely that they must be adults, citizens of the country concerned, sane and so on, but in other cases they may be more restrictive. The President of the United States must be born a citizen of that country, at least thirty-five years of age and resident in the United States for fourteen years. Similarly, United States senators must also be citizens (though not native-born), at least thirty years of age and resident in the states they represent. We have, of course, already noted other legal restrictions which may limit the circumstances in which an office-holder may be re-elected. On the whole such restrictions are not particularly severe, and other aspects of electoral systems – the extent to which the right to vote (or franchise) is restricted and the way in which votes are cast and counted – are more important.

Universal adult suffrage is the most common basis of electoral franchises, but this is usually restricted by such factors as citizenship, sanity and criminal records. In some political systems these restrictions are taken further and include other criteria, such as literacy, residence and property qualifications. In the past some of these restrictions have been very severe and the electorate has therefore constituted only a minority of the population. Indeed, only as recently as 1920 was the vote granted to women in Canada and the United States, and in Britain full women's suffrage was not granted until 1928, while Switzerland continues to restrict its federal franchise to men. In some cases restrictions on the franchise have been based on philosophic arguments regarding the extent to which members of the electorate should be 'responsible' persons or capable of making rational decisions in exercising the vote, thus stressing the possession of the latter as a privilege involving duties as well as a right. The struggle over the extension of the franchise in Britain constantly revolved around arguments of this sort. In other cases restrictions have been used more crudely to deny the vote to particular sections of the population. This was one of the means used to limit the political participation of Negroes in the southern states of America: literacy tests and the linking of payment of taxes with right to vote were among the most common methods.

Restrictions on the franchise are likely to have an important effect on voting behaviour and therefore on who is elected to political office. This is especially true where restrictions apply to particular sections of the population who are likely to remain unrepresented until they are at least partially enfranchised. This was an important factor, for instance, in limiting working class representation in many countries and Negro representation in the

United States. Furthermore, the sectional extension of the franchise may be linked with the subsequent polarization of electoral behaviour where parties arise specifically to represent these sections of the population. In many European countries the rise of parties seeking to represent and mobilize the working classes have resulted in the latter securing far greater legislative representation than has been the case in the United States, where no viable working class party exists.

Restrictions on the franchise are, for the most part, historically important in helping to explain party alignments and electoral polarization, and their impact is rather different from that of the way in which votes are cast and counted. Electoral systems based on the simple plurality (or 'first past the post') exaggerate the proportion of seats that the winning party secures in the legislature in relation to the votes cast in its support at the expense of its opponents, particularly third or minor parties. Thus in the British general election of 1966, the winning Labour party secured 48·1 per cent of the votes cast and 57·8 per cent of the seats in the House of Commons. Conversely, the Liberal party secured 8·5 per cent of the votes and only 1·9 per cent of the seats. In fact no party has won an absolute majority of the votes cast in a general election since 1935, yet in every election since then either the Conservative or the Labour party has had an absolute majority in the House of Commons. This is because the country is divided into single-member constituencies in which the candidate with the most votes wins – he does not need an absolute majority; he may win by one vote or by 20,000, the result is the same. Since the balance between the two major parties is fairly equal and the electoral swing is usually evenly spread and in the same direction over the whole country, the result in a significant number of constituencies is decided by relatively few votes, so that the party winning the general election secures a higher proportion of seats than it does of the national vote. Furthermore, parties like the Liberal party accumulate considerable minority votes in a substantial number of constituencies but do not win a commensurate number of seats. This means that in Britain a general election is, in effect, a choice between the Conservative and Labour parties, and that it is difficult for the Liberal party or any other party or parties to secure enough seats to make the formation of a coalition government necessary. Occasionally the election result is sufficiently close to necessitate a minority government, but coalitions are normally reserved for times of emergency.

In many other countries, coalitions are the norm and their likelihood is often facilitated by electoral systems based on proportional representation. The variety of types of proportional representation is considerable, and each type is associated with particular results: some types favour large parties, some small; others favour well-organized parties, and so on; but each seeks to apportion seats in the legislature in accordance with the support that parties secure at an election. This means that it is more difficult for a party to secure an absolute majority in the legislature than it is in Britain: assuming a minimal degree of distortion in the electoral system, proportional representation demands an absolute majority of the votes cast to secure an absolute majority of the seats.

Countries like Britain and the United States adopted electoral systems that were regarded as simple and obvious, and all subsequent attempts to secure their modification have been successfully resisted, if only because they are advantageous to the major parties. Other countries have chosen systems more deliberately in order to achieve particular results, either a proportional distribution of seats generally, or, more specifically, with the intention of creating some advantage or disadvantage for particular parties. West Germany, for example, uses a mixture of the simple plurality and proportional representation, but no party is allowed any seats in the Bundestag unless it secures a minimum proportion of the votes cast. This system has allowed the larger parties to secure relatively proportional representation in the Bundestag, but has contributed to the exclusion of the extremist N.P.D. France has, throughout its history, experimented with many electoral systems, often seeking to remedy the perennial problems of the fragmented French political system. Australia, on the other hand, adopted the alternative (or preferential) vote in order to avoid the problem of a candidate being elected with a minority of the votes cast in any constituency by taking voters' second preferences into account where no candidate secured an absolute majority. This system, however, has been largely responsible for the failure of the Australian Labour party (A.L.P.) to win an election since 1955, because its rival, the Democratic Labour party, advises its supporters to give their second preferences to the Liberal–Country party coalition. Not surprisingly, the A.L.P. would like to see a reversion to the simple plurality which would facilitate its return to power.

The relationship between electoral systems, voting behaviour and party systems is complex: that there is a relationship cannot be doubted, but it cannot be said, for instance, that the simple plurality causes two-party systems, nor that proportional representation causes multi-party systems. Party systems are the product of the social characteristics of the society concerned, not the electoral system. The latter is likely, however, to facilitate the maintenance of particular party systems: a two-party system is more often associated with the simple plurality; proportional representation is more often associated with a multi-party system. The reverse in each instance is not normally the case: a number of countries use the simple plurality but do not have a two-party system; other countries which use proportional representation and have multi-party systems would probably have such party systems regardless of the type of electoral system used.[1]

A somewhat less important factor is the method of casting votes. Before the introduction of the secret ballot, possibilities and incidence of bribery and corruption were considerable; open voting was clearly an important factor in elections, especially in the era of the limited electorate. Other factors concerning the casting of votes remain important, however. The placing of party labels on the ballot papers clearly assist those electors, probably a majority, who wish to vote for a party rather than a candidate; the introduction of the voting machine in the United States facilitates the practice of 'voting the party ticket' instead of making a large number of individual choices for each office at stake; electoral systems involving preferential voting may create problems for the voter because of their relative complexity and problems for the parties in guiding their supporters in making second or lower preferences; the order in which the candidates' names are placed on the ballot paper may be important where the result is likely to be close, since there is evidence that those higher on the list have an advantage if the voter is uncertain of

---

[1] For a discussion of the relationship between party systems and electoral systems, see Duverger, *Political Parties*, Book II, Chapter 1, and Douglas Rae, *The Political Consequences of Electoral Laws*, New Haven, Conn., 1967.

which candidate to support; a candidate possessing a name the the same as or similar to public figures or a name which is clearly identified with a particular section of the electorate may benefit electorally; in some countries voting is compulsory, while the extent to which voting by post or by proxy is allowed may also be important. These are all examples of how voting methods may be significant.

In the majority of elections the contest is between *parties* as much as it is between individual candidates, since the majority of electors identify themselves with a party. Even those electors who may be described as 'floating voters' probably see electoral contests at least partly in party rather than individual terms. A presidential election in the United States, highly personalized as it is, rests on a basis of party conflict – independent candidates do not win. In some countries the party conflict is institutionalized by the placing of party names on ballot papers, or, more importantly, by the practice of presenting the voters with lists of party candidates and requiring the voters to choose between *parties* rather than individual candidates. This latter practice can only be introduced in conjunction with a system of proportional representation and may itself be subject to many variations. Israel, for instance, treats the whole country as a single constituency: the electors vote for the party of their choice and seats in the Knesset are allotted proportionately; a similar process occurs in the Netherlands. A number of European countries, however, use party list systems based on multi-member constituencies in which the seats are allotted proportionately within each constituency rather than nationally. In the case of Israel, candidates are selected by the national party organizations, but in most other countries regional or local party organizations control candidate selection.

The choice made by the parties is therefore important, but its importance is substantially increased where a party's support is heavily concentrated, as is likely to happen, in particular constituencies, so that to secure the party's nomination in such a constituency is invariably a guarantee of election. Even in those constituencies in which the outcome is in some doubt because the parties are evenly balanced, the effective choice is between the leading party candidates, minor party and non-party or independent candidates being at a considerable disadvantage. This is especially true where the electoral system in force is the simple plurality. Electoral systems based on proportional representation normally provide lesser parties and independent candidates with a greater chance of being elected, of course, but this does not obviate the concept of the 'safe' seat, since in a multi-member constituency based on proportional representation the leading parties can normally expect to secure one or more seats out of those at stake, so that to secure the nomination of these parties remains a substantial guarantee of success. Proportional representation only increases the chances of independent candidates and the majority of those elected are still party nominees, again stressing the importance of party connections.

Securing the nomination and support of a party (preferably a major party) is therefore an important step towards electoral success for individual candidates and an important part of the process of political recruitment. Despite the fact that nationally organized parties normally dominate elections, it is misleading to assume that the selection of candidates is dominated by central party organizations: in most cases responsibility for candidate selection is concentrated at regional or local rather than national level, although in some cases the national organization can formally or informally veto the selection of particular individuals. Even in such cases where a national veto is possible, it is essentially a negative weapon, enabling the party leadership to prevent the nomination of someone it dislikes but denying it the means of securing the nomination of someone it likes. This does not preclude some degree of centralization, but this is usually at regional level (as in West Germany) or at state level (as in the Australian Labour party).

Regional or local control does not necessarily mean the selection of candidates abhorrent to the national party, nor does it exclude co-operation between national and other levels of party organization. It normally means that selection is carried out within a procedural framework common to the party as a whole, and often supervised by the national organization, but it also means that the effective choice of candidate is made at regional or local level. This appears to be the case with the majority of countries for which information is available. There are, of course, significant differences between and within various countries, but these do not invalidate the generalization that candidate selection is subject to substantially local control. Again, in most cases, that control is in the hands of the regional or local *party* organization, but there is a major exception to this rule – the use of primary elections in the United States and, to a lesser extent, local convention in Canada.

Leon Epstein links this major difference to the virtual absence of *organized party membership* in the United States and Canada.[1] To what extent it is a causal relationship is more difficult to say. V. O. Key argues that:

> The adoption of the direct primary opened the road for disruptive forces that gradually fractionalized the party organization. By permitting more effective direct appeals by individual politicians to the party membership, the primary system freed forces driving toward the disintegration of party organizations and facilitated the construction of factions and cliques attached to the ambitions of individual leaders.[2]

Conversely, Epstein suggests:

> Less a cause than a symptom, the primary may have been adopted as an expression of an organizational weakness and individualism that was coming to be widely accepted in American candidate selection. Party organizations must already have been losing what strength they had, if so apparently disruptive a method as the direct primary could have been adopted.[3]

Moreover, as Epstein points out, the most common method of candidate selection in the United States prior to the adoption of the primary was the party convention, a method which is more akin to the primary than to the oligarchical intra-party methods used in most other Western democracies. It is reasonable to argue that where a strong party organization based on mass membership exists, there will be considerable resistance to open the process of candidate selection to the wider electorate, but where the political process is traditionally more open, as in the United States, innovations like the primary are more difficult to resist.

The use of the primary election may be regarded as significant in three respects, compared with alternative methods of candidate selection. First, as practised in the United States, the conduct of primary elections is governed by law (the same is also true of candidate selection by convention) and candidate selection is

[1] See Epstein, *Political Parties in Western Democracies*, Chapter 8.

[2] V. O. Key, Jr, *Politics, Parties and Pressure Groups*, New York (5th edition), 1964, p. 342.

[3] Epstein, *Political Parties in Western Democracies*, p. 210.

therefore subject to public regulation to a degree unknown else-where. Secondly, the primary election allows a greater proportion of the electorate to participate in the process of candidate selection than is possible elsewhere. Finally, it provides a means by which a relative 'outsider' can secure a major party nomination.

The fact that primaries are legally required in all but five states, means that would-be candidates must be prepared to fight a public election campaign to secure nomination. The form of the primary varies, however: in some cases the primary is *open*, and any voter may participate, although in most cases he may only vote in one party's primary; in other cases the primary is *closed*, and participation is limited to those who are, by various means, registered as party supporters. Furthermore, although the primary undoubtedly facilitates political participation, it is important to note that turnout varies considerably. As Key points out,

> Comparatively few voters determine who are to be the candidates in the general election campaign. In about three-fourths of the primaries held in a sample of states . . . less than 35 per cent of the potential electorate voted on the nomination of gubernatorial candidates.[1]

Moreover, turnout tends to be highest in the primary of the electorally dominant party and lowest in that of the weaker party, while, where the parties are evenly divided, turnout is often minimized because efforts within each party are made to negotiate agreement on nominations. The provision of fierce intra-party competition in one-party states allows,

> . . . party candidatures [to be] assumed by individuals and groups able to win primary elections. In winning, they are likely to seek at least the informal help of those identified as party leaders or workers, but in much the same way as they seek the help of others outside party ranks. There may be no 'party' to approve or disapprove of candidatures.[2]

Party candidates for most political offices in the United States are chosen by primary elections, although, as we have already seen, not all primaries are of equal significance. The major exception to the practice of selecting candidates by primary elections, at least in the direct sense, is the choosing of presidential candidates. In both major parties this is done by party conven-

---

[1] Key, *Politics, Parties and Pressure Groups*, pp. 580–1; see also pp. 290–1 and 378–80.

[2] Epstein, *Political Parties in Western Democracies*, p. 205.

tions consisting of delegates from each of the states. It is important to bear in mind, however, that the delegates to a convention may be pledged or at least influenced by the result of a presidential primary which has been held in their state. Approximately a third of the states conduct presidential primaries, some of which allow voters to choose between several candidates for the party nomination; but others are concerned merely with selecting state delegates and offer no opportunity of expressing any direct candidate preference. The influence that these primaries can exert is thus complicated, not only because not all states use them and delegates are often not bound by their results, but because a good or bad showing in one or more of the important primaries can have a crucial effect on a candidate's chance of securing the party nomination at the convention. One of the most striking examples of this was

> . . . the 1952 'Minnesota miracle', when over 100,000 persons took the trouble to write in the name of Eisenhower in the primary [and] Republican leaders all over the land could see that a vote-getter had arrived on the scene.[1]

The primary election is a method of selection peculiar to the United States, and although some Western European countries provide for the participation of party members in the selection of candidates, it is neither as extensive nor as open as the American method. In West Germany, for example, selection may be by a ballot of all party members, but in practice oligarchical control is more common. Similarly, in Norway selection is undertaken by delegate bodies following consultation with local party members. The nearest equivalent to the American primary, however, is found in Sweden and Belgium. In Sweden some parties consult the party membership by means of a postal ballot, and others hold a ballot of all members if this is requested by a quarter of the district delegates. In Belgium parties run primaries which are restricted to party members, who may choose candidates from lists submitted by the party leaders.[2] In no case, however, is selection conducted by means of a public campaign, nor is participation extended beyond party members to those who are merely party supporters.

Canada bears some similarity to the United States in candidate

---

[1] Key, *Politics, Parties and Pressure Groups*, p. 411.
[2] See Epstein, *Political Parties in Western Democracies*, pp. 226–8.

selection in that the two older parties, the Progressive Conservatives and the Liberals, select their candidates through party conventions, and these conventions are sometimes open to all who consider themselves party supporters.[1] Practice varies, however, in both parties, while the New Democratic party (N.D.P.) restricts participation in selection to party members. Nevertheless, there is a further Canadian parallel, and this is the practice of Canadian parties of selecting their leaders through national conventions rather than following the British model of confining this to members of the parliamentary party. As in the American case, the convention consists of delegates from party organizations in each province and is preceded by public campaigning by the aspirants. With the exception of the N.D.P., in which the leadership is subject to election every two years, conventions are held only when necessary, which is normally when the leadership becomes vacant or, more rarely, when the incumbent leader is prevailed upon to allow his position to be challenged, as happened to the Conservative leader, John Diefenbaker, in 1967.

Britain provides an example of the main alternative method of selecting candidates. The two major parties use a two-tier method by which

> . . . a relatively small body examines the applicants [in the Conservative party] or nominees [in the Labour party] for the vacancy and makes certain recommendations to a larger [representative] body, which in turn normally elects one of the recommended candidates . . . selection remains in the hands of comparatively few people, not only within the constituency but within the local party itself.[2]

The control exercised by the national party organizations is basically negative, as we have already noted, and the selection of parliamentary candidates in Britain is subject to considerable local autonomy – a greater degree of autonomy than is often found in other Western democracies, where regional party organizations sometimes have effective control over candidate selection. In countries like Britain, where selection is an internal party affair and not subject to a common legal framework of the sort provided by the American primary system, there are often significant procedural differences between the parties:

[1] See Howard Scarrow, 'Nomination and Local Party Organization in Canada: A Case-Study', *Western Political Quarterly*, **17**, 1964, pp. 55–62.
[2] Rush, *The Selection of Parliamentary Candidates*, p. 276.

Selection in the Labour party is subject to the rules laid down in the party and C.L.P. [Constituency Labour Party] constitutions and no C.L.P. may depart from the prescribed procedure. Under this procedure no individual may *apply* for the vacancy; he must be nominated by a party or affiliated organization. There is no formal procedure for interviewing nominees prior to their appearance before the selection conference and, apart from the general adoption meeting held shortly before the election campaign (which for obvious reasons must be a formality), the decision of the selection conference is final as far as the C.L.P. is concerned. The N.E.C. [National Executive Committee] may overrule the G.M.C. [General Management Committee] and refuse to endorse its choice, but this is the exception rather than the rule. At no time, therefore, is the selected candidate submitted to the approval of the general membership of the C.L.P., other than when the withholding of such approval would be virtually unthinkable.

There is no *formal* selection procedure in the Conservative party, however, although a fairly detailed advisory pamphlet is made available by [the Conservative] Central Office and most local associations follow a basically similar procedure. At the same time, variations in procedure are not only permissible but fairly common. Individuals may apply for vacancies and there is no system of nomination. The interviewing of applicants prior to short-listing is normal, after which successful applicants appear before a body similar in form and composition to the Labour G.M.C. The decision of the executive council [of the local association] is subject to the approval of a general meeting of the association. A *second* general meeting is held at the beginning of the election campaign, when the candidate is formally adopted. The selection is *not* subject to the formal endorsement of the national party, since approval is sought prior to selection.[1]

Procedural differences of this sort are often important in affecting the whole process of selection. For instance, the whole federative nature of the Labour party, with its formal organizational divisions representing trade unions, the Co-operative party, individual members and so on, is reflected in its selection procedure and is the basis of many of the cross-pressures which arise in Labour selections. Similarly, the system of nomination of possible candidates by local party organizations used in the Labour party tends to limit the choice of local parties much more than the system of applications used by the Conservatives.

Despite these differences both within and between political

[1] ibid., pp. 276–7. For a description and discussion of selection in other British parties, see Michael Rush, 'Candidate Selection and its Impact on Leadership Recruitment', in J. D. Lees and R. Kimber (eds.), *Political Parties in Britain: An Organizational and Functional Guide*, London, 1971.

systems in the methods used to select candidates, there is a wide-spread tendency for the major decisions in candidate selection to be concentrated at local or regional rather than national levels. The principal difference, therefore, between the American primary method and those methods more common to other Western democracies is that in the latter the selection of candidates is conducted *within* the party organization: participation at its very widest is limited to those who are party members – to be a declared party supporter is not enough.

A more significant difference in many respects stems not from the degree of party control over selection, but from constitutional doctrines of the separation and fusion of powers. The separation of powers in the United States (and in those Latin American countries which have adopted American-style constitutions) means that there is a procedural separation in the selection of candidates for the executive on the one hand and the legislature on the other. Thus even though candidates for both executive and legislative positions may be selected by the same or similar procedures, the actual selections are separate and allow the primary electorates (or party organizations in the absence of a primary) a direct voice in the choice of candidates for these positions. In those political systems in which there is a fusion of powers, however, and members of the executives are normally drawn from, and are members of, the legislature, candidates are selected initially as potential members of the legislature rather than the executive. This means that the career patterns of leading office-holders in the two types of system tend to be different.

In Britain the majority of ministers, especially those holding the most important portfolios, are drawn from the House of Commons. They will therefore have had some legislative experience. Most of those ministers who are not M.P.s are members of the House of Lords and will also have had legislative experience. Moreover, the legislative experience of senior ministers usually amounts to at least a decade, while a prime minister is likely to have spent as many as twenty or more years in Parliament before assuming office. Harold Wilson, for example, had been in Parliament for nineteen years when he became Prime Minister in 1964. The majority of his Cabinet colleagues had had at least eleven years' parliamentary experience, while all but a few of those appointed to posts outside the Cabinet had at least five years' experience. Furthermore, depending when the party last held office, a significant proportion of those appointed to ministerial positions (especially those at senior level) may have had previous ministerial experience.

Generally speaking, the longer a party retains office the more likely it is that those who eventually hold senior government posts will have had to work their way up through the ministerial hierarchy. Where a party has had a long period in Opposition, however, the appointment of those without such experience to senior posts (including membership of the Cabinet) is more likely when office is eventually achieved. This was the case with the Labour Government of 1964, of which only two members had previous experience as Cabinet ministers, although a number had held non-Cabinet posts between 1945 and 1951 when the Labour party had last been in power. Those who achieve the office of prime minister usually combine both legislative and ministerial experience. Indeed, the only prime minister in this century to assume office without first having held a Cabinet post was Ramsay MacDonald, the first Labour prime minister, and even he had considerable legislative experience.[1] From time to time individuals with no legislative or ministerial experience are appointed to the Cabinet, but these are the exception rather than the rule.[2]

The career patterns of American presidents and members of their cabinets are likely to be far more varied. Excluding those presidents who succeeded to office as vice-presidents through the death of the incumbent, and who served only the expiry of that term, twenty-two of the thirty-two presidents elected from 1789 to 1968 had had executive and legislative experience prior to election, while seven had had executive experience only, and three legislative experience only. It should be noted, however, that although executive experience includes having held a Cabinet post or having been a state governor, it also includes having held high military command or having been vice-president. If these last two categories are excluded on the grounds that military command is not strictly political experience, and that experience as vice-president varies considerably from one administration to

---

[1] See Philip W. Buck, *Amateurs and Professionals in British Politics, 1918–59*, Chicago, 1963, Chapter 5 and Appendix 4, Tables 20–3.

[2] See F. M. G. Willson, 'Routes of Entry of New Members to the British Cabinet, 1868–1958', *Political Studies*, 7, 1959, pp. 222–32.

another and is sometimes almost a sinecure, then the number of presidents who have had executive and legislative experience is reduced to fourteen (less than half the total), and those with executive experience only to four. Presidential candidates may be drawn from a wide field, and although often active in politics prior to nomination, their strictly political experience may be limited or negligible. This is even more likely with members of the Cabinet, who may be drawn from a variety of spheres and whose political experience may be non-existent.

This is not to suggest that executive or legislative experience is necessary for these posts, but merely to point out the way in which career patterns may be shaped by the institutional arrangements of the political system. Thus legislative experience is virtually a prerequisite of holding political office in Britain, and executive experience generally precedes appointment to the most senior positions. In the United States, on the other hand, executive and legislative experience, while common, is far from being a prerequisite, especially for those holding Cabinet posts.

Much of what has been said applies to the other Western democracies, although career patterns in these countries have been less widely documented. France, for instance, provides an interesting example of how institutional changes can alter the pattern of recruitment. Under the Fourth Republic there existed a fusion of powers, and ministers were generally members of the National Assembly and career politicians. With the establishment of the Fifth Republic in 1958, however, a modified separation of powers was introduced by which ministers could not be members of the legislature, although they could address it from time to time. This facilitated the recruitment of civil servants, businessmen and other non-politicians as members of the Cabinet, with significant results.

Unfortunately, little is known about the selection of political office-holders in developing countries beyond the fact that the principal vehicles of recruitment are, as in Western democracies, political parties. It seems likely that the processes of recruitment are far less formalized in such systems, since the organizational development of political parties is less extensive and more fragmentary than that found in most industrially advanced countries. Many developing countries are, in territorial terms, of such recent origin that any emphasis on such questions as executive and legislative experience is hardly possible, while the transformation of independence movements into effective political parties presents considerable recruitment problems. Experience is likely to be interpreted in terms of the struggle for independence, but as the achievement of independence becomes accepted, the struggle for power, the responsibilities of government and the problems of social, economic and political development create tension which may fragment the often precarious unity of the former independence movements. Recruitment is likely to be conducted through informal channels based on traditional tribal, ethnic or regional groups. Efforts to avoid social and political fragmentation may be made through the creation of comprehensive nationalist parties seeking to unite as many groups as possible under the aegis of a common ideology – Apter's 'political religion'. This may lead in turn to one-party states of the sort found in Kenya and Tanzania which have, for the most part, sought to absorb and contain opposition elements within a single party. Alternatively, the emphasis may be upon the suppression of these elements, as in Ghana (under Nkrumah) or a number of former French colonial territories. Whatever devices are used, however, the importance of the traditional methods of political recruitment (even through modern institutions such as trade unions, which may be linked with parties) involving informal relationships of kinship and tribal and ethnic origin are likely to predominate.[1]

Although the political systems of those developing countries which have enjoyed independence from colonial domination for many generations (or of those which have never been effectively subjected to colonial rule) have had longer to establish legitimacy, they are, in most cases, subject to as much instability and lack of legitimacy as many more recently-established political systems. None the less, social institutions tend to be less subject to change in such areas as Latin America and parties are often more firmly established there than in other developing areas. Recruitment may therefore be channelled through the more formal party structures, although the social divisions between urban and rural areas, between the traditional and the modern, and the long-standing systems of social stratification almost certainly remain crucial.[2]

[1] See Almond and Coleman (eds.), *Politics in the Developing Areas*, Parts 1–4.
[2] ibid., Part 5.

In contrast to political recruitment in developing societies, where the process tends to be relatively unsystematic, in totalitarian societies it is highly systematized. In addition to exercising general control of the educational system, the totalitarian state seeks to train a party élite for political and governmental office. In Nazi Germany, for example, a three-tier system of élite training was established. At the lowest level the most promising members of the Hitler Youth were sent to Adolf Hitler Schools from the age of twelve and subjected to intensive leadership training. These schools were run by the Hitler Youth. Above these were the National Political Institutes of Education, supervised by the S.S. and providing a combination of strict military training with special instruction in National Socialist ideology. Finally, the leading graduates from these two levels were sent to the *Ordensburgen*, where they received six years' training in the 'racial sciences' as well as political and military instruction.[1]

A similar situation is found in the Soviet Union, although systematic study of the recruitment is inevitably difficult, especially in the field of party recruitment. Fainsod describes three types of party school: (1) Higher Party Schools, 'designed to train leading party officials for republic and oblast level duties and . . . reserved for those having a higher education and considerable experience in responsible [party] work'; (2) Inter-oblast and Republic Higher Party Schools, providing courses for less senior party officials; and (3) Republic and Oblast Schools, dealing with lower level officials.[2]

RECRUITMENT TO ADMINISTRATIVE OFFICE

The systematic training and recruitment of *political* office-holders finds no parallel in Western democracies, but it does bear some comparison with the recruitment of *administrative* office-holders. In Western democracies, the latter are systematically recruited and, usually, trained by the state to fulfil particular roles in the bureaucracy. Recruitment is based primarily on merit, and entrance to the bureaucracy is generally achieved by some form of examination designed to test merit.

[1] See Shirer, *The Rise and Fall of the Third Reich*, pp. 255–6.
[2] Fainsod, *How Russia is Ruled*, pp. 242–4.

Countries like Britain and France, however, differ from the United States in that they adhere to the principle of a politically neutral civil service. Thus leading members of the bureaucracy retain their posts regardless of the party or parties in power, whereas in the United States federal civil service a change of party (or to a lesser extent of president, even though he may be of the same party as his predecessor) means changes of personnel in the higher echelons of the bureaucracy.

It has been estimated that 95 per cent of the personnel of the federal civil service are recruited through the *merit* system, rather than the 'spoils' system, but the importance of the latter (apart from the patronage it places in the hands of the party and president in power) lies in the fact that it is the means by which *key* officials are recruited. It is, of course, grossly misleading to suggest that posts are distributed to party supporters merely in response to the demands of patronage. The latter is more important in rewarding party supporters with minor posts which still remain within the purview of the 'spoils' system, posts such as chauffeurs, stenographers and the like. What the 'spoils' system does mean in political terms is that the highest posts are likely to be filled by 'outsiders' who are not career civil servants.

The philosophy behind this system is not difficult to understand, nor impossible to justify. Although Andrew Jackson was the first prominent politician to give articulate expression to the 'spoils' system, its use was already widespread in many states and by no means unknown at federal level when Jackson gave it the presidential accolade. Patronage, which was the common basis of recruitment in most countries at the time, was rationalized by the argument that changes of personnel were healthy and democratic, that the offices concerned required no special skills, and that the party in power needed bureaucrats who were sympathetic to its aims and would not seek to undermine its actions.

The wholesale use of the 'spoils' system as a means of recruitment has, as the figure mentioned earlier makes clear, been vastly reduced and recruitment on grounds of merit introduced, beginning with the Civil Service (Pendleton) Act 1883. The merit system has gradually been extended by the systematic classification of grades and pay, the introduction of pensions plans (both of which were closely linked with merit schemes) and by direct extension through federal legislation and executive orders.

Following the two world wars, however, the merit system was modified by the preference given to veterans (or ex-servicemen). Thus, between 1920 and 1940, 20 to 25 per cent of those appointed to positions in the federal civil service were veterans, while a decade after the Second World War approximately 60 per cent of those employed by the service had had veterans' preference. The 'spoils' system, however, applies in practice only to a small minority of administrative office-holders (if these veterans are excluded) in the United States, but they are a very significant minority.

Although most civil servants are now recruited through the merit system (veterans still receive preference, but must still reach certain required standards), recruitment is not centralized and each department conducts its own examinations and makes its own appointments. Furthermore, the view that no special skills are required by administrative personnel has militated against the training of civil servants. As the United Comptroller-General remarked in 1910, '. . . it is presumed that officers and employees when appointed and employed have the necessary education to perform the duties for which they were appointed.'[1] This doctrine of initial competence remained inviolate until 1921, when the Graduate School of the Department of Agriculture was established, and this was followed in 1924 by the founding of the Foreign Service School. Thereafter in-service training became more acceptable and widespread, especially with the developments introduced during the New Deal.

Even though Britain and France may be contrasted with the United States in establishing politically-neutral civil services, there are important differences between these two countries. Britain gradually eliminated patronage (though it was not linked with partisan control or turnover of office, as in the United States) during the nineteenth century following the Northcote-Trevelyan Report of 1854 and the establishment of a Civil Service Commission, which was made responsible for the recruitment of all administrative personnel. At the same time, the principle of recruitment by open competition was accepted and subsequently introduced. The civil service was divided into grades according to the nature of the work concerned and personnel for the three

[1] Quoted in Arthur D. Kallen, 'Training in the Federal Service – 170 Years to Accept', *Public Administration Review*, 19, 1959, p. 37.

main groups (the clerical, executive and administrative classes) were separately recruited through the Civil Service Commission, although internal promotion from one class to another remains an important source of recruits.[1] Open examination of an academic nature are held, but these are supplemented in some cases by intensive interview methods, particularly for the highest group, the administrative class. Occasionally personnel are recruited from outside the civil service, but such appointments are exceptional, although in times of emergency, such as the Second World War, the recruitment of non-career civil servants may assume significant proportions.

Until recently the training of British civil servants was based on the concept of in-service or vocational training, and little in the way of special instruction was provided. The lowest rank in the administrative class, that of assistant principal, is therefore a training grade. This was later supplemented by the establishment of a Centre for Administrative Studies, which provides courses for assistant principals soon after they join the service. The concept of specific training has now been taken further by the founding of a Civil Service College, which will provide a wider basis of training for civil servants.[2] The emphasis remains, however, on in-service training, and therefore upon recruitment based primarily on educational qualifications not necessarily related to or specifically preparation for a civil service career.

France rationalized administrative recruitment rather earlier than Britain, and has, moreover, developed more intensive training techniques for civil servants. French civil servants are recruited by open examination and, as in Britain, the bureaucracy is divided into classes according to their functions. Entry to the higher echelons of the civil service in France differs, however, in that intensive pre-service training forms the basis of recruitment. This pre-service training is provided by the École Nationale d'Administration (E.N.A.) and the École Polytechnique. The E.N.A. was founded in 1945 as part of the extensive civil service reforms carried out in the immediate post-war period. Its role is

[1] The present system of classes in the Civil Service is being replaced by a unified grading structure, following the recommendation of the Fulton Report.

[2] See *The Civil Service* (The Fulton Report), Cmd 3683, 1968, Vol. 1, pp. 35–40, and Vol. 4, Section VI. For further discussion and information, see ibid., Vol. 1, Chapter 3, and Vol. 4, Section III.

both to recruit and train higher civil servants, and candidates are selected either by open competition (based on examinations in subjects broadly related to a career in public administration), or by limited competition open to existing civil servants of lower grade. Once they have entered the E.N.A., recruits are salaried civil servants and subsequently undergo a two-year period of administrative training, which includes a year working in a local prefecture and a much shorter period in a private company, as well as various forms of instruction in central administration and policy-making. The E.N.A. thus recruits and trains members of the French civil service who are to fill the chief administrative posts. Recruitment and training of technical specialists for the higher echelons of the civil service is undertaken by the École Polytechnique, although, unlike the E.N.A., the Polytechnique also trains graduates for the armed services and for private industry. The stress in France is thus on training recruits to the bureaucracy specifically for careers in the public service, whereas in Britain and the United States there is less emphasis on training and more on recruiting 'suitable' individuals into the bureaucracy.

Suitability is, in practice, the major factor in administrative recruitment, except where patronage is the sole determinant. Suitability may, however, be variously defined in terms of competence, political loyalty, socio-economic background, ethnic origin and so on. Western democracies tend to emphasize competence, for example, although most demand minimal political loyalty to the state. Socio-economic background is often important in that it is directly or indirectly associated with competence, while ethnic origin is of significance in countries like Canada, where some balance is sought between English- and French-speaking civil servants. In other countries, however, much greater stress is laid upon such factors as political loyalty and ethnic origin. In developing societies formerly subject to colonial rule, strenuous efforts are often made to create a bureaucracy drawn from the indigenous population, although reliance upon members of the former colonial administration is common in the early years of independence. Demands for 'Africanization', for example (demands not necessarily restricted to the bureaucracy), in former British and French colonies often make it difficult to recruit enough competent civil servants. Furthermore, there may be disproportionate recruitment from particular ethnic or tribal groups, as in Nigeria, while the demands of political loyalty, particularly in one-party states, and the extensive use of patronage in some developing countries present additional problems.[1]

Clearly totalitarian societies lay considerable stress on political loyalty, as the Preamble of the German Civil Service Law of 1937 makes clear:

> A professional Civil Service, rooted in the German *Volk*, saturated with a National Socialist commitment, based on personal fealty to the Leader of the German *Reich* and *Volk*, Adolf Hitler, constitutes the pillar of the Nationalist Socialist State.[2]

At the same time, because they are complex modern societies, totalitarian states necessarily emphasize the importance of competence. Thus, in the Soviet Union,

> Every sector of industry and administration has its parallel system of advanced schools and institutes which feed their graduates into the branch of public administration for which they prepare.[3]

The ultimate aim of any totalitarian society, as the Nazi Civil Service Law makes clear, is to create a bureaucracy in which political loyalty is absolute and takes precedence over competence. Indeed, under such circumstances no bureaucrat whose political loyalty is in doubt can be regarded as competent. This, however, presents particular difficulty in periods of change or transition.

When there are fundamental changes in the political system, the accompanying turnover of political and administrative office-holders holders is often considerable. Political office-holders are, of course, subject to a greater turnover, but it is misleading to assume that this is simply the replacement of one group by an opposing one, as Lewis Edinger has shown in his study of the transition from the Nazi régime to the West German Federal Republic. The process is inevitably complicated, and even conscious efforts to replace one 'élite' with another are unlikely to result in a total change of personnel. Thus, despite the efforts of the Allies to control political recruitment in post-war Germany, Edinger found that,

[1] See Richard L. Harris, 'The Role of the Civil Servant in West Africa', *Public Administration Review*, 25, 1965, pp. 308–13; James R. Shuster, 'Bureaucratic Transition in Morocco', *Human Organization*, 24, 1965, pp. 53–8; and Almond and Coleman (eds.), *Politics in the Developing Areas*, Parts 1–5.

[2] Quoted in Elke Frank, 'The Role of the Bureaucracy in Transition', *Journal of Politics*, 28, 1966, p. 742; see also Carl Beck, 'Party Control and Bureaucratization in Czechoslovakia', *Journal of Politics*, 23, 1961, pp. 279–94.

[3] Fainsod, *How Russia is Ruled*, p. 415.

Most members of the 1956 élites were recruited from the ranks of those who had belonged neither to the Nazi élite nor to the counter-élite, who had neither been strong opponents nor strong supporters of the totalitarian régime, neither strongly involved in running that régime nor in fighting it . . . about 24 per cent may be considered to have been supporters of the régime, 57 per cent to have been ambivalent, neutral or oscillating during the twelve years of Nazi rule, and no more than 19 per cent to have been more or less consistently opposed.[1]

Much depends, of course, on the nature of the changes in the political system. Where the transition is from a totalitarian to a non-totalitarian régime, then the changes in personnel may be limited to the holders of the more important political offices, but the establishment of a dictatorial or, more particularly, a totalitarian régime demands more extensive changes of personnel. None the less, it is important to note that even in the latter case (as in the example of developing societies formerly subject to colonial rule) totalitarian régimes are likely to be dependent upon the administrative office-holders of the previous régime. For example:

While trusted Bolsheviks held strategic positions at the top of the administrative pyramid, the lower levels of the bureaucracy were still composed of old-régime carry-overs whose knowledge made them indispensable and whose skills frequently enabled them to determine the policies of the institutions with which they were connected.[2]

Similarly, despite the law of 1937, a study of the German Foreign Office found that the Nazi régime had had to retain most of those already established in the service, and of these approximately a third *never* became members of the Nazi party. This particular study concluded that both the Weimar Republic and the Third Reich were too short-lived to establish bureaucracies which accepted the legitimacy of the régime.[3]

WHO IS RECRUITED AND WHY

The literature on who achieves political and administrative office is extensive. Moreover, as far as modern democracies are con-

[1] Lewis J. Edinger, 'Post-Totalitarian Leadership in Élites in the German Federal Republic', *American Political Science Review*, 54, 1960, pp. 72 and 75.
[2] Fainsod, *How Russia is Ruled*, p. 92.
[3] Elke Frank, 'The Role of the Bureaucracy in Transition', *Journal of Politics*, 28, 1966, pp. 725–53.

cerned, there is general agreement that political and administrative office-holders are invariably unrepresentative of the general population.

Table 25. *Educational background of political and administrative office-holders in the United States*

HIGHEST LEVEL ATTAINED	Presidents, vice-presidents, Cabinet members (1877–1934)	United States Senators (1949–51)	United States Representatives (1941–3)	State governors (1930–40)
	%	%	%	%
None	–	–	–	–
Grade School	11	3	–	3
High school	10	10	12	20
College	79	87	88	77
Totals	100	100	100	100

HIGHEST LEVEL ATTAINED	Missouri State legislators (1901–31)	High-level civil servants (1940)	Population over 25 years of age (1940)
	%	%	%
None	–	–	5
Grade school	30	–	54
High school	13	7	31
College	57	93	10
Totals	100	100	100

SOURCE: Donald R. Matthews, *The Social Background of Political Decision-Makers*, New York, 1954, Table 6.

Table 25 shows clearly that those who have held various types of political and administrative office in the United States are educationally unrepresentative of the general population, and a similar pattern is found if the occupational backgrounds of some of these groups is examined (Table 26). A similar pattern emerges if the backgrounds of political and administrative office-holders in Britain are examined (Table 27).

The pattern found in Tables 25, 26 and 27 is repeated in other countries, although there are, as the tables illustrate, important variations. What is probably of greater significance, however, is the fact that a similar pattern is found in some developing countries (Table 28).

Table 26. *Occupational backgrounds of political office-holders in the United States*

OCCUPATION	Presidents, vice-presidents, Cabinet members (1877–1934)	United States Senators (1949–51)	United States Representatives (1941–30)	State governors (1930–40)
	%	%	%	%
Professions	74	69	69	60
Proprietors and officials	21	24	22	25
Farmers	2	7	4	11
Low-salaried workers	1	–	1	1
Wage-earners	2	–	2	1
Servants	–	–	–	–
Farm labourers	–	–	–	–
Unknown, not classified	–	–	2	3
Totals	100	100	100	101

OCCUPATION	State legislators (1925–35)	Labour force (1940)
	%	%
Professions	36	7
Proprietors and officials	25	8
Farmers	22	11
Low-salaried workers	4	17
Wage-earners	3	40
Servants	–	11
Farm labourers	–	7
Unknown, not classified	10	–
Totals	100	101

SOURCE: Matthews, *The Social Background of Political Decision-Makers*, Table 7.

Source and note for table 27

SOURCES: Cabinet ministers: W. L. Guttsman, *The British Political Élite*, London, 1963, Table XV.

M.P.s: J. F. S. Ross, *Elections and Electors*, London, 1955, Tables 71, 77, 87 and 91.

Civil servants: A. H. Halsey and I. M. Crewe, 'Social Survey of the Civil Service', *Fulton Report*, Vol. 3(1), Tables 2.3, 2.7, 2.8 and 2.9.

* The sum of these figures exceeds the total proportion of graduates because of attendance at more than one university.

Table 27. *Background of political and administrative office-holders in Britain*

	Cabinet ministers (1916–55)	M.P.s (1945)		Administrative class civil servants (1967)
(A) CLASS BACKGROUND	%	%	Father's occupation	%
Aristocracy	20	8	Professional and managerial	67
Middle Class	58	} 92	Skilled non-manual and manual	23
Working class	22		Semi-skilled	4
			Unskilled	2
			Other	4
Total	100	100		100
(B) EDUCATIONAL BACKGROUND				
School				
Elementary	20	34	} 42	
Secondary/grammar	20	21		
Public school	52	44	55	
Other	8	–	3	
Totals	100	99	100	
(C) UNIVERSITY BACKGROUND				
Oxford and Cambridge	47 } 59	28* } 42	49* } 76	
Other	12	18*	28*	
None		41	58	24
Totals	100	100	100	

	Cabinet ministers (1916–55)		M.P.s (1945)	
	%		%	
(D) OCCUPATIONAL BACKGROUND				
Professions	37	Professions	53	
Officials of trade unions, etc.	15	Workers, including TU officials	27	
Commerce and industry	13	Employers and managers	17	
Landowning	12	Unoccupied	2	
Rentier	11			
Civil service, public administration	6			
Armed forces	4			
Manual workers	1			
Totals	99		99	

Table 28. *Occupational and educational background of members of legislatures in Ghana and Nigeria*

	Ghana %	Nigeria %
(A) OCCUPATION		
Education	30 ⎫ 46	30 ⎫ 50
Professions	16 ⎭	20 ⎭
Business	17	27
Farmers	4	6
Manual and clerical workers	6	3
Local government (including chiefs and officials)	16	11
All other	11	3
Totals	100	100
(B) EDUCATION		
Pre-secondary	44	33
Secondary	42	37
University	14	30
Totals	100	100

SOURCE: James S. Coleman, 'The Politics of Sub-Saharan Africa', Table 8, in Almond and Coleman (eds.), *Politics of the Developing Areas*, p. 342.

Furthermore, the pattern of recruitment among administrative office-holders, as measured by the occupational class of the fathers of higher civil servants, is similar in modern democracies and developing societies (Table 29).

Table 29. *Occupational class of the fathers of higher civil servants in selected countries*

COUNTRY	Middle class %	Working class %
Denmark (1945)	87	13
Britain (1949–52)	97	3
France (1945–51)	96	4
United States (1959)	81	19
Turkey (1960)	90	10
India (1947–56)	96	4

SOURCE: V. Subramaniam, 'Representative Bureaucracy: A Reassessment', *American Political Science Review*, **61**, 1967, Table 1, p. 1016.

It is, of course, important to bear in mind that in many cases the categories used in these tables are not strictly comparable, especially in dealing with such phenomena as class and educational levels. The validity of the data does not depend on absolute comparability, however, but in demonstrating the extent to which political and administrative office-holders are drawn from particular groups in society, a phenomenon which, it has been argued, is found in all societies in the form of an oligarchy, political élite or ruling class.

Political Recruitment and Élite and Class Theories. In seeking to explain why political and administrative office-holders are drawn substantially from particular social groups in a society, a number of theorists have suggested that these groups constitute élites or classes in whose hands political power is concentrated. Their existence is not accidental but, it is argued, is the result of various forces in society which create some form of social stratification. The basis of social stratification can, of course, vary – it may be based on economic divisions in society, or on the concept of a religious hierarchy, or on some form of status differentiation, or on ethnic divisions and so on. In practice it may well be a combination of these, but particular societies illustrate each type: modern industrial democracies are often cited as societies divided into upper, middle and lower classes according to occupational and other economic criteria; the Hindu caste system is clearly an example of religiously-based stratification; feudal societies were instances of status differentiation; while the position of Jews in Nazi Germany, Negroes in the United States or of Indians in many Latin American countries provide examples of some degree of ethnic stratification. It is further argued that the distribution of power within societies is determined by and directly related to the system of social stratification, and that the particular group wielding such power constitutes a political élite or ruling class.

A similar but separate theory suggests that those who wield power are always a small minority or oligarchy, since all organizations consist of an active minority and an inactive majority. The active minority, it is argued, can always out-manoeuvre the inactive majority because it has the advantage of being organized, and such a minority can only be replaced or overthrown by another minority possessing superior organization. This is Michel's 'iron law of oligarchy'.[1] Thus even an organization

[1] See Robert Michels, *Political Parties*, Part Six.

which, by its rules, grants formal power to its whole membership, is in practice subject to control and manipulation by a minority of active members; or, in the words of one of its leading proponents, Gaetano Mosca:

> In all societies – from societies that are very meagrely developed and have barely attained the dawnings of civilization, down to the most advanced and powerful societies – two classes of people appear – a class that rules and a class that is ruled.[1]

Mosca, however, attributes the dominant position of the minority not only to its organizational advantages, but further argues that the minority possesses these advantages because it consists of superior individuals, superior not necessarily because they are more able, but because they have characteristics which are valued by their particular societies. Mosca calls this minority a *ruling class*; his contemporary and rival, Vilfredo Pareto, calls it a *political élite*. Both Mosca and Pareto agreed that there was a division between rulers and ruled, between the political minority and majority, and that the composition of the ruling class or political élite could change over a period of time, either by the recruitment of members from the non-élite, or by the establishment of a counter-élite, a process which Pareto called the 'circulation of élites'. They differ, however, in that Mosca stresses that the relationship between minority and majority may vary significantly from society to society, whereas Pareto argues that the relationship is fundamentally similar in all societies. Mosca also offers a broader explanation of the circulation of élites.[2]

Other writers have developed the arguments of Mosca and Pareto by arguing that modern industrial societies develop particular types of ruling class or political élite. James Burnham, for instance, suggests that such societies ultimately become dominated by a *managerial élite* whose power rests on their control of the means of production, and that this control is maximized when the state nationalizes all industry.[3] C. Wright Mills, on the other hand, argues (at least so far as the United States is concerned) that

[1] Gaetano Mosca, *The Ruling Class*, edited by A. Livingston and translated by H. D. Kahn, New York, 1939, p. 50.

[2] For a discussion of the theories of Mosca and Pareto, see James H. Meisel (ed.), *Pareto and Mosca*, Englewood Cliffs, N.J., 1965, and T. B. Bottomore, *Élites and Society*, London, 1964.

[3] See James Burnham, *The Managerial Revolution*, New York, 1941.

there is a *power élite*, comprising the heads of the largest business corporations, the political leaders and the leading military personnel, whose dominance rests on the 'coincidence of economic, military, and political power'.[1]

The development élite theories was in many respects a reaction against, and an endeavour to refute, the class theories of Karl Marx. Marx argues that in all societies there is a ruling class and one or more subject classes. These classes are economically based and the power of the ruling class depends upon its control of the means of production, which gives it substantial or absolute control of the means of coercion in society and of the development of ideas. Thus Marx stresses the importance of economic control and organizational advantage, but differs from the élite theorists in arguing that there is an inevitable conflict between classes which will lead not to some circulation of élites, nor to the predominance of a particular élite, but to the dominance of the most numerous class: the working class.

Apart from Marx's assertion that the working class will ultimately secure political power and that, because of working class homogeneity and class consciousness, and because men's basic needs will be satisfied, a classless society will result, there are other differences between the élite and class theories. Both regard the distinction between rulers and ruled as fundamental, but élite theorists attribute this solely to the minority being organized, the majority unorganized, whereas Marx attributes it to the specific organizational advantage of controlling the means of production. According to élite theorists, change is brought about by the circulation of élites, which may occur by a variety of means, whereas Marx attributes change to the conflict between ruling and subject classes. Similarly, both theories assume that the ruling minority is bound together by cohesive social forces, but élite theorists attribute this to a variety of factors, such as similar social background, general identity of interest and so on, whereas Marx is in no doubt that cohesion is based on a common economic interest.[2]

T. B. Bottomore suggests that it is possible to identify various élites as 'groups which have high status (for whatever reason) in a society: a *political class*, consisting of 'all those groups which

---

[1] C. Wright Mills, *The Power Élite*, New York, 1956, p. 278.

[2] See T. B. Bottomore, *Classes in Modern Society*, London, 1965, as well as his *Élites and Society*.

exercise political power or influence, and are directly engaged in struggles for political leadership'; and a *political élite*, comprising 'those individuals who actually exercise power at any given time'.[1] This having been done,

> we can attempt to distinguish between societies in which there is a ruling class, and at the same time élites which represent particular aspects of its interests; societies in which there is no ruling class, but a political élite which founds its power upon the control of the administration, or upon military force, rather than property ownership and inheritance; and societies in which there exists a multiplicity of élites among which no cohesive and enduring group of powerful individuals or families seems to be discoverable at all.[2]

The principal criticism of élite and class theories is that they are both dependent on group cohesion and group consciousness. It is not difficult to establish, as we have already seen, that the holders of political and administrative office are frequently drawn from particular social groups in society; nor is it difficult to demonstrate that members of these groups have common interests by virtue of belonging to their respective groups; but it is an entirely different matter to show that these groups are conscious of those interests and act cohesively in response to them. This is not to say that political élites or ruling classes do not exist in the sense that those who wield political power may be drawn from particular segments of society, but merely to question why they exist.

TOWARDS A THEORY OF POLITICAL RECRUITMENT

The fact that particular groups in society are disproportionately represented among political and administrative office-holders is often attributed to the forces of *demand*. This is clearly so in a limited way with the formal qualifications that are sometimes laid down for candidates at elections, and to a much greater extent in those laid down for administrative office-holders. There may also be less formal demands related to personal background, ability or representativeness, for example. It should be recognized, however, that political recruitment is also a question of *supply*, as the model illustrated in Figure 4 suggests.

---

[1] Bottomore, *Élites and Society* (Pelican edition, 1966), p. 14.
[2] ibid., p. 44.

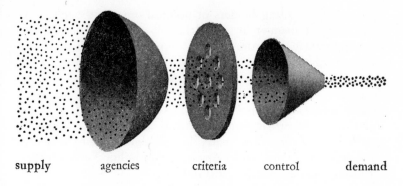

| supply | agencies | criteria | control | demand |

Figure 4. A simple model of political recruitment

Apart from the demand for, say, more women M.P.s in Parliament or fewer lawyers in Congress, it is also important to consider whether supply exceeds or falls short of demand. It does not follow, for instance, that because the demand for women M.P.s is low that this alone accounts for the under-representation of women in Parliament. As far as Britain is concerned, there is evidence that, although supply exceeds demand, the election of *all* those women *seeking* parliamentary candidatures would still leave women considerably under-represented.[1] Conversely, the fact that the legal profession provides a useful basis for a political career may well be a partial explanation of the over-representation of this occupational group in many legislatures – a product of supply as well as demand. Or again, the educational qualifications laid down for higher civil servants are often fairly high and, should it happen that the educational system is such that those who secure these qualifications are disproportionately drawn from particular social groups, then this will be reflected in recruitment to the bureaucracy.

The forces of supply and demand are also influenced by the various agencies of political recruitment, by the criteria that may be applied, and by the degree to which the process is controlled. Some of these agencies work more or less formally (such as administrative recruiting commissions), others entirely informally (such as 'political' families or certain interest groups). Political parties are clearly the most important means in most political

[1] See Rush, *The Selection of Parliamentary Candidates*, pp. 63 and 223.

systems of recruiting holders of political office, although as we have seen the manner in which they do so varies considerably. The importance of parties as agencies of recruitment is illustrated by the extent to which particular parties provide vehicles for the recruitment of working class office-holders: this function is performed, for instance, by the Labour party in Britain, the Communist and Socialist parties in France, the Social Democratic party in West Germany, and the A.L.P. in Australia, whereas the absence of a comparable party in the United States may well account for the much lower proportion of political office-holders of lower socio-economic status in that country.

It is also possible that the general absence of agencies of administrative recruitment comparable to the working class party is partially responsible for the virtual absence of those of lower socio-economic origins from the ranks of administrative office-holders. The principal informal recruiting agencies for the latter are often particular educational establishments which provide individuals with the necessary formal qualifications and the informal incentive to consider a career in the public service. For example, in Britain institutions like Oxford and Cambridge, and in France the Institut des Études Politiques, supply a disproportionate number of higher civil servants, not only because they produce able applicants, but because such a career is traditionally associated with these institutions. Thus, even where an attempt is made to widen the pool of recruitment, as there was in France after 1945, the results may be minimal – in 1966 fifty out of the sixty-five entrants to the E.N.A. came from the Institut.[1]

The agencies of recruitment will normally lay down a variety of criteria embodying the characteristics and skills that they regard as appropriate to the office concerned. These criteria will, of course, reflect demand, but they will also affect supply by encouraging or discouraging those with particular characteristics or skills. It is likely, for instance, that women are discouraged from seeking political office in many countries, and this in itself limits the supply of would-be women politicians. Different parties encourage different types of individual. Donald Matthews suggests, for instance, that American Senators can be divided into four types:

---

[1] Anthony Sampson, *The New Europeans*, London, 1968, p. 338.

1 *Patricians*, who come from 'political' families of fairly high social status, and found in both parties (7 per cent of the Senators in Matthews's study).

2 *Amateurs*, who are usually of somewhat lower social status, but often wealthy, and supplying rather more Republicans than Democrats (34 per cent).

3 *Professionals*, who have worked their way up through a variety of political offices, and supplying rather more Democrats than Republicans (55 per cent).

4 *Agitators*, who are usually of low social origin and have secured office by their own efforts (4 per cent).[1]

Similarly, the criteria applied by the same party in different electoral districts may vary significantly. In Conservative-held constituencies in Britain, for instance, the type of candidate chosen tends to vary in relation to the safeness or marginality of the seat and the extent to which it is rural or urban. Local Conservative associations in safe seats are more likely than those in marginal seats to select candidates who have attended a public school (especially one of the more prestigious schools), and who are university graduates (especially of Oxford or Cambridge) – tendencies which are reinforced in rural constituencies. In the Labour party candidates sponsored by the trade unions tend to be concentrated in the northern half of the country, those sponsored by the Co-operative party in the southern half, reflecting in both cases the distribution of the membership of these movements. In both parties there are important distinctions between the types of candidate chosen by the party holding the seat and that which does not.[2]

Comparable data may be found in a study of congressional recruitment in Chicago, which found significant differences between the candidates selected by the major parties in the inner city districts (generally safe Democratic areas), the suburban districts (generally safe Republican) and the outer city districts (generally marginal). For example, the safe Democrat districts were usually subject to strict control by the Democratic party machine and individuals prominent within the party organization

[1] Donald R. Matthews, *U.S. Senators and their World*, Chapel Hill, North Carolina, 1960, pp. 61–5.

[2] Rush, *The Selection of Parliamentary Candidates*, Chapters 3 and 6–8.

were most likely to be selected; but in the safe Republican districts, there was less party control and the primary electorate played a more important part, while in marginal districts there was more variation in the types of candidates selected.[1]

The extent to which political recruitment is subject to various types of control is also important in affecting supply and demand. As we have noted, there may be formal qualifications laid down for would-be holders of office. Some of these may be laid down by the agencies themselves, others may be laid down by the state. In either case, this is likely to affect the process profoundly. The educational qualifications normally required for bureaucratic positions reflect not only a demand for a particular type of applicant, but are a limit upon the supply of such applicants. Of more general significance, however, is whether the recruitment process is relatively open or closed. A system of administrative recruitment based on patronage is relatively closed; one based on open examinations is relatively open: both are the results of types of control. Moreover, such control may affect different groups in different ways: a system of patronage will be very open to those who are in a position to influence its distribution, but virtually closed to those who have neither money nor the necessary contacts; whereas an examination system widens the field of possible applicants in some respects and narrows it in others. In the same way some political parties have extensive control over the selection of candidates, others do not. In Britain the *national* party organizations have relatively little control over candidate selection, but there is very considerable *local party* autonomy, so that selection remains effectively under the control of the party. Conversely, in the United States the presence of the primary militates against party control. Nevertheless, in both cases the recruitment process remains relatively open.

This is not the case in totalitarian societies, however, since political recruitment is an area of vital importance and is therefore subject to stringent control. Of course, as we have already seen, extensive changes in personnel normally take time, especially in the administrative sphere, but one of the most important methods of effecting fundamental changes in the political system is through control of the process of political recruitment. Thus the régime in

[1] Leo M. Snowiss, 'Congressional Recruitment and Representation', *American Political Science Review*, **60**, 1966, pp. 627–39.

a totalitarian society endeavours to control the recruitment of all political and administrative office-holders, rather than leave this to autonomous or semi-autonomous agencies. In Germany between 1933 and 1945 and in the Soviet Union the National Socialist and Communist parties respectively are the principal agencies of political recruitment, and as such may fundamentally alter the results of that process. Under the Weimar Republic, for example, recruitment to political office (as measured by the backgrounds of Cabinet personnel) became more open than it had been under the monarchy, but the advent of Hitler resulted in marked changes: the proportion of Cabinet members of aristocrat background increased, those of middle and working class origin declined. Similarly, the proportion of those with military and business backgrounds also increased significantly.[1]

The extent of this control is well illustrated by the U.S.S.R., where significant changes in the composition of the Politburo have occurred since the establishment of the Communist régime in 1917. Most of the leaders of the Russian Revolution and of the Politburo from 1917 to the death of Lenin in 1924 were middle class intellectuals, but between 1924 and 1938, when Stalin was establishing and consolidating his position, the composition of the Politburo changed markedly in terms of the social origins of its members. Whereas the members during the earlier period were typically of middle class, urban origin and had had some higher education, under Stalin the typical member was of lower class, rural origin and had had no higher education.[2] We have, moreover, already seen how the régime has exercised control over the recruitment of party members in the Soviet Union.[3]

The problems of studying political recruitment are well illustrated by the examination of the role of supply in the process. Since this is a more difficult area to examine than demand – the problems of investigating the backgrounds of those who *seek* office are immense compared with the problems of measuring demand – there is a lack of systematic studies of this vital aspect of political

[1] See Maxwell Knight, *The German Executive, 1890–1933*, Hoover Institute Studies, Series B, No. 4, Stanford, California, 1952.

[2] See G. K. Schueller, *The Politburo*, Hoover Institute Studies, Series B, No. 2, Stanford, California, 1951.

[3] See Chapter 3, pp. 108–9 above.

recruitment. Central to the question of supply is finding out what impels individuals to seek or offer themselves for political and administrative office, especially the former. A few studies exist: Philip Buck, for instance, found that of a group of eighty-two British M.P.s, 61 per cent had been invited or persuaded to stand for Parliament (usually by friends or through some other political activity), and 39 per cent had actively sought candidatures.[1] Kenneth Prewitt and his colleagues found interesting differences between the levels of political office and the stage at which individuals became interested in politics in a study of state legislators and city councillors in the United States. The two most important reasons of those who became interested in politics during pre-adult life were 'admiration for particular politicians' and a 'sense of obligation', whereas those whose interest in politics had come in adult life placed 'sense of obligation' first and a 'sense of indignation' second. Thus it was not surprising to find that the 'adults' were more likely to be influenced by local conditions and issues, and the 'pre-adults' by presidential, gubernatorial or senatorial campaigns or particular administrations. Furthermore, 'adults' were more likely to be recruited through non-political activities. Prewitt and his colleagues also found that state legislators were more likely to cite 'admiration for particular politicians' and 'ambition for political power', while city councillors were more likely to cite a 'sense of indignation' or a 'sense of obligation'.[2]

These studies are, however, limited in scope and much remains to be done in this area of political recruitment. Furthermore, the links between supply and demand and the characteristics of those who both seek and secure office remain largely unknown. In another article, Kenneth Prewitt argues that the crucial variable may be *'exposure to politics'* – the extent to which individuals come into contact with political phenomena – and cites a number of studies which show that *political* leaders are subject to a greater exposure to politics than the general population.[3] How far such an

---

[1] Buck, *Amateurs and Professionals in British Politics*, pp. 67–9, and Appendix IV, Table 35.

[2] Kenneth Prewitt, Heinz Eulau and Betty H. Zisk, 'Political Socialization and Political Roles', *Public Opinion Quarterly*, **30**, 1966, pp. 569–82.

[3] Kenneth Prewitt, 'Political Socialization and Leadership Selection', *Annals*, **361**, September 1965, pp. 96–111.

explanation is applicable to *administrative* recruitment and to political recruitment as a whole is not known, but in suggesting political exposure as the crucial variable, Prewitt is in effect arguing that the processes of political recruitment and political socialization are inextricably linked: those links, however, await further investigation.

5 · Political Communication

PATTERNS OF POLITICAL COMMUNICATION

Political communication – the transmission of politically relevant information from one part of the political system to another, and between the social and the political systems – is the dynamic element of a political system,[1] and the processes of socialization, participation and recruitment are dependent upon it. The communication of knowledge, values and attitudes is fundamental to all three, since it is these which determine the political activity of individuals.

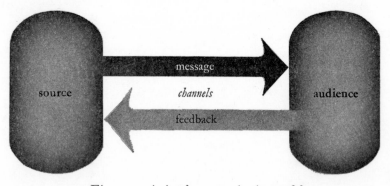

Figure 5. A simple communication model

The elements of a communication system are shown in Figure 5. These comprise the source of the message (or information), the message itself, the channel through which it passes to the audience

[1] See Karl W. Deutsch, *The Nerves of Government: Models of Political Communication and Control*, New York, 1963, *passim*.

(or recipient of the information), and a process known as 'feed-back', by which the positions of source and audience may be reversed in the form of a reaction to the message from the original audience to the original source. Thus in a system of political communication, a typical source would be a candidate for election to a political office; his message would be a series of policy pro-posals; his channel a television broadcast; his audience those members of the electorate who happen to watch the broadcast; and the feedback (or audience reaction) approval or disapproval of his proposals.

The various elements of a system of political communication are not necessarily a structural part of the political system, nor is their role in the process necessarily continuous and it may vary from one situation to another. In one situation an individual is the source of a message, in another he is the audience, and in another he may be the channel through which the message is conveyed. Thus in one case a political office-holder is the source of a message to the electorate, but in the event of some reaction from the latter, their roles are reversed, while in a third situation the office-holder may pass on to the electorate a message from another source. Moreover, some sources are specific, others diffuse: a political leader is an example of the first, an electorate of the second. In any society there is a complex network of communication and a simi-larly complex network is found in any political system. This net-work is characterized by a great variety of sources, audiences and channels. It is not simply a question of vertical but also of horizon-tal communication – communication laterally between individuals and groups who occupy a common level in the political system. For each individual and each group of individuals in the political system, however, there is a discernible communication network.

For a political office-holder, for example, his sources of infor-mation will include his immediate colleagues in office, the adminis-trative office-holders associated with his post, various political associates (both supporters and, probably, opponents), a variety of less political contacts (such as interest group leaders), the mass media, and, possibly, periodic contact with other members of society through such devices as electoral campaigns, public speeches and visiting different parts of the country. His audiences and channels of communication will be similarly composed and similarly diverse.

For other, less active individuals sources, audiences and channels will tend to be more limited and the whole process of political communication more intermittent. In spite of differences between political systems it is likely that the channels of information for most individuals are generally similar, as Table 30 suggests.

Table 30. *Main channels of political communications in France, Spain and Iran*

CHANNEL OF COMMUNICATION	France	Spain	Iran
	%	%	%
Newspapers, magazines, etc.	22	38	36
Radio and/or TV	59	37	57
Personal contacts, other sources, etc.	7	22	5
No answer	12	3	2
Totals	100	100	100

SOURCES: France: main channels of information on the presidential campaign, 1965; IFOP, August 1965.
Spain: main channels of information on the plan for economic social development, 1965: IOP, October–November 1965.
Iran: main channels of information about important world events, 1962: NIP, Teheran, Summer 1962– literates only.

Clearly there are some variations from one country to another, as the data in this table shows. For instance, radio and television appear to be considerably less important in Spain and personal contacts and other sources more important than in either France or Iran. None the less, there is a basic pattern in all three countries in which the principal channels of information on political questions are the mass media.

The role of the mass media in political communication illustrates the way in which the whole process is integrated with the societal communication network in that only the more specialized of the mass media are normally wholly or overwhelmingly political in content. Newspapers, radio and television are usually intended to inform their users about a very wide range of matters of which political affairs are a minority, while the entertainment content of radio and television in particular is often predominant. Only particular parts of their output are normally specifically political. Furthermore, there are important differences among the mass media. For example, radio and television audiences tend to be relatively undifferentiated compared with those of the printed mass media. This means that, although particular programmes may be broadcast with a particular audience in mind, radio and television networks are not normally able to cater more or less exclusively for a particular audience in the way that the printed media can and do. Quite apart from specialized publications, such as those serving a particular occupation or interest or seeking to promote specific views, many newspapers have, despite their diffuse contents, clearly identifiable readerships (Table 31).

Table 31. *Newspaper readership, class and party support in Britain*

	READERSHIP	
NEWSPAPER	Predominant class	Predominant voting intention
The Times	Middle	Conservative and Labour
Guardian	Middle	Labour
Daily Telegraph	Middle	Conservative
Daily Mail	Middle and Working	Conservative and Labour
Daily Express	Working and Middle	Conservative and Labour
Daily Sketch	Working	Conservative
Sun	Working	Labour
Daily Mirror	Working	Labour

SOURCE: based on NOP, July 1967.

Given the identity of readership shown in this table, both in terms of class position and party support, each newspaper is able to choose and present its material in the manner best suited to its readership. In other words, each newspaper will normally reach only a particular section of the population and will seek to meet the particular needs of that section. This is clearly the case in Britain, where there are a number of national newspapers whose readerships differ in socio-economic and political identification, and similar differences may be found elsewhere. In some countries, however, the sheer size of the country, involving the existence of time zones, and economic trends in the newspaper industry have reduced, sometimes eliminated, competition between papers, so that one newspaper often enjoys a monopoly in a particular area. Nevertheless, such newspapers still serve a particular readership – in this case identified less in socio-economic or political terms and more by locality. While the same is true of local radio and television networks, it should be noted that these networks, unlike newspapers, often face competition from other networks, and, furthermore, that many programmes that they broadcast (especially television networks) are not of local origin and are not aimed at specifically local audiences.

We have already noted that the significance of the mass media in general and of any one medium in particular varies from one country to another. It is not therefore surprising to find that the extent to which people follow public affairs also varies, often considerably (Table 32).

Table 32. *Proportion of population following accounts of political and governmental affairs in the United States, Britain, West Germany, Italy and Mexico*

FREQUENCY	United States	Britain	Germany	Italy	Mexico
	%	%	%	%	%
Regularly	27	23	34	11	15
From time to time	53	45	38	26	40
Never	19	32	25	62	44
Others and don't know	1	1	3	1	1
Totals	100	101	100	100	100

SOURCE: Almond and Verba, *The Civic Culture*, p. 54.

The number of people who regularly follow public affairs varies in the United States, Britain and Germany, but the major dichotomy shown in this table is between these three countries on the one hand, and Italy and Mexico on the other. Thus, when Almond's and Verba's respondents were asked whether they followed reports of public affairs in newspapers, magazines and radio or television, the proportions replying that they did so at least weekly in respect of newspapers and radio or television, and 'ever' in the case of magazines, were in the range 21 to 58 per cent for the United States, Britain and Germany, but 16 to 31 per cent for Italy and Mexico.[1]

Each political system develops its own network of political communication and the significance of particular sources, channels and audiences will differ accordingly. Except in primitive societies or in those still dominated by traditional cultures, which are characterized by low literacy levels and which lack the technological skills and means to develop modern mass media, the printed word and broadcasting are the major means by which political information is transmitted in any political system. At the same time, other channels of communication are very important

[1] Almond and Verba, *The Civic Culture*, p. 56.

and often more obviously political. Interest groups and political parties, though varying from one system to another, are vital to the communication process by providing channels through which contact between those holding political and administrative office and the general populace can be maintained. Membership of political and quasi-political organizations may involve the individual in only intermittent political communication, but the more active participants are involved in more frequent communication in which information is passed vertically from them to those holding higher positions in the hierarchy of participation and horizontally between members active at a common level, both as members of the same organization and between organizations. Compared with the mass media, which may be regarded as a general means of political communication, interest groups and political parties are more specifically and frequently involved in this process.

Apart from the mass media and formal organizations, there is a third important channel of communication – informal contact between individuals and groups of individuals. Clearly such contact is not in practice isolated from either of the other two major channels, but it is analytically important to deal with it separately, partly because it is not entirely covered by the mass media and formal organizations, and partly because it forms the basis of an important theory of communication.

Informal contact or face-to-face relationships are the most common and frequent means of communication in any society, although its role in *political* communication is probably related more to the formation of *public opinion* than merely to the transmission of political information; and it is in the first of these two roles that the theory of the *two-step flow of communication* has been developed. The two-step flow theory was first postulated by Paul Lazarsfeld and his colleagues in their study of voting behaviour, *The People's Choice*,[1] and it argues that the influence of the mass media is mediated to individuals through 'opinion leaders'. These opinion leaders are 'very much alike and typically belong to the same primary groups of family, friends and co-workers'.[2] Elihu Katz examined a number of studies in both politics and sociology

[1] Lazarsfeld, Berelson and Gaudet, *The People's Choice*, p. 151.
[2] Elihu Katz, 'The Two-Step Flow of Communication: An Up-to-Date Report on an Hypothesis', *Public Opinion Quarterly*, 21, 1957, p. 77.

which sought to test the theory and concluded that inter-personal relations of this type were important in three respects: first, as actual channels of information; secondly, as sources of social pressure upon individuals to adhere to various norms of attitude and behaviour; and thirdly, as sources of support for such norms and therefore for group cohesion. It is important to appreciate, however, that as channels of *information* opinion leaders are primarily subordinate to the mass media and other channels we have mentioned and that their significance is greatest in the realm of public opinion, which involves the evaluation of this information, and with which we shall be dealing later in this chapter.

The particular pattern of communication that a political system develops is, inevitably, dependent upon various factors in society. The most important of these are physical and technological, economic, socio-cultural and political factors. Communication is ultimately dependent upon physical and technological factors, and these stress the importance of examining communication from a temporal point of view. The historical development of communication networks is closely linked to physical and technological factors. In the past the pattern of communication has been largely dictated by the relative ease or difficulty of physical communication and by various technical limitations, which have severely restricted the extent to and speed with which information can be disseminated. Communication networks therefore tended to be relatively isolated and inter-communication between networks was limited. The ability, for example, of the various colonial powers from the sixteenth to the nineteenth centuries to communicate effectively with their colonies was limited by their reliance upon slow-moving sea transport, and there is little doubt that such events as the American War of Independence and wars between the colonial powers were complicated by problems of communication. Even in relatively limited areas in which the physical barriers to communication were not unduly severe, such as a number of European countries, communication was slow and difficult. Newspapers were either non-existent or had only limited circulations, and the dissemination of news was fragmentary and haphazard. Technological advances, however, subsequently overcame many of these problems. In so doing, however, they created not new communication networks but added a further dimension to existing networks.

Physical barriers, such as mountains, deserts, forests, seas, lakes and rivers, are often important in determining an initial pattern of communication. In physical terms, there may exist a natural communication pattern – along rivers, valleys and coastlines, for example – which is subsequently developed into a communications system of land and water transport linking various communities. The relative isolation or integration of these communities within a particular society is obviously profoundly affected by the sort of communication pattern that develops. This was, as we have already suggested, especially true before the development of modern means of communication facilitated by technological advances. Moreover, notwithstanding these advances, physical factors remain of considerable importance in many societies. For instance, the larger a country is the greater the problems of communication, regardless of the existence of natural barriers to such communication. Countries like the United States or Canada, with a considerable east–west span, are divided into time zones which militate against national newspapers and radio and television networks, whereas smaller countries like Britain, or larger ones like Japan even, which fall into a single time zone, are not faced with this problem. Even where a modern communications system exists its affects may be partially offset by physical barriers. The populated areas of Australia, for instance, are mainly around the coastal periphery and its hinterland, with the result that communication is made more difficult. In less advanced countries, physical barriers may constitute even greater barriers to communication, and since many of these countries are in parts of the world which are characterized by formidable physical obstacles, this is a problem common to most developing countries.

In most countries, however, technological changes have reduced many of the problems presented by physical factors and have profoundly altered communication patterns. Modern technology has not only greatly increased the ease and speed with which people and materials can be transported from one place to another, but has also brought about an equal if not greater revolution in the communication of information. The availability of the printed and spoken word has been extended almost beyond measure, while the speed of communication that is now possible across vast distances is itself an important factor. Furthermore, inventions such as the transistor and the miniaturization of communication equipment which it has made possible have also made important contributions.

The extent to which physical barriers are overcome and to which technological advances are significant, however, is closely related to economic development, as Richard Fagen has shown (Table 33).

Table 33. *Relationship between level of economic development and level of mass media development*

MASS MEDIA	GNP *per capita*
Daily newspaper circulation per 1,000 population	·80
Radio receivers per 1,000 population	·85
TV sets per 1,000 population	·75
Cinema attendance *per capita*	·65

SOURCE: Richard R. Fagan, *Politics and Communication*, Boston, Mass., 1966, Table IV.I, p. 58, constructed from data in Russett *et al.*, *World Handbook of Political and Social Indicators*, pp. 272 and 274–5. The figures shown in this table, and in Table 34, are product-moment correlation co-efficients; for an explanation of how they are calculated, see H. Blalock, *Social Statistics*, New York, 1960, pp. 285ff. The closer the figure to 1·00 the more significant the correlation.

As the table suggests, the higher the level of economic development the more extensive the development of the mass media. It is also likely that there will be greater reliance upon the mass media as channels of *information* than upon informal face-to-face contacts, but of greater importance is the relative uniformity of communication that is likely to be found in economically developed societies. Not only are more people involved in the communication system, but they are reached by the same channels and so the information likely to reach them will be more uniform. In developing societies, however, the communication system will usually be more fragmented because it relies less on the mass media and more upon limited and informal channels of communication that reach only particular sections of the population. These patterns of communication will also be affected by a variety of socio-cultural factors. An obvious factor is the level of literacy (Table 34).

Table 34. *Relationship between level of literacy and levels of the mass media and economic development*

MASS MEDIA AND ECONOMIC DEVELOPMENT	Literacy (Population age 15 and over literate)
Daily newspaper circulation per 1,000 population	·88
Radio receivers per 1,000 population	·80
TV sets per 1,000 population	·69
Cinema attendance *per capita*	·71
GNP *per capita*	·80

SOURCE: Fagen, *Politics and Communication*, Table IV.2, p. 62, constructed from data in Russett *et al.*, *World Handbook of Political and Social Indicators*, p. 283.

Apart from limiting the impact of the printed media, illiteracy also limits the impact of the spoken word since it is inevitably linked to educational attainment. In such circumstances, face-to-face contacts assume immense importance and are the principal means of communication. A study of communication patterns in Egypt vividly illustrates this. The survey on which the study is based was conducted in a number of villages near Cairo. Only a fifth of the respondents were literate. Approximately the same proportion read newspapers, but more than half listened to the radio, and 45 per cent said that they discussed local and national news. Discussion of politics in particular, however, was less important than discussion of village affairs and farming among the men and the least important subject among the women respondents. The most important finding of the survey was that a two-step communication pattern existed between literate and illiterate respondents – the literates passing on news to the illiterates during the day, this being followed by discussion in the evenings.[1]

We have already seen in Table 31 how newspaper readership may vary according to social class and party identification. An American study of the experiences of respondents in an area ravaged by a tornado found that eye-witness accounts varied

[1] Gordon K. Hirabayashi and M. Fathalla El Khalib, 'Communication and Political Awareness in the Villages of Egypt', *Public Opinion Quarterly*, **22**, 1958, pp. 355–63.

according to class. Lower-class respondents described the incidents they had seen solely from their own perspective and did not report any accounts of other witnesses. Their narratives were fragmented, their imagery generally concrete and simple, and they usually felt little need to explain the context of their accounts. In contrast, the accounts of middle-class respondents were usually seen from a multiple perspective; their narratives were coherent and organized, their imagery more varied and conceptual, and they frequently explained the context of their remarks.[1]

The whole question of physical, technological, economic and socio-cultural factors is aptly summed up in a study of the communication problems of an island off the coast of Korea. The island, Cheju-do, lies sixty miles off the Korean peninsula and is a province of South Korea. The very fact that it is an island and does lie so far from the mainland presents obvious communication problems as far as contact with the latter is concerned. This physical separation has resulted in the people of Cheju-do regarding themselves as distinct from the people on the mainland, while the island itself is further fragmented by its mountainous terrain. The island's transport system is rudimentary and inadequate, especially as a means of disseminating information, while the mountains reduce the efficiency of radio communication. The effectiveness of the radio network is further reduced because so few people possess receivers, since they are expensive items which are regarded as of little or no use by most of the population. The radio network is, however, supplemented by local newspapers, and both are economically supported by the South Korean government. This provision of mass media is a costly exercise and is further complicated by the high rate of illiteracy on Cheju-do, by the widespread use of the English and Korean languages for oral communication and Chinese characters for written communication. Efforts by the government to surmount some of these problems by the use of simple documentary films and face-to-face contacts have not been successful, largely because of the long history of resistance by Cheju-do to interference from mainland Korea.[2]

[1] Leonard Schatzman and Anselm Strauss, 'Social Class and Modes of Communication', *American Journal of Sociology*, **19**, 1955, pp. 329–38.

[2] Richard A. Garver, 'Communication Problems of Underdevelopment: Cheju-do, Korea, 1962', *Public Opinion Quarterly*, **26**, 1962, pp. 613–25.

It is clear from the case of Cheju-do that political factors – the desire of the Korean government to establish a system of communication which will enable it to disseminate certain political information, and the traditional resistance of the islanders to mainland interference – are often of very great importance in determining the pattern of political communication. In Cheju-do the traditional resistance of the islanders is largely reinforced by the physical, technological, economic and socio-cultural problems of communication in the area. In other cases, however, these problems may be less formidable, and this is more likely in more advanced societies which tend to facilitate rather than hinder technological advance in particular.

In Nazi Germany, for example, the channels of communication were subject to close supervision, and this was largely effective because the régime was able to exert a large measure of control over the content of information in the mass media and to ensure that it secured a wide circulation – the technical apparatus at the government's disposal made it possible. German newspapers received daily instructions from the Propaganda Ministry telling them what to publish, how it was to be presented, what editorials were required, and so on. All editors had to be politically reliable and racially 'pure', and their actions were subject to constant scrutiny. Any newspapers which failed to follow their instructions were either suppressed or suffered appropriate staff changes. The German radio network was subject to even stricter control, which was facilitated in the early days of the Nazi régime by the fact that it was already state-owned. It is a measure of the effectiveness of the Nazi control of political communication that William Shirer, in spite of his access to foreign newspapers and broadcasts, was led to comment:

> A steady diet over the years of falsification and distortion made a certain impression on one's mind and often misled it. No one who has not lived for years in a totalitarian land can possibly conceive how difficult it is to escape the dread consequences of a régime's calculated and incessant propaganda.[1]

The impact of the mass media was reinforced by the face-to-face contacts between individuals, especially those involving party members, who could be relied upon to disseminate only the

[1] Shirer, *The Rise and Fall of the Third Reich*, pp. 247–8.

'truth'. Such a system, as Shirer points out, often results in this 'truth' being so widely believed that to question it is utterly useless.[1]

Substantially the same situation exists in the Soviet Union, for substantially the same reasons:

> The Soviet régime has developed one of the largest and most complex systems of public communication in the world. The Communist party has forged a parallel system of control which is more elaborate and thorough than any other still in existence in the postwar era. Both the system of communication and the control apparatus are oriented toward a single goal. They must serve as instruments through which the party and government mobilize the mind and will of the population; they must see to it that what ought to be done *is* done, what should be thought and felt *is* thought and felt.[2]

The mass media in the U.S.S.R. are subject to strict party and governmental control, and this involves close supervision of all types of newspapers, periodicals and books and their availability, strict control of all broadcasting, and careful scrutiny of all products of the Soviet film industry. This control of the mass media rests firmly on the extensive system of 'agitators' who disseminate party propaganda and political information:

> the . . . agitator makes his contribution to effective party leadership primarily at the level of bringing party policy to the people and seeking to enlist their support. But he plays an important part in bringing the leaders information that they must have as a basis for determining policy, and he has a central role in securing execution of policy.[3]

The role of the 'agitator' in the Soviet Union emphasizes the extent to which political communication consists of a complex network of channels carrying messages between a great variety of sources and audiences, and that such a system involves a process of feedback, by which reactions to messages are received by the original source. The way in which such a system is established has been shown by a study of the development of communication patterns during the Communist occupation of South Korea. The Communist régime concentrated its efforts on three channels of communication: the mass media, the education system and face-to-face contacts. Complete control was exercised over

---

[1] ibid., p. 248.
[2] Inkeles, *Public Opinion in Soviet Russia*, p. 317. (Original italics.)
[3] ibid., p. 121.

the mass media, and newspapers using the Korean phonetic alphabet (and not Chinese characters) were specially prepared for South Korean consumption. Newspapers were the principal means of mass communication, but their impact was reinforced by radio, posters and parades and demonstrations. The education system was harnessed to propagate political information and great efforts were made to increase literacy levels in order to facilitate the use of printed media. Face-to-face contacts were organized through party organizations, mainly by means of group discussions and instruction. This system was based on three concepts: first, of a *monopoly* (as far as possible) by the authorities of all means of communication: secondly, of *concentration*, on the belief that a message was more effective if it was simple and constantly repeated; and thirdly, of *reinforcement*, the use of all channels for the same message at the same time. The authors of the study suggest that the communication system that developed was more effective as a means of communication from the political authority to the people rather than vice versa. It is likely, however, that this was a function partly of the fact that Korea is and was a developing society and partly of the short period of the Communist occupation. The study none the less illustrates the methods used by a régime intent on securing control of the system of political communication in a society.[1]

The total control of political communication is, of course, one of the major characteristics of a totalitarian society, and political factors are therefore paramount in the development of the pattern of communication in such societies. In modern democracies the degree to which communication is subject to political control, is limited, and total control is neither one of their aims nor one of their characteristics. Political factors remain important, however. We have, for instance, already stressed the importance of face-to-face contacts in all communication systems, and modern democracies are no exception. Thus, much will depend on attitudes towards the dissemination and exchange of political information, as Almond and Verba showed in their five-nation study. They found that not only did the proportion of people who discussed politics vary from 76 per cent in the United States

---

[1] Wilbur Schramm and John W. Riley Jr, 'Communication in the Sovietized State, as Demonstrated in Korea', *American Sociological Review*, **16**, 1951, pp. 757–66.

to 32 per cent in Italy (with Britain and West Germany approximating to the American position and Mexico to the Italian), but that there were considerable variations in the degree to which people in these countries felt free to discuss politics. Approximately a quarter of the American and a third of the British respondents did not feel free to discuss politics or felt free to do so with only a few people. Compared with this, more than half the German and Italian respondents and over two-fifths of the Mexican adopted these views.[1] Attitudes such as these are obviously of great relevance to the formation of public opinion, which is one of the major functions of a communication system.

THE FORMATION OF PUBLIC OPINION

We have already seen how totalitarian societies seek to control the communication system in order to control public opinion. Indeed, it is clear that the system itself, or particular parts of it, are deliberately developed to facilitate such control. Richard Fagen notes, for example, that the Committees for the Defence of the Revolution in Cuba were

> first formed by Castro in 1960 to act as a grass-roots defence against counter-revolution. Organized on a geographical basis, they soon became multi-purpose citizen groups used by the leadership for recruiting, administering, and proselytizing in the service of the revolution.[2]

Public opinion is, as the above quotation suggests, formed not in isolation, and is not only an integral part of the process of political communication, but also of the processes of socialization, participation and recruitment. Public opinion is closely involved in each process, because what people know (or think they know) and believe – their knowledge, values and attitudes – is a crucial factor in determining their political behaviour.

It is common to speak of public opinion as though it were massive and united, almost as if it were applicable only to one matter. Even where some division of opinion is acknowledged, it is usually thought to be in clearly-defined groups. In practice, of course, there are an infinite number of 'public opinions' on an infinite range of matters. It is true that on certain matters the

---

[1] Almond and Verba, *The Civic Culture*, pp. 79 and 83.
[2] Fagen, *Politics and Communication*, p. 34n.

overwhelming majority of people in a society may adhere to a common attitude and hold certain values in common, but that it is not to say that such near unanimity extends to all matters on which the public may have opinions. Thus there may be a general agreement about the 'arrangements of society', but it is less likely that such agreement will apply to matters which affect some individuals (or groups of individuals) and not others, which affect some more than others, and which affects some in one way and others in a different way. It is quite likely, therefore, that public opinion on any particular matter will be divided or, as Robert Lane and David Sears suggest, public opinion will have *direction*.[1] This means that some individuals will be in favour of a particular point of view, others against it. Others, of course, may be uncertain or prefer to qualify their opinion in some way. Various studies have shown, for instance, that the higher a person's level of education, the more likely he is to give a qualified answer to a question. Excluding those who have no view at all on a particular matter, most points of view may be seen on a 'pro-con' basis.

Direction is the fundamental characteristic of an opinion, since it indicates its basic form, but there are two other characteristics which indicate its importance. The first of these is the *intensity* with which the opinion is held. If an individual holds an opinion very strongly, he may be more likely to act upon it than another individual who holds the same opinion less strongly. This is especially important where an opinion is strongly held not just by a single individual but by a group of individuals.[2] Clearly the question of intensity is of importance in political participation in general and recruitment in particular.

The second important characteristic is closely related to intensity, but is also concerned with the relationship between the various opinions that an individual may hold. Since some of these opinions may be more important than others, it is possible to speak of the *salience* of particular opinions.[3] In the case of political behaviour, it is possible than an individual may regard his political opinions as paramount, and this may lead to a high level of participation.

[1] Robert E. Lane and David O. Sears, *Public Opinion*, Englewood Cliffs, N.J., 1964, pp. 6–9.
[2] ibid., pp. 9 and 94–113.
[3] ibid., pp. 15–16 and 78–81.

Saliency is also important, however, in considering another aspect of a person's opinions: the extent to which they may be regarded as consistent. A series of opinions may be inconsistent in either of two ways. First, a person may hold opinions that are to some degree contradictory, and secondly, particular opinions may be inconsistent with the knowledge that a person possesses. For example, 74 per cent of the respondents of a survey in California agreed with the view that the state university and colleges should be independent of the political control of the state governor and legislature, but 63 per cent of the respondents in the same survey also agreed that the 'tax-paying public' should have more say in the way the state university and college system was run (CAL, April 1967). While these views are not entirely contradictory, they are somewhat inconsistent in that the tax-paying public normally exercises the sort of control it appeared to be seeking through its elected office-holders. The relationship between salience and consistency is important, since it often offers an explanation of apparently contradictory attitudes. In April 1966, for instance, a survey in Britain found only 27 per cent of its respondents in favour of the nationalization of the steel industry (SOC, April 1966), yet, a month before, 'public opinion' had returned a Labour government pledged to nationalize steel. In fact, the questions put to the electorate in March 1966, and to the opinion poll respondents in April, received apparently contradictory answers not because of the lapse of time, but because one offered a choice of governments and the other a choice on a single policy. It may well have been that those who voted for the Labour party in 1966, but nevertheless opposed steel nationalization, were prepared to regard the latter as part of the price of Labour victory which they otherwise favoured, or else that they were unaware that it was part of that price.

It is, in fact, misleading to assume that, because people are willing to express opinions on various matters, thay are 'well-informed' or have 'sufficient' information on these subjects. Thus, in 1965, no less than 60 per cent of the respondents in an Italian poll said that they did not know how much Senators and Representatives in Italy were paid. Furthermore, the same proportion said that they had not heard that the pay of Senators and Representatives was a 'public issue'. None the less, nearly 90 per cent were prepared to express an opinion on the issue (DOXA, October

1965). Levels of knowledge may vary very considerably from one country to another, as a series of polls asking the same questions in Norway, Poland and France show (Table 35).

Table 35. *Levels of knowledge in Norway, Poland and France*

	Correct answers			Don't know/No answer		
	Norway	Poland	France	Norway	Poland	France
	%	%	%	%	%	%
Range	37–97	28–88	19–83	2–34	11–48	12–55
Median	73	64	47	14	25	43
Mean	70	61	50	16	29	36

SOURCE: VC, winter 1964–5.

The international survey summarized here asked the respondents in each country a series of *factual* questions on a wide range of political matters. They were asked whether they could name the location of the headquarters of the United Nations; to identify the Test-Ban Treaty; to say which of a series of named countries were members of NATO and the Warsaw Defence Pact; and to identify the political leaders of several countries. It is clear from the table that the highest proportion of correct answers and the lowest proportion of 'don't knows' came from Norway, and the lowest proportion of correct answers and the highest proportion of 'don't knows' from France. The level of knowledge not only varies considerably from one country to another, but, as the table shows, the actual amount of information possessed by an individual on a particular matter may be fairly limited. Thus, in France, as many as 22 per cent of the respondents did not know whether or not France was a member of NATO. But, as we have already pointed out, this does not necessarily prevent people from having and expressing *opinions* on matters of which they may have only limited knowledge. They may, of course, find it easier to hold opinions on some matters than others, as another international survey shows. In this instance respondents in eight countries were asked a series of political questions about whether they thought the power of the United States, the Soviet Union and Communist China would increase or decrease in 1967; and a series of questions asking them to estimate the economic prospects of their countries in 1967.

Table 36. *Level of 'don't knows' on matter of opinion*

	Political questions	Economic questions
	%	%
Range	14–64	3–42
Median	36	17
Mean	38	19

SOURCE: Gallup International, winter 1966–7.

As Table 36 shows, respondents found it easier or were more willing to answer the economic than the political questions: on all three political questions, the proportion of 'don't knows' was higher. Comparing the proportions of 'don't knows' in Tables 35 and 36 is difficult, since the questions and countries vary in the two surveys. None the less, it can be seen that on the whole the proportions of 'don't knows' were lower on factual questions than on political questions, and about the same on economic questions. It is important to bear in mind, however, that although the respondents in this second international survey were being asked their opinions, they were also being asked to make predictions of political and economic developments. This would make these questions almost 'factual' to many respondents and illustrates the closely-woven relationship between fact and opinion. Evidence from other studies shows that, as in the Italian case, informational levels are generally fairly low and 'more people are willing to report on what the government ought to be doing than are able to say what it is doing . . .'[1]

At the same time there is, for any particular opinion, a requisite level of information necessary for its formation. That some minimal point of contact is necessary is clear from an opinion poll in India which asked respondents their attitudes towards various countries: the proportions of 'don't knows' was much higher for countries like Japan, France, West Germany and the United Arab Republic than they were for the Soviet Union, the United States, Communist China and Britain (IIPO, January-February 1966). In this case the respondents found it easier to express opinions on countries with which India had had close contact (friendly or otherwise) than on those countries with which India's relations were more remote.

The whole question of levels of information and willingness to

[1] Lane and Sears, *Public Opinion*, p. 61.

hold opinions is part of the wider problem of *rationality* in the formation of public opinion.

> To be rational [Lane and Sears argue], a man must expose himself to congenial and uncongenial matters alike; he must be able to look at both and perceive them as they are, not merely as what he would like them to be, and he must be able to retain this information in undistorted form.[1]

A rational individual is thus open to information, is able to process it objectively and is able to assess effectively the relationship between his values and the information he receives. Some matters, such as those concerning religious, ethnic or ideological issues or matters involving personalities, are more liable to irrational pressures; while others, such as those based on economic or socio-economic differences, are more subject to rational pressures. Thus certain conditions are more likely to result in irrational responses – situations involving individuals with low social status or subject to poverty, or where there has been an undermining of traditional culture, or where there are problems of family stress, or where the individual is socially isolated, or where educational levels are low, are all examples of such conditions.[2] Much therefore depends upon the societal context and, as we have already argued in our chapter on political socialization, knowledge, values and attitudes are determined by the interaction between social environment and the individual. Public opinion, all opinion, results from the influence of face-to-face contacts and the mass media: from the influence of parents, education, peer groups, work and leisure groups, and opinion leaders on the one hand, and from the influence of newspapers and other printed media, and the broadcasting media on the other. Not all these influences are of equal importance, of course, and much will depend on the *evaluation* of each by the individual.

There is, for example, a good deal of opinion-poll evidence on people's evaluation of the mass media, which, as Table 30 shows, are the main source of information for most people. A Dutch poll found in 1966 that 75 per cent of their respondents regarded newspapers and magazines as giving an accurate or generally accurate picture of events in the Netherlands, but only 56 per cent agreed that this was the case with television (ATTS, August-September 1966). In Norway two-thirds of the respondents in a

[1] ibid., p. 73.   [2] See ibid., Chapter 7.

similar poll said that the newspapers were 'mostly correct' in their reports (PRIO, November-December 1964), but in France only 33 per cent of the respondents agreed that the state-controlled television network (O.R.T.F.) was impartial (IFOP, November 1965). The problem of source evaluation takes on immense proportions during time of national crisis, as the Vietnam war has forcibly demonstrated in the United States. A poll conducted in Minnesota found that 43 per cent of its respondents felt that the mass media were giving an 'honest picture of what is going on in Vietnam', while 47 per cent disagreed, leaving 10 per cent who were uncertain. The reasons why people felt that they were not getting an 'honest picture' were, however, very varied: 35 per cent thought that news was being held back or that war news was inevitably inaccurate; 18 per cent thought that the government was controlling the dissemination of news (possibly for security reasons); 8 per cent said that the true situation was being hidden to avoid public alarm and panic (MINN, September 1966). Thus, even though a substantial minority of these respondents agreed that their news of Vietnam was distorted, they were less united on why this was so. Lack of faith in the mass media or particular sections of it will result either in a low level of information, because the individual ignores this source, or in distorted information, because the individual relies more heavily than usual on his interpretation of the information. In some cases the process may rely very heavily on interpretation or 'reading between the lines' in the manner of the 'Kremlinologist' or 'Pekinologist'.

The question of evaluation, however, applies not only to the audience in its evaluation of the source, but also to the source in its evaluation of the audience. This is particularly the case in political communication, since messages are so frequently calculated to achieve a particular effect. The political leader endeavours to formulate, deliver and address his messages in the manner, at the time and to the audience which will achieve the greatest impact, but in so doing he makes certain assumptions about his message, his audience, his channel of communication, and himself as the source of the message. He assumes that his audience will wish to hear or can be persuaded to listen to his message. Thus, should his message be unpleasant, he assumes that his audience will regard him sufficiently highly as a source to overcome their distaste for it. He assumes that he has chosen the most effective channel of communication and that he will reach his proposed audience, and he assumes that the moment is propitious for the delivery of his message. Often of greatest importance, however, is the relationship between these various assumptions and the changing of public opinion.

The influence of political leaders is not, of course, the only means by which public opinion may change. Indeed, as we suggested in Chapter 2, knowledge, values and attitudes change in response to a great variety of factors. The role of leaders in such change, however, illustrates one of the crucial characteristics of public opinion, that it is both subject to change and a factor in change:

> Public opinion places considerable restraint upon the ability of a leader successfully to advocate important measures which do not accord in some degree with public opinion. Even the most prestigious public figures cannot achieve general opinion change in the face of significant opposition President Roosevelt could not 'pack' the Supreme Court, popular as he was, and Woodrow Wilson was unable to get the United States into the League of Nations. . . . Many an important public figure has fallen from power because he advocated too radical a change, and was himself devaluated by the voters.[1]

The way in which opinion can change in response to events is well illustrated by changing attitudes in India towards Britain and the Soviet Union. Before the war in 1965 between India and Pakistan, 63 per cent of the respondents in a survey of urban centres in India described their attitude towards Britain as 'good' or 'very good', compared with 80 per cent for the Soviet Union. Following the Tashkent talks, in which Russia successfully mediated between the two sides, there was a dramatic change in attitudes towards Britain: only 25 per cent of the respondents now regarded Britain (which had officially adopted a neutral stance during the war) as 'good' or 'very good', 24 per cent regarding Britain as 'bad' or 'very bad'. The change in attitudes towards the Soviet Union was relatively small, but after the Tashkent talks 90 per cent regarded Russia as 'good' or 'very good' and no respondent placed Russia in the two categories of disapproval (IIPO, January-February 1966).

Change in public opinion depends on two factors: firstly, upon the amount of resistance to change that exists, and secondly, on the evaluation of the source or sources of information on which

[1] ibid., pp. 49–50.

the opinion is based. Clearly resistance to change is dependent upon the intensity and salience of opinions: the more strongly opinions are held and the more important they are among the whole range of opinions held by an individual, the less likely is some change of opinion. Similarly, the greater the faith of the individual in the source of information the greater the significance this may have on the likelihood of a change of attitude. It is important to appreciate, however, that faith in a source may be a factor to encourage as much as to discourage change. Resistance to change may be overcome because the source is trusted, and it is on such trust that many political leaders pin their hopes of effecting widespread societal reform. Whether the vehicle and motivating force in such change is a leader, a party or an ideology, its ultimate success depends upon the establishment of a sufficient degree of trust (unless change is, of course, effected by force). This is not to suggest that change may be initiated only from above, although the opportunity for taking such initiative is obviously greater for those holding some sort of formal office. In practice, initiative for change may be taken by those who hold no formal office and who have hitherto been politically inactive. Indeed, the formation of public opinion frequently leads to such initiative, since strongly held opinions may be the decisive factor leading to some form of political participation. It may, for instance, be a factor in the use of violence to effect change, or, as we noted in Chapter 4 in Kenneth Prewitt's study, in the recruitment of state legislators and city councillors in the United States, to take a more specific example.[1] Furthermore, the fact that an opinion is widely held, perhaps by a majority of people, is clearly of importance (regardless of the political system), but this is generally likely to be a reflex factor, a factor of importance not so much in the taking of an initiative but as a reaction to it. It does matter how many people hold an opinion, but it probably matters more *who* these people are. Whatever democratic theory might suggest, the opinions of the prime minister or the president are normally more important than those of the solitary voter; and even at election time the solitary voter is of significance only in combination with his fellow voters – most especially in a marginal situation.

Even so, important as the opinions of certain individuals in a

[1] See p. 158 above.

particular society may be, their level of information may only be marginally greater than that of less important persons, while the degree to which their opinions are rational is not necessarily a function of their importance. Information in any context, but especially in a political context, is seldom 'pure', and in the realm of public opinion it can hardly be expected that it should be. Information, in this sense, means not only the 'facts about a situation', but also 'facts about other people's opinions'. Moreover, the nature and the amount of information received varies considerably from individual to individual, and in each case it must be sifted through the individual's perceptual screen. The result is that each individual has a personalized view of each item of information and develops his opinions accordingly. It is not therefore, surprising to find, as Bernard Cohen did in a study of the development of attitudes towards the peace treaty between the United States and Japan, that 'members of the Executive and Congress received somewhat different images of "public opinion" on the treaty, because different groups and individuals communicated different things to them at different times.'[1] These people received different images, not only because their information, the sources of that information and the times when they received it varied, but also because it is likely that there were existing variations in their perceptual screens – in their knowledge, values and attitudes. We suggested in Chapter 2 that these basic orientations regarding their knowledge, values and attitudes were acquired through the process of political socialization. We also argued, however, that these orientations were subject to possible change under the impact of an individual's experience and that political socialization was a continuous process applicable not only to childhood and adolescence, but also to adult life. If this is so, then changes in particular attitudes or opinions may be accounted for by the same process – by the constant resifting of knowledge, values and attitudes under the impact of experience.

The role of political communication in this process is that of catalyst in that it provides the dynamic element – the means by which politically relevant information reaches the individual and shapes his political orientations. These orientations, which are by no means immutable, may lead in turn to varying degrees of

[1] Bernard C. Cohen, 'Political Communication and the Japanese Peace Settlement', *Public Opinion Quarterly*, **20**, 1956, p. 27.

political participation and ultimately to the holding of political office, and therefore to the consideration of political recruitment: in each of these processes political communication plays its part, but most of all in the process of political, social and economic change. We would therefore agree with Lane and Sears when they assert that 'a political system is shaped and guided by two things: what its members believe, and the way they learn and change their beliefs.'[1]

[1] Lane and Sears, *Public Opinion*, p. 114.

6 · Conclusion

We defined political sociology in Chapter 1 as the examination of the links between politics and society, between social structures and political structures, and between social behaviour and political behaviour; and in discussing its development and the approaches and methods appropriate to its study, we touched upon the problems of objectivity and the study of values and ideas in political behaviour. These are, of course, problems common to the whole of social science – the extent to which its practitioners can be objective in their studies and whether values are of legitimate concern to them. The behavioural approach in particular stresses the need to separate facts from values, though it does not necessarily hold that the latter should be ignored.

The concepts of political socialization and political communication, as we have defined them, are concerned with values, in that they are closely involved with the political behaviour of the individual. No one acts in complete isolation of values, although their existence may not be recognized and may be denied in particular cases. Similarly, a set of values may form a coherent pattern based on a rational process of thought, or appear to be a jumbled mass of contradictory or unconnected reactions to various phenomena. It may, moreover, be difficult, perhaps impossible, to establish any firm or significant relationship between values on, say, political matters on the one hand, and those on economic matters on the other. In a study of the relationship between personal values and political attitudes, for example, Brewster Smith found a correlation between holding *liberty* as a value and concern about the policies of the Soviet Union, but there was no significant relationship between holding *economic security* as a value and attitudes towards the Soviet Union. In 1947, at least, when this survey was conducted, it appeared that attitudes towards Russia in the United States were part of a democratic-totalitarian syndrome rather than an economic syndrome. Smith also found that those respondents holding liberty as a value generally had broad interests and were likely to be active in community affairs, whereas those holding economic security as a value generally had narrower interests and were less likely to be active in community affairs.[1] The political sociologist is therefore deeply concerned with the values held by individuals, with the way in which they are acquired and the way in which they change, since values hold the key to political behaviour; and the problems of studying values in no way lessens that concern.

Political participation and political recruitment can be analysed in terms of the social and other characteristics of the persons involved, but they can only be explained in terms of the values held by those persons. Quite apart from the relative ease with which data on the characteristics of people can be obtained, compared with data on their values, studies of social behaviour suggest that there is often a link between particular characteristics and particular values. Such a link is not necessarily causal, but merely suggests that individuals with certain characteristics are more likely than those with different characteristics to hold certain values. It may well be, of course, that the characteristic concerned, whatever its causal significance, suggests a useful hypothesis to explain the link. In this sense the concern of the political sociologist is primarily with the particular values of the individual or those of groups of individuals.

Values are also important, however, in the form of ideologies, since the development of related values into a consistent or relatively consistent pattern has been, and remains, a powerful force in social and, more especially, political behaviour:

> At the present day, we are better able to recognize the important role of ideologies in social change, because we have the experience of the achievements of Marxism . . . as an ideology which powerfully assists rapid industrialization, and on the other hand, of the retarding influence of traditional creeds in such underdeveloped countries as India.[2]

[1] M. Brewster Smith, 'Personal Values as Determinants of a Political Attitude', *Journal of Psychology*, **28**, 1949, pp. 477–86.

[2] Bottomore, *Élites and Society*, p. 28.

The two examples suggested by Bottomore of the role that ideology can play can, of course, be supplemented by many more, and the very names of many political parties and movements are a convincing testimony of the role of ideas in political behaviour. The very example of political parties, however, serves as a reminder that ideologies and ideas do not function in a vacuum. The relationship between an ideology and the political party which claims to adhere to it is seldom simple: not only may the ideology be silent on many matters, but also, like the party which is its vehicle, it is often subject to change. Such changes are often subtle and difficult to detect, and may even be denied by proponent and opponent alike. Where they are detected they may be subject to exaggeration out of all proportion to the change as the full force of ideological conflict exerts itself. The periodic clashes between left and right in the British Labour party, the brief triumph of the Goldwater forces in the American Republican party in 1964, the conflict between pro-Chinese and pro-Russian elements within various Communist parties and within the world Communist movement, and the formation of the Democratic Labour party in Australia after a split in the A.L.P., are all examples of such conflicts. Where there is little apparent conflict to emphasize ideological commitments it may be more difficult to discern the influence of ideas, and even the names of parties may be confusing: thus it has been suggested that the French Radical Socialist party is neither radical nor Socialist, and the Canadian Progressive Conservative party is neither progressive nor conservative, while many observers have experienced difficulty in finding any ideological distinction between the Republican and Democratic parties in the United States. The very fact, however, that parties (and other social and political institutions) claim to adhere to particular values or a particular ideology, and that their members (or some of them) believe in them, is of considerable importance in itself. It also illustrates, as Crick points out, that

institutions are the framework of political behaviour and must be studied as the 'institutionalization' of particular styles of politics and social aspirations; political ideas are then the theories and doctrines about how institutions are, can and should be worked.[1]

[1] Crick, 'The Tendency of Political Studies', p. 683.

The political sociologist is thus concerned with the relationship between political institutions and values, with how institutions are shaped by values and how values are shaped by institutions in a reciprocal process of change. Some of the relationships between particular political institutions and values are not difficult to see. For example, a relationship between the British Parliament and the value of liberty as expressed in certain legislation is apparent; while a relationship between the values held by party leaders in Communist-controlled countries and the political institutions that have been established is clear enough. In most cases, however, the relationship is less clear and is extremely complex, especially where institutions have become, on the one hand, semi-independent, developing a life of their own, and on the other, inextricably linked to certain values and to other institutions, so that a complicated process of interaction results. It is at this stage that the problem of values becomes crucial to the political sociologist and to the social scientist generally.

Not only may ideas and ideologies influence political behaviour, but, as Bottomore argues, '. . . every sociological concept and theory has an ideological force by reason of its influence upon the thoughts and actions of men in their everyday life'.[1] The political sociologist is no exception to this rule, and it may be seriously questioned whether objective inquiry in social science is possible. It may, therefore, be necessary to agree with another writer on the subject, 'that it is in the nature of social science that it may be influenced in its methods and results by the character of the observer'.[2]

The two founding fathers of political sociology, Marx and Weber, both believed that they practised a value-free social science, although Weber recognized the importance of values. The standard has since been taken up by the advocates of the behavioural approach to the study of social phenomena. The criticism has not been effectively answered, however, and the problem remains. The fact that the problem is acknowledged rather than ignored is in itself important, and we may agree with Runciman when he suggests that

---

[1] Bottomore, *Élites and Society*, p. 20.

[2] Leon Bramson, *The Political Context of Sociology*, Princeton, N.J., 1961, p. 152.

... political sociology – that is, an explanation or set of explanations of political behaviour – must depend for its vocabulary on some kind of philosophical position. This derives directly from the fact that the social sciences deal with actions and not events. It does not ... require us to abandon all notions of scientific method in sociological enquiry; [and though it may be that] complete scientism is unattainable ... it is nevertheless worth trying.[1]

THE ROLE OF POLITICAL SOCIOLOGY

Our definition of political sociology suggests its principal role – to explain the connection between social and political phenomena. In order to fulfil this role, however, it is necessary to develop theories and methods which will link the social sciences together, particularly sociology and political science. The four concepts which we have defined and discussed in the earlier chapters are an attempt to contribute to the task of developing political sociology as a theoretical and methodological link between sociology and political science. In dealing with each concept, we have endeavoured to draw our examples from as wide a field as possible (while maintaining a degree of continuity to illustrate the way in which the concepts are linked), so as to demonstrate not only the wealth of material available and the need for its systematic treatment, but also to show that political sociology has no inherent ideological commitment, despite our earlier discussion of values. Those values which influence its use are those of the observer, and they therefore vary from observer to observer. It also follows that political sociology is as relevant to the study of political behaviour in the United States or Britain as it is to the study of political behaviour in Ghana or Indonesia, Russia or China. Thus to argue, as some observers have done, that political sociology involves 'a political commitment to the values of democratic institutions',[2] and that its main task is 'the study of the social conditions of democracy as a social system',[3] is unreasonable as well as placing unacceptable limits on political sociology. While

[1] Runciman, *Social Science and Political Theory*, pp. 16 and 66.
[2] Reinhard Bendix and S. M. Lipset, 'Political Sociology', *Current Sociology*, 6, 1957, p. 81.
[3] S. M. Lipset, 'Political Sociology', in R. K. Merton, L. Brown and L. S. Cottrell Jr (eds.), *Sociology Today*, New York, 1959, p. 108.

political sociology has thrown considerable light on the conditions under which democracy is likely to flourish and has done much to illuminate the democratic process, we believe there is sufficient evidence in this book to support the view that political sociology is methodologically applicable to the study of *any* political system.

How far it is possible at present to apply political sociology to *any* political system is a different matter, but this is because

> . . . the establishment of political sociology as a real interdisciplinary approach, as a balanced cross-fertilization, between sociologists and political scientists, is more a task for the future than a current achievement.[1]

This book seeks to contribute to that task.

[1] Sartori, 'From the Sociology of Politics to Political Sociology', p. 200.

Bibliography

GENERAL

Almond, Gabriel A. and Coleman, James S. (eds.), *The Politics of the Developing Areas*, Princeton, 1960.

Almond, Gabriel A. and Powell, G. Bingham, *Comparative Politics: A Developmental Approach*, Boston, 1966.

Almond, Gabriel A. and Verba, Sidney, *The Civic Culture*, Princeton, 1963.

Bendix, Rheinhard and Lipset, Seymour M., 'Political Sociology', *Current Sociology*, 6, 1957, pp. 79–98.

Bramson, Leon, *The Political Context of Sociology*, Princeton, 1961.

Crick, Bernard, *The American Science of Politics*, London, 1959.

Crick, Bernard, *In Defence of Politics*, London, 1962.

Crick, Bernard, 'The Tendency of Political Studies', *New Society*, 3 November, 1966, pp. 681–3.

Dahl, Robert A., *Who Governs? Democracy and Power in an American City*, New Haven, 1961.

Easton, David, *The Political System*, New York, 1953.

Easton, David, *A Framework for Political Analysis*, Englewood Cliffs, New Jersey, 1965.

Easton, David, *A Systems Analysis of Political Life*, New York, 1965.

Herbele, Rudolf, *Social Movements: An Introduction to Political Sociology*, New York, 1951.

Inkeles, Alex, *What is Sociology?*, Englewood Cliffs, New Jersey, 1964.

Janowitz, Morris, 'Political Sociology', in the *International Encyclopedia of Social Science*, New York, 1968, Vol. 12, pp. 298–307.

Johnson, Harry M., *Sociology: A Systematic Introduction*, London, 1961.

Kornhauser, W., *The Politics of the Mass Society*, London, 1959.

Lasswell, Harold D., *Politics: Who Gets What, When and How*, New York, 1936.

Lasswell, Harold D., and Kaplan, A., *Power and Society: A Framework for Political Inquiry*, New Haven, 1950.

Lipset, Seymour M., *Political Man*, Garden City, New York, 1960.

Lipset, Seymour M., *The First New Nation*, London, 1963.

Lipset, Seymour M., 'Political Sociology' in Merton, Robert K., Brown, L. and Cottrell, Leonard S. Jr (eds.), *Sociology Today*, New York, 1959, pp. 81–114.

Mackenzie, W. J. M., *Politics and Social Science*, London, 1967.

Michels, Robert, *First Lectures in Political Sociology*, trans. de Grazia, Alfred, Minneapolis, 1949.

Runciman, W. G., *Social Science and Political Theory*, London, 1965.

Sartori, G., 'From the Sociology of Politics to Political Sociology', *Government and Opposition*, 4, 1969, pp. 194–214.

Weber, Max, *From Max Weber: Essays in Sociology*, trans. and ed. H. H. Gerth and C. Wright Mills, London, 1948.

Weber, Max, *Theory of Social and Economic Organization*, trans. A. M. Henderson and ed. Talcott Parsons, New York, 1947.

Young, Oran R., *Systems of Political Science*, Englewood Cliffs, New Jersey, 1968.

POLITICAL SOCIALIZATION

Aberle, David F., 'Culture and Socialization' in Hsu, Francis L. K. (ed.), *Psychological Anthropology: Approaches to Culture and Personality*, Homewood, Illinois, 1961.

Adorno, T. W., Frenkel-Brunswik, Else, Levinson, Daniel J., and Sandford, R. N., *The Authoritarian Personality*, New York, 1950.

Apter, David E., 'Political Religion in the New Nations', in Geertz, Clifford (ed.), *Old Societies and New States*, New York, 1963, pp. 57–104.

Argyle, M. and Delin, P., 'Non-Universal Laws of Socialization', *Human Relations*, 18, 1965, pp. 77–85.

Bar-Yoseph, Rivkak, 'The Pattern of Early Socialization in the Collective Settlements of Israel', *Human Relations*, 12, 1959, pp. 345–60.

Benedict, Ruth, *The Chrysanthemum and the Sword*, Boston, 1946.

Child, Irvin L., 'Socialization' in Lindzey, G. (ed.), *Handbook of Social Psychology*, Cambridge, Mass., 1954, Vol. 2, pp. 655–92.

Coleman, James S. (ed.), *Education and Political Development*, Princeton, 1965.

Converse, Philip and Dupeux, Georges, 'Politicization of the Electorate in France and the United States', *Public Opinion Quarterly*, 26, 1962, pp. 1–23.

Davies, James C., 'The Family's Role in Political Socialization', *Annals of the American Academy of Political and Social Science*, 361, September. 1965, pp. 10–19.

Dawson, Richard E. and Prewitt, Kenneth, *Political Socialization: An Analytic Study*, Boston, 1969.

Dicks, H. V., 'Personality Traits and National Socialist Ideology', *Human Relations*, 3, 1950, pp. 111–54.

Easton, David, 'The Theoretical Relevance of Political Socialization', *Canadian Journal of Political Science*, 1, 1968, pp. 125–46.

Easton, David and Hess, Robert D., 'The Child's Political World', *Mid-West Journal of Political Science*, 6, 1962, pp. 229–46.

Easton, David and Hess, Robert D., 'The Child's Changing Image of the President', *Public Opinion Quarterly*, 24, 1960, pp. 623–44.

Easton, David and Dennis, Jack, 'The Child's Acquisition of Régime, Norms: Political Efficacy', *American Political Science Review*, 61, 1967, pp. 25–38.

Easton, David and Dennis, Jack, *Children in the Political System: Origins of Political Legitimacy*, New York, 1969.

Eisenstadt, S. N., *From Generation to Generation*, London, 1956.

Estvan, Frank and Elizabeth, *The Child's World*, New York, 1959.

Eysenck, H. J., *The Psychology of Politics*, London, 1954.

Froman, L. A., 'Personality and Political Socialization', *Journal of Politics*, 23, 1961, pp. 341–52.

Fromm, Erich, *Escape from Freedom*, New York, 1941.

Geiger, Kent, 'Changing Political Attitudes in Totalitarian Society: A Case-Study of the Role of the Family', *World Politics*, 8, 1955–6, pp. 187–205.

Goldrich, Daniel and Scott, Edward W., 'Developing Political Orientations of Panamanian Students', *Journal of Politics*, 23, 1961, pp. 84–105.

Greenstein, Fred I., *Children in Politics*, New Haven, 1965.

Greenstein, Fred I., 'Personality and Political Socialization: the Theories of the Authoritarian and Democratic Character', *Annals of the American Academy of Political and Social Science*, 361, September 1965, pp. 81–95.

Greenstein, Fred I., 'Political Socialization' in the *International Encyclopedia of Social Science*, New York, 1968, Vol. 14, pp. 551–5.

Greenstein, Fred I. and Wolfinger, Raymond E., 'The Suburbs and Shifting Party Loyalties', *Public Opinion Quarterly*, 22, 1958, pp. 473–82.

Hyman, Herbert, *Political Socialization: A Study in the Psychology of Political Behaviour*, Glencoe, Illinois, 1959.

Iisager, Holger, 'Factors Influencing the Formation and Change of Political and Religious Attitudes', *Journal of Social Psychology*, 29, 1949, pp. 253–65.

Inkeles, Alex, 'National Character and Modern Political Systems' in Hsu, Francis L. K. (ed.), *Psychological Anthropology: Approaches to Culture and Personality*, Homewood, Illinois, 1961.

Inkeles, Alex, *Public Opinion in Soviet Russia: A Study in Mass Persuasion*, Cambridge, Mass., 1958.

Inkeles, Alex, 'Social Change and Social Character: the Role of Parental Mediation', *Journal of Social Issues*, 11, 1955, pp. 12–13.

Jennings, M. Kent, 'Pre-Adult Orientations to Multiple Systems of Government', *Midwest Journal of Political Science*, 11, 1967, pp. 291–317.

Jennings, M. Kent and Niemi, R. G., 'The Transmission of Political Values from Parent to Child', *American Political Science Review*, 62, 1968, pp. 169–84.

Jaros, D., Hirsch, H. and Fleron, F. J., 'The Malevolent Leader: Political Socialization in an American Sub-Culture', *American Political Science Review*, 62, 1968, pp. 564–75.

Koff, David and van der Muhl, George, 'Political Socialization in Kenya and Tanzania: A Comparative Analysis', *Journal of Modern African Studies*, 5, 1967, pp. 13–51.

Kuroda, Yasamusa, 'Agencies of Political Socialization and Political Change: the Political Orientations of Japanese Law Students', *Human Organization*, 24, 1965, pp. 328–31.

Lane, Robert E., *Political Ideology: Why the American Common Man Believes What He Does*, New York, 1962.

Lane, Robert E., 'The Need to be Liked and the Anxious College Liberal',

Annals of the American Academy of Political and Social Science, 361, September 1965, pp. 71–80.

Langton, Kenneth P., 'Political Partisanship and Political Socialization in Jamaica', *British Journal of Sociology*, 17, 1966, pp. 419–29.

Langton, Kenneth P., 'Peer Group and School and the Socialization Process', *American Political Science Review*, 61, 1967, pp. 751–8.

Langton, Kenneth P. and Jennings, M. Kent, 'Political Socialization and the High School Civics Curriculum in the United States', *American Political Science Review*, 62, 1968, pp. 852–67.

Lasswell, Harold D., *Power and Personality*, New York, 1948.

Levin, Martin L., 'Social Climates and Political Socialization', *Public Opinion Quarterly*, 25, 1961, pp. 596–606.

Le Vine, Robert, 'The Internalization of Political Values in Stateless Societies', *Human Organization*, 19, 1960, pp. 51–8.

Le Vine, Robert, 'Political Socialization and Culture Change' in Geertz, Clifford (ed.), *Old Societies and New States*, New York, 1963, pp. 280–303.

Lipsitz, Lewis, 'Work Life and Political Attitudes: A Study of Manual Workers', *American Political Science Review*, 58, 1964, pp. 951–62.

Litt, Edgar, 'Education and Political Enlightenment in America', *Annals of the American Academy of Political and Social Science*, 361, Sept., 1965, pp. 32–9.

McClintock, Charles G. and Turner, Henry A., 'The Impact of College upon Political Knowledge, Participation and Values', *Human Relations*, 15, 1962, pp. 163–75.

McClosky, Herbert and Dahlgren, Harold E., 'Primary Group Influence on Party Loyalty', *American Political Science Review*, 53, 1959, pp. 757–76.

Maccoby, Eleanor E., Matthews, Richard E. and Morton, Anton S., 'Youth and Political Change', *Public Opinion Quarterly*, 18, 1954, pp. 533–6.

Mann, Erika, *School for Barbarians: Education under the Nazis*, London, 1939.

Murphy, Raymond J. and Morris, Richard J., 'Occupational Situation, Subjective Class Identification and Political Affiliation', *American Sociological Review*, 26, 1961, pp. 383–92.

Nogee, Philip and Levin, Murray B., 'Some Determinants of Political Attitudes among College Voters', *Public Opinion Quarterly*, 22, 1958, pp. 449–63.

Oakeshott, Michael, 'Political Education', in Laslett, P. (ed.), *Philosophy, Politics and Society*, Oxford, 1956, pp. 1–21.

Orren, Karen and Peterson, Paul, 'Presidential Assassination: A Case-Study of the Dynamics of Political Socialization', *Journal of Politics*, 29, 1967, pp. 388–404.

Pethybridge, Roger, 'The Assessment of Ideological Influence on East Europeans', *Public Opinion Quarterly*, 21, 1967, pp. 38–50.

Prewitt, Kenneth, Eulau, Heinz, and Zisk, Betty H., 'Political Socialization and Political Roles', *Public Opinion Quarterly*, 30, 1966, pp. 569–82.

Reading, R., 'Political Socialization in Colombia and the United States', *Midwest Journal of Political Science*, 12, 1968, pp. 352–81.

Riesman, David, *The Lonely Crowd*, New Haven, 1950.

Sigel, Roberta S., 'Some Explorations into Political Socialization: Children's Reactions to the Death of a President', in Wolfenstein, Martha and Kliman, Gilbert (ed.), *Children and the Death of a President*, New York, 1965, pp. 30–61.

Singham, A. W., 'The Political Socialization of Marginal Groups', *International Journal of Comparative Sociology*, 8, 1967, pp. 182–98.
Skrzypek, Stanislaw, 'The Political, Cultural and Social Views of Yugoslav Youth', *Public Opinion Quarterly*, 29, 1965, pp. 87–106.
Szyliowicz, Joseph S., 'Political Participation and Modernization in Turkey', *Western Political Quarterly*, 19, 1966, pp. 166–84.
Tannenbaum, P. H. and McLeod, T. M., 'On the Measurement of Socialization', *Public Opinion Quarterly*, 31, 1967, pp. 27–37.

POLITICAL PARTICIPATION

Abrams, Mark, 'Social Trends and Electoral Behaviour', *British Journal of Sociology*, 13, 1962, pp. 228–42.
Agger, Robert E., Goldstein, Marshal N. and Pearl, Stanley A., 'Political Cynicism: Measurement and Meaning', *Journal of Politics*, 23, 1961, pp. 477–506.
Alford, Robert R., *Party and Society*, Chicago, 1963.
Almond, Gabriel A. and Verba, Sidney, *The Civic Culture*, Princeton, 1963.
Barnes, Samuel H., 'Participation, Education and Political Competence: Evidence from a Sample of Italian Socialists', *American Political Science Review*, 60, 1966, pp. 348–53.
Bauer, Raymond A., 'Some Trends in Sources of Alienation from the Soviet System', *Public Opinion Quarterly*, 19, 1955, pp. 279–91.
Bowman, Lewis and Boynton, G. R., 'Recruitment Patterns among Local Party Officials: A Model and Some Preliminary Findings', *American Political Science Review*, 60, 1966, pp. 667–76.
Brass, P. R., 'Political Participation, Institutionalization and Stability in India', *Government and Opposition*, 4, 1968, pp. 23–53.
Butler, David E. and Stokes, Donald E., *Political Change in Britain*, London, 1969.
Campbell, Angus, Gurin, Gerald and Miller, Warren E., *The Voter Decides*, Evanston, Illinois, 1954.
Campbell, Angus, Converse, Philip E., Miller, Warren E., and Stokes, Donald E., *The American Voter*, New York, 1960.
Erbe, William, 'Social Involvement and Political Activity', *American Sociological Review*, 29, 1964, pp. 198–215.
Gleitman, Henry and Greenbaum, Joseph, T., 'Hungarian Socio-Political Attitudes and Revolutionary Action', *Public Opinion Quarterly*, 24, 1960, pp. 62–76.
Katz, Fred E. and Piret, Fern V., 'Circuitous Participation in Politics', *American Journal of Sociology*, 69, 1964, pp. 367–73.
Key, Jr, V. O., *Politics, Parties and Pressure Groups* (5th edition), New York, 1964.
Key, Jr, V. O., *Public Opinion and American Democracy*, New York, 1961.
Lane, Robert E., *Political Life: Why People Get Involved in Politics*, Glencoe, Illinois, 1959.
Levinson, Daniel J., 'The Relevance of Personality for Political Participation', *Public Opinion Quarterly*, 22, 1958, pp. 3–10.

Lindenfeld, Frank, 'Economic Interest and Political Involvement', *Public Opinion Quarterly*, 28, 1964, pp. 104–11.

Lipset, Seymour M., *Political Man*, Garden City, New York, 1960.

Lipset, Seymour M., Lazarsfeld, Paul F., Barton, Allen H. and Linz, Juan, 'The Psychology of Voting: An Analysis of Political Behaviour', in Lindzey, G. (ed.), *A Handbook of Social Psychology*, Vol. 2, New York, 1954, pp. 1124–75.

Lipset, Seymour M. and Rokkan, Stein (eds.), *Party Systems and Voter Alignments*, New York, 1967.

Litt, Edgar, 'Political Cynicism and Political Futility', *Journal of Politics*, 25, 1963, pp. 312–23.

McClosky, Herbert, 'Political Participation', in the *International Encyclopedia of Social Science*, New York, 1968, Vol. 12, pp. 252–65.

Maccoby, Herbert, 'The Differential Political Activity of Participants in a Voluntary Association', *American Sociological Review*, 23, 1958, pp. 524–32.

McKenzie, Robert T. and Silver, Allan, *Angels in Marble*, London, 1968.

Milbrath, Lester W., *Political Participation: How and Why Do People Get Involved in Politics?*, Chicago, 1965.

Mussen, Paul H. and Wyszynski, Anne B., 'Personality and Political Participation', *Human Relations*, 5, 1952, pp. 65–82.

Nordlinger, Eric, *Working Class Tories*, London, 1967.

Olson, Marvin E., 'Alienation and Political Opinion', *Public Opinion Quarterly*, 29, 1965, pp. 200–12.

Rokkan, Stein (ed.), 'Approaches to the Study of Political Participation', *Acta Sociologica*, 6, No. 1–2, 1962.

Rokkan, Stein, 'The Comparative Study of Political Participation', in Ranney, Austin, *Essays on the Behavioural Study of Politics*, Urbana, Illinois, 1962.

Rose, Arnold M., 'Alienation and Participation: A Comparison of Group Leaders and the "Mass" ', *American Sociological Review*, 27, 1962, pp. 834–8.

Rosenberg, Morris, 'Some Determinants of Political Apathy', *Public Opinion Quarterly*, 18, 1954, pp. 349–66.

Srole, Leo, 'Social Integration and Certain Corrollaries: An Exploratory Study', *American Sociological Review*, 21, 1956, pp. 709–16.

Stokes, Donald E., Campbell, Angus and Miller, Warren E., 'The Components of Electoral Decision', *American Political Science Review*, 52, 1958, pp. 367–87.

Townsend, James R., *Political Participation in Communist China*, Los Angeles, 1967.

Truman, David B., *The Governmental Process*, New York, 1951.

Wright, C. R. and Hyman, Herbert H., 'Voluntary Association Memberships of American Adults: Evidence from National Sample Surveys', *American Sociological Reviews*, 23, 1958, pp. 284–94.

POLITICAL RECRUITMENT

Barber, J. D., *The Lawmakers: Recruitment and Adaptation to Legislative Life*, New Haven, 1965.

Beck, Carl, 'Party Control and Bureaucratization in Czechoslovakia', *Journal of Politics*, 23, 1961, pp. 279–94.

Bottomore, T. B., *Elites and Society*, London, 1964.

Bottomore, T. B., *Classes in Modern Society*, London, 1965.

Buck, Philip W., *Amateurs and Professionals in British Politics*, 1918–59, Chicago, 1963.

Burnham, James, *The Managerial Revolution*, New York, 1941.

The Civil Service (The Fulton Report), Cmd. 3683, HMSO, London, 1968.

Downs, Anthony, 'A Theory of Bureaucracy', *American Economic Review*, Papers and Proceedings of the American Economic Association, 55, 1965, pp. 439–46.

Diament, Alfred, 'A Case-Study of Administrative Autonomy: Controls and Tensions in French Administration', *Political Studies*, 6, 1958, pp. 147–66.

Edinger, Lewis J., 'Post-Totalitarian Leadership in Élites in the German Federal Republic', *American Political Science Review*, 54, 1960, pp. 58–82.

Epstein, Leon, *Parties in Western Democracies*, New York, 1967.

Eulau, Heinz and Sprague, John, *Lawyers in Politics: A Study in Professional Convergence*, Indianapolis, 1964.

Frank, Elke, 'The Role of Bureaucracy in Transition', *Journal of Politics*, 28, 1966, pp. 725–53.

Guttsman, W. L., *The British Political Élite*, London, 1963.

Harris, Richard L., 'The Role of the Civil Service in West Africa', *Public Administration Review*, 25, 1965, pp. 308–13.

Kallen, Arthur D., 'Training in the Federal Civil Service – 170 Years to Accept', *Public Administration Review*, 19, 1959, pp. 36–46.

Kim, Young C., 'Political Recruitment: the Case of Japanese Prefectural Assemblymen', *American Political Science Review*, 61, 1967, pp. 1036–52.

Knight, Maxwell, *The German Executive*, 1890–1933, Hoover Institute Studies, Series B, No. 14, Stanford, California, 1952.

Lasswell, Harold D., Lerner, Daniel and Rothwell, C. Easton, *The Comparative Study of Élites*, Stanford, California, 1952.

Marvick, Dwaine, *Political Decision-Makers*, Glencoe, Illinois, 1961.

Marvick, Dwaine, 'Political Recruitment and Careers', in the *International Encyclopedia of Social Science*, New York, 1968, Vol. 12, pp. 273–82.

Matthews, Donald R., *The Social Background of Political Decision-Makers*, New York, 1954.

Matthews, Donald R., *U.S. Senators and their World*, Chapel Hill, North Carolina, 1960.

Meisel, James H. (ed.), *Pareto and Mosca*, Englewood Cliffs, New Jersey, 1965.

Michels, Robert, *Political Parties*, originally published 1911, first English edition 1915; latest edition, translated by Eden and Cedar Paul, with an introduction by Seymour M. Lipset, New York, 1962.

Mills, C. Wright, *The Power Élite*, New York, 1956.

Mosca, Gaetano, *The Ruling Class*, ed. A. Livingstone and trans. H. D. Kahn, New York, 1939.

Pareto, Vilfredo, *The Mind and Society*, ed. A. Livingstone and trans. Andrew Bongiorno and A. Livingston, New York, 1935.

Prewitt, Kenneth, 'Political Socialization and Leadership Selection', *Annals of the American Academy of Political and Social Science*, 361, September 1965, pp. 96–111.

Rae, Douglas, *The Political Consequence of Electoral Laws*, New Haven, 1967.

Ranney, Austin, *Pathways to Parliament*, London, 1965.

Ross, J. F. S., *Elections and Electors*, London, 1955.

Ross, J. F. S., *Parliamentary Representation* (2nd edition), London, 1948.

Rush, Michael D., *The Selection of Parliamentary Candidates*, London, 1969.

Rush, Michael D., 'Candidate Selection and Its Impact on Leadership Recruitment', in J. D. Lees and R. Kimber (eds.), *Political Parties in Britain: An Organizational and Functional Guide*, London, 1971.

Scarrow, Howard, 'Nomination and Local Party Organization in Canada: A Case-Study', *Western Political Quarterly*, 17, 1964, pp. 55–62.

Schueller, G. K., *The Politburo*, Hoover Institute Studies, Series B, No. 2, Stanford, California, 1951.

Seligman, Lester G., 'Political Recruitment and Party Structure', *American Political Science Review*, 55, 1961, pp. 77–86.

Seligman, Lester G., 'Élite Recruitment and Political Development', *Journal of Politics*, 26, 1964, pp. 612–26.

Shuster, James R., 'Bureaucratic Transition in Morocco', *Human Organization*, 24, 1965, pp. 53–8.

Snowiss, Leo M., 'Congressional Recruitment and Representation', *American Political Science Review*, 60, 1966, pp. 627–39.

Subramaniam, V., 'Representative Bureaucracy: A Reassessment', *American Political Science Review*, 61, 1967, pp. 1010–19.

Weber, Max, 'Politics as a Vocation', in *From Max Weber: Essays in Sociology*, trans. and ed. H. H. Gerth and C. Wright Mills, London, 1948, pp. 77–128.

POLITICAL COMMUNICATION

Almond, Gabriel A. and Verba, Sidney, *The Civic Culture*, Princeton, 1963.

'Attitude Change', *Public Opinion Quarterly* (special edition), 24, 1960, pp. 163–365.

Barker, Anthony and Rush, Michael D., *The Member of Parliament and His Information*, London, 1970.

Bauer, Raymond, Inkeles, Alex and Kluckhorn, Clyde, *How the Soviet System Works*, Cambridge, Mass., 1965.

Berelson, Bernard R., Lazarsfeld, Paul F. and McPhee, William N., *Voting: A Study of Opinion Formation in a Presidential Election*, Chicago, 1954.

Childs, H. L., *Public Opinion*, Princeton, 1965.

Davison, W. Phillips, 'On the Effects of Communication', *Public Opinion Quarterly*, 23, 1959, pp. 343–60.

Cohen, Bernard C., 'Political Communication and the Japanese Peace Settlement', *Public Opinion Quarterly*, 20, 1956, pp. 27–38.

de Sola Pool, Ithiel, 'Political Communication' in the *International Encyclopedia of Social Science*, New York, 1968, Vol. 3, pp. 90–5.

Deutsch, Karl W., *Nationalism and Social Communication: An Enquiry into the Foundations of Nationality*, New York, 1953.

Deutsch, Karl W., *The Nerves of Government: Models of Political Communication and Control*, New York, 1963.

Dexter, Louis Anthony, 'What Do Congressman Hear in the Mail?', *Public Opinion Quarterly*, 20, 1956, pp. 16–27.

Fagen, Richard R., *Politics and Communication*, Boston, 1966.

Garver, Richard A., 'Communication Problems of Underdevelopment: Cheju-do, Korea, 1962', *Public Opinion Quarterly*, 26, 1962, pp. 613–25.

Hirabayashi, Gordon K. and El Khalib, M. Fathalla, 'Communication and Political Awareness in the Villages of Egypt', *Public Opinion Quarterly*, 22, 1958, pp. 355–63.

Jacobs, Milton, Farzanegan, Farhad, and Askenazy, Alexander R., 'A Study of Key Communicators in Urban Thailand', *Social Forces*, 45, 1966–7, pp. 192–9.

Katz, Elihu, 'The Two-Step Flow of Communication: An Up-to-date Report on an Hypothesis', *Public Opinion Quarterly*, 21, 1957, pp. 61–78.

Katz, Elihu and Lazarsfeld, Paul F., *Personal Influence: The Part Played by People in the Flow of Mass Communication*, Glencoe, Illinois, 1955.

Klapper, Joseph, T., *The Effects of Mass Communication*, Glencoe, Illinois, 1960.

Lane, Robert E. and Sears, David O., *Public Opinion*, Englewood Cliffs, New Jersey, 1964.

Lazarsfeld, Paul F., Berelson, Bernard R. and Gaudet, Hazel, *The People's Choice: How the Voter Makes Up His Mind in a Presidential Election Campaign*, New York, 1948.

Packard, Vance, *The Hidden Persuaders*, New York, 1957.

Pye, Lucian W. (ed.), *Communication and Political Development*, Princeton, 1963.

Schatzman, Leonard and Strauss, Anselm, 'Social Class and Modes of Communication', *American Journal of Sociology*, 60, 1955, pp. 329–38.

Schramm, Wilbur, *Mass Communication* (2nd edition), Urbana, Illinois, 1960.

Schramm, Wilbur, *Mass Media and National Development: the Role of Information in Developing Countries*, Stanford, California, 1964.

Schramm, Wilbur and Riley Jr, John W., 'Communication in the Sovietized State, as Demonstrated in Korea', *American Sociological Review*, 16, 1951, pp. 757–66.

Smith, Bruce Lannes, Lasswell, Harold D., and Casey, Ralph D., *Propaganda, Communication and Public Opinion: a Comprehensive Reference Guide*, Princeton, 1946.

Smith, M. Brewster, 'Personal Values as Determinants of a Political Attitude', *Journal of Psychology*, 28, 1949, pp. 477–86.

Sussman, Leila A., 'F.D.R. and the White House Mail', *Public Opinion Quarterly*, 20, 1956, pp. 6–16.

Index

Aberle, David S., 17n
Abrams, Mark, 83n, 102n
Adenauer, Konrad, 71
Administration and policy, distinction between, 115–17
Administrative office-holders: in Britain, 140–1, 147, 148; in France, 141–2, 154; recruitment of, 116, 138–44; social characteristics of, 145–9; training of, 140, 141–2; in United States, 139–40, 145, 148
Adolescence and childhood, political socialization in, 30–45, 50–4, 55, 56–8, 65–6
Adorno, T. W., 26–7
Adults, political socialization of, 45–50, 55, 61–2, 66–7
Agger, Robert, 92, 96
'Agitators', role of in USSR, 61–2, 110, 172
AIPO, 101
Alford, Robert R., 46n, 112n
Alienation, 49–50, 69, 80, 93–100; definition of, 93–4, 97; Marx's theory of, 4; and political participation, 80, 93–100; and violence, 97–100
Alker, Hayward R. Jr, 82n
Almond, Gabriel A., 9, 10, 13, 21n, 42, 48–9, 69, 84n, 86, 88, 93–4, 103–4, 137n, 143n, 148n, 164, 173
American Negroes, political socialization of, 49
Anarchists, Russian, 99
Anomie: definition of, 94–6, 97; and political participation, 94–7; in United States, 95–6
Apathy: and cynicism, 93; definition of, 90–2, 97; and political participation, 79–80, 89–101; reasons for, 91–2
APOP, 51
Appalachian region, political socialization in, 49
Approaches and methods, 9–12, 188–9

Apter, David E., 66
Argentina, legitimacy of political system in, 70–1
Aristotle, 17
Atatürk, Kemal, 66–7
Attitudes, and values, 185–6. *See also* knowledge, values *and* attitudes
ATTS, 179
Australia: candidate selection in, 127; Democratic Labour party, 125–6, 187; electoral system in, 125–6; Liberal-Country party coalition, 125–6; party identification in, 51
Australian Labour party (ALP), 125–6, 128, 154, 187
Authoritarian personality, 26
Authority, development of attitudes towards, 32–7
Automaton personality, 26

Bagehot, Walter, 7
Barker, Anthony, 45n
Barton, Allen H., 112n
Bar-Yoseph, Rivkak, 54n
Bauer, Raymond A., 70
Beck, Carl, 143n
Behavioural approach, 10, 188
Belgium, candidate selection in, 131
Bendix, Reinhard, 189n
Benedict, Ruth, 27n
Berelson, Bernard R., 47n, 112n, 165n
Bluntschli, J. K., 25
Bolsheviks, 99
Bottomore, T. B., 150–1, 186n, 187, 188
Bramson, Leon, 188n
Britain: administrative recruitment in, 140–1, 147, 148; Cabinet, recruitment of, 134–5, 136; candidate selection in, 132–4, 153–7 *passim*; Conservative party, 87, 88, 119, 132–5; cynicism in, 93; discussing politics in, 84, 103, 174; dissatisfaction with political system, 73; elec-

LIMERICK CITY LIBRARY

Phone 314668
Website:
www.limerickcorp.ie/librarymain.htm
Email: citylib@limerickcorp.ie

The Granary,
Michael Street,
Limerick

This Book is issued subject to the Rules of this Library.
The Book must be returned not later than the last date stamped
below.

Class No. ..... *CF* .... Acc. No. ..... *C* **14148**

Date of Return	Date of Return	Date of Return	Date of Return
07 APR 10	0 5 FEB 2016		
	2 8 MAR 2017		
	2 6 APR 2017		
05. OCT -15	NOV 2011	0 8 AUG 2018	
07 DEC 0			
0 5 JUN 2012			
2 0 JUL 2012			
- 1 SEP 2012			
2 JAN 2014			

RAPIDS

RAPIDS

Tim Parks

Secker & Warburg
London

Published by Secker & Warburg 2005

2 4 6 8 10 9 7 5 3 1

First published in Great Britain in 2005 by
Secker & Warburg
Random House, 20 Vauxhall Bridge Road,
London SW1V 2SA

Random House Australia (Pty) Limited
20 Alfred Street, Milsons Point, Sydney,
New South Wales 2061, Australia

Random House New Zealand Limited
18 Poland Road, Glenfield,
Auckland 10, New Zealand

Random House (Pty) Limited
Endulini, 5A Jubilee Road, Parktown 2193,
South Africa

The Random House Group Limited Reg. No. 954009
www.randomhouse.co.uk

A CIP catalogue record for this book
is available from the British Library

ISBN 0 436 20559 9 (hbk)
ISBN 0 436 20585 8 (pbk)

Typeset by Palimpsest Book Production Limited

Printed and bound in Great Britain by
Clays Ltd, St Ives, plc

To all those who taught me
not to be afraid of the water,
and never to fight it.

The following pages are fiction. No reference to any living person is intended or should be inferred. While the place names are real, scenery and circumstance have been somewhat altered to suit the plot. There is no campsite at Sand in Taufers. In particular, the rapids of the river Aurino are not exactly as described. Canoeists beware! This book is not a guide for a safe descent.

A STOPPER

This isn't the right world, he told her. For us. He unrolled a sleeping bag and laid down on the planks. Be strong, he said. Earlier, immediately on their return, they had tried out the stretch downstream from Sand in Taufers. Filthy cities, Clive muttered. Michela looked taller and slimmer in her wetsuit beneath the large backdrop of the Alps, if possible even younger. Filthy Milanese, he insisted, pulling tight his spraydeck. Old misanthrope! she laughed. She was happy. It was right to go, she said, I don't regret it at all, but great to be back.

So it was. They seal-launched from the bank. The river was high. It slid solid beneath the bridge. She knew she loved him and so was thinking only of the practical arrangements: the campsite, the pitches, the food, the equipment. This is the big day. These are her duties. I hope they don't bring any basket cases, she called. Clive was already away downstream. He broke in and out of the swift flow. The merest hint of an eddy was refuge enough. He was so stable on the flood. He used so few paddle strokes, so little energy. Michela darted behind. She was aware that basket case was

I

his expression. She was aware of emulating his deft certainty in the strong water. It's not my element yet. Clive broke out again. His yellow boat slewed to stop with its prow in only a handkerchief of stillness behind the lure of something submerged. The river tugged by. Move off! she called. The current was faster. Make room! He shook his head. He was laughing. The eddy was too small for two. Meanie! Now she must take the rapids first.

Suddenly alone, the river's horizon comes to meet you. There's a certain glassiness to it and as the roar swells the water grows more compact, it pulls more earnestly. The mountains around and above are quite still. Already you are past the point of no return. You must choose your spot. Michela knows the right place, slightly left of centre. But just before the plunge, she sees it has changed in their week away. The river is constantly changing. A rock has gone under. A heavy log is caught in the larger boil of the stopper. Perhaps still in the spell of last week's drama, or half focused on the group that will arrive this evening, she tries at the last second to change her line. She isn't used to leading. It's a mistake. The surface is already curving down. The pull is fierce. She throws in a sharp paddle stroke on the right to avoid the log, tries to straighten on the left. But already she's in the quick of it. Not quite in line with the current, the kayak is sucked abruptly back into the stopper, sideways to the flood.

For a second the young woman allows the elements to take over. A moment's inattention is more than enough. The water pounds on the spraydeck, forcing her head down into the rush. Her helmet bangs on the log. The red kayak spins on its axis. Her face is under now, in the foam. Again the helmet grates. But Michela is calm and lucid. She is always calm when it actually happens, when she's gone below and the world is blurred and swirling dark. She has her paddle gripped tight. As the stopper spins her up, head downstream, she leans out across the water to block the rotation, the bottom of the boat exposed now in the drumming cascade of the fall. At once she's steady, held in the churn of the stopper, but with her face just above water, her arms reaching to scull for support on the troubled surface. The log bangs and bangs on the hull. She's stuck.

There's someone shouting now, but the roar of the rapid is too loud. She glances up. Clive is already there in the eddy she was headed for. He's watching her. He beckons. He's so near. Slide out this way! Her boat is pointing towards him. Beyond its prow the stopper runs on for a couple of yards or so, a line of transparent water pouring over a ledge of rock to spin white beneath the surface. Every piece of flotsam dragged down the river is held there, for hours, perhaps for weeks, turned and turned in this liquid trap. The water flows on, but not the driftwood. Or the coke cans. Or even a dead rat, or sheep. Michela is caught. It's all she can do to keep her head above water.

Just beyond the stopper is the complete stillness of the eddy where she should be, sheltered by a spur of rock. Clive is grinning, beckoning, motioning to show how she can use the paddle to edge along the line of foam. She knows that of course. In theory. But in this position she can't get the boat to move. It won't budge. The underside grinds against the rock and the log. The water drums. And she can't hear Clive's voice either, if only because her right ear is actually in the icy water. The river is snowmelt. I must be strong, she thinks. But now she sees he's about to toss a line. He's passed it round a sapling on the bank and is waiting for her to understand. The throw-bag falls exactly over her arms. She grasps the line quickly with her left, twists it round a wrist, almost loses her precarious balance, then has it passed round the paddle and is gripping tight. Cautiously, Clive starts to tug. He seems to be savouring the resistance of the stopper, balancing the two pulls exactly, the water, the rope. Inch by inch, the boat slides along the ledge of the fall, approaching the eddy. Then it rocks free so suddenly that the girl capsizes and has to swing the paddle wide to roll up, drenched.

Idiot! Clive laughs.

All at once Michela can hear again. The world is calm and still and warm, unusually warm for the mountains. There are flies and river-bank smells. Only a couple of yards away, the roar of the crashing water seems remote and unimportant.

You should see your face, he says.

If you'd led the way, it wouldn't have happened.

You can't always be following me. Actually, you did brilliantly. He's smiling at her, water glinting on his thick beard, his eyes narrow against the sun. It's not easy to come out of a spin. Most people would have pulled the deck and swum.

Why didn't you leave the eddy to me?

There was room for three!

There was not!

You didn't try.

She would have liked to kiss him now, he was so steady with his wet beard, glinting eyes, thick forearms, but Clive is already shifting his boat round hers to move into the stream. By the way, he asked, how do you say eddy in Italian?

I told you, no one speaks Italian in this part of Italy.

I just want to know, so I can sound knowledgeable if people ask.

La morta, she said. You say *entrare in morta*.

With one stroke he was in the stopper. A simple move

4

of the hips lifted the underside of the boat to meet the falling water pouring over the ledge. At once the hull locked in, trapped in the tension between fall and reflux. Now he was in the same position she had been, though facing the other way. It looked easy. With long strokes that seemed to caress the surface of the water downstream of the boat, he moved slowly to the other side and popped out. He motioned for her to try. Michela shook her head and pulled into the flow below the fall. Evidently they would have to start the weaker paddlers further down.

The group arrived towards eight. They had driven all the way from England. Michela was waiting at the gate. Michela loves English people. Michela loves all things English and despite having lived only six months in the country Michela speaks and writes a near-perfect English. The fact that it isn't perfect is a torment to her. You have no accent, Clive explains: To be perfect, people would have to know where in England you come from. Michela comes from Brescia. She doesn't want Clive to learn Italian. It won't be necessary. Not in the South Tyrol. Her destiny is England and English. She feels this deeply. To become truly strong, she must leave Italy. They are only here because English people like to go abroad for their holidays, because the South Tyrol is so unspoiled and beautiful. Is there anywhere unspoiled in Europe aside from the Alps? They are only here for the summers. Then they'll go back to England. I don't like to speak Italian, she told him. I hate my mother tongue. I hate this country. Clive was thinking about other things. When not on the water, he is troubled, concerned. He is checking a kit bag, or looking through paperwork. Michela likes the impression he gives of always thinking, always foreseeing and forestalling some accident. It's an important moment in their lives. This is the

first group they have brought here. They have made an investment.

Weren't there supposed to be thirteen of you? The van
bounces on the rutted track turning into the campsite. It's a
dirty white. The driver hits the horn in celebration. Am I
driving carefully? asks a sticker on the back. There's a phone
number and the name of a county council. The trailer with
all the camping equipment and a couple of personalised kayaks
bumps and trundles behind. Then people are spilling onto the
grass, shouting, laughing, shaking hands. Mandy, Keith, Adam.
Who's got the bloody trailer key? Who's got the duty list?
Sugar! A tall chinless man in early middle age is trying to
make a call from his mobile. At once Michela is excited, but
anxious. The English are never quite the English she would
like them to be, the English as she thinks of them when they
are not there. One of the men is decidedly paunchy. It's their
language she loves. Mandy too turns out to be robust and
squat. They are shaking hands. Miserable crick in the neck!
the older woman complains. She wears a shabby smock and
clutches a digital camera. The boy who runs into her is in
his gormless early teens. Clot! Mandy tells him abruptly. Her
accent is unmistakably South London. You're on the cooking
tent, Adam. Water canisters, please! Out of the e-mail and into
the wetsuit, laughs the fatter, older man. I'm Keith. He grasps
Michela's hand with both of his. His eyes are glassy and jolly.
Mandy takes a photo. One for the website. Weren't there
supposed to be thirteen of you? The girl asks again. Two
coming separately, Keith explains. Already on holiday somewhere down south. Lucky sods.

The campsite is a cosmopolitan patchwork. The van moves
slowly through a chequer of tents and chalets, the clutter of
washing lines, cooking equipment, loud cries in Dutch, in
Spanish, of children playing ball. Three grim teenagers are

6

sitting around African drums, transmitting a nervous rhythm to the twilight. Suddenly the forests above are black, the mountains stark. We've got the pitches nearest the river, Michela explains. Furthest from the loos, a spindly girl moans.

Speech! Keith announces as soon as the van has stopped. Men and women, kids and kayakers, lend me your lobes! So here we are in Wopland at last. Okay, it's been a long journey, I know, we've had a couple of sense-of-humour break-downs, it's only natch, but what we need now is maximum co-op-er-ay-shun! It's nearly dark. We're going to have to move fast. From this moment on nobody thinks of them-selves until the kitchen tent is up, the van unpacked, the water canisters filled and supper under way. Is that clear? We before me, okay? Thine before mine. Then you can put up your own tents and get yourselves sorted. Remember: this is not, repeat *not* a holiday; it's a *community experience*, right! As soon as we're all done and we've eaten we'll have the evening meeting and plan out tomorrow's activities. Oh, and don't forget to prepare your nominations for Wally of the Day!

As he finished speaking – and an Indian boy was already on top of the van furiously undoing tie-ropes – Michela saw Clive emerge from their chalet. His face more than ever expressed a contained, manly perplexity, a faint smile at the corner of the bearded mouth. Long time no see, he said, shaking hands with his old teacher. Wonderful place you found for us, Keith enthused. As the last light shrank behind the peaks, the valley was suddenly chill. How's the river? High, Clive said. The glaciers are melting. Mallet please! someone was shouting. Mall-et!

Sorry to be so silent, Vince told his daughter. Once again the autostrada had come to a standstill. These are his first words of the drive. The air-conditioning hummed. The girl was changing CDs. Head down, lips pursed she looked at him sidelong, half smiled. What's there to say? she asked. He felt ashamed. You've put up with Florence, he said. Now you get your fun, see some friends. Louise laughed: I *liked* Florence!

Then the car was shaken with an urgent rhythm. May I? She turned it up even louder. He nodded. He hated the music. It was shameful that he had nothing to say to her. Nothing has been said about Gloria. His daughter was staring intently, tapping on her knees. The landscape trembled with heat. For at least a mile ahead the cars glittered stationary, as if a great river sweeping down from the Apennines had solidified in the summer haze. The planet is burning up, he thought. An asset long since amortised. He felt quite untouched, shivery.

Swaying her head, his daughter smiled, still with a faint hint of compassion. She is thinking of her mother, he decided. How can a holiday like this do anything but make us think of her? Yet it isn't really Gloria I am thinking of. He knew that. It was to do with Gloria, but it wasn't her. I don't *see* Gloria. He was suddenly anxious. I don't *hear* Gloria's voice when I remember the things she said. You think of nothing at all, he told himself. But so intensely. Life had not prepared him for this.

The pulse of the music became an obsessive repetition, a hectic running on the spot. The car throbbed. The song went on long beyond the point where you'd heard enough. The traffic stewed. Abruptly Louise turned the volume down: There is one thing though: if we're camping, how am I supposed to recharge my phone? Vince was gripping the steering wheel, willing the cars to move. Dad? Sorry, what was that? How am I supposed to recharge my phone? In what sense? We're camping, there won't be plugs.

8

He looked at her. No idea, he said. He managed a smile. Do without it for a week. Live free. Dad! She shook her head and turned up the volume again. Only now did he notice she was cradling her mobile in one hand, as if expecting some vital call. She has been fondling her mobile all week, he thought. I haven't even made fun of her. All at once the fierce drumming of the car stereo was challenged by the sound of a distant siren speeding along the emergency lane. Somebody has died, he decided. Someone won't be going home.

Michela felt keenly how different tonight's meeting was. Still, she had no presentiment of what was about to happen. Last week she and Clive had slept in the squalor of a *centro sociale* in Milan; more than two hundred people were spread across the floor of an abandoned warehouse. Many were smoking dope. There were angry speeches and chants, which she translated more or less for Clive. Sometimes someone stood up and spoke in English, or French, or German. They were speeches punctuated with slogans that everybody could repeat, whatever their language. Michela wasn't sure if she was enjoying it, but felt keenly that they were right to be here. They shared a cause. Everything precious was under threat. Some final barrier was about to come down, some crucial dam would burst releasing the final great wave of destruction. They must be strong to resist. They must protest. She joined in the chants. There were people of all colours and nations, mainly young, all scandalised. Our world is a scandal, somebody stood to say. Quite probably it will end in our lifetime.

Clive rolled his cigarettes. Despite the crowding, the intense heat, they had managed to make love every night, a slow, strong, silent love. We are two torrents flowing together in the dark, she whispered. During the meetings she sat between his legs. She had never felt more protected. Her man was solid, solemn. Free trade is just the free transfer of wealth from the poor to the rich, a young man explained. Loans are theft! It is criminal to ask for interest payments from the starving! It is lunatic to cut down the forests and burn more and more oil!

People clapped and cheered. Everywhere they went throughout the week they were met by the same impenetrable line of riot shields and truncheons. Police vans blocked the entrance to a square. Helmeted men with teargas launchers sprouted from hatches above. The heat was oppressive. Thirty-eight degrees. On the Thursday they tried to force the cordon round Palazzo Marino as President Bush arrived. They assumed it was President Bush. Usually so calm, Clive heaved wildly behind a thick Plexiglas screen they had made to push against the police. He was beside himself. *Issa!* the Italians shouted. Heave! *Issa! Issa!* Scores of photographers were crammed into a specially protected paddock. Heave!

The crowd surged. Some of the men had balaclavas, or motorcycle helmets. When the police counter-charged, two demonstrators were killed. That is: a barrier collapsed alongside the road and a dozen or so people were forced under the wheels of an oncoming tram. There was a chaos of sirens and scuffles. They had a policeman on the ground. That could easily have been us, Clive shouted. It could have been you! He was angry beyond anything she had seen before. They've fucked everything up, he kept repeating, everything. A rump re-formed across the street by La Scala. Multinational murderers! they chanted. No surrender!

For perhaps twenty minutes the situation was out of control. Michela felt proud of her man. We shall not be moved, he sang. She pulled him away from the truncheons. Dozens were being dragged to police vans. That evening the dormitory was alive with angry debate till three or four in the morning. Thunder rumbled across the city. A teenager with a guitar sang a song: You can't bomb your way to peace, Mr President. His amplifier was faulty. Clive bought some dope. To forget, he said. It was expensive in the strict economy of their lives. They still had equipment to purchase before heading back to the mountains. The jeep needed new tyres. Michela's mother had offered no help. They were poor and in debt. Michela stroked his high forehead, his straggly hair. I am living intensely, she told herself. Let me stroke you, she said as he lay on his back, smoking in the dark. His body was rigid. He is crying, she thought.

But this evening in the South Tyrol, Keith, the English group leader with the glassy eyes, the paunch, invited all the kayakers to say who they were and why they'd come on this trip and what they expected to get out of it. They were sitting in a circle on the hard dusty ground between pine trees and guy-ropes. Only one or two had seats. The others shifted on their hams. Starting on my left, Keith said. He was warm and avuncular. I know most of you know each other, but some don't. He had a fold-up canvas chair with wooden arms. Come on, don't be shy.

I'm Amelia. This was a wiry girl with bony white legs. I live just outside Maidenhead. The accent was moneyed. I did my three-star paddler with Waterworld last month. I love kayaking and can't wait to get some experience on white water. She seemed to have finished, then as if some explanation were required added. Oh, I'm fifteen. All right! someone cheered. Amelia forgot to say, Keith intervened, that she won the Girl Scouts Southern Counties Speed Kayaking competition last year. The girl looked at the ground. Aren't we modest, Mandy shouted. Then her camera flashed.

In a deadpan voice, rolling gum in her mouth, the fat, freckled girl beside Amelia said very quickly: Caroline, fifteen, from Gillingham, hoping to have a good holiday because I love the water and all.

Name's Phil, announced the gormless boy beside Caroline. His eyelids drooped. He too was chewing. Love playing on the water, like, but I've only done weirs n'all so I'm hoping I'll get on something well fast and dangerous. Never been to Italy before. I've done some surf, though. Like off Broadstairs. Wicked. That's it. In the sudden silence, everybody tittered. Phil seemed puzzled. He has a thick lower lip over a broad chin. Then he raised a fist and shouted: Chuck me in the rapids and I'll go for it! Again someone yelled, All-righty, sir! Respect! said Amelia solemnly.

Keith had to intervene: Fun aside, kids, this trip is not about playing. White water is serious. Okay Phil? The first skill we have to develop is looking out for each other. Making sure no one gets hurt. Too true, Mandy said. I want people constantly watching to see that someone else is not in trouble. Constantly, is that clear? You're always checking that everyone else is okay. That's how a group survives when things get dangerous. Never forget that your personal safety depends on other people looking out for you. We don't want to lose anyone.

It was dark now. A small gas lamp was hung on the lower branch of a pine. The next voice to speak came from a lean, chinless man in his late thirties. He was fingering a mobile. My name's Adam. As you probably all know, I'm a level-two instructor at Waterworld. I'm hoping to improve my skills here and move up to level three, though obviously my main job is to instruct those of you who haven't been on white water before. Anyway, I hope I'll be part of giving you all a good and useful time, so that you have something to take home with you. He turned the mobile round and round in his hand.

Thanks Adam.

Already a sort of embarrassed routine was creeping into these introductions, but Keith seemed to savour this, as if the very embarrassment had a social function. Mint anyone? offered the Indian boy. All the youngsters reached. I'm Mark, said one of them, sitting back. The voice was barely loud enough to be heard. Adam's me dad. There was a silence. You could say a bit more than that, suggested the father. I'm, like, seventeen, you know? And I've come to do my best. Is that all? Adam asked again. What am I supposed to say? the boy wanted to know. Even sitting, he was lanky and awkward. His long hair fell on his face. I'm here, like. He seemed belligerent. And I'll do my best. Oh, I love camping, he added.

Tom? Keith put in quickly.

Yes, I'm Tom. I'm twenty-one. This voice was deeper, the face immediately handsome in the dim light. Every feature was even and warm and strongly moulded, the teeth sharp and white, the hair polished, eyes bright. I study at the LSE. Haven't had a paddle in my hands for a few years now, but some other folks let me down for the holiday we were going to take, so at the last minute I signed up for this. Now I'm here I can't wait to get on the water.

Tom didn't say, but he rows for his university, Keith announced.

You all know me, Mandy said. She was opposite Keith. They exchanged glances. This must be the twentieth trip I've been on, and I'm telling you, after you've done all the admin you feel you deserve to be here. I'm the first-aid person and the menu planner, so any complaints, cuts or bruises or special requests this way. I'm also the trip photographer. She held up the camera, pointed it Keith's way, and set off the flash. So if you have to do anything idiotic, do it in front of me so you can look stupid on the website. And here's hoping this trip will be as exciting as all the others.

Three boys spoke now in quick succession. I'm Maximilian, but you're allowed to call me Max. Come to develop my skills and have a shot at my four-star and it's not true I'll be trying to avoid the washing-up. Oddly, this boy was wearing a proper shirt. Emerald green. And proper grey flannel trousers. He sat on his own camp stool. If anybody's heard snoring, folks, it's not me!

No one laughed.

I'm Brian. Same as Max really. Oh, I'm sixteen. So's Max. Come for the obvious reasons: drink, drugs, sex and underwater swimming. The boy stopped and blushed.

Be just like being at home then, Keith said generously.

Sex! Gormless Phil sniggered. Our Brian, sex!

Quiet kids, Adam protested.

I'm Amal. The Indian's voice was embarrassingly high-pitched. I love Waterworld. It's like a family for me. I'm seventeen. I've done plenty of white water in an open canoe – I did the Canadian trip – but this is my first time in a kayak. I'm sure it'll be a doddle.

Bloody open-canoeists, Max said.

Then in the straining light with the sound of low drums still beating in the fresh alpine air and the moths circling the gas lamp, attention shifted to Michela. There was a short pause; it was the first time perhaps that people had had a chance to see what a beautiful creature she is. Her black hair is cropped tight around a white, perfect oval face where the eyes are steady and dark. I'm Michela, but please call me Micky. Me and Clive here have been setting up this trip for you. We've scouted the rivers which are not traditionally much used for kayaking, so we won't have any problems with traffic. We've sorted out what level is what and who can go where. Or Clive has. He's also selected and bought fifteen good Pyranhas and all the equipment, so this is quite a big moment for us. I've mainly been doing things like booking the campsite, accounts, paperwork and so on. We really care about your having a good experience in a beautiful environment, leaving it as you found it and hoping it will change you for the better.

She stopped. Hear, hear! Keith said. You English? Caroline asked. The fat girl was squatting on her haunches, elbows on her thick knees, chin on hands, chewing. Michela hesitated: I'm Italian, she said, and turning quickly to Clive she asked him what he wanted to add.

As the others also turn, they find themselves looking at a powerful man with a thick beard and broad forehead. I was one of Keith's first pupils years back, he says. His thinning blonde hair is shoulder-length. And I survived to tell the tale. Somebody titters. Clive sits cross-legged, hands forward as if warming himself at a trekker's fire. I've always thought kayaking was more than a sport. I mean, more than playing squash or tennis or something. It teaches you to respect nature, to read it carefully and understand it. One day your life may depend on how well you read the river. Then, when you spend time by the river and on the river, you can't help but understand how dull and squalid a lot of so-called civilised life is. That's why Michela and I have been trying to make it our job to get people involved. He paused.

Anything else? Keith asked. Want to give us some kind of idea about what we'll be doing?

Clive still hesitated. It was the first time Michela had seen him address a group. She couldn't imagine he was nervous. The river Aurino, Clive said, or Ahrn as the Germans call it, rises in the glacier above Sand in Taufers. He gestured with a thumb up the dark valley. On the Austrian border, more or less, about twenty miles away. It's what the Italians call a *torrente*, rather than a river. Until Taufers it's fast and wild. There's a stretch there we might try on the last day, with those of you who are up to it, that is. But I'm warning you, you'll have to convince me and Keith that you really are up to it. The water is powerful and there's no space to breathe. Either you make the eddies and break out perfectly or you'll be carried straight down the river and trashed on the rocks. Anyway, we'll start by working the stretches downstream of Taufers. Plenty of interesting rapids, but usually a good space to roll up and generally relax afterwards if you've got the worst of it. Further down, between Bruneck and Brixen, there are stretches where you'll have to deal with a lot of volume. One day we'll have a go on a slalom course on the river Eisack, north of Brixen. That'll be a bit of a drive.

Any waves? Maximilian asked. He has a public-school voice. Stoppers? Phil wanted to know. Holes? So far they had only heard tell of holes.

Plenty of everything, Clive promised. But actually, what I really wanted to say was . . . You see, last week, Michela and I were at the anti-globalisation demonstration in Milan, you probably heard about it, where two people were killed. I don't know, maybe we're still a bit upset. Anyway, I'd like you to know that we feel the work we're trying to do here is part of the same campaign. You know – to help people respect the world before it's too late.

Yes, that's an interesting thought, Keith said. There was a

pause. Adam said: Actually I'm not sure I can go along with that. My own impression is . . .

Okay, okay, Keith intervened. No politics, not on the first night. We're here to help each other and learn about the water. Now, let's have the Wally of the Day nomination before we break up.

It seemed every evening – Michela could never have imagined this side to Englishness – that a small furry toy of vaguely teddy-bear shape called Wally was to be hung around the neck of whoever had done something particularly stupid during the day. The culprit would then have to perform some demeaning act, after which he or she must keep Wally about him until the following evening and be constantly ready to show it on request. Failure to show Wally at any time, even in the kayak, would lead to further humiliations.

Who gets today's Wally award?

Mandy nominated Keith himself for the incredible cock-up he had made reading the map outside Mainz, as a result of which they had gone west instead of east and arrived two hours late. Maximilian proposed Adam for having tied the kit on the roof so badly. A suitcase had slipped onto the windscreen just before Munich. It wasn't me, Adam quickly explained. It was too, Dad! protested the boy beside him. Yes it was! said Caroline. From a strictly legal point of view, Maximilian said, your name was on the duty sheet, Adam, so it was your responsibility. Oh shut up. The instructor was irritated. But the majority voted Keith. Punishment: a performance – Mandy proposed – of Ken Charles, Outdoor Activity Director for Kent County Council, giving his famous awards speech. Keith jumped to his feet. His glassy eyes shone. He is overweight, his cheeks round and red as a child's. He fixed Wally sideways under his chin like a bow-tie and ruffled up his hair. Ladies and gentlemen, he began, in a pompous bass, strutting back and forth. Everybody cheered. If you had but the teeniest inkling of what your dear offspring have achieved at Waterworld this week, you would be agog with wonder. Drinks! Max jumped up to shout. Everybody to the bar for drinks before it closes. Alrighty, sir! Phil was on his feet. No alcoholic beverages for the under-sixteens, Mandy ordered. Is that clear. I promised your parents.

The group moved quickly off through tents and caravans to where there was still music coming from the top of the campsite. Karaoke perhaps. Michela and Clive went with them. Then, towards midnight, in one of the site's chalets where they had lived for some three months now, Clive watched his girlfriend climb into their bed. He was seventeen years older than her. Aren't you coming? she asked. He kept pottering with bits of equipment. There was a spraydeck to mend, a repair kit to sort out. She waited. He was smoking more than he usually did. The room was rough wood with only the barest necessities. They had to share the outdoor bathrooms with the rest of the site. What's wrong? she asked. You just sleep, he told her. Then he said: What a prick that guy Adam is! Can you believe we're going to have to spend the week with a chinless wonder like that. What's wrong? she repeated softly. You can just see he's a prick, Clive insisted. A tight-arsed prick. Bet he's an estate agent or something.

Michela waited. Clive continued to potter about the room. Now he was sorting out clothes. This isn't the right world, Micky, he eventually told her. Not for us. He had found his sleeping bag in the big cupboard. Be strong, he said. Squatting, he unrolled it on the floor. She sat on the bed and stared. They had been lovers for two years. What are you doing? she demanded. I've been thinking about it a lot, he said. His voice was low and tired. We can't sleep together anymore.

She sat still. He was fiddling with the zip on the bag. Bastard thing! It had snagged. He wouldn't look up. What did I do? she asked. Her voice quavered. What's happening? Clive wouldn't speak. He had coaxed the zip past its snag. Slowly, as if he were squeezing into a new kayak, he sat down on the floor and put one leg after another into the sleeping bag. You hit the light, he said. The switch was just above the bedside table. Michela threw back the bedclothes and stood to grab a dressing gown hanging from the door. She pulled the waistband tight. What 'ave I done? There was an edge of disbelief in her voice. She felt sick. What in the name of God 'ave I done? She was standing over him. He lay face up, but his eyes were fixed on the ceiling. Nothing, he said. It's me. You haven't done anything. Look, don't worry, Micky. Everything will be just the same, the kayaking and the camp and the money and so on. But this isn't the world for us.

Don't slam the door! Vince stopped the car. It would wake people, he said. The need to respect others seemed to have snapped the driver out of his unhappy reverie. He let the car roll along the dirt track, passenger door still open. Louise trotted beside, making little forays among the pitches to check the vans for the Waterworld logo. It was almost two a.m. The autostrada had been jammed for hours. The sleeping campsite was illuminated only by the neon glow from the bathroom block. Everything was tied down and zipped up. Where are they? Louise rushed off between two tents again. Sweeping slowly round the corner at the bottom of the site, the car's headlights picked out a slim figure in silhouette sitting beneath a pine, back bent, face in hands. Vince touched the brake and the passenger door swung forward.

If he leaned back a little, he saw a head of dark hair framed against bushes. *Mi scusi*, he began. Dad! Louise came running, then tripped and fell heavily. Vince climbed out. Don't yell! They're over there! The girl was dusting herself off.

Are you looking for the English kayak group? The seated figure had got to her feet now. A young woman offered a wan smile of welcome. I'll show you to your pitch.

Vince parked beside a screen of trees that sloped steeply down to darkness. The night was quiet, but you had a distinct impression of the proximity of moving water, of a strong pull beneath the stillness of the branches. They haven't left you much room, Michela apologised. Heaving out their camping stuff, Louise tripped again. A torch shone out through orange nylon beside them: If this tent collapses, a posh voice announced, you'll hear from my lawyer!

Vince was surprised that the young woman appeared to be staying to help. You weren't waiting up for us, I hope? he said in a whisper. But Louise had the giggles now, trying to sort out tangled guy-ropes. Maximilian, or perhaps it was Brian, was making an obscene shadow play with torch and fingers on the tent wall.

Kids! Don't wake everyone up, Vince hissed.

I'm Michela, the woman said. I'm responsible for arranging things this end. But please call me Micky.

Oh come on Dad! Louise was laughing helplessly. We're on holiday! The girl's solid body had turned to jelly. We're supposed to be having fun. She laughed madly.

Michela took the guy-ropes from the younger girl's hand and untangled them. She seemed to know exactly how their tent was to be put up. The ground's too hard to push the pegs in with your foot, she warned. Go to the kitchen tent, there's a mallet just inside on the left.

The kitchen tent was a big, hut-shaped canvas structure open at both ends. Inside, between a dozen cardboard boxes with provisions, Vince's torch flashed over two figures asleep on the floor, in separate bags but face to face. Vaguely, he took in the sharp fine features of the one girl, the dull heavy jowl of the other. When he returned, Michela already had the tent up. Louise was complaining she had put the door at the wrong end. Don't look, Dad, she said some time later when they were undressing. It was cramped inside. They were lying on their backs, barely a foot apart. What? Don't look! Of course, sorry. That Max is so stupid, Louise complained. She huffed and puffed, turning this way and that for a comfortable position. Vince lay still.

Half an hour later he had to get up to pee. This was what he always hated about camping. Two zips to undo, shoes to find, struggling to your feet in damp grass to pick through the guy-ropes. Gloria loved it, he remembered. I always refused. In Florence, he had taken Louise to an air-conditioned, four-star hotel. The weather had been torrid. Here instead the night was chill and smelt strongly of pine resin; the sky was solemn with stars. But he didn't raise his head. As he arrived at the bathrooms, the urinals all flushed of their own accord under ghostly neon. I hate campsites, he thought. Why had he come?

Then walking back – it must be three a.m. at least – he saw that the young woman was still sitting where they had found her earlier. He hesitated. He had forgotten her name. She was hunched among the pine roots, face in hands. Somewhere nearby a clock chimed. Perhaps she was expecting another late arrival. There was a church tower just outside the entrance to the site. What if I'm not up to it, Vince worried, crawling back into his sleeping bag. He was a weak kayaker. Before the most ordinary outing he felt a shiver of fear. Maybe that was why he had come.

Then four hours later everybody was woken by a wild clanging of bells. For this is how the day always begins in Sand in Taufers. Christ Almighty, Louise yelled.

A WAVE

The first thing is padding up. Michela stands beside Clive while he gives his little lesson. The course that they have been advertising in canoe clubs all over England is called An Introduction to White Water: Five Days in the South Tyrol. A year ago, Vince Marshall would never have dreamed of coming.

You have to be tight in the cockpit. Okay? This isn't the Thames Estuary. Tight tight tight. The perfect fit.

Like sex? ventures a voice. Brian has a fuzz of red hair, a small snubbed nose, droll expression.

Actually no, not like sex at all, says Clive patiently. He is wearing a khaki cap. The girls are giggling. As somebody might know, if he had a minimum of experience.

Cru-el!

With sex, Clive continues in his measured sensible voice, two entities move constantly in relation to each other, *n'est-ce pas*?

Two what? Phil demands.

Michela's hand is just touching Clive's as he speaks. Vince, who hadn't been paying attention, is suddenly caught by this. He stares.

There is a certain amount of lubricant, Clive insists, with only a faint smile beneath his beard. Of give.

I do beg your pardon, Mr Riley, but what time of day is it? Mandy asks.

Two what! Phil whispers to Amal now.

Whereas if you're properly padded up in your kayak, kids, there should be *absolutely no movement at all*. Got that. None. You and the boat move welded together in the water.

May I venture to say, then – Max's facetious voice pipes up – that this is more like the male member's relationship with a condom.

Oh do shut up! Adam complains.

Only hazarding an ay-nalogy, smirks Max.

Anal? Phil demands.

I said, shut up! Adam insists. Let's remember some basic rules of decency.

Well, the condom would certainly be a more accurate description, Clive acknowledges wryly.

Let's just get on with it, can we? Adam is a scout leader. His son is watching him.

My sentiments entirely, says Amelia. For a second she keeps a straight face. She has pretty freckles round a prim nose, long straight black hair. Then all the adolescents burst out laughing. Even the fat Caroline. Even the older Tom.

Oh, I'm going to pee myself, Louise gasps. Vince now notices that his daughter has the top of her wrist pressed into her mouth.

Kids! Keith steps in. Kids, concentrate! If someone wants their four-star paddler this week they'll have to do more than crack jokes.

Wally! Phil shouts. Where's Wally!

Keith is aghast. Oh no! Eternal damnation! Then the older

man reaches into his open shirt and conjures the little effigy from his armpit. Fooled you!

Clive invites Michela to sit in a boat on the grass at his feet. They have lifted one of the Pyranhas down from the trailer beside the chalet. She's wearing jeans. She unlaces her trainers, puts a hand each side of the cockpit and slips in. The boat is a bright new blue. They have bought them with a loan. Clive squats down beside her. His beard, just greying from red, is close to her cheek. His blonde hair flows out of his cap in the manner of the American pioneer.

How are the feet?

Loose.

The footrests – gather round, kids – have to be so tight that the upper part of the thigh is jammed, I repeat, jammed under the cockpit here.

Clive puts a strong hand on her knee and pushes it laterally, then waggles it hard back and forth.

Too much give. See?

Michela shoots a glance at him.

They are a couple, Vince tells himself. He can't concentrate.

Michela gets out and Clive shows the others how to adjust the footrests. The trick is, set it so it's as snug as can be, right, then tighten up one more notch. Okay? Tight as possible. And then *again* one more. That's the secret. If it's not uncomfortable, it's not right. It has to hurt. At least at first.

Michela gets in the boat again. They are in the small clearing in front of the kitchen tent. Now she has trouble forcing her knees under the cockpit edges. She wriggles, smiles, grimaces, eyes closed, eyebrows lifted. Youch! It is another expression she learned from Clive.

If condoms hurt that much, a voice mutters, I'll do without.

Adam twists his head. He seems to be appealing to Keith to put a lid on this.

Brian's freckled face assumes a saintly glow.

I believe that's why the Pope is so against them, Max remarks boldly. The boy is wearing a broad-brimmed straw hat, as if at some public-school picnic.

Rock the boat, Micky, Clive is saying. Please, watch carefully everybody. Rock it from side to side.

Sitting upright, Michela leans to the right. She wears a white T-shirt that leaves a hand's-breadth of stomach visible. Vince looks away. Above the tents and the coloured clutter of the campsite, he lifts his eyes to climb solid slopes rising steeply through gleaming meadow and dark pine to shreds of bright cloud that drift among barren walls of rock. The instructor's voice fades. Then, further above, even in this month of August, Vince sees patches of snow shining distantly to cap dizzying cliffs of dark stone, gritty corrugated peaks. He breathes deeply. You're on holiday, he tells himself. To the north a tiny cable car crawls up the gigantic back of the mountain.

See how the body moved first, Clive explains, *before* the boat? Did you see that? All at once the voice is louder and insistent. Did you? Vince turns and finds Clive's eye on him.

It is absolutely essential that you take this on board.

Michela shifts her hips, raises a knee, so that the rounded hull of the kayak gradually tips while her torso remains upright. Clive thrusts a hand between the girl's thigh and the edge of the boat. That's the space we've got to pad out and eliminate. Okay? Any give between you and the cockpit, and the sheer fact is, as soon as you're in serious water you're going to be trashed. Which means of course that someone else is going to have to take time out to rescue you. Most of all, remember – now he raises his voice –

26

please, all remember: to do an Eskimo roll successfully in white water, you and the boat have to be one thing, moulded together. Okay? The boat *is* your arse.

Oh me dearie! Max exclaims, tugging on the brim of his hat.

Clive upturns a big cardboard box full of black poly-styrene blocks in plastic wrapping. Everybody was to pair up, get the boats off the trailer, set footrests, then help their partners to pad up, cutting the blocks to the right width.

You can use an ordinary knife for that. There are tubes of glue when you're sure you've got it right. Oh, and do it in your swimming kits everybody. Make it tight. That way it'll be even tighter when you've got your wetsuits on. I want you to feel like you're in a vice.

Vice is nice! Brian immediately joked. Nobody laughs. There is a general sense of anxiety. It's time to choose boats.

Louise was already paired off elsewhere. Vince saw Caroline grab her friend Amelia. Adam was giving his son useful instructions.

Us oldies should stick together, Mandy said, taking Vince's arm. Keith's brought his own boat, she explained. A mauve costume clung to her shapeless body. She has a round face, short hair dyed coal-black and carelessly cut. The two joined the bustle by the trailer. As they lifted a boat down, Vince was aware of being physically weaker than he would have wanted. Mandy sat in the kayak on the ground. They worked at the blocks of padding. I'm such a fat old sow, she was saying. She had strong wrists and forearms. And she said: Oh by the way, Adam told me about your wife. I'm so sorry.

Thanks, Vince acknowledged.

How has the girl taken it? she asked.

He pressed the foam block between her thigh and the

27

boat. She pulled a face. For all its rotundity, her flesh was solid. I really wouldn't know, he said.

Yaiiii! Towards ten-thirty a scream exploded on the water. Even before Amelia had her spraydeck on, Keith thrust her boat off the bank from behind and Clive, standing in four feet of still water, spun her upside down.

The first thing, kids – Keith now shoved Max off before the boy could grasp what was happening – the first thing, once you've got yourselves as tight as can be in your boats – I hope your ankles are killing you – is to make bloody sure you can get out of them in an emergency. Right, Phil? Another boat splashed in. Clive promptly capsized it.

From the dark water a red helmet popped up. Yaiii!!! Amelia shrieked. It's frigging freezing! It's ice!

You forgot your three slaps on the hull, Keith told her. Nobody comes out of the boat without banging three times on the hull. Otherwise how is a rescuer supposed to know that you're not still planning to roll up.

Then it was Vince's turn. The boat slid off the grassy bank and out across the water. It was a quiet spot downstream from the campsite where the river spread out in a slow curve across flat pastureland before taking the next dive. The nose of the kayak hit the water. Even before Clive could grab it, Vince leaned over and capsized. The shock of the cold water on his face was extraordinary. He was suddenly wide awake, forced into presence. Because he had secured the spraydeck and was watertight, he waited a moment, hanging upside down in the cockpit, to feel the full effect of the river's chill on face and hands. The water was unusually bright and clear after the estuary. He could see his fingers, even the pale gold of his wedding ring, as if in a swimming pool. Okay. He slapped three times without urgency on the sides of the boat, then reached for the tab on the elastic deck. The tab wasn't there. Why not? His hands felt rapidly round the rim of the cockpit. Everything was perfectly visible. The black deck, the blue boat. But he had secured the stretch-rubber top with the release tab tucked inside. In two years of kayaking he had never made this most elementary of mistakes.

Now he banged again on the hull. Another boat must have followed him. Clive was turning it over. He sensed noise and laughter and people scrambling out of the water. He was underneath, unseen, shut away. If he'd come in with his paddle he could have rolled up. But he hasn't. People can't hear, they can't see. I could die, he suddenly thought. He started to claw with his fingers, trying to pull the elastic from the cockpit rim to expose the tab and pull the deck. Nothing. Did they imagine he was showing off staying under so long? He put both hands on the cockpit, tried to pull his knees to his chest to force the deck off. It wouldn't pop. They are made not to pop. It is new and stiff and tight. Then he threw himself violently from side to side, twisting his head for air, shouting into the water, banging on the side of the boat. There was splashing all around. Firm hands grasped him and turned the boat. As he came up, blue-faced, he was looking straight into Adam's grey eyes. The man was shaking his head like some disappointed schoolmaster.

Wally! his daughter yelled. Dad's going to be Wally tonight!

What a fool! Vince shouted. He was furious. I'm such a fool! Damn and damn. He was taken aback by the violence of his own reaction. The youngsters were watching him. Respect, someone said.

Holding his boat on the other side, Michela said quietly,

Better in fun than when it's for real. This was another thing that came from Clive.

The sun was hot, as it had been all summer. They used the slack of the meander to get used to the boats and paddles. Clive had bought good paddles of a new nylon material, light and fast. Altogether it was a big investment. The instructors checked that everybody could roll. Capsize, kids. Go for it. Only Tom had difficulty. It was strange that such a strong, apparently expert boy should be the one to fail. In his eagerness to breathe, he tried to bring his head up too soon. Your head is the last part to come up, Keith repeated. But everybody knows this. Amelia and Louise stationed their boats beside his and gave advice. Tom is so handsome, a slim, straight, powerful young man with a good jaw, deep eyes. He tried again. His head struggled out of the water too soon and sank back. Amelia prodded her boat against the red hull. Tom felt for the bow and pulled himself upright holding that. His strong torso came up, dripping water, his fine face clouded with annoyance. Don't worry, Louise chirped. It took me ages.

Meantime the younger boys were turning their boats over and over in every possible way. Phil capsized, passed his paddle from one hand to the other over the bottom of the boat, head under water, then rolled up. All the time he was chewing gum. Can you do a helicopter roll, Bri? A reverse screw roll? Mark, Adam's quiet son, seemed particularly expert. Look at this one, Dad. He rolled up with the paddle behind his head. Adam watched. Anyone can do that kind of thing in calm water, he said soberly. In calm water anyone can be an expert. Amelia knew how to roll her boat with just her hands, no paddle. You sort of sway your body, like, from one side right to the other, she explained to Vince. He shook his head. It seemed impossible. I don't panic, Tom repeated to Keith. Really I don't.

I used to be able to do it. Swimming away from his boat, his young manliness seemed to be deserting him.

The kayaks spread out across the meander, tipping over and popping up.

What about the other side, Clive approached Vince.

Sorry?

Can you roll the other way round, with your paddle on the other side?

Never tried. As soon as Vince was alone, his mind lapsed back, not so much into thought, but a sort of intense, wordless inner paralysis. There are moments, Clive explained, in white water when it's only possible to come up on one side of the boat, because of the current, or you're stuck against a rock maybe. Vince tried it. He tipped over. Under water, instead of thrusting the right hand forward and across to his left side he did the reverse. His paddle felt for the surface. He pushed the arms far up and away towards a glow of daylight. It is strange how different it feels making a movement you know well, but with the other side of the body. He is disorientated. Like writing with the left hand. Or walking arm in arm with someone you're not used to. Concentrating, upside down in the glacier-fed water, he pulled the left arm through a wide arc and leaned his head back. To his surprise the boat turned, his body came up. For a moment it stopped, it seemed he might fall back. Vince thrashed with his paddle and suddenly he was upright. He felt proud. He had done the right thing to come on this holiday. Clive was sceptical. See if you can do that in turbulence, he said.

They picnicked. On the bank people peeled off closed smock jackets with tightly sealing rubber cuffs and necks. Everybody has strips of neoprene hanging off them, or wet T-shirts, or towels round their necks. It is uncomfortable. At the back of the Kent County Council van where the sandwiches have been stored, Vince found himself beside Michela. There are cheese sandwiches and crisps and melting chocolate, bottles of water. To his surprise, the Italian girl came to sit beside him on the grass. She had pulled down the top of her wetsuit so that the shoulder-straps hung round her thighs. Vince felt vaguely embarrassed by the thought that his daughter would see them sitting together. But this was ridiculous because now all the adults came to eat in one group, the adolescents in another. Your daughter is relieved to be out of your company, he thought. I am relieved too. They would never live together again.

Clive said how hard it was to predict river levels with this global warming. The glaciers retreated each year. The hot weather came too soon. This summer more than ever. The full melt was on you before you expected it. By now they were paddling on the snows of centuries back, the blizzards of the Middle Ages. There were more thunderstorms, perhaps, but less of the same steady release of the winter's snow. The river could be bony or even dry before you knew it. It's amazing they do nothing about the greenhouse effect, he went on. What was the temperature in Milan during the demonstration the other day? Thirty-six degrees? Thirty-eight? No wonder people went crazy.

He was sitting on a rock beside Michela. She leaned her back against him. I can't believe, he insisted, how enthusiastic they are when car sales are up. Keith nodded, eating. The world cooks and dries up and they worry about car sales! There was a silence. Mandy was rubbing sun cream into her shoulders. I should take a picture, she said. You wonder, Clive went on, if they will ever really open their eyes before something major simply forces them to.

Like what, Adam asked coolly.

A drought, Michela said at once. A flood.

Well, which? He had a wry smile.

Vince was not following. His eye had again been drawn upward to the hugeness of the mountains above them. The majesty of the place was crushing. It appeased some obscure desire in him. At the same time he was intensely aware of the young woman, of the fact that her belligerence now, saying something about multinationals, was to do with her being together with this bearded instructor, this strong capable man. Suddenly, he was stumbling to his feet.

We've bored Vince to death, Keith said.

Hearing his name, he managed to turn. He shook his head. Not at all. He tried to smile. Just need to cool my feet in the water. He had kept his wetsuit on.

The climate changes anyhow, Adam was saying. This whole thing is being exploited by people who have an axe to grind and time on their hands.

Vince sat on the upturned hull of his boat with his feet in the water. It seemed impossible that he would get through these days and months without asking someone for help. He watched the youngsters throwing themselves in the water. You hold an important position, he reminded himself. In a major organisation. For some reason he had a recurrent image of a needle penetrating the skin between his fingers. It would bring relief. It would dissolve the pressure in his mind. Then Tom insisted on swimming right across to the opposite bank. He was a strong swimmer. He had been the weakest in this morning's rolling lesson. Louise, Brian, Amelia and Caroline were trying to follow.

Your buoyancy aids! Keith arrived at a run. He was yelling. No one in the water without buoyancy aids! The swimmers protested. We must keep an eye on them, the group leader told Vince. There was a hint of reproach. Out! He raised his voice. It's a question of insurance. There are rapids round that bend.

But we're here, Amelia complained. You can't accuse us of being round the bend!

Caroline wallowed beside her. Respect, she said.

Out of the water at once, Keith insisted.

Wally! Show Wally!

I'll show Wally when you get out.

Only as they came out on the mud did Vince realise that one of the boys had a club foot. The red-haired lad with the sly face. He had trouble getting to his feet. It was a serious malformation. I've forgotten their names, Vince told himself. He breathed deeply.

Crazy as it may sound, we now paddle upstream, Clive told them. Remember, no one said this was a holiday. In about quarter of a mile, we get to some white water and we can have our first go at a wave. But getting there is going to be a sweat.

Hear that, Phil? Keith asked. Neoprene jacket unzipped, the man's paunch was in evidence.

Doddle, the boy said. On the back of his helmet he has a skull and crossbones and the words, Don't follow me!

Clive smiled. Okay, basically, the thing to do is to use whatever slack water you can find, in the eddies by the bank, or behind the rocks midstream, to keep moving upstream. It's an exercise in reading the water. Anyone in despair, there's a path behind those bushes on the other side. You can always carry the boat.

There was a minute's unpleasantness pulling the damp wetsuits back on, a minute's sleepiness, perhaps. The day was clouding over, as so often in the mountains at noon. It was muggy and chill by turns. There were midges and dragonflies. The air hummed. As soon as Vince was back in his boat, paddle in hand, life seemed possible again.

All right, Mark? he asked Adam's son, when they were on the water. He knew that name.

Fine, the boy said. He had an earnest, slightly vacant face. Just me feet going numb. Like having your legs jammed up yer arse.

You look good on the water, Vince said.

Tell me dad that!

No sooner had they rounded the bend, upstream, than the river narrowed. The water began to flow more swiftly. The boat wobbled. Wake up, Vince told himself. There was a constant gurgling. He was concentrated, nervous. Lean back when you break into the stream from the eddy, Keith warned. Lean back, you're crouched! You're tense. How can your shoulders work like that? Relax.

The kayaks zigzagged, gaining in the slack water behind rocks and spurs, fighting to cross the swift flow in the centre. Show your butts to the stream, everybody. Make the river carry you across! Vince rested behind a boulder. His eyes moved over the water ahead. From brown it had turned black. Perhaps that was the sky growing darker. There was no time for the landscape. He looked for the flat swirling of water that marked the lower part of an eddy.

Break into the current with the hull scraping your rock, Max! Clive called. Scraping it, I said!

I'm Brian, the boy complained. Max is the fairy.

Bugger you, Bri.

See what I mean!

Vince watched. Brian then was the boy with the club foot – concentrate – Max the blonde lad who had worn the straw hat. He was surprised to find how well he was doing. Never in his life had it been so difficult to get through a day, or even a single hour. There had been weeks and months of misery. But now, when you spoke to someone for a moment, or managed to cross a big rush of water and hide behind a low rock, then a little time passed unnoticed. He felt a sense of achievement. Life was flowing again. I'm doing fine, he thought. By the end of the holiday, I'll be cured.

But now there was a more serious obstacle. They were trapped behind a spur. You fight up the cushion of water, Clive explained, then, at the critical point – don't worry, you'll sense it – you throw your weight forward and paddle for it like crazy.

Vince's paddle caught on the rocky spur. The water rushed towards him. I'm gasping. I'm sweating like a pig. He hung on the surge of the current, fought it, paddled wildly, then was carried down, had to struggle just to get back in the same eddy. Meantime, all the others had passed. He was last.

Try again, Clive told him. The key is the angle when you enter the flow. Vince tried and failed. The strokes weren't powerful enough. Or weren't placed right. He sensed the strain in his shoulders.

Just keep working at it, Keith said patiently. He had come back for them. But you have to believe you're going to make it. Use your shoulders, not your wrists. Punch the stroke through.

The sheer fact is, Clive laughed, there's a difference in the ratio of strength to body weight between us and the youngsters. We adults sink deeper. We're heavier. They just try and they fly.

Between *me* and the youngsters you mean, Vince said grimly. Suddenly he was again telling himself he shouldn't have come. I'm making a fool of myself. He should have stayed home to wait out this mental state. To wait till he became himself again.

Go for it!

Vince looks hard at the solid curve of water coming down from above the spur and doesn't understand how all the others have done it. Even tubby Caroline. He throws himself at it again. He gives it everything. The left side of the bow grazes the rock. He lifts the left edge to meet the current. The boat is pushed to the right. Paddle like crazy, someone is shouting. Now! Weight forward! Now! Vince paddles. One stroke goes in with surprising power. It feels different. He's done it. He's on top. It wasn't even that difficult. Now he just has to fight to the slack by the bank to avoid being carried down again.

Mandy is there, her head among the branches of a willow. Waiting for my heart rate to come down a little, thank you very much, she laughs. Even on the water she has the camera attached to her jacket, apparently waterproof. She squints at the little screen. You're red as a lobster! This'll be good. Vince's skull is pounding under his helmet. Did it! he finally finds the breath to shout. Did IT! He punches the air. He is overreacting.

At that moment a red hull swirled by, a kayak floating upside down. Immediately alert, congratulating himself on the fact, Vince broke from the eddy to meet it. They must look out for each other. That was the rule. But even as he pulls into the current, swept back towards the rush he has just climbed from, a paddle breaks the surface beside the hull and in a second the boat has flipped right side up. Phil is grinning gormlessly, chewing, nose dripping under a green helmet. Vince crashes into him as they go down the rush by the spur together. See that! There's a flurry of water and paddle strokes. The boy seems to do everything instinctively. See that tail squirt I did! I was bloody vertical. No sooner are they back in the lower eddy than Phil climbs the rush again,

apparently without effort, and is gone. Vince is exhausted. After
one failed attempt to get back to Mandy, he paddles the boat
the other side of the rock and over to the bank.

There's a heavy smell of dank vegetation here, exposed
willow roots with water flowing through them, a buzz of
flies. Vince pulls his boat up on the bank, then flounders,
looking for a break in the nettles. Now there are raindrops
pattering all around. His foot sinks into black mud. Hey!
Clive reappears in the eddy behind the rock. You should tell
me if you're getting out. He's irritated. Otherwise I'll be
worried we've lost you. I'll go searching downstream.

But how could Vince have told him, if the others were all
ahead? The path squeezes through dense woodland. On his
shoulder the heavy kayak knocks against trunks and branches.
It's dark here among the trees and there's a dull roar of water
coming from up front. Or is it traffic on some road? Now
the rain pours down. Summer storm rain. The boat knocks
against his head. He has to crouch to get the thing through
a thicket. The ground is broken. The earth smells strangely
warm and resiny. Stumbling into a small clearing, he almost
bangs into a low makeshift hut put together with blankets
and tarpaulin, blue nylon string and hunks of driftwood. On
a sheet of cardboard in the mud by the entrance, a thin, heavily bearded man jumps to his feet. Vince stops. Immediately,
the man waves a bottle and begins to speak excitedly.

Capisco niente. Vince says. *Verstehe nicht.*

The small man is gesticulating, perhaps warning him. His
eyes are red. There's an unpleasant smell. His jacket looks as
if it too might have been pulled from the water, like the
driftwood of his home. There are fish-heads lying in the
mud. The man goes on shouting. In his early forties maybe.
Or older. His eyes are fierce.

Verstehe nicht, Vince repeats. He turns and pushes on. The man screams after him. He hurls his bottle into the bushes over Vince's head. Vince finds the path, and after five or six paces the trees open up on the river bank. He sees the rapids and again the hull of a boat floating upside down. Blue this time. The boys are playing at breaking into the stream with the tail edge dipped towards the current. The back of the kayak is forced deep into the water, the nose lifts in the air. Tail squirts. Phil's boat rears up like a mad horse, or a motorcycle raised on its rear wheel. For a moment, the boy holds it there, yelling Yahoo, alrighty! The boat collapses back on top of him.

Vince watches, his face tense.

The river here is squeezed through a gap of only four or five yards then immediately opens out with big turbulent eddies swirling against each bank. A stone ledge stretching halfway across the flow at its fastest point causes the water to drop in a deep trough that then curls up into a tall, steady wave. Adam is showing the girls how to break from the side of the river and surf on the crest of the wave. The water is high and fierce and Caroline refuses to try. She has hooked an elbow round a sapling on the bank. Not my bag, she says, chewing. Adam repeats the same movements, simple and mechanical. Unlike the boys, he seems to take pleasure not in the thing itself, but in knowing how to do it, the control, the communication of technique. He is reassuring, but cold. Amelia ventures into the trough of the wave. The little girl seems so small in her long green boat, so hesitant. For a few moments the wave holds her, then the boat is tossed out like a cork.

Too cautious, Louise misses the trough altogether, spins round when the bow hits the crest of the wave, almost capsizes but, seemingly unconcerned, regains the bank. Vince is proud of her.

At the same time, over and over, the boys throw themselves into the turbulent stream, pushing to the front of the eddy, ignoring any queue the others have formed. Brian with his club foot has an uncanny balance in the boat. He never capsizes.

You selfish brats! Mandy yells. She is dragging her boat out of the water having failed to roll up. She shouts at Max and Phil as if it were their fault. You've got to watch out for each other!

Clive and Keith are sitting a few yards down from the action, ready to help any swimmers. The Indian boy Amal is also playing helper. He has an air of pleased diligence about him.

Try it, Mark, Adam invites his son.

Me arms are aching, the boy complains. I need a rest.

It doesn't require any strength, Adam insists.

I'm well tired, the boy repeats. I got pins and needles. He won't do it.

Vince reaches the top of the eddy. So how do you do this? he asks the instructor.

Okay. Adam holds his boat. You put your nose in the current, pointing upstream and just a little across. You break into the flow and lift your right knee to give a hint of an edge. You shouldn't even have to paddle if you get it right.

Vince is nervous. He is facing a rush of water such as he hasn't seen before. It foams, silver and black, over the stones, moss-green here, marbly grey there. He recalls the bearded face of a few moments before, the alcoholic shouting in German, throwing his bottle. What if I get it wrong, capsize, hit my head on a rock?

Go, Adam says. Don't shilly-shally.

As he shifts his boat out of the eddy, Vince finds it suddenly drawn towards the submerged ledge over which the water is surging so powerfully. He is being sucked upstream and under. This is quite unexpected. How can I be pulled upstream?

Lean back! Adam shouts.

Vince tries to correct, back-paddling, but this has the effect of sending the boat careering sideways, rocking violently. A mountain of water piles down on him. Vince tries to raise the edge of the kayak to meet it, but it's too late, he is down. His head hits the foam.

The experience is quite different from any other capsize he has known. You are no longer in slow water with time to reflect. You are in the quick of it – this is life – eyes open but blind. An icy flood rears and tugs and swirls. The paddle is being dragged away from him. He can't push it to the surface. It won't move, it's trapped against the boat. He tries the rolling motion anyway. The boat half turns. His head breaks the surface. For a split second, comic no doubt to the onlooker, he can catch a breath. He has a vague impression of the world rushing by. Someone's shouting. Then he's down again. Now the helmet scrapes, again he fights with the paddle, again fails to right the boat. This time his fingers find the release tab. The spraydeck pops. The freezing water floods the cockpit and he swims out. Hold on to your paddle! Don't let go of the boat! Turn it upright. As his head breaks the surface, Keith is already there with a tow-sling and a clip. And you forgot to bang on the sides!

All afternoon they keep at this. It's today's lesson. Very soon they are in three groups. There are those who take few risks, happy with what they can do; those who seem to have no trouble with anything – the elect – and then those who will keep trying and trying though almost always beaten.

Time and again Vince approaches the top of the eddy. Fascinated, he watches how others – Michela, Amelia and

Louise now too – penetrate the current and glide across to the wave apparently without expending energy or taking risks. How is this? There is some hidden place, it seems, between eddy and flow, between the soft grey water milling on shallow stones and the fast dark stream pouring into the wave, some place where the river can be unlocked. A secret entrance. You're admitted directly to the heart of things. You're privileged. You can sit on the wave in a miracle of exhilarating speed and reassuring stillness. This mystery is denied to him. The entrance isn't there when he approaches. The explanations – do this, do that – don't seem to corre- spond to the experience.

In the eddy, Michela brings her boat alongside his. She is laughing. She seems happy. She shows Vince exactly the point of entry, the movement of the paddle and hips. Clive will come round, she has decided. It's so fine to be near him. He is so strong. Those deaths in Milan have brought on a crisis. It will pass. Speaking English makes her feel cheerful. He gives me strength too. Relaxed and determined, she tells the older man to go with the flow. Don't fight it, she says.

Vince grips his paddle. The rain pours on the rushing water. Unnoticed above, the mountains have dissolved in cloud. And take it easy when you capsize, Michela repeats. You're hurrying. There's always more time than you think. Imagine you're in a swimming pool.

Dad, don't overdo it, Louise shouted. You've got to drive me home, you know.

On the fourth attempt, having once more capsized with- out reaching the wave, Vince rolls his boat upright in the worst of the turbulence. The paddle is suddenly in the right place. He arches the arm, moves his hips and with no effort at all there he is, tossed out on a boil of water, disorien-

42

tated, floundering, but up, breathing. Things could still go right.

Last night, Keith was saying later, I asked everybody to introduce themselves. But then, as you know, there have been two late arrivals.

It was raining still, but uncannily warm. They had trailed the boats back to camp. They had strung up lines between the trees to hang the equipment. At least if it doesn't dry, the rubber won't stink. They had showered. The Louts had cooked. The three teams are the Louts, the Pigs and the Slobs. This had been young Max's idea during the trip out. A spirit of healthy emulation, he said in his precocious little lawyer's voice from beneath the straw hat. Now they were all crowded into the kitchen tent in the light of the gas lamp. Across the site the French boys were drumming under their awning. Occasional thunder rumbled over their heads. The church clock has just chimed eight. It was time for the evening meeting. Sitting in his canvas chair again, Keith wears a permanent smile of self-congratulation.

Louise?

Yeah, I'm Louise, Vince's daughter said. You all know me anyway. Fifteen. Chatham Grammar. Not cool, I know, but there you are. I'm here because I love the water and the company.

All right, Brian clapped.

That's all. She was trying to catch Tom's eye.

Verdict on today? Keith insisted. There was something evangelical about the man.

Great. Really. Learned a lot. Apart from having Phil push in front of me about every two seconds in the eddy by the wave.

Yes, a Wally nomination coming up there, I suspect. Vince?

43

Sorry?

Could you introduce yourself?

Vince still doesn't understand. His mind has been captured by the drumming.

Let people know who you are. A few words.

Someone sniggered. It was a beat that seemed to go round and round in rapid circles.

Yes, of course.

He was standing by the entrance of the tent. Michela noticed that his eyes were clouded, his mouth always slightly open.

Well, I work in a bank.

There was an adolescent groan.

Vince smiled. Right, he agreed. Very boring. Anyway, probably some of you will have known my wife, my wife Gloria, since she was an instructor with Waterworld until a year or so ago. He took a breath. Anyway, after . . . after what happened, well, she had booked a place on this trip, and I just thought I would . . . He couldn't go on. The drums pattered.

Vince's wife, Keith cut in, was national sprint champion in her age group at Henley, when was that, Vince?

Vince was staring at the lamp-lit faces under canvas.

1998, Adam said.

In the night, he opened the fridge and she was crouching there inside. He wasn't surprised. The fridge was her domain. I can live for ever here, she told him. He was looking for eggs to scramble. What else can I cook? He took them from her hand and closed the door, then went back and opened it again. There was something I should have said. She didn't seem cramped. She was in her gym kit. No need, she said. Her smile was condescending, like a mother's. There's some-thing I want to ask, he insisted. Don't keep the fridge door

44

open, love, you'll waste the cold. She smiled. You're wasting electricity, love. There's something . . . It's precious. Close it. He closed the door. But he was in the flat in London, not at home. Gloria never comes to his London flat. The fridge is tiny. There's something I have to ask. He rushed across the room to tear the door open. The fridge, as always in his flat, was empty. Gloria! He shouted. Gloria!

Dad, you're snoring! From her sleeping bag, his daughter woke him. The girl was sitting up. They were unnaturally close in the tent. She seemed eager to turn away.

I'm sorry. He lay still on his back. The ground is uneven and uncomfortable. But it's not that. The blue canvas flickers from time to time with the torchlight of people heading for the bathrooms. Did I make myself come camping as a punishment? he wondered. Vince put his hands behind his head. His body ached. The day on the river has exhausted him. Then, as always after these nightmares, in the alert, sleepless mood they induce, he played over the sudden last moments of his marriage, the end of life as he had known it. Vince, I'm dying, her voice says. She has called his mobile. He is just climbing the stairs from the Underground at St Paul's. I'm dying. I've phoned nine nine nine. I'm paralysed. It's a stroke. I'm sure. I know the signs . . . It must have been at that point of the call that he had shouted, Gloria! He had stopped in the crowd. People were pushing past. It was early morning at St Paul's. He was standing still, rigid, in the hurrying crowd. Gloria, for God's sake! My head is filling with blood, she cried. Oh, I'm dying Vince. I'm so, so sorry.

The curious thing, as he let each evening's tears fill his eyes, was the clarity of her voice in his head. Freed from the crackly quality of the mobile on the stairs outside the Underground, it spoke directly in his head. I'm paralysed. It's a stroke. The change of tone from her normal matter-of-fact, rather bossy self to something piercingly intimate could not have been more marked. Oh, I'm dying Vince, I'm so so sorry. It was as if right at the end it hadn't been her, or rather it had been her *at last*, someone he had never known. My wife. His mind was caught there, turning and turning in this unexpected maelstrom. Why had she said she was sorry? Why did he feel so ashamed? Very soon, I must become someone else; Vince knew that. He couldn't break out of this churn of thought. After six months, it was a wonder he hadn't already drowned.

A RAPID

At breakfast Tom joined the adults, rather than the children. Those bells! The young man seems in turns uncertain of himself and aggressively assured. Vince had been woken ten minutes before the morning ringing by the arrival of a text message on his daughter's phone. They stood in the mud by the kitchen tent. Who pays the bloke to get up so early every day? Adam was shaking his head. Mandy wanted to know how on earth Michela had learned English so perfectly. She had only been in the UK a few months. She hadn't even studied at university. With the grass damp, people ate standing up. Tea in the pot! Keith announced. I was born in the wrong country, the young woman laughed. The sun was just touching distant peaks, but the valley lay in shadow. The church tower was topped with a gleaming bronze onion dome, quite new obviously.

Neither of your parents speaks English, though?

I would never have learned if they did. It's hard to explain, I always knew from as soon as I could think, I should have been English.

Too much of a class act to be a Brit, Tom said earnestly. Oh thank you so much! Mandy objected.

Michela wasn't eating. She looked at the young man without seeing him. Too much to do in a world that's too ugly, Clive had said last night. Once again he had insisted on the sleeping bag on the bare floor. It was a punishment. Again she had walked out after midnight and sat on the roots of the big pine tree above the group's pitch. In a tent the other side of the track a man and woman were murmuring in a language she didn't know. She sat with her spine against the damp bark. Why now? Why had he chosen this of all moments?

Again, sometime after one o'clock, she had seen the thin, older Englishman head for the bathroom. He sneezed twice. That was the river in our noses. He is carrying a burden, Michela thought. She drew into the shadow so he wouldn't see her. She thought in English. She would not use the language of her father and mother. She would not let Clive see her cry. I must be strong, she decided. If you want to go back to your mum, Micky, he said from the darkness as she pulled the door to, I'd understand perfectly. We could sort out the money side. She waited some minutes before answering. She undressed and got into bed. I'd rather kill myself, she told him.

Her man did not watch as she undressed. He knew her body. He knows how avidly she makes love. The room was dimly lit from a lamp outside. It smelled of bare wood and river kit. A good smell. I checked my e-mail this evening, he said finally. He had driven into Sand in Taufers. They're talking of chartering a plane for Berlin. Will you come?

Of course, she said.

He had not looked as she undressed, but now, over cornflakes, Clive was watching Michela carefully. Vince caught the man's intense gaze and knew he was in love. For months, he thought, I keep noticing people in love. It was almost the only thing he did notice.

But you have a pretty high position, don't you? Adam was speaking to him. He named one of Britain's major clearing banks. The tall instructor was already wearing a wetsuit, the shoulder-straps hanging at his side. I mean, you're one of the big guns, aren't you? He seemed extremely respectful of Vince, eager to get to know him. His hair was neatly combed, his receding chin closely shaved. Clipped to his belt, a waterproof case held his mobile.

Well . . .

I remember your wife saying something.

He only pretty well runs the whole bloody bank! Louise arrived hungry. There was a bag of Chocos she was after, under Tom's elbow. Move over macho! The girl wore no bra under her T-shirt.

One shouldn't exaggerate, Vince began.

Oh, come on Dad! You know you run it.

Adam seemed to be expecting a response. I imagine, he insisted, that someone like yourself has to be in touch even while you're away. I mean at certain levels of responsibility . . .

But now a new noise captured everybody's attention. There was a tinny jingle. Oh no! shrieked the young Max, his straw hat tipped back. On the table in the kitchen tent, beside the milk carton, a white hamster, about a foot high on its hind legs, had begun to beat a tin drum. Legs and paws moved with mechanical grace, while the solemn head made slow turns from side to side. A recorded voice in his innards crooned:

I think I love you, but that's what life is made of.

Amelia and Caroline were bent double with giggles. The

big girl grabbed Phil. Was it you? She had to pull off the headphones of his Discman.

And it worries me to say, the voice crooned on, that I've never felt this way.

Who stole my hamster? Mandy demanded. The bristly white muzzle was hilariously wise. The voice was that of some twenties vaudeville entertainer. Picked up in a service station, the toy had been a constant joke on the long journey from England. Amal was grinning broadly.

Do you think I have a case, the hamster sang, won't you tell me to my face?

Who's been in my tent? Mandy insisted. This is a happy British holiday, Vince told himself. I must participate. Adam smiled sardonically. Who was it? Mandy shrieked. Everybody was running around, giggling. Who stole my hamster? Guilty! Keith peeped a ruddy face from behind Michela's pine tree. Was it possible, Vince wondered, that the group's leader and their administrator had something going together? You cheeky bastard, Mandy made a half-hearted dash. Nosing in my stuff! Oh a serious impropriety! Max shouted in his most camp voice. Photograph! someone shrieked. One for the website! When Vince turned he saw Michela was hurrying away to the trailer where the boats were loaded and locked up. How lithe she was. You are under a spell, he told himself. It was an expression he would sometimes use at work to describe this or that commodity or currency. Coffee is under a spell. There's no other explanation. The dollar is under a spell. But now Tom was saying politely, Mr Marshall, actually I was wondering—

Vince, I'm called Vince.

Sorry, I was wondering if I might pick your brain on money supply at some point? There are a couple of things they've been teaching us at university that I really don't understand.

Listen, don't talk about my work, Vince told Louise quietly as they gathered their kit together for the day's outing. His cag was still damp. She couldn't find her towel. She was sure she'd left it on the line. Please, he said. They fussed about the fly-sheets. It bothers me. What else is there to talk about with you, Dad? she asked. You never do anything but work. He asked if the message she had received this morning had been from her cousins. No, she said. She smiled very brightly. Adam had promised her she could charge her phone on his car charger.

They already had the boats on the water before the sun climbed over the mountainside and poured its warmth into the valley. This time they ran the section from the camp-site to the village of Geiss. Never do anything but work, Vince is thinking. His daughter's words have soured his morning. Yet he hadn't called the office so far this holiday, as his colleagues no doubt expected. He hadn't even read the papers or listened to a radio. Quite probably they are trying to contact him. He hadn't turned on his mobile. He hadn't bought a car charger. He had no idea what the market was up to. For thirty years you give your whole life to something, he thought, you build up a solid career; and then in the space of a couple of weeks, it's forgotten. I have lost my daughter, Vince told himself. This holiday is confirm-ing that loss. First in Florence, now here. I have lost all sense of purpose. All I notice is people in love. From what you tell me you are clinically depressed, his brother-in-law had advised him. Jasper worked in that field. He ran a psychi-atric clinic in South London. You should be on drugs, he said. Vince was afraid that drugs would cloud his judgement. It was a difficult moment in foreign equities. It is always a difficult moment. He had stopped performing after Gloria died. He knew it. He knew they knew it. Why had he let Louise go to live with her cousins? I have no home now. Suddenly, Vince feels a grating under the boat. Wake up! The kayak is broadside to a bank of pebbles rising from below the grey water. The river slides forward with a strong steady pull. He should have seen the tell-tale rippling on the surface. It's too late. Vince finds himself being turned over in only six inches of rapidly flowing water. His shoulder bangs along on the stones. Wally nomination! Phil shouts. Phil has the creature tied round his neck for his behaviour yesterday. What a fool! Vince curses himself. He is livid.

Only a few minutes later, Clive orders: Stop paddling everyone and listen. There are still patches of early-morning mist rising on the calmer stretches of the water. The boys are splashing each other. Listen up! Adam complains. It seems to irritate him that Clive and Keith won't impose discipline more firmly. Mark, I said listen! he tells his son. Stop paddling.

The fifteen kayaks with their bright plastic colours drift on the glassy surface. The thin mist is luminous and the water wide and apparently tranquil, pressing steadily forward. Three ducks are flapping along the bank in front of them. Faint in the distance from beyond the trees is the repeated beep of a truck reversing, in some quarry perhaps. Brian giggles, Mysterious!

Shush!

Leaning back, arching until her helmet rests on the deck behind, Michela gazes upward. Among high white clouds, the tall mountains slowly revolve. It's dizzying. The current is turning the boat. The high rocks seem precarious. They will tumble down. A buzzard swoops above the tree line and the girl feels as if she herself has fallen from there. She is still falling, the mountains turning. It's so calm. She doesn't believe what has happened. She is living an intense swan-song of adoration and denial. She has given herself completely to Clive. My family is behind me. I will go anywhere you go, she told him last night. She lets her hands trail in the water and the chill climbs up her fingers to wrists and forearms. You know I can't go home.

Then Vince hears it. Beyond the still-beeping truck, a low roar emerges, a dark line floats up on the auditory horizon. At once the water takes on a new urgency. They are gliding past narrowing banks of steeper and steeper stone. Alrighty! Phil breaks the silence. River-left! Clive shouts. He is paddling backwards, facing the others. As he tells them what to do, he is sensible, steady, entirely manly. But Michela recognises the hint of impatience in his voice, the energy restrained. He wishes he were in another era, exploring virgin territory, commanding soldiers. She loves this in him. Kayaks are plastic toys, he complains when he is depressed. There's nothing *necessary* about them. They're not natural. One evening he asked over and over, Do you understand, Micky, what I mean by something being *necessary*? Clive is old never to have settled; she knows that. She saw the mad intensity of his eyes at the demonstration in Milan.

Keith is shouting names and numbers. He has to yell now over the roar of the rapid, swollen with yesterday's rain. Amal five, Amelia six, Louise seven. They must follow Clive's line. Three boat-lengths apart. Don't get too close.

One by one the kayaks drop below the horizon. Each hull with its bright colour slips suddenly away, then the helmet. Louise's helmet is white. Number seven is gone. Next to last, with only the expert Adam behind him, Vince dips into a slalom of rushing water and rock. The acceleration is dramatic. For the first time he finds himself actually looking downhill, in the water. No time to be frightened. The boat is flung to the side. The boulders come very fast. Vince steers and turns and braces. His mind is absolutely concentrated, his body is wired and reactive. Suddenly, a boat is blocking his path. Mark is pinned against a boulder to one side of the narrow central chute. The water is piling on his deck. He's shouting. Vince crashes into the boat. Mark is bounced free, but capsizes in the rush. Somehow, Vince does something instinctive, some strange banging of paddle on water, an unexpected elasticity of ageing hips, that keeps him upright in the race. Now he is plunging down into the terminal stopper. The water is frothing. Paddle! a voice shouts. From the eddy behind a rock, everybody is shouting. Paddle hard! The churning white water grabs hold of him. The stern is pulled down, as if arms under there had clutched him. They want him under. *Paddle, for Christ's sake!* Vince paddles and the boat rears and pops out. Safe.

Vince enjoys, then, as on waking every morning, about two or three seconds of complete contentment. He fights his way out of the white water. He sees his daughter's radiant pink face. She is rafted up against Tom in the eddy. My daughter is bursting with excitement and happiness! Their first real rapid. What a rush of adrenalin! Then after this flash of pleasure, the dark returns, with an awful inevitability. You give everything to work, Gloria would say. You have no other life. Bizarre phrases come to his mind. I am *excluded*. He wants to shout the words. Gloria excluded me. I'm so so sorry, she said. What did she mean? Vince is boiling with rage. Whipping the boat round as he crosses the eddy-line, he sees only now that the instructors have passed a rope across the river at the stopper and Clive is in there pulling out Mark. I forgot the boy. I forgot him! Mark is retching. His face is white with panic.

That evening everybody began to drink. The afternoon had been uncomfortably warm and Keith insisted on splashing and playing the fool and putting everyone in a party spirit. How could the idiot get himself pinned in a grade-two rapid? Adam kept repeating of his son. Three more rapids were run without incident. In the spaces between, Amal insisted on pairing up with Vince and chattering in his queer, high-pitched voice. His father had died ten years ago, his mother was obliged to work all hours in his uncle's shop. Waterworld is like a family to me, he repeated two or three times. Amelia had been his girlfriend when they were both on the Canadian trip. She was nice. That was open canoes. But they had agreed to split up.

You run a bank, don't you? he said. They were paddling the last tame stretch to Geiss between high banks of brushwood. Your wife taught me once, he explained. My two-star. She was the one with her hair in a bun, right? And she worked in a hospital. That's right, Vince said. Good teacher, Amal said. Very strict. Didn't let you get away with doing things even slightly wrong.

It was curious how good-looking the Indian boy was, with bright dark eyes and high cheekbones, and how completely the shrill voice and over-eagerness to please undercut this attraction. My brother Vikram is handicapped, he said. He can't kayak except in those special day-out things they give handicapped people, you know. Louise is improving, though, Amal said appreciatively. She has a great hip-flick. Vince felt oppressed, the day was really too warm. Everyone was dipping hands and arms in the water to cool off. He couldn't decide whether to call the office the following morning perhaps. He couldn't see any way forward, only his old self, his old life. Wally, Amal was explaining, is supposed to be the spirit of a drowned paddler, you know. He protects us, like. But only if we protect him. Is that so? Vince managed. That's why it's so important not to lose him, Amal said. The older man wanted to scream.

Then, checking the duty rota back at the camp, Vince read: PIGS, *Wednesday*, <u>Shopping</u>. See list. In twenty-five years of marriage, he had hardly shopped at all. Perhaps I let Louise go, he wondered, because I was scared of shopping. Team! he called. Hey! Pigs! He assumed the joking voice everyone else was using, the holiday voice. We're on shopping. In the car, team! We'll use mine. He had Amelia, Tom and Max.

Do you know where to go? Tom asked. We can't buy this lot at the camp shop. The list stretched to two pages. Micky! Sitting in the passenger seat the young man buzzed down the window. Michela was standing in the no man's land between chalet and tents. Micky! Vince moved the car a few yards. She crouched by Tom's window and gave directions. I can come, if you need help, she offered. Oh, us Brits have a long tradition of bossing about the natives, Max assured her. He was wearing his straw hat, a yellow cotton shirt with button-down collar. As they drove up the rutted track, Vince watched the young woman bob in and out of the mirror. He didn't like the way she called herself by a boy's name. It seemed wrong. Nice girl, Tom said. The young man's powerful hands rested on his knees. For a Wop, Max agreed. She's Clive's girlfriend, isn't she? Amelia reminded them. By the way, can someone give me the shopping list? Sure, Vince said. Am I the only one, he asked, with a pain when they rotate their elbow? Amelia leaned forward between the seats: Tom, why don't you choose the beer and all the crisps and snacks? That'll save time. Me the whisky and bog paper, sang Max.

Beyond the campsite, a fast road ran through an area of warehouses and light industry. Timber milling, it looked like, building materials. Ahead, where the valley narrowed above the cluster of the small town, a castle dominated the scene, a *schloss*, shamelessly picturesque on a tall spur of rock with the dramatic mountain gorge behind. It was hard not to feel you had seen it in some film. How old is your daughter, Mr Marshall? Tom suddenly asked. I mean Vince, sorry. Fourteen, Vince said. I'm almost sixteen, Amelia remarked. You *are* not, Max objected. Only three months! You could be dead before then! the boy shouted. Max, please, Vince begged. Age is so much to do with how you behave, though, isn't it? Tom said sagely. Badly! Max shrieked. Shut up, the girl hissed.

Then they were in Sand in Taufers: swept streets and big square Austrian-style houses, all with the same steep roof, the same wide, pine-fronted balconies, the same fierce geranium displays blazing in the early evening light. Everywhere there were *Zimmer frei* signs and gift shops, a general impression of regimented colour, authorised souvenirs. Posters in three languages proclaimed a festival of traditional horn music. A photograph showed a bearded man in lederhosen blowing into a horn at least six feet long, resting on the ground in front of him. The little supermarket, when they found it, was called EuroSpin, its windows plastered with international brand names, credit card signs. It was curious, Vince thought, how nothing seemed unfamiliar anymore, excepting one's state of mind, perhaps. He found it strange how at ease he felt with these kids.

A stiff little man in a white coat, his eyes bloodshot, turned from stacking Nestlé's snacks. *Guten abend*, he said throatily. Velcum to mai umble 'ome, Max whispered. Are we in Italy or what? *Guten abend*, Tom replied politely.

Vince found a trolley. Remember, everything we get is for fifteen, okay? Almost at once the youngsters were giggling at the sausage section. Great curved turgid things wrapped in red and yellow cellophane. You don't see these in England. *Wurst und wurst!* Amelia cried, picking up a particularly obscene example and waving it at Tom. The shopkeeper shifted from the doorway to keep an eye down their aisle. You choose, Amelia was telling the boy.

The store had the cluttered shelves of a restricted space trying to satisfy every need. Again the attendant moved as they rounded the end of the aisle. Ve arr being voched, Max whispered. Everything Vince chose – there were sandwich things to get and chicken pieces for this evening's dinner – Amelia asked Tom if it was right. Don't you think we'd be better with long-life milk? She had straight black hair clipped in a fringe above a puckered, solemn forehead and at a certain point she contrived to pick up a can of peeled toma-toes that Tom already had his hands on. The young man studied the labels intently, until, to everybody's surprise, Max walked straight down the aisle and addressed the shopkeeper in fluent German. He spoke for at least a minute, with some expression, gesturing at the shelves. The stiff man smiled, took him to the meat counter, then another shelf. That's the sauce for the chicken casserole, the blonde boy said. His shirt seemed freshly ironed, likewise the white cotton trousers. The spuds are round the corner. Brilliant, Vince told him. I did French, Tom advised Amelia. He took her by the elbow.

Vince bought sun cream, matches, a roll of duct tape and a second tray of beers. Actually, we don't need those, Tom said. We've already got a tray. But there are thirteen of us, Vince explained, fifteen with Clive and his girlfriend. Seven or eight are under age, Tom pointed out. Oh come on, Max protested. This is piss beer, this Kraut stuff. Most of us were swigging stronger stuff than this before we could walk. Mandy said no, Tom insisted. Amelia couldn't make up her mind whether to support him or not. I have to get something for Caroline's chapped lips. Does your dad let you drink? Vince asked the girl. She wore a short skirt over thin, coltish legs. Sometimes, she said. Aping the adult, she folded her arms, shifted her weight. I believe Mandy actually signed something, Tom was saying now. He seemed genuinely concerned that a rule might be broken. We could add a tray of Cokes, he suggested, for the kids.

Vince gave the black wallet with the Waterworld kitty to Max and told the boys to carry out the boxes. Then he invited Amelia back into the shop and with his own money bought two more trays of beer and various goodies: marshmallows and skewers, in case they made a fire, and three bottles of sparkling wine. Since we're the Pigs, let's be pigs, he announced. He felt cheerful. You're a tempter, Mr Marshall, Amelia laughed. Vince, he again insisted. Why couldn't they use his name? You don't call Keith Mr Whatever, do you? Bags I the front seat, Max rushed. Tom and Amelia were quiet in the back.

No! Mandy said. No drinking! No, no, no! Keith overruled her. The group leader seemed extravagantly, even brutally merry. Suck on that. He gave a can to Caroline, another to Amelia. Adam was evidently irritated. He gets like this, Mandy shook her head. Soon he'll be flirting with the under-sixteens. It's only beer, Keith insisted breezily. Drink, he told Mark. You're not on the river now. A holiday's a holiday. Even when it's a community experience, Amelia chipped in. And if you want to be really English – Keith handed another can to Michela – you'll have to get in training. You know the British government's thinking of introducing an alcohol test for citizenship: ability to imbibe five pints a day, five days running. A working week, no less, Brian observed. Mark took his beer and sat on the ground beside Amal. The boy had barely spoken after his accident at the rapid. On the table in the kitchen tent, the hamster began to beat his drum. I think I love you. Oh no! the children groaned. Turn the beast off! I think I hate you, Phil laughed. Vince couldn't help noticing the way he and Caroline leaned on each other as they sat.

At the meeting, after the casserole, Louise nominated her father for Wally and the vote was unanimous. Only an idiot could capsize in six inches of water. Public humiliation! Keith demanded. On his third beer, Vince was nervous and pleased. I am becoming part of the group, he thought. But what was the punishment to be? Something really degrading! Louise shrieked, can in hand. Gloria had never let her drink. Uncle Jasper's family was even stricter. You decide, Mandy told Caroline. Vince had seen how carefully the older woman brought in everybody. There would be no faces missing from the website. The big girl grimaced and chewed, then looked to Amelia. There was an old complicity between the two. They burst out laughing. The Chicken Song! Both struggled to their feet, stood side by side in the tight circle of the tent, where the gas lamp was throwing shadows as the twilight faded. Caroline was almost a head taller than her friend, her thighs heavy, wrists and ankles thick, her manner timid, but when she began to dance there was a mad energy and unexpected elegance to her. Incongruous together, the two girls kicked their legs, flapped their arms. I'm a chubby chicken, ready for the chop, they'll cut my pretty head off, stricken, plop, but still I run around and kick 'em. Hop Hop! The girls pulled faces, lolled their heads, broke one one way and one the other, running round the group kicking at people.

Pathetic! Brian and Max shrilled. Naff!

I have to do that? Vince asked.

You're getting off lightly, Mandy told him. She smiled indulgently. Everybody was looking.

With the actions or without?

He took his place in the centre of the circle. Michela is watching me, he saw, and my daughter. Vince danced, Vince who never danced. He was wearing corduroys and a thin sweater. I'm a chubby chicken, he sang. He heard his voice singing. He and Gloria had never danced. He tried to do it well. He was absurd. Gloria did every kind of sport, but didn't dance. It was strange at fifty to be making yourself so ridiculous. I am director of all overseas accounts, he told himself. The kids were giggling. He tried to remember the words. Ready for the chop! The others were clapping and as he made to kick at them, they jumped to their feet and dashed out of the tent. Rise, Sir Wally, Keith said, dropping the creature over his head on a piece of string. Thou must take care of he who protects us. Pathetic! Phil shrieked.

And they went up to the camp bar. On a low stage a local band were playing music for karaoke. There were people of all ages and from all over Europe, Austrian bikers and ageing Dutch nature lovers. The tables were spread over a wide terrace. The kids disappeared, Amelia and Louise dragging Tom with them. It seemed there was an internet café up the road. Everybody has a life elsewhere, a message to send. We'll need you to order the drinks, the girls protested. Tom turned a lingering glance to Michela, but the young woman never noticed. Mark was boasting to Louise about something he had done on a previous expedition, in an open canoe. He has started to talk again. Only Amal stayed with the adults. The boy seemed eager to agree with everything everyone said.

How the twit could get pinned in the world's easiest

rapid, I do not know, Adam repeated, taking his seat. Leave the kid be! Mandy cried. She ordered a round of large beers from the waiter. And no, I'm not being inconsistent, she turned on Keith. It's fine when it's us and not the kids whose mothers I've promised. The man brought half-litre glasses. Some middle-aged Germans were trying to sing 'Maggie May'. Maggie I vish. Drink up, and stop fussing, the stout woman told Adam. My new cag is giving me a rash, Keith complained. Bottoms up.

The music grew louder. A group of Spanish children were playing hide-and-seek among the adults. Vince got the next round. It was years since he had had more than a couple of beers. A strange excitement was fizzing up. Unasked, he started to talk about the man he had seen on the river bank the other day, in the ramshackle hut. Every river has one, Keith said. People who've dropped out and they're just drawn to the river. The river is life, Clive said rather solemnly, sheer life. Michela was beside him. Oh, they're just alkies, Adam objected. He kept playing with his mobile, apparently sending and receiving text messages. It's just easy for them to get driftwood and water by the river and you can crap off the bank. They leave a lot of rubbish around. Shouldn't be allowed. He tapped on the keypad.

The bloke threw a bottle at me, Vince said.

There you are.

Clive began to speak about a man he had got to know by a river in the Canadian Rockies. This guy had lived there for years in brushwood shelters, hunting and selling pelts, sleeping in animal skins. After a rainfall he could tell you exactly when the river would rise and how much. To the inch. He even knew when a tree had fallen into the water upstream or a cow. The birds and fish behaved differently.

Oh I find that very hard to believe, Adam said.

Let's karaoke, Keith interrupted. Come on. Let's ask for some oldies. Be sentimental. But Mandy had launched into an intense attack on someone or something. It's all either technical, she was complaining to Amal, like, we all have to do every stroke in the regulation BCU style; or commercial, you know, if we take an extra instructor, we won't break even, or if you have an end-of-season party, you'll lose money. I must have missed something, Vince thought. His eye had settled on Michela's slim wrist as she poured some of her beer into Clive's glass. They were sitting round a large white plastic table. Clive was drinking a lot. He had rolled himself a Golden Virginia. They will make love later, Vince told himself. He looked away. Adam was consulting his mobile again. The man doesn't see, Mandy was explaining, that that's not really what people are after. They don't come to Waterworld for that. Or not *only* that.

Who are we talking about? Vince asked Keith. Amal was nodding in agreement. Ron Bridges, Keith told him. District Superintendent, Kent Sports and Recreation. The boss. He lowered his voice: Mandy applied for the job, but they wouldn't give it to her.

And the thing is – the squat woman was almost shouting – I don't know how or why, but we never finished a year in the red till he came along. Can you believe it? I remember Sylvia saying, Soon we'll have lost as much as the film *Waterworld*, remember? Hollywood's biggest flop. He's been a bloody disaster! She slammed her beer down, wiped her mouth. People want to have fun, don't they, and to feel their life is being given some sense – she was evidently repeating things she had said before – in a group together, you know? Out in nature. They want excitement and friends. You can't persecute them just because they can't do a reverse-sweep stroke exactly the way the British Bloody Canoeing Union prescribes.

Keith stretched his arms: Attaboy, Mandy!

You should have seen, she shrieked, the list of instructions he gave us for this trip. The length of that list! We wouldn't have had any fun at all. We'd have spent the whole time practising low braces in the first eddy.

Adam again clicked his mobile shut. Still, you do have to teach the strokes right, and you do have to break even.

Of course you bloody do, of *course* – the woman leaned forward across the table. But that's not *the point* of it all, is it? It's not *why* we do it.

Adam began to object, but a beep indicated the arrival of another message. The missus? Keith asked, with an arching of bushy eyebrows. The mistress? Mandy echoed.

What sad minds! Adam shook his head. He began to tap out a response. Across the table, a dangerous expression of scorn had settled around Clive's lips. He rubbed the knuckle of one thumb back and forth in his beard across his chin. There is no *one* way to do any stroke, he began very deliberately. It's a question of *attitude*. Vince for example knows the strokes. You tell him what to do and he does it. But his attitude's wrong.

Vince asked: How?

Clive half smiled. He bit the inside of his lip. Watch Amal, he said.

Me? The dark boy sipped his beer and looked at them over the glass. I don't know anything.

No, tell me now, Vince said. Explain. Then I can work at it.

Keith chuckled: Clive's right, watch Amal, then you tell us.

But I only started kayak last year, the boy protested in his oddly high-pitched voice.

Oh you've been on the water since as long as I can remember, Mandy said approvingly. You're a natural.

I'll watch him too, Michela told Vince. I'm constantly thinking I must be doing something wrong.

Again Adam snapped his phone shut. Your problem is— he began.

Don't! Clive cut in. He'll learn better watching Amal.

Since it's my problem— Vince began.

Wally! Keith cried. Produce Wally or prepare to face total humiliation.

Present and correct, Vince pulled the little effigy from his pocket. He smiled. He liked Keith.

It'll all sort itself out, the leader reassured him, in good time. It's an intuitive thing.

But Adam wouldn't leave be. This mysticism is silly, he said. It's a way of giving yourself airs. Like stories of riverside alcoholics with uncanny powers of divination. Why don't you tell him he sits too far back in the boat? There's no great philosophical wisdom to kayaking. It's the same with the anti-globalisation stuff, to be frank. People want to feel they have a good, semi-religious cause – save the planet, and so on – because then they've got an excuse for breaking things and causing trouble. They release a bit of energy and imagine they're saints.

The chinless man said all this in a relaxed, even cheerful voice, as if it was hardly a criticism at all. At once Michela was frantic.

How can you say that? she demanded. Do you have any idea how many people are dying of hunger while their governments are forced to spend the money that could save them to pay back loans to Western banks?

Not the loans, Clive cut in. He was leaning forward on his chair, smoking intently. Not the bloody loans, the *interest* on the loans. The interest! It's scandalous. I'd feel like a worm if I didn't do something about it. I wouldn't feel human. I'd die of shame if I didn't get involved. You don't have to go *looking* for a good cause these days. The miracle is that some people manage to hide from them. They sit in their air-conditioned offices and pretend the climate hasn't changed, while the rest of the world roasts.

Adam said calmly: If somebody asks for money from a private organisation, what is that organisation supposed to do, give it them for free?

But there are whole continents dying of AIDS, Michela pleaded. She seemed on the verge of tears. Because the drug companies don't want to lower their prices.

That is true, Mandy observed. She mentioned a TV programme.

What a petty morality! Clive cried. A petty, petty morality! Like the money-lender demanding his pound of flesh when the victim and his children are starving. As if we weren't all part of the same human family.

Ask the September 11th people about that.

All we are saying, Keith began to hum, is give peace a chance! He placed his beer mat on the edge of the table, flipped it in the air and caught it. Chill out, folks. Let's talk about tomorrow's paddle.

Why don't *you* explain to them? Adam suddenly said, straight-faced. He twisted his lean neck and turned to Vince. You understand it better than anyone here.

I think we could do with an expert opinion, Mandy agreed. Clive snorted.

Keith sent half a wink that invited Vince to calm the waters. Waiter, he called. He pointed to their beers. It was after eleven now. The three youngsters on stage with their keyboard and rhythm machine were trying to persuade someone to do the Macarena. Two Scandinavian children obliged, then two couples in swarthy middle age. Slavs

66

perhaps. Above the open terrace, the sky had cleared and was seething with stars.

Bit of a far cry, Vince tried hesitantly, from my kayaking problems, isn't it?

Actually, perhaps not, Clive said in a knowing voice. Maybe not at all.

Oh come on, Adam laughed. If you treat everything as a deep and mysterious secret we won't be able to talk about anything at all.

Vince saw Michela's hand gripping Clive's now. He sighed. He pursed his lips. I've been involved, of course, in negotiating and renegotiating loans to Third World countries. What can I say? Actually the bank directors do think a lot about the human consequences of their decisions. It's a complex situation.

What's complex, Clive cut in, about people dying of hunger? You should be ashamed of yourself.

Ease off, Clive, Mandy said.

By the way, Keith put in, check out those Wops! A pair of young Italian women were wriggling back to back. The band played with more enthusiasm.

On the other hand, Vince went on, as a bank, our primary responsibility, inevitably, is towards our shareholders. He stopped: I wish we were discussing my paddling problems.

Perhaps we are, Clive said.

Oh *come on*! Adam looked up from his phone. Michela was grim. She took the tobacco herself now. Her fingers were trembling.

When we've finished, I'll explain, Clive insisted.

Okay, Vince said. I'll give you a typical example. So, a large organisation, maybe even a country, asks us, in consortium with other banks most likely, to extend them a loan. A big loan. We know that this country needs money to develop its economy and improve its people's lot. So we agree, having negotiated certain collateral of course and despite the fact that we are accepting a lower rate of interest than usual. The client is creditworthy we tell the shareholders. Then something happens. The government changes. There's a drought. They start a war. They make a disadvantageous contract with some multinational commodities set-up. The currency market shifts. They spend the money on arms. All of a sudden we have a debt crisis and our shareholders are looking at losses. Now the question is, how far can we be charitable on their behalf? That's not why ordinary people invested their money in our bank.

All you're saying, Clive said. He had to raise his voice because the music was louder now. All you're saying is that the normal, comfortable mechanisms for accumulating fortunes have broken down. Tough bloody luck. But when you're looking at kids with swollen bellies and maggots in their lips, there's only one real question: How can I help?

Vince hesitated. A fourth beer was before them.

And how have you helped, Adam cut in. He had a light, sardonic smile. What have you ever done?

Come on, Adam, Keith said. Chill.

From what I gather you go to a demonstration and shout your head off, but then at the same time you're setting up your own little business in the tourist trade, which is what kayaking is in the end.

Adam's even voice was barely audible above the throb of inane music. The Italian girls had attracted others to the dance floor. The instructor had a hint of a smile at the edge of his mouth, as if what he was saying were not offensive at all. When I teach kayak, he went on, two evenings a week on the estuary, I do it free, for underprivileged kids, in my spare time. You're making money and pretending you're involved in some cause to save the world.

There was a very short pause. As in a collision on the road there was a split second in which everybody realised that they were involved in some kind of accident, without yet knowing how serious.

Enough, let's talk about tomorrow's paddle, Keith said determinedly. I was saying to Clive, I think it might be time to split up into two or three groups around ability levels.

Clive had climbed to his feet. He reached across the table and slapped the chinless man hard across the face. Clive has a knotty, powerful arm, a solid hand. Adam fell sideways against Amal. The boy held him. Something clattered to the tiled terrace floor. The phone. A beer glass had gone over.

Prick!

Michela stood and pulled him back, put her arms round him.

Clive! Mandy shrieked. For God's sake!

He pushed the girl away, stepped backwards knocking over his chair, and walked off. Michela fell back and burst into tears, crouched by the table. Stupid, she was shaking her head. Stupid!

From their scattered tables the other campers were watching. One of the Spanish children was hiding behind Mandy's chair. Amal picked the phone from the floor and wiped the beer off it with the front of his T-shirt.

Since those people were killed, Michela got out, in Milan, he's been so tense. She stifled her tears, sat on a chair. Vince was in a trance. He felt exhilarated, upset. Only now did he notice there was beer dripping in his lap.

If he's broken my phone . . . Adam began. But the mobile was already beeping with the arrival of another message.

I'd better go and talk to him, Keith stood up.

Later, it turned out that Adam's sister-in-law in Southampton had given birth to a healthy little boy. They should have been celebrating.

KEITH'S ROCK

Vince watched Amal. This was the Rienz below Bruneck, a broad brown swirl of summer storm water rushing and bouncing between banks thick with brushwood, over-hung with low, grey boughs, snagged in the shallows with broken branches that vibrate, gnarled and dead, trapped by the constant pressure of the passing flood. A hazard.

Amal sits alert and relaxed in his red plastic boat. They are ferry-gliding, crossing the river against the current. The Indian boy waits his turn in the eddy, chatting with the others. The boats rock and bang against each other. Someone is humming the hamster song. Then one firm stroke and the prow thrusts into the flood. The leading edge of the boat is lifted to meet the oncoming water. The current is wild and bouncy, not the steady strong flow of the narrower torrent, but the uneven tumbling of scores of mountain streams gath-ered together in the lower valley and channelled into a space that seems to resist their impetuous rush. The water piles on top of itself. It comes in waves, fast and slow.

The hull of the boat lifts. Amal has sunk his paddle on the downstream side as brace and rudder. Without a further stroke, the diagonal steady, the trim constantly adjusted, the kayak is squeezed across the flood and, without apparent effort, slides into an eddy against the further bank. The boy sits there steady, helmet wreathed in willow twigs. What is he doing that I can't?

Vince is familiar with the notion that kayaking is an activity where words, instructions, will take you only so far. In her first bossy excitement at having finally persuaded her husband, two years ago, to take up a sport, Gloria had given Vince a book, the BCU handbook, that taught all the strokes. There were diagrams, photographs, tips. Vince studied them. The stroke that most concerned him then was the Eskimo roll. He hated the embarrassment of having to swim out of his upturned boat and be rescued, perhaps by a twelve-year-old girl or a sixty-year-old man, on the muddy shore of the Thames Estuary.

But text and diagrams were not enough. He who understood the most complex accounting procedures at a glance, who oversaw the foreign activities of one of the world's top ten financial institutions, could not get his mind around the co-ordinated movement of hands, hips and head that would take you from the upside-down position, face blind and cold in the slimy salt water, to the upright, sitting steady again, paddle braced in the wavelets, the stinging breeze in your eyes. Even when he learned the movement, when he began to come up nine times out of ten, it was still as if some conjuring trick were being performed, something subtracted even from the most attentive gaze, an underwater sleight of hand. Only that now it was being performed through him. Whatever his motives for starting the sport, he knew that this was the reason he had continued, not the health advantages his wife nagged him about for so long, out of love, no doubt (she feared the businessman's thrombosis), but this stranger business of his body having learned things that his mind would never know, the idea of access to a different kind of knowledge; and, together with that, an edge of anxiety. There was always the tenth time when you didn't come up and didn't know why. All at once, he found he needed this excitement.

Vince! It was his turn. He paddled to the top of the eddy and out. Do I have the angle right? The boat was tossed up, thrust sideways. Now he was paddling like mad on the downstream side to keep the angle. The further bank was slipping by. Already he was downstream from Amal. He was working, sweating in the heavy jacket with its double layer of rubber. I'm inefficient. I'm messy. The hull scraped on a thick branch poking out in a swirl of brown water. For a second Vince was unnerved by the sheer volume of the water piling at him, so muddy and broken. Finally, he fought his way into an eddy a good fifty yards down from the Indian boy.

What do you think is wrong with my paddling, he had asked Louise last night in the tent. After the ridiculous argument between Clive and Adam, there had been a long and tedious conversation with Mandy about her divorce and difficult teenagers – she seemed determined to compare notes, as if a separation could be compared with a bereavement – and when at last he had managed to get back to the tent he had lain in his sleeping bag, waiting for his daughter's return. In the shadows, a glint caught his eye. Something yellow. He switched on the torch. On her copy of *The Lord of the Rings*, in the corner by her pillow, Louise had lined up the contents of her cosmetics bag. A thin oval bottle was catching the light. There was a yellow liquid inside. Suddenly the idea of femininity was intensely present in the soft curves of the glass, the pale colour of this cheap scent. Beside it lay a puff of pink cotton wool. Vince thought of Michela and Clive. They will be in each other's arms. My daughter won't want to share a tent with me next year, he decided.

Crouching to push between the flaps, Louise stumbled. Sorry, Dad. Were you asleep? It was past midnight. He told her about the argument: So then Clive just leans across the table and whacks him one, I mean, really hard! What idiots, the girl said. I'd never go for an older bloke like that, if I was Michela. They're in love, Vince said. He's not that old. Sitting on her sleeping bag, the girl had put on a long night-dress and was removing things from underneath. It was something her mother had always done. Love! the girl snorted. She even sounded like her mother. Well, Tom isn't exactly your age, Vince suggested. Louise giggled. She was brushing out her hair. I'm only doing it to piss off Amelia. Suddenly she was indignant. The way she's acting, you'd think he was already her property! Vince asked: Now you've seen me for a couple of days, what do you think is wrong with my paddling?

Don't be boring, his daughter said.

No, tell me, I'm getting obsessed.

Probably that's the problem then. With sports, the more you think about it, the more you screw up. Phil is such a prick, though. She was studying her toenails with the torch. He kept downloading these dirty pictures and trying to get us to look. Honestly. Then there's the fact that you never wanted to do it in the first place.

What?

Kayak, silly. You only started because Mum forced you. God knows why. And you only came on this trip to be on holiday with me. Probably you'd rather be at the office.

But now I'm here, I want to forget the office, he told her.

73

God, I'm exhausted. I've got a blister on my thumb. She threw herself back on her sleeping bag. This is so bloody uncomfortable.

Lying in the dark – his daughter had started to tell him some news from her cousins, something about her having to change room while they decorated – Vince thought back to that odd period when his wife had absolutely insisted he try this sport. There had been an atmosphere of crisis in the family, but with no substance, as when the market crashes without even a rumour of bad news. Perhaps that was why he had finally agreed. It seemed so much more important to her than he could understand. He began to take lessons Saturday afternoon, out on the estuary. But not long after he started, Gloria had stopped. You don't want me always telling you what to do, she said. She concentrated on her tennis. In the blue dark of the tent, Vince announced: I've been thinking it would be nice to live together again, next term, Lou. Me and you. His daughter didn't reply. Are you asleep? A patter of rain had begun to fall on the tent.

Vince followed Amal down the river. Whatever it was he was supposed to learn, he thought, had to do with the boy's calmness. His muscles were perfectly relaxed as a wave smacked into the boat. When he slalomed between stones, the upper body swayed in supple response. This is something more easily observed than emulated. Ahead, Tom was thrashing with determination. He is trapped into being a man to the girls. Amelia, Louise and Caroline were always beside him, pestering, giggling, offering themselves. Mark tagged doggedly after them. Vince rather likes Mark. Adam was precise, steady, executing textbook strokes. Phillip looked for every opportunity to turn his kayak on end, spin it round, force it over a rock and into the stopper behind. The skull and crossbones are visible on his helmet. Max and Brian were splashing each other. But Amal seemed to flow around the obstacles like the water itself. A safe pair of hands, Vince had begun to repeat to himself as he paddled. A safe pair of hands. More and more he would allow his consciousness to be submerged in the rhythm of the repeated phrase. Don't fight the water, go with it. Don't fight, don't fight. Behind him, Michela performed every manoeuvre as if it had been learned, very correctly, only moments before. She is a determined disciple in the wake of her guru. Clive has said not a word today. He is stony, silent, embarrassed by last night's madness. From bend to bend, eddy to eddy, they descended the river in a plastic line until, shortly before lunch, Keith injured himself.

Let's learn something new, kids, their leader shouted. Tail dips, Keith proposed. His eyes had their glassy brightness. We're late for lunch, Adam objected. People are getting tired.

Okay, so what we're going to do is to use this rock to push the tail under the oncoming current where it pours over.

The rock was about two feet across with the current pressing hard all round. Keith allowed his boat to be drawn up the eddy, then turned it and paddled backwards so that the tail of the boat was pushed under the water pouring over. The effect was immediate. First the stern was sucked down, into the oncoming rush, then quite suddenly the whole boat was forced vigorously upward and forward as if launched from a catapult.

Wey hey! Keith shouted. It was a pantomime of adolescence. With the exception of Mark and Caroline, the kids were enthusiastic. Cool! But Clive was shaking his head, arms folded in resignation on his paddle. Vince was torn between his interest in the manoeuvre itself, and his awareness that both of yesterday's antagonists disapproved. They don't want their sport to be a game.

Should be able to go vertical, Keith announced, if you get the entry right. He repeated the performance. His face glowed with a sort of second youth. This time, as the tail was sucked under, Keith let his heavy, paunchy body go right back with it. The boat rose, higher and higher until it seemed to stand still a second, vertical on its tail, then toppled backwards into the rush. Oh yeah! The kids clapped. Ace!

With enviable ease, Keith rolled up at once. He had hardly been under water a second. But he let out a loud cry. Across his wrist was a long deep gash. Swinging the paddle, he had caught a rock edge, or something very sharp. More than two inches of skin had opened up wide, ragged, deep and red. Keith stared. Oh! He was bleeding profusely. Already Adam was beaching his boat in the shallows. He had a first-aid kit under his seat. Blood was pumping out of Keith's arm. There were squirts of it. Eventually a bandage was found. They tied it tight. But the man must go to hospital. Suddenly the day has a purpose.

The main group was left to eat their lunch while four boats raced down five miles of busy river to the get-off point where the minibus had been parked: Keith, Mandy, Michela, Vince. The two men with coaching qualifications must stay with the kids. Keith had been adamant about that. Those were the BCU rules. He looked the two of them in the eyes. Clive is in charge, he said.

Hurrying down the river, with no plan for playing or learning, just one goal, to get the man stitched up, Vince finally found himself at home on the water. The sudden purposefulness made it easier, and the trust they had put in him. The bow swept into the current. He paddled. He reached determinedly for his strokes. The river was swollen, but straightforward. Perhaps I am a canoeist, he decided. They smacked into a wave train. He laughed. His face ran with sweat and spray. But Keith was evidently in pain. The bandage was soaked in blood. The man was gritting his teeth. Mandy was scolding him for always taking risks, showing off to the kids. How could he have known? Michela objected. She was panting. It was one in a million to catch a sharp edge like that.

At last they were paddling across a low lake at the bottom of the run. A storm of ducks rose from the water. Keith and Mandy were already approaching the beach, the get-out point. The air was humming with flies. Vince had waited to let Michela catch up. He was elated by the speed of the descent. Okay? She looked at him, flushed with effort, eyes shaded beneath black helmet. Exhausted, she said.

Course, if I go to hospital, Keith complained, they'll tell me I can't paddle for the rest of the week. He was up front in the minibus. You're bloody well going, Mandy told him. She had a proprietorial manner. You'll need stitches, I'm afraid, Vince said. Keith blew out his cheeks and sighed. Photo of my war wound, please, he asked.

With Michela to interpret, the injured man was left at the hospital in Bruneck, while Mandy and Vince drove back to the campsite to get a car. It was ten miles up the valley. What Keith was really worried about, the woman explained, was the last day, the stretch of river above Sand in Taufers, the grand finale of the trip; he wouldn't be able to be there, which meant Clive and Adam running the show together, who hated each other. Keith played the fool, but in the end he only did it for the group. He was totally dedicated.

Vince was driving. Well, the combatants seem to have agreed a truce today, he said. It was the first time he had driven a minibus. Actually, I can't help thinking Clive is right really. At least in general. I mean, when one of us gets hurt, like now, we immediately rush to help. But we don't do anything for people we don't know.

Nor do they for us, the woman said sensibly. She was still wearing wetsuit shorts, and a soaking T-shirt on a stout body. The thing is there's helping, she said, and there's shouting about helping.

It was mad to hit him, Vince agreed.

No, but apart from that, don't you think, it's all very well him having this cause and so on, we all agree with it, but in the end it's easy rushing about and chanting at demonstrations. Clive's never had to deal with things like a divorce, or you losing Gloria like that. He's always worried about people on the other side of the planet.

Can't blame him for not having suffered a catastrophe, Vince thought.

All I'm saying is, I judge a bloke by his personal life, what he makes around him, not his ideals.

He looks like he's got something pretty nice going with Michela, Vince said. He glanced in the mirror.

I've seen him the same way with half a dozen others.

Really? Well, good for him, I suppose.

Turning towards her a second as he spoke, he found the woman looking at him quite intently. Her chubby right knee jerked up and down under her hand. I think blokes like yourself, she said quietly, I mean who've been husbands all your lives, don't understand men like Clive. And vice versa. You're chalk and cheese. But women understand. They have to. Look at Keith, for example, married too young, then has affairs, everybody knows, but won't leave home, like. He has his responsibilities.

Doesn't sound like my idea of being a good husband.

He's stuck at it, Mandy said. While Clive is always talking about universal justice.

And Adam? Vince was aware of a social circle drawing him in. Perhaps, having lost his wife, he should become part of the Waterworld community. He would go to all the club's events. He could gossip and be gossiped about. Except, of course, that there was nothing to say about him. What have I ever done?

Adam's wife's handicapped, Mandy said. MS. No, handi-capped's the wrong word. She shot Vince an enquiring glance. Actually, I think your Gloria looked after her in hospital.

I'm really sorry, Vince said. I had no idea.

Campsite! Mandy shouted. Don't miss the turn.

They crossed the bridge, passed the church, trundled down the track between the tents in the bright sunshine. Mandy took over the driving seat of the minibus to head back to the river and pick up the group. Vince went to get his own car to return to the hospital. This was what he'd been brought along for. Fifteen minutes later, on impulse, trapped behind a tourist coach on the narrow, bendy road to Bruneck, he opened the glove compartment of the car, found his mobile and turned it on. There were no messages. Then, driving, he called the office. It was strange. In a matter of seconds he was in touch with London, with reality. His secretary was a small Chinese woman in her fifties. Of course you're needed, she told him, but everybody's agreed to wait till you're back. That would be Monday. So nothing urgent? he asked. It'll be urgent on Monday, Mr Marshall, but not before. She asked him if he were having a good break. It was blis-tering in London, she said. She couldn't remember a year like it. He told her he felt immensely refreshed.

Vince drove past stacks of timber, sawmills. The sun was fierce. There was an open yard full of wooden weathercocks, machine-carved, life-size crucifixes, curious trolls. We come here to play on the river and have no contact with the locals, he thought. A lean old man in a broad-brimmed hat and blue overalls was scything the steep bank above the road to the right. Quite probably he had never been on the water that raced through his valley. Is it really possible I'll be back in the City on Monday? Vince was conscious of enjoying the drive, of deliberately looking out for everything foreign and unusual: the wide wooden balconies, the gothic script over shops and hotels, the weathercocks, the hay hung on wooden trestles up steep slopes, the little children in lederhosen, the onion domes of the churches. Did I ever belong to anything aside from the bank? he wondered. Was I part of any community outside the office? Important decisions were being taken without him. I mustn't miss the turn to the hospital, he worried.

They're seeing him now, Michela looked up and smiled. The waiting room was a mix of tourists and locals, sitting round the walls, flicking through provincial newspapers, international glamour magazines, nursing wounds and coughs. Two or three men kept glancing at the tall Italian girl in her neoprene shorts and white bikini top. Only since Gloria's death had Vince become acutely aware that he had never been with any other woman but his wife. He had never 'picked up' a woman. They had found themselves, he and Gloria, in adjacent rooms in Durham university dorms. It would have been hard to establish a moment when either deliberately chose the other. By a process of happy osmosis they had married. If you removed that boulder, Keith had been talking to the group yesterday about reading the river, which way do you think the water would go? How many things downstream would that effect? Suddenly Vince is in trouble again. With a determined effort, he asked the girl:

How many of these groups will you be getting then?

Sorry? Michela looked up from a magazine.

Will you be having another group right after ours?

Four altogether. We have a week's break after this one for a demonstration in Berlin. Then one after another right through to the end of August.

And then?

How do you mean?

I suppose you have some other job.

We'll go back to England, do courses there through the winter. In England the only real white water is in winter. Here it slows up when the glaciers stop melting. She laughed: We must look crazy dressed like this.

Me more than you, he said. He was wearing a grey thermal top and swimming shorts. She raised an eyebrow.

Being so much older, Vince explained.

You're younger than Keith.

And you won't miss anyone in Italy?

No, she grimaced.

There must be someone.

I hate Italy.

All the English love it.

She turned to him. Suddenly she was wry and sophisticated. You want to know? Everybody seems to think I'm such a mystery. I'm not. Just that all the Italian I heard before I was ten was my parents arguing, hating each other and me. Understand?

I'm sorry, Vince said.

But the girl wouldn't let him off the hook. And when I was in my teens it was my mother on her own telling me she didn't want to live anymore. She regularly took overdoses. The hospital, the stomach pumps, at least a dozen times. Okay? Got the idea?

Vince sensed the girl was trying to crush him by the

completeness of this disaster and the sarcastic lightness with which she spoke of it. There was nothing he could reply. He looked at the young woman, her short glossy hair, tall neck, smooth olive cheeks, lips parted, eyes clouded. She thinks I'm inadequate, bland. Michela smiled rather sourly: I watched Disney films and read comics in English. English was escape for me. It was another world. Does that make sense now? Has the mystery dissolved?

Vince still couldn't see how to reply.

She eased off: Then just when things are looking promising, Clive goes and makes a scene like that last night.

Did he apologise?

Not yet.

Might be wise, Vince said quietly.

It's not up to me to tell him what to do. She was sharp again.

Actually, Vince went on, I agreed with him, you know, in a way . . . with what Clive was saying. In the end, it's a position you can only respect.

How do you mean?

Well, that as communication speeds up and the countries of the world come closer to each other, it gets harder and harder to avoid the impression that we have a responsibility towards those who are suffering.

If you bloody well agree, why don't you do something about it?

Like hit Adam?

Oh don't be funny. She was scathing.

Vince was finding this difficult. To agree with someone, he said, doesn't mean that you share their passion.

They were sitting side by side on green plastic seats in what might be any waiting room in Western Europe. She was holding a copy of the Italian magazine *Gente*, leaning forward, feet tucked under the chair, girlish and belligerent. He realised he had adopted the condescending voice he found himself using so often with Louise. He didn't know how else to speak to someone so young.

Well, it sounds like an excuse to me, she said. I mean, what would it take before someone like you actually did something about the state of the world? Would some huge natural catastrophe be enough? Or would it have to happen right in central London before you woke up? Will people never see what's going on?

Before he could answer, she started to tell him that she admired Clive so much because of the intensity of this concern he felt. Only he couldn't find a channel to express it. Do you understand? They went to demonstrations and so on, they had to. But it didn't *achieve* anything. Clive really means it, she insisted, when he says we want to use these kayak trips to get people to think differently about the world, to notice that the glaciers are melting, that the planet is being ruined. Obviously we have to make enough money to live, but that's not why we're doing it.

Vince listened. As she spoke, the girl grew more and more fervent. She is pleading, he thought. Her whole face was animated. Her urgency was beautiful. Other men in the room were watching. You can't split up the world, she was telling him now. You can't care for this and not that, the Third World's problems, but not global warming or GM foods. Do you see what I'm saying? It's all part of the *same* campaign. There's a right and wrong behind . . .

Keith emerged from a tiled corridor. His arm was in a sling, his bearded face was pale, but he was smiling. Only eight stitches, he told them, and an order to do absolutely nothing for a month. Great. Now I need a drink.

They found a café in the centre of Bruneck where Vince

83

noticed that Keith flattered the young woman in every possible way, winking, joking, passing remarks, until at last she relaxed and accepted an ice cream laced with rum and Keith said in all his experience he had never heard of anyone getting such a deep wound from doing a simple roll in an apparently innocuous patch of water. It was as if there were an open switchblade just under the surface. Waiting for me! Kismet! he laughed. Or kiss me, as the case may be. His eyes are twinkling.

Michela hadn't understood. Keith launched into an explanation. Vince's mind began to wander. The café tables around them spread out over a recently renovated square of fresh porphyry cobbles and clean stone-and-wood façades. A lot of money is being invested here, Vince thought. It was a big collective effort, to capture the tourists, but also to maintain their identity. There were baskets of hanging flowers and, beside the café door, a large wooden troll carved from some gnarled tree trunk with a face at once grotesque and madly benevolent, pipe in warped lips, hat on a knotty head, axe held in crooked fingers. Not unlike the drunk with his shack down by the river bank. Oh Vince! Earth to Vince! Have an ice cream as well, mate, Keith insisted. It's great with rum. You paddled brilliantly, by the way. Huge improvement. Come on, the others won't be back yet. Yes, have an ice cream, Michela joined in. She smiled with a long spoon in her lips. Come on, Ageing Mr Banker, enjoy yourself. You look like you don't enjoy yourself enough.

Where's Wally? Phil demanded.

Vince couldn't find the thing. He searched everywhere. He was upset. I can't believe how seriously you're taking it, Louise said. It's only a cheap toy. Mark came to their tent to tell the girl she was supposed to be helping with dinner. The Louts are on. Vince just couldn't find the stupid puppet. He was sure he had tied it to his cag.

Vincent has lost Wally! Phil shrilled. He ran from tent to tent. Wally missing believed drowned! Re-drowned! Stock market'll be tumbling, Adam remarked. He was hanging out the wet kit. Wally wasn't on Vince's cag, nor in his dry-bag. Enormous fines, the chinless man insisted, shaking his head, smiling wryly, if only to pay the increase in our insurance premium. A grave breach of trust, Max mocked. Unspeakable punishments. There were decades of literature on Wally, Keith said. He was a mythical figure, a patron saint of river communities, the archetypal paddler. Went over Niagara, Mandy joined in. His disappearance presages disaster. Vince looked everywhere. The boat, the minibus, the tent. There'll have to be a funeral, Amelia announced solemnly. Ask not for whom the bell tolls. Someone who's lost Wally, Caroline announced, has to buy a substitute and wear it for the rest of his life. She tried to hold a gloomy face, then burst into giggles. It was time to eat spaghetti bolognaise.

We have a new feature on the landscape, Mandy announced as the meal was finishing. Let's drink to Keith's Rock, a remarkable underwater geological feature discovered by the Yorkshire man Keith Graham. There was applause, and a toast: To Keith's Rock! but immediately followed by a chant, from all the children, Where's Wally, Where's Wally? They were sitting in a circle on the ground, their plates on their laps. The sun had long since gone behind the mountain beyond the town, but the evening was still bright, the air warm. Then Michela stood up from beside Clive and came round the circle to whisper in Vince's ear, They've stolen it, silly. They're teasing you.

May I say a word? Vince asked. He cleared his throat.

Pigs, Slobs, Louts. He paused. It is with regret that I must inform you that while the eminent discoverer Mr Graham was in hospital after the christening of his remarkable rock, I was unfortunately obliged to go to the police station, to report a, er, serious theft. Indeed a kidnap. Wally, a character, or rather a spirit, a haunting presence, whom we all agree, I think, is the ghostly heart and soul of our community, without whom, etc. – Wally, or at least the effigy he is obliged to inhabit following his untimely decease, has been taken from us and is presently being held against his will. Now I must warn you all that the Italian *carabinieri*, if not the Austrian *Polizei*, will be arriving in just a few moments to question everyone and search all the tents. The criminals face summary execution. You have just a few seconds to own up.

His daughter, he noticed, was smiling. Then suddenly Wally was flying up in the air in the middle of the circle. The tiny bear wore a small red and white scarf. Who had it? Who stole it? It fell without a bounce beside a stack of dirty plates. Nobody owned up. The creature was awarded then to Max who had forgotten to replace the drain plug in his boat after emptying it at lunchtime and had almost sunk before he realised what the problem was. I shall cherish our patron paddler and protector, he announced, more carefully than has my predecessor. Oh aren't we affectionate, Brian said. His prede–what? Phil demanded. As on every evening, the boy had returned his food almost untouched.

Serious note now folks, Keith interrupted. Serious announcement to finish the evening. No doubt word has got around that our two illustrious instructors had a bit of a barney yesterday evening. About politics, would you believe? Politics! Brian groaned. What's that? They've made it up, of course, but from now on, the rule is, *no discussion of politics* for the rest of the trip. Okay? Anyone caught discussing anything that could remotely be considered to be political will be obliged to run round the whole campsite in just their underpants. Yes, please! Max shouted. Oh shut up! What matters here is us, our paddling, learning to help each other, making the group work. Is that clear? Any outside or personal interests, however noble, must be sacrificed to those goals for as long as we're together. Now, tomorrow will be a half day; we're going to drive out to a slalom course for the morning and do two or three runs to sort out who will be able to do the tough trip on the last day. Then it's rest time for the afternoon. You can go into town or take the cable car up to the glacier.

The Pigs were on washing-up duty. Amelia and Tom stood side by side at the big sinks outside the bathrooms. You've left a bit, the girl complained. She had tied her hair in a ponytail. It's a mark on the plate, Tom said. In the plastic, look. They bent their heads over it. No it isn't. Yes, it is. They nudged elbows and pushed each other and giggled, both clutching the plastic plate. Beneath the inevitable straw hat, Max made faces to Vince. I think I love you, he began to croon, but that's what life is made of. The boy did an excellent imitation of the hamster's mechanical movements, imaginary microphone in one hand, drumstick in the other. It's a manufacturing defect, can't you see! Tom shouted, but he let the girl hold his wrist. They were tugging, laughing in each other's eyes. And it worries me to say that I've never felt this way. Max dropped his tea towel over their heads. Idiot, Tom yelled, but the economics student seemed perfectly happy with the situation.

Someone tapped Vince on the shoulder. Dad? Louise had put a skirt on, and a short top. She wore earrings. Can I have some money to go to the bar? Just behind her, Mark was hovering nervously, a polite smile on his face. Handing over a note, Vince felt old and disorientated. The Pigs were now occupying three sinks with piles of dirty dishes and the kids doing nothing but fool around. Come on team, he told them, let's get going and do it properly. Tom. Amelia! Come on now. When Amelia started carrying the plates back to the kitchen tent, Tom suddenly became earnest again and asked Vince how far it was really possible for a government to establish the true volume of the money supply. A professor at LSE had shown them an unbelievably complex calculation. Discovering the exact quantity of the supply was largely irrelevant, Vince said. What mattered was to establish whether it was going up or down, which actually was all too easy. Ooh, I know, Max laughed, I know!

Afterwards, weary of company and conversations, Vince went for a walk around the large campsite on his own. A Jaguar with Dutch plates was parked in front of a luxury caravan. Through the window he glimpsed an elderly couple and, on the table between them, a goldfish in a bowl. He stopped and looked again. Why would anyone drive from Holland with a goldfish? A tiny child on a tricycle circled a waste bin. Somewhere out of view Italian voices were singing to the accompaniment of guitar and accordion, while behind the surface buzz of the site, thunder rolled faintly in the peaks.

Vince looked up. The glacier beyond the castle was obscured by mist. Shining from behind the nearest mountains, a last flare of summer light had turned the vapour to bright milk above the sombre gorge below. It was like some of the skies they had seen in old paintings in Florence, Vince thought: cosmic drama above tortured saints. He stopped. There was no passion between myself and Gloria, he said out loud. To his left was a low tent with a large motorcycle beside it. A haggard woman in early middle age sat cross-legged in black leather pants, smoking, reading a thriller. The thunder came louder. Was that what she meant when she said, I'm so sorry? He began to walk again. The week in London – all work – year in year out; the weekend, full of domestic chores. There was no passion, he repeated. He stepped aside for a car carrying four bicycles on its roof. But does that matter? There's always something so stupid about passion, Vince told himself. That girl, he thought, is more intelligent than to say those things she said to you. As if the world's sick could all suddenly be healed. She says those things, he thought, to be in love.

Come on, a voice interrupted: You haven't got Wally to talk to now, you know. Adam was beside him. Loos are cleaner this side of the campsite, he explained. Want a walk? It's going to rain, Vince said. So we'll get wet, Adam smiled. He suggested they climb the hill behind the group of houses at the entrance to the site. There was a church poking out from the woods above, perhaps half a mile away and a few hundred feet higher. There must be a path. But what if there's a storm? Vince worried. We'll get drenched, Adam said equably.

They walked quickly, out past the camp shop and bar, the larger church in the valley that rang its bells every morning. Finding a signpost, they struck off up the hill and were soon among thick pine trees. You were talking to yourself, Adam repeated. Getting old, Vince said. The chinless man seemed in good spirits. He said how wonderful the air was here. He worked in insurance, he explained, policy design, risk calculation, dull stuff. What did Vince think about the government's plans for new banking regulations? Watch it, Vince objected. We'll be running round the site in our underpants next. He didn't like the way people kept insisting on his professional life. Oh, I'm not about to whack you round the chops if we don't agree. Adam stretched the corner of his mouth and touched it gingerly. Bloke's a primitive. Well-meaning, but primitive.

Vince said nothing. This is an attempt to make me an ally, he thought. The path crossed a meadow, then was back in the wood again. Odd this thunder, he observed, always there but always far away. It's up on the plateau, Adam said, at seven thousand feet. You know? Different world. After a while they heard the sound of water splashing on stone. It was getting nearer. In the twilight, beneath the dark-green pines, they stood on a small log bridge over a stream that fell towards them down mossy black rock. Adam chose this moment to say how sorry he had been about Gloria. He really should have come to the funeral. We taught a couple of courses together, you know, a few years back. Then we did the Ardèche trip of course. She was really kind to my wife when she was in hospital.

Thanks, Vince said.

Gloria was a wonderful woman, Adam insisted. So full of energy. She gave her time so generously.

Vince had heard this description of his wife from various sources. We'll get caught walking down in the dark if we don't hurry, he said. But Adam wanted to press on. They were almost at the church. Your main problem with your paddling, he began to say, is the way you sit too far back in the boat, as if you were afraid. Apart from breaking in and out, you're usually safer leaning forward, in the attack position, reaching for it.

The path climbed steeply and was stony now and damp. The air had taken on a cool, sweet smell. Vince was wearing sandals and his foot slipped. Eventually they reached a low wall; a gate led into a churchyard with just a few dozen graves. Neat lines of black wrought-iron crosses stood at the head of thin rectangles of shale. In the centre of each cross was a photo of the deceased, a name, some dates. When they both stopped a moment by a fresh grave, smothered in yellow flowers, Adam rather cautiously asked Vince where he had had Gloria buried. She was cremated, he said. I scattered the ashes in the estuary. Oh. Adam seemed taken aback. I really should have gone to the funeral, he repeated.

The church itself was closed. Opposite the door, beyond the graves, a bench looked out across the valley. They leaned on a low parapet. Down below, the road from Bruneck to Sand in Taufers streamed with headlights, but above, the slopes were already colourless and vague with just here and there, high, high up in the forests opposite, an occasional solitary light: some lonely *baita*, a family with their cattle on the high meadows. Strange being so cut off, Adam murmured. With sudden intuition, Vince announced: You know what the last thing Gloria said to me was? His voice was hard and angry in his throat. I am so, so sorry. He was almost croaking. Those were her last words. She had just a few seconds to speak – she phoned me, you know, she knew she was dying, she recognised the symptoms and managed to phone – and that's what she said: I'm so sorry. Turning, he found Adam staring at him in alarm.

It had begun to rain. The drops were clattering on the tents when they got back. Vince went to the bathroom then lay on his sleeping bag to wait for Louise's return. The rain came harder. It drummed on the kayaks roped to the trailer, on the kitchen tent where Phil and Caroline had begun to kiss. Adam was also lying alone, concerned that his son was late, thinking about that moment in the graveyard with Vince. I miss you so much when I'm away, he texted his wife. The bedridden woman sent a reassuring reply. Sarah's baby was doing fine.

The thunder cracked louder now. In the chalet just beyond their pitch, Michela and Clive had been talking round in circles. You just want me to leave, don't you? she repeated. No, I need you, he said. We're in this business together. We invested the money together and we'll have to pay it back together. He began to talk about an e-mail he had received from Diabolik, one of the members in their militants' news group. There was to be a big demonstration at the American airbase in Vicenza. Some people were going to break in and sit on the runway.

The rain fell harder on the roof. Michela watched her man as he spoke. She had made herself a camomile tea. Her stomach was unsettled. He had insisted on whisky. He was smoking. Come to bed, she said softly. He shook his head. The river will be rising, he said. He picked up the book he'd been reading. *The Case Against Nestlé's*. Then the thunder cracked right overhead and the rain fell with loud slaps against the windows.

Towards three a.m. those who had managed to sleep were woken by a wild clanging. The church bell, not a hundred yards away, had begun to ring. In boxer shorts, pulling a plastic waterproof about him, Vince ran squelching from his tent and banged into Mandy. Did it mean there was going to be a flood? There was something gothic about the woman in her white nightdress in the teeming dark. She was fighting with an umbrella. The guy-ropes need tightening, he said. She clutched at him and almost fell. The nightdress was soaked. It was odd to feel the embrace of her body, the heavy breasts.

The church bell rang and rang. Four or five people had already abandoned their sleeping bags for the big kitchen tent. Phil claimed he would be rained out if it went on. Is it a warning or what? He would have to sleep here with

Amelia and Caroline. Then Michela appeared. Above long tanned legs, she wore a heavy mountain oilskin. She was smiling. Listen up, everybody. It's just a habit here that they ring the bells when it rains really hard. She had come to reassure them. The noise of the bells is supposed to break up the clouds. Certainly breaks up any hope of sleep! Why would it do that? Vince asked. She smiled at him. She had a way, he understood, of seeming seraphic beyond her age. I've no idea, she said. It's a faith they have here, a tradition.

Borrowing an umbrella, Vince made his usual trip to the loo. As always the urinals mysteriously began to flush as he approached. It should be reassuring, this sense of being integrated into the world's sensible automatisms. Your arrival is foreseen, you are provided for. Faith in what? Louise demanded, when he crawled back between the fly-sheets. She had been reading a text message. The little screen glowed. The bell rang incessantly. The rain was trying the quality of Gloria's old tent. Gloria loved camping. There were beads of water running along the seams. I know he acts a bit of a loser, but he's sweet, Louise said of Mark. It's his dad on at him all the time that makes him shy. Oh, it turns out they knew Mum quite well, by the way. She visited his mum who's stuck in bed or something. His dad plays in the same tennis club. I know, Vince said. After a moment he asked, Who's the message from? None of your business, Louise laughed.

They were lying on their beds while the rain drenched the fabric above them and the bell clanged on. Funny, Louise eventually said, her head on her hands, the impression Mum made on people. Mark says he liked her a lot. It was the first time in ten days together that she had spoken to him about her mother. I suppose we all make different impressions on people outside the family, Vince said cautiously.

Suddenly, his daughter began to cry. She lay still, crying quietly. Vince leaned across and put his hand on her forehead, stroked her hair. To his surprise, she didn't push the hand away. It was a pleasure to feel the soft hair under his fingers, the warm skin.

Later, after the rain eased off and the bell stopped, he lay awake, listening to distant voices, the clatter of drops blown off the trees, rustling fly-sheets, zips. He imagined the Italian girl unzipping her waterproof. Clive would be embracing her. Gloria, he whispered. He wasn't jealous. Many evenings he went to sleep this way. The rehearsal of that final phone conversation, then the quiet mouthing of her name. Gloria. In Excelsis Deo, she liked to add primly. But he couldn't hear his wife's wry laugh in the dripping tent with his daughter gently snoring. There was no passion, he whispered. For a moment he imagined getting up again and going to the window of their chalet. You are sick, he thought, Vince Marshall. Sick.

KATRIN HOFSTETTER

Max had hung Wally from the brim of his straw hat. The talismanic bear swung from side to side at every bend. Mandy insisted that everyone buckle up their safety belts. No exceptions! The slalom course was almost thirty miles away. People had slept badly. Caroline had cried off altogether. Don't you think 'sort out the men from the boys' is a pretty sexist expression, Brian was enquiring of Clive. I mean, women don't even get a look-in. Anyway, the boys are usually better than the men, Phil boasted. It was the drooping eyebrows that gave him such a gormless look. Oh you think so too, do you, dearie, Max cried. The minibus pulled its trailer along the Bruneck–Brixen road. Amelia and Tom had their heads bowed over the BCU's manual of correct recovery strokes. They seemed seriously absorbed. Vince felt his stomach tight. He had had to crap twice before departing. The course has sections that are grade four, Amal told him solemnly. That means there's only one line to take through the rapid and you have to get it right. Or kaput! The Indian boy smiled. Why do I feel so determined, Vince wondered, to be on this suicide trip tomorrow? What do I have to prove?

About four hundred yards of river had been carefully reorganised to present more or less every troublesome white-water feature: a stopper, a hole, a couple of daunting waves, rocks in the most trying places. Being dam-fed, the water levels were fairly constant. Criss-crossing over the river was a system of wires from which perhaps forty slalom gates were suspended so that their red- or green-and-white posts were just clear of the water. But this extra subtlety, the weaving back and forth in a set course among obstacles, was for the long, slim slalom boats, the experts. All you have to do, Clive explained earnestly – but he in particular had slept little and badly – at least for the first two runs, is to show me that you can break out of the current at every single eddy on the course, then break back in again without any trouble. Okay? We go down in groups of four. At the bottom you get out and carry your boats back to the beginning again. Keith will be stalking the bank taking notes and giving advice.

Vince ran his fingers round the rim of the cockpit to check that the spraydeck was sealed. The tab was out, ready to pull. He was with Mandy, Amal and Phil. At once he sensed he would have felt safer in a group with one of the two instructors. The water rushed down, grey and gleaming, to where they sat ready on the low bank. But of course, not to be with an instructor was a compliment. The pour-overs were larger and fiercer than any they had run before. There were places where even a small mistake would lead to getting pinned against a rock. It's years since I did something as tough as this, Mandy muttered. She was checking the strap on her helmet. Slalom courses are always a doddle, Phil said knowledgeably. They've taken out any sharp stuff you could hurt yourself on, haven't they? Nobody ever gets killed. He seemed disappointed. You lead, Vince told Amal. The Indian boy launched himself from the bank.

Pointing upstream, Amal ferried from the bank to the first rock and signalled to Vince to follow. First his finger indicates the person who is the object of the message, then the place he has to arrive at. As Vince moved out, Amal was already leaving his small refuge to drop down behind the first spur. One by one the group followed. First in the eddy, then back into the flow and through a fierce stopper. Take it close to the left, Keith was shouting from the bank. He had his arm in a sling. Right against the rock! The rocks are your friends!

Vince raced down. The deceleration as you punched into the eddy, raising the bottom of the boat to the still water, was fearsome. At the third he misjudged and was pulled over by the inertia. He rolled up on the second attempt. It was freezing. The cold gripped his head. He was excited. He signalled to Mandy to follow and broke back into the current again. As the least likely to come to grief, Phil was at the back to pick up anyone who got into trouble.

Certainly beats banking, Vince told Mandy at the bottom when they'd completed the first run. Once again, the concentration required and the physical effort had cleared his mind of all pain. You looked good, Mandy said. She had taken a couple of photos from eddies. Pretty dull, Phil thought. He wanted to play in the big stopper. They heaved the boats onto their backs and trudged up to the top.

On the second run, Amal tried a ferry-glide just below the stopper. It has a hole as well! Keith warned them from the bank. It's grabby. They are behind a spur of rock looking upstream into a fierce churn of white water beneath a drop of about three feet. A cold spume fills the air, causing small rainbows to form in the bright sunshine. The world has a glitter to it, a powerful presence. Everything is immediate. Just downstream of the white water, the surface is irregular and turbulent and there must be a point – you know this – where if you push too close to the froth, the backflow in the stopper will begin to pull you in. The boat will sink and spin in the soft, oxygenated water. But to make it over to the eddy that Amal has spotted way on the opposite bank, you can't let yourself drift too far down. You must ride close to the stopper and its deep white hole. Amal steers his kayak out into the stream. His ability to set the angle and edge of the boat is uncanny. With no effort, he glides across.

Vince follows. He's too vertical, pointing straight upstream. The hole begins to pull. He back-paddles, suddenly loses almost ten yards, but fights his way across with a huge expenditure of effort. Panting, relieved, he signals to Mandy to come across and join them. There's room in the eddy for all four. They can regroup. As she looks across to him, Mandy's face is grim and Vince guesses at once that she isn't going to make it. The woman is hunched. Her posture betrays her nerves. She is here for the group, Vince is aware, for the companionship that expeditions like this can offer a single woman in middle age, for the photographs and fun.

Mandy's first tentative stroke leaves the tail of the boat still anchored in the eddy. Before she's halfway across, she's lost at least twenty yards to the current. Barely breaking the surface, there's a stone in the middle of the river here. She could rest the bow of her kayak behind it, take a break, decide what to do next. But she hasn't seen. She isn't thinking. She drifts against the stone sideways, paddling like mad. It surprises her. With the unexpected contact, the bow is shifted the other way, back to the left bank. She fights the shift, but half-heartedly. The river has got her now. Grey and bouncy, the current swirls towards a smooth black boulder by the bank where it piles up in a tense cushion before being forced back into the centre to plunge down the next drop. All this would be easy enough to negotiate if taken face on, but Mandy is pointing upstream. She is still trying to turn the boat back across the flow when the current pushes it sideways onto the boulder. Immediately she's pinned, the underside of the kayak against the rock, the water crashing on the spray-deck.

Vince is watching all this from the safety of his eddy on the opposite bank, thirty yards upstream. He sees the woman try to brace her paddle against the oncoming water to keep her head up. He has a picture of the blue helmet, the orange paddle-blade. But it's only a fraction of a second before she's down. Now she will pull out and swim. She doesn't. Arm in a sling, Keith is scrambling down the bank. But there are thick brambles between himself and the rock. He can't get to it. Mandy is still under. Amal! Vince looks round. The boy is locked away from the stream by Vince's boat. Vince looks for Phil. Incredibly, he is fooling around in the hole. He's let his kayak be sucked in and is throwing the boat this way and that, tail up, tail down, in the spongy water. He hasn't seen anything. He can hear no screams.

Amal is trying to force a way round Vince to the stream, but now Vince breaks in himself. He will get to her first. In one stroke he's in the quick of it. The power of the current tosses the boat round. It's a matter of seconds. He is bearing straight down on Mandy's boat, still pinned upside down against the rock. The bank is to the right, the next rapid to the left. I have no idea how to do this, Vince thinks.

Keith is shouting something, but Vince can't hear, can't listen. Instead of fighting the pull of the current onto the rock, Vince speeds towards it, as if to spear Mandy's boat as he goes down. Lean into it! Keith is yelling. Vince pays no attention. Just before he hits the submerged boat, he lets go the paddle with his right hand and throws his body towards the rock to grab the bow-handle of the boat. His arm is wrenched violently, but the boat shifts. It's free. Dragged over, Vince thrusts his hand down on the bow of Mandy's boat to bounce up and prevent himself from capsizing. Now he's spun backward and dropping into the rapid. He's just got both hands back on his paddle when he hits a stopper sideways and goes down. This time he rolls up without thinking, as if rolling in white water were the easiest thing in the world. Mandy is swimming. Keith has already got a line to her. Amal is chasing the upturned boat down the river. Exhausted, mentally more than physically, Vince pulls over to the bank.

The deck just wouldn't pop, Mandy is repeating. There's a note of hysteria in her voice. She is stumbling up on the rocks. Her body is shaking. The water was so powerful, it wouldn't pop. I couldn't get out. I was drowning. Thought I might have to take a swim there, Keith laughs. Stitches or no stitches. Then the woman insists on embracing Vince. You saved my life. Nonsense! Later they worked out that the whole crisis had lasted no more than twenty seconds. Nursing the pain in his shoulder, Vince understood he had booked himself a place on tomorrow's trip.

The chair-lift begins a mile or so above Sand in Taufers. It took them up in threesomes, their feet dangling a few yards above the tall pines either side, the cables humming and clicking above them, the air cooling around their faces, the valley falling away dramatically behind. The kids giggled and took photos of each other. Amelia was quiet beside Tom. Max dangled Wally below his seat on a string amid shrieks of fake horror. Somebody had begun to sing 'Inky Pinky Parlez-Vous'.

At the top, a large timber-built hostelry, flying the vertical red and white banner of the Tyrol, sits in a wide meadow hemmed in on three sides by even steeper slopes leading up to a ridge at almost nine thousand feet. But the youngsters really don't want to walk. The sun has a sharper, brighter quality here. They could buy Cokes at the hostel, fool around and sunbathe. Since Bri can only hobble, we've all decided to keep him company, Max laughed. Keith and Mandy had stayed behind, to explore Bruneck, they said. The woman had needed a rest. So for the walk up to the glacier there were just Vince, Amal, Adam, Clive and Michela. Adam tried to persuade his son to join them. Risking nothing, the boy had survived the slalom course well enough. He doesn't want to, Vince said softly. It was clear there was something going on between him and Louise. Adam insisted. It would do everybody good to stretch their legs after being cramped in the boat. Mark didn't even reply now. He turned and ran after the others.

Then no sooner had the walkers set off up a path that zigzagged steeply through walls of flint, than Clive suddenly stopped to apologise to Adam. Michela didn't expect it. The party was brought to a halt on the narrow path. I shouldn't have hit you. A clouded look came over his handsome face. Dead right, you shouldn't, Adam agreed. Then the instructor said, Forget it, but grudgingly, Michela thought. They climbed in single file up the steep slope under bright afternoon sunshine, and as they walked and she watched Clive's strong legs in short trousers and his powerful back bending to the slope, she began to feel angry. You shouldn't be apologising, she began to speak to him in her mind. He isn't worth it. And you shouldn't be wasting time, doing stupid, touristy things, taking groups up mountainsides. The kayaking was a mistake, she told herself now. If we aren't to be happy together, what point is there in arranging these trips? She was thinking in English. What point for a man like Clive? Suddenly she understood that he must do something *serious*. That's why he has never married. He is preparing himself. Michela knew that Clive had lived with two or three other women before her. He couldn't marry because he must do something important. It's crazy for him to lead ungrateful people up a mountain, when they just want to hang around at the *rifugio* and flirt and sunbathe. He must do something that *changes the world*. Yes. Oh, but it made her so furious that he could break off their relationship, he could stop making love, just like that, before there was really any need, and that he could do it without missing her body at all, without any sense of loss. Why did I have to find a saint? she complained. I'm his last temptation. You're a saint, Clive. The voice in her head was louder now. So what are you waiting for? she demanded of him. It sounded like a scream. Whatever it is you have to do, do it!

They climbed slowly, in silence, but in her mind the noise is loud and angry. Why had he apologised? You have a cause, a goal, the voice insisted. She couldn't stop it. She doesn't want him to have doubts. Do something then! If we are not going to love again, at least let me be proud of you. Let me admire you. She stumbled. She put a hand down. How gritty and unrelenting the ground was. She felt dizzy. I haven't been sleeping enough. Above them the slope was a mass of ugly shards. Only far away did it make sense, the peaks ranged in line after line, quivering in the slow convection of the sunny afternoon. There are so many mountains, and so empty. Michela loves them for their emptiness. She loves the miniature look of distant villages in the valley bottom, the thin threads of plunging streams, this placing yourself far away in utter emptiness to look back and down on it all.

From way below came the clang of the cowbell: the beasts, the herd. Why had he humiliated himself like that? Why was he so knotted and tense and thwarted? Clive! She could have helped him. She wanted him to be free. When they stopped at a vantage point, she said out loud: I don't think I can get through the whole summer like this.

She was speaking to Clive, but quite loudly. She feels exhausted. I really can't, she said. The voice was matter-of-fact. It echoed in her head. The others didn't understand. Vince put it down to some momentary slip in English, some conversation he had missed. The climb had been long and steep. He is panting. The panorama was extraordinary. Drink? He offered her his bottle. But people were already moving again. As they walked, Vince was constantly aware of her girlish body swaying after Clive's, the man's powerful tread, her feminine lightness and flexibility. It was strange to be so attracted to a couple like this, to be so conscious of their bodies, of femininity and masculinity, their togetherness. He had seen the girl catching her man's eye. Were Gloria and I ever like that? He wanted to tell them that he approved. He imagined them twining together in love. His interest disturbs him. I approve of their loving and their politics, he thought. Two people cleaving to each other, and caring about the world too. You approve because your own life is so empty. But he did not feel unhappy this afternoon. Being near them, the taciturn man, the urgent girl, seemed to cheer him.

Then after only ten more minutes Amal asked for another stop. I'm getting a headache, he said. Pressure, Adam told him. At this point when I climbed it two years ago, we were already on the ice, Clive said. All around them, the ground was arid flint. Again Michela said out loud, I won't get through the whole summer like this.

Again no one responded. She said it in such a strangely detached way. Slim and tall against the sky, it was as if she wasn't quite among them. Or she is just complaining about the path. Look at this, Amal said. On a plaque nailed into the rock there was an oval photograph of a young woman's face. Vince went close to read. Katrin Hofstetter: 19.1.1979–31.8.1999. The face was bright and the woman's long blonde hair had been brushed forward to fall on her shoulder. Actually, that's about the fourth of those, Adam said. First woman though.

Eventually, they reached the snow and began to walk around the horseshoe of the ridge, so as to descend behind the hostelry. They were on top of the world here. Only far to the north, in Austria, were there taller peaks with larger glaciers. When the ice is gone, Clive explained to Vince, but he evidently wanted Adam to hear, you won't get that slow storage and release of water you get at the moment. It'll either be bone-dry, or, after it rains, you'll get great surges ripping down the slopes and flooding the valleys out. Obviously, the less snow there is, the more the temperature goes up and the more the glacier melts, so there's a built-in acceleration to it all.

Standing on the crusty grey ice, Vince turned to look in all directions at the phenomenon of the Alps. It was curious how something could be at once awesome and vulnerable. Your instinct was to shiver at the majesty, yet you were being told you had destroyed it. Amal asked if anything could actually be done. Only if the whole world changes its lifestyle, Clive remarked, and drastically. Then Adam said: A hawk, look. Apparently he has decided not to argue. Below them a large bird was slipping across the air-stream that rose from the valley. Same principle as a ferry-glide, the Indian boy said. See how he sets the angle and lets the wind squeeze him sideways. Standing right on the edge, where the ridge fell away into the valley beyond, Michela had taken Clive's hand. The couple stood together looking out over an ocean of empty air. The drop is dizzying. The hawk closed its wings and went down like a stone. Clive slipped an arm round her waist. How can I ever go back to the bank? Vince wondered.

Then Michela said: You must do something serious, Clive. She squeezed his hand hard. He turned and found her face flushed with the sun and the glare from the ice. Her eyes were melting in the bright light. Not just demonstrations, she told him. He was staring at her. They were standing on the edge. One forward step and they would be gone right out of things. Had he understood? We have to move, Clive announced. Or we'll be late. This is where the path turns down. Careful not to slip now.

Where are you taking us? someone shouted. Driving back to Sand in Taufers, the minibus had turned off the road down a dirt track. Suddenly the river was beside them, swirling through a deep gully. We're going to look at the get-out point for those of you who are on the trip tomorrow. Clive had his solemn, almost religious expression. When he speaks, Michela thought, it's as if he knew vastly more than anyone else could imagine. He hasn't told me anything.

The bank was steep but easy enough to get down. Basically, Clive pointed upstream, when you come under the bridge, there, where the road crosses, you have about two hundred yards more to paddle, and you're looking for the long flat spur on your right, here, below us. Everybody crowded round. Doddle, Phil said. As ever, he gave the impression of being let down. Yes, it's easy, Clive said. Oh, check out the marker someone's tied on the tree there. A few yards upstream, a long ribbon of orange plastic dangled from the drooping branch of a spruce. And now, Clive said, let me show you what would happen if by chance you fell asleep and drifted a few yards further down.

The dirt track turned abruptly away from the river and up the mountainside through stands of larch. Leaving it, they scrambled down a steep narrow path through brushwood and saplings. This was the gorge that made such a dramatic backdrop to the castle of Sand in Taufers as seen from the campsite. You can see why Long John Silver stuck to ocean-going craft, Brian complained. His club foot slipped. He had hurt himself. Max and Mark stayed to help. Vince grabbed a thin branch and leaned out over the water. Narrowing, the river tumbled rapidly in jumps of five, six and even ten feet, swirling between boulders and rushing against smooth walls of rock.

Clive stopped on a patch of mud and waited for the others to catch up. X-treme! Amelia breathed. They were looking down into a boil of water as the main stream went over a ledge to crash and froth around a huge dark rock just visible in a torment of backwash. This, Clive said, is grade five, verging on six. Give us the BCU definition, Amal. In his high-pitched voice, the boy sang: Only one line to follow, as with grade four – but harder to find and more technical to negotiate. Failure to follow line is seriously life-threatening. He seemed pleased with himself. Ambulance waiting at the bottom sort of thing, Louise said. Hearse more like it, Amelia added. Wicked! Phil approved. He was excited. Wally says this is nothing to Niagara, Max remarked. He was holding the bear to his ear, as if they were whispering together.

Mark stepped back. It's not do-able, though, is it? he asked. He looked worried. I mean, like, I don't see how anyone could get through that. They'd never try. Adam had been gazing with folded arms. Now he invited his son to come and stand beside him. He squatted down, pointed: Punch through the stopper to the right of the rock. There's just room, okay? You use the hole behind to brake and turn, but without falling into it. Then a determined ferry over to the far side, spin just before the bank and take the next drop where that tongue of water shoots through the debris down into the next pool.

They all considered this hair-raising manoeuvre. Vince tried to imagine the effect of gravity in the drops, the power of the water. Perhaps it was possible. Is this the hardest bit, then? Tom enquired. To look down with more safety, Amelia had put an arm round his strong waist. It was curious how she was both the gawky schoolgirl and the society snob. Louise, Vince thought, has a coarser, franker energy. Let's go and look, Michela said. She seemed to have cheered up. The sheer energy of the river was a source of pleasure.

They worked their way down a further hundred yards, scrabbling on stones and mud, occasionally pushing through the wet grass to the edge of the gully from which a soft spray drifted upward with the impact of water falling onto stone below. Immediately you looked down, the eye was captured by a kaleidoscopic shifting of dark-green and brown rock, white foam and blue transparent pools.

Fun to be had with the log there, Adam said. He was shaking his head. Life hath many exits, quoted Max. You just don't have to hit the bloody thing, do you, Phil said boldly. Hard to avoid, Amal thought. A thick tree trunk was wedged between boulders right below a pour-over. Unless you're mad enough to run river-left, that is. They were all relishing this contemplation of dangers they would never undertake. The water boomed. Almost belligerently, Mark again demanded: But nobody's ever done it, have they? Sure they have, Clive replied. He had a smile on his face. There's almost nothing people haven't done. The boy wasn't satisfied. He pushed back the hair that fell on his eyes. But, like, someone you know, you've seen them?

I've done it, Clive said.

Wow! The announcement caused excited reaction. Michela looked at her man sharply. I mean Wow, wow, and triple wow! Louise said. When you went to visit your mother, Clive whispered quickly. Michela couldn't take it in. Why would he lie like this?

How many of you? Adam asked. The kids were all shaking their heads. Respect! Re-spect!

Two local guys, Clive said. From the rafting centre.

But you don't know any local guys, Michela thought.

In the Pyranha? Amal enquired. Wouldn't you need something with more volume?

And you fixed throw-lines and things? Adam asked.

No, no support on the bank, Clive said. They told me the line to follow and we went for it. River-left to avoid the log. The gap is just big enough.

You're mad, Mark declared.

I could do it, Phil said. Bet you I could do it, if someone would let me.

And you never capsized?

Everybody was looking at Clive's bearded face, the pioneer ponytail. She loves him, Vince thought again, catching Michela's gaze.

Sure I did. Three times, Clive said. See that rock there? Downstream of the pour-over, it's invisible as you approach. I came crashing over the ledge, see, and speared it. Bang on. Boat went vertical and I was down. Vince asked: How on earth did you come up? They were looking at a storming torrent of water plunging through boulders.

I've no idea, Clive told him.

The Slobs had cooked curry. Everybody had picked up a bit of colour in the afternoon sun up on the mountain. If you never eat what's on your plate, Mandy asked Phil, whence do you draw your sustenance, my boy? My what? Supply of Mars bars in his tent, Brian said. He must have about a hundred. Caroline kept setting off the hamster to general groans. It worries me to say, that I've never felt this way. Was that what you were saying to yourself, Max asked Mandy, when you were pinned underwater on the slalom course? The hamster never tired of his song. He beat his drum and waved his microphone. I was saying to myself, Mandy laughed: I think I love life, but this is what death is made of. Oh, it wasn't even a close shave, Keith protested. You could have taken a photo or two, under water. Wally had been ceremoniously handed over to Amelia, who had dropped a shoe coming down on the ski-lift. It's his fault, the girl cried, poking Tom. The young man grinned with embarrassment. She did it on purpose, Caroline scoffed, so's she'd have to lean on him, like, walking back to the car park. Slander! Amelia shrieked. She hung the red-scarfed little effigy round her neck and pushed it down inside her T-shirt between the small breasts. Let's see if anyone dares to steal it there! I consider that an invitation, Brian cried. Please, Adam said. Kids!

Keith was looking relaxed. Perhaps it was a relief not to have to paddle. Debrief, he shouted. Tomorrow's the last day. Some of you are going to run a very serious river, let's hear from the river leaders who the chosen victims will be. The others will be rerunning the stretch from the campsite down to Geiss and getting in some much-needed practice. After which we'll eat in a restaurant since it's the last night.

The last announcement caused much excitement. Shush everyone! Adam's got the list, Clive said quietly. We decided it together. Standing up by the door of the kitchen tent, Adam announced: First, I want to thank Amal, who has offered to play river leader for those who won't be going on the upper Aurino. Chicken! Phil yelled. He's scared! Shut up, idiot. So, if we can be serious a moment, folks, the participants will be – and Adam read: Clive, leader. Myself deputy. Then: Vince, Amelia, Michela, Max, Brian, Mark and Phil. Max, Brian and Phil will be assessed for their four-star paddler.

There was a surprised silence. Vince tried to catch his daughter's eye. It wasn't clear to him why she had been excluded. They were in the clearing between the tents. The girl had her head bent knotting a red scarf round her neck. What about me? Tom asked. I'm sorry, Adam said, but we can't take people who don't get their roll at least ninety per cent of the time. But I never turn over, Tom said. Keith cut in brightly. We have to accept the river leader's decisions. Mark's going and Tom isn't? Amelia protested. That's crazy. Clive said, Mark rolled up twice this morning in white water. If Tom doesn't go, then neither do I, Amelia said. Adjourn to the bar, Max was already shouting. Drinks! With Brian's foot still killing him, the lame boy had to lean on his friend as they made off between the guy-lines.

In their cabin, Michela was determined to get things straight. Why did you tell that story? Clive was cross-legged on his sleeping bag, rolling himself a cigarette. It wasn't a story. Want a smoke? You don't know anyone from the rafting centre. He admitted this was true. I went alone, he said. He tossed the tobacco to her. But I couldn't tell them that, because of all their strict rules. I mustn't seem irresponsible. Otherwise we'll have people like Phil chucking himself down there.

You're lying, she said. You just wanted to show off after making a fool of yourself in this thing with Adam. You're weird, she went on quickly. Really weird. It's not normal just to tell me we're not making love, then imagine we can go on as before. You're crazy sleeping on the floor. It's stupid. And I meant it today, you know, when I said I couldn't go on like this. I meant it.

Clive lit his cigarette. He seemed to be waiting until she had finished. The tobacco was damp and didn't draw well. I wasn't lying, Micky. He puffed. He seemed calm. Before Milan, remember when you went ahead to ask your mother if she could lend us something? That's when I did it. I ran it alone. Three times actually on three consecutive days. It's not that difficult. I did worse in New Zealand.

She stared at him. So why didn't you tell me?

He shrugged his shoulders. Why should I?

But this is even weirder. You go and do something completely suicidal and you don't even tell me. Her hands were shaking with the lighter. He used an old paraffin thing from at least twenty years ago.

It's suicidal to smoke, he said.

Yeah, I set myself alight and die. It's different, and you know it.

I didn't want you to worry about me, he said. You had worries enough with your mother. They gazed at each other across the cabin. The space was lit with a naked, 40-watt bulb. He was cross-legged, swaying slowly backward and forward, smiling softly. He seemed to have regained all the confidence, the slightly mystical impenetrability that had been threatened that evening with Adam. She was on the bed. It's clear she isn't a real smoker. She rolls cigarettes because she is with Clive. I go kayaking because I'm with Clive, she thought. She knew that. I say a thousand things Clive says. I share his opinions. Seeing the shake of her hand, she felt her closeness to her mother. It had been a disastrous visit. My hopeless, hopeless mother. I hope you understood, she finally asked, what I meant when I said you must do something serious. Did you? I think you owe it to me.

He seemed to relish the distance that had been established between them. Swaying, he pressed his lips firmly together. Yeah, I understood. He tapped the thin ash of the roll-up into his cupped hand. But I've been thinking the same thing myself, for years. Obviously, I have to do something serious.

So what are you going to do? Not just these stupid demonstrations. They do nothing. Or are you just going to start hitting idiots like Adam?

Why are you so aggressive? he asked.

If you don't understand that then you're really stupid!

The demonstrations are important, he said calmly. It's important the world is constantly reminded that there are people who care. You know that. Over the years I think they have a cumulative effect. More than people admit. But, I am thinking of something bigger.

Like what?

I'm working on it.

Like paddling down a grade-five river on your own and getting your spine smashed. You'll be a photograph on a wet rock. What good is that going to do anyone?

They stared at each other. There was a soft look in his eyes. Suddenly she feels sure that he loves her. Somehow this is worse. He loves her but it makes no difference. You said we would live together and have children. I believed you.

He held her gaze. I meant it, Micky, but this isn't the world for us. Leave be, now.

What world, then, she demanded. When will there be a world for us? This is the only one we've got.

Clive was silent.

She stood up and went to pull on her shoes by the door. You're weird, she said. I'm going to go out and fuck someone else. Okay?

He sat still, watching and smoking.

I said, okay?

Go.

She walked through the campsite. I've lost control now, she decided. Good. At least something would happen. Her mind was feverish. Everywhere there was barbecuing or the clatter of washing-up, or singing, the hum and rhythm of people at ease and pleased with themselves at the end of another day away from home. A curse on them! A young man and woman were arm in arm on the ground by a gas stove. Under her breath Michela began to mutter in Italian. *Maledizione! Siate maledetti e stramaledetti!*

The scene at the bar was the same as on all the other evenings: the second-rate band with their rhythm machine, the desultory karaoke. At a couple of tables pulled together, Adam and Vince and Mandy were sitting with Tom, Amelia, Caroline, Phil, Brian and Max. Overdoing the English accent, Michela asked, Anybody need topping up? What are you having? She stood behind them, wallet in hand. She has so little money. The kids clamoured for beers and Adam and Mandy tried to deter them. I told your parents no. Let's say you didn't see, Phil protested. You thought it was apple juice. We disobeyed you. Like, we're impossible, aren't we? Unmanageable.

The tall girl turned to the bar. Vince saw at once that she

was excited. Tom stood politely to help her. Michela slipped an arm around his and smiled straight into his eyes. At the bar she switched to Italian and ordered eight beers and a gin and tonic for Max. It was more than she had spent all week. Sounds lovely when you speak Italian, Tom told her. Again she smiled warmly. Want me to teach you a few words, Tommy? Hardly that much time now, he said stolidly. I'm not even going to be with you tomorrow, which is a bit of a bugger. The nights are long, she said coolly. She was purposeful. For a moment she put a hand round his waist. Tom seemed unable to respond. *Le notti*, she repeated, *sono lunghe*. Think you can repeat that? *Lunghissime*.

Back at the table the Italian girl squeezed in between Tom and Brian. Amelia was on Tom's other side. The children grabbed their beers. Adam was sending messages again. My wife, he explained. Text messages had been the bedridden woman's salvation. Is Clive not coming out this evening? Amelia enquired. The girl has smelt danger. Mandy was talking to Vince about her son's motorcycling obsession. Single parents should form a club, she said, for mutual support. Michela had downed her beer in a gulp. I don't know what Clive's up to. She looked dazed. Why? Amelia didn't reply. Phil and Caroline were sharing a cigarette. Hope it rains, the fat girl was giggling. She clearly has a problem with chapped lips. Oh not the mad bell-ringer again! Max laughed. Brian leaned across the table towards Amelia: You know you look like you've got three tits. He was referring to Wally. Except the one in the middle is the biggest! Phil shouted. He slapped a hand on the table and laughed. Shut up! Amelia was on the brink of tears. She was chewing a strand of hair. Michela now had a leg pressed against Tom's. Anyone could see.

Adam stood up and offered to go and fill Michela's glass.

As soon as he set off for the bar, Tom began to talk excitedly. Can anybody really understand why I'm not going tomorrow and Mark is? The young man has a pretty dimple in his chin, a square jaw, high cheekbones. He is handsome, virile and vulnerable. Because Adam's his dad, Phil said, puffing on his cigarette. Kids! Mandy intervened. The instructors know best on these matters. They can't take any risks. I'm not a kid, Tom protested. In his ear, Michela whispered, You can say that again. Vince saw her lips move. Her eyes are too shiny. Mark doesn't even want to go himself, Caroline remarked. He just does it for his dad. Actually, Tom, Max leaned across the table, the real reason for your exclusion is, Mandy's got the hots for you. She wants to have you all to herself tomorrow. Oh for God's sake, Max! Mandy was laughing. Then just as Adam returned with the beer, Amelia pushed back her chair. The girl was so abrupt it fell over. Without stopping to right it, she turned and hurried away across the empty dance area. What's wrong? Melly! Brian dragged himself up and began to hobble after her. Ow! He had to hop. Max got up after him. There was a vigorous flounce to Amelia's backside as she crossed the brightly lit space. Tom half stood. Michela put a hand on his arm. I'd better go and see what's going on, Mandy said.

In just a few confused moments, Vince found himself at the table with just Adam, Phil and Caroline. From the corner of an eye he was aware of Michela and Tom standing together on the far side of the dance floor where the bright light of the terrace and the dark of the field beyond seemed to fizz together. The band leader was introducing the next song with weary cheerfulness. What was all that in aid of? Adam asked. His phone beeped the arrival of another message. Vince was conscious of a desire to watch, to follow them even.

Amelia got upset, Caroline explained, because Brian said

something shitty about her being flat-chested. Adam frowned over his message. All the more beer for us! Phil cried. Theatrically surreptitious, he began to pour from Amelia's glass into his own and Caroline's. The girl had the coarse, hearty look of someone who couldn't be enjoying themselves more. I thought you were Amelia's best friend, Vince said. Speaking, he realised that these were almost the first words he had addressed to Caroline. So? the girl asked. I was just surprised to see the others rush away after her and you stay put. Her men! Caroline said archly. She doesn't need me. Brian's got a crush, Phil explained. Hopeless case.

Adam was shaking his head. Can't keep up with you youngsters, he complained. Vince asked if the message was serious. Adam began to explain that his wife tended to get a little hysterical when she knew they were going to run a difficult river. Why d'you tell her, then? Caroline demanded. Phil drained his own beer and reached for Brian's. I didn't, Mark did, Adam said. The idiot! He seemed to enjoy shaking his head at the perversity of the world. That was what was so great about Gloria, he turned suddenly, enthusiastically, to Vince. Like, nothing fazed her, you know, whatever river . . .

Now Vince pushed back his chair. Need a pee, he announced. He walked across the dance floor and around behind the bar, very conscious of the slight unsteadiness that three beers can bring on. I won't sleep well tonight, he knew. I must be on form for tomorrow. Instead of going into the loo, he crossed the track beyond the entrance to the site and walked into the pine trees beyond. This is where they must have come.

The ground sloped steeply down towards the river bank. The trees were scrawnier here, but closer together. Vince stopped. The cushion of pine needles beneath his feet created an impression of silence, though he could still hear the beat of music from the bar. It was as though the distant sound actually increased the silence in the wood. When the path became too dark to follow he stopped and listened. I am completely disorientated. He stood still. The drink made him sway. This week has rubbed out my ordinary life. It was amazing how dark it could be, black even, and so near to where he had been in bright light and company. It has rubbed out the pain, but all the things that made sense too. Gloria was never fazed, Adam said.

Vince breathed deeply. What a powerful smell there was, of freshly cut wood and dung and smoke. He took a step, caught his foot, lurched. Even staying vertical is a hard thing when the darkness is so complete. Then he heard a little cry and a giggle. Vince was electrified. They *had* come here. But why did I follow? What do these shenanigans mean to you? He was swaying on his feet. He didn't know which way to tread. A fifty-year-old widower with a big job in the City? Should I tell Clive? Now there was a sharp intake of breath, followed at once by a quiet whimper, and this time a boy's laugh. I'm so, so sorry. Get out of here! Vince began to move. He stumbled. Gloria was never fazed. Which was the way back? Twigs cracked. Shit! In a second's stillness he was aware of low voices. Then someone else was banging through the undergrowth. It's a dream. The noise was so loud. I must go the other way. Just as he turned, a bright light flashed up from very low. He was on the edge of a steep bank. The torchlight swung towards him through the trees. There was a cry. Vince ran away from it, up the slope.

Back in the tent he went through his bedtime routine with great deliberation. The branches had scratched the back of his hand, the side of his neck. Don't think anything, he kept repeating, don't think till your mind is calm. He slipped off his socks and put them in his shoes under the fly-sheet. But now there were rapid footsteps. Dad! No sooner had he stretched out on his sleeping bag than a torch shone in. Louise dived into the tent. Dad, weirdest thing happened. Just now. God! She plunged on her stomach. Turn that thing off, he complained. You're blinding me. Really frightening! Tell me. Vince began to pay attention. Are you okay? I was with Mark, you know. I guessed, Vince said. Oh, he's all right. We were just kissing a bit, in the trees behind the bar. The other side of the track where it goes down to the river. Kissing? Oh, nothing heavy, Dad, come on! When this pervert comes along trying to spy on us. Really! Like, he was only a yard or two away. I mean, he could have been a serial killer or something. It was like a horror movie. I pretty well wet myself.

Vince lay back on his sleeping bag. Did you see him? Mark did. He turned on the torch and made a dash, saw the bloke running away. Some old guy. Anorak type. Wasn't it a bit dark, Vince asked, to be fooling around in the woods? He knew what he had heard there. No, there's plenty of light when you get used to it, she said. Oh God, the phone, she announced then. The torch came on again and in the glow Vince watched his daughter's face as she rummaged in her rucksack. There was a healthy blush on her cheeks. Strands of blonde hair fell over her eyes. Where did I hide the damn thing? There. Sure enough, just a few moments after she turned it on there came the beep of a message arriving, followed by a low giggle, the sound of a thumb on the keypad. Vince said: You have a boyfriend back home, don't you? That's what all these messages are about.

None of your business, she laughed. Then she said. Course I've got a boyfriend. What do you think?

Only that you're two-timing him, obviously.

What a funny expression.

I don't know what the current word is.

And so?

Well, it's not altogether nice, is it?

Altogether?

It's not nice.

I'm enjoying it.

Louise, I'm trying to talk seriously for once! By the way, your clothes smell of cigarettes.

He'll never know, she said.

And Mark?

I told him.

And he doesn't mind?

Dad, it's a *holiday*! Everybody does this on holiday. It's what they're for. And even if you don't, everybody imagines you do.

I thought it was a community experience.

She giggled. More like an orgy sometimes. But I mean, Phil and Caroline, Amelia and Tom, it'll all be over when they're home. You can't believe Tom doesn't have a girl-friend, can you? At college. A fab-looking bloke like that.

Was it you smoking or Mark?

She said, Mark.

I'll try to believe you.

She leaned over and kissed him. You're a treasure, Dad. Then he knew she had been smoking. Do your teeth, he said.

When she came back from the bathroom, he asked:

And what if I did the same thing?

How do you mean?

Went kissing in the woods.

Dad!

Because we're on holiday.

when he had felt less in control of his life, more subject to the flow of volatile emotions. Now there was just tomorrow's river run, then Sunday the drive home, and Monday he would be back in the bank: the busy bright foyer, the lift, the fourth floor, the coffee machine, fluorescent lighting, e-mails, meetings, phone-calls. Before the week was out, they would begin final preparation of the balance sheets. He would be anchored again, not by the breathing of someone beside him in the dark of the tent, but by the exhausting routine. The world would close in. August was the moment to finalise the foreign accounts. There would be pressure to present things other than as they were. And even if you don't, he heard his daughter's laugh, everybody imagines you do. Cheat. But actually Vince didn't. He never has. I never fudged a single figure. My career, he knew, has been based more on absolute probity and solid common sense than any genius. You'll never get rich, Gloria would tease. He can hear her voice. But we *are* rich compared with most others, he told her. She said she loved him for this. There was a condescending note. Vincent Marshall, incapable of guile, she laughed. But we *are* rich, Gloria, he insisted. The top five per cent. Isn't that enough? You don't have to stay at the hospital, you know, he always told her, if you don't want to.

Suddenly Vince was back in a particular weekend, in the rather empty comfort of their sitting room. Again, Gloria had been telling him he must take up a sport. They were speaking across the polished dinner table. It was stressful, she said – she'd just finished a week of nights in Intensive Care – to watch people dying all the time. That's why she needed to do so many physical things. You don't have to work, he told her. You could be a woman of leisure. Me? She had laughed. She put a hand on his: Come on, come down to the club tomorrow. Why don't you? You'll feel better if you get your blood moving. How can they? she asked a little later when there was some documentary on aid workers in the Third World. The television showed a boy picking maggots from his scalp. They were sitting together on the sofa, but without touching. About half our bad loans are to Third World countries, Vince remembered now. He lay in the tent listening to his daughter's breathing. How pleased with herself the girl was, to have kissed one boy while texting another. She felt alive. Then at last a real question presented itself: When was the last time Gloria and I made love together?

Vince sat up, slipped out of his sleeping bag, unzipped the tent, set off for the bathroom. I'm better integrated with the photo-electric cells of the toilet-flushing system than I was with my wife. Coming back he could see the light in their chalet was on. There are eight chalets arranged either side of a central track. Vince stopped. A blind had been pulled down but there were chinks shining through. Theirs was the last in the near row. What had happened this evening, he wondered, with Michela? With Tom? It was strange.

He checked his watch, turned left into the track between the chalets, skirted round the last building at the end. The window on the far side showed chinks of light too. None of your business, Dad, Louise said. What is my business? Vince asked. I was away week in week out doing my business, in London, then home Saturday and Sunday and Gloria obsessed by the idea I must be stressed, I must take up a sport. What was it all about? Cautiously, Vince took a step or two beyond the track towards the chalet. I am a widower with a job that makes me co-responsible, with others, for the management of billions of pounds. Gloria betrayed me, Vince decided. My daughter hardly recognises my authority. I can't tell her anything about smoking or sex. Continents away, people die like flies, as a result of our carelessness, perhaps. Or our prudent decisions, our need to balance books. It's none of your business. Vince stood in the dark on the edge of the campsite. I'm just a man, he suddenly thought. For some reason the words were reassuring.

In the safety of the shadow on the further side of the chalet he approached the window. The room is empty, he saw. Where are they? He frowned, then something moved and he realised there was a figure on the floor. Stretched out on a blue sleeping bag, wearing a pair of glasses hung round his neck on a string, Clive was studying a stack of papers in a folder. Invoices perhaps. Why wasn't he on the bed? Vince watched. Clive was underlining things, circling figures. He turned back and forth among the papers, handsome forehead frowning. It was odd.

Then the bearded face looked up, alert. The sound of footsteps set Vince's heart racing. He crouched low. Someone is coming along the track, walking quickly. The door squeaked. He didn't dare stand up yet. A pervert, Louise protested. An anorak type. Yet Vince felt sure it was his business. He heard their voices, low, flat, couldn't make out their words. He listened. They weren't arguing, but there was no warmth either. It is my business. For years I paid no attention. I let things slide. I was an excellent bank director. He waited a little longer then stood. Clive had rolled on his stomach, head sideways on a pillow of folded clothes. For just a second Michela crossed Vince's line of vision. She is naked. Her hand stretched out and the light was gone. He saw a pale blur re-cross the cabin and stretch out on the bed.

I thought they were lovers, Vince repeated to himself as he hurried back to the tent. You are a fool! You understand nothing. Gloria never walked around naked. She always put on her nightdress before removing bra and pants. I paid no attention to her. She was never fazed. Perhaps Adam honestly only meant: by river trips. She wasn't fazed by rapids and pour-overs. I saw the girl's sex, he thought. Perhaps Gloria honestly only meant, she needed her sports if she was to watch people dying every day, if she was to look after the invalid wives of canoe-club friends. Why had she stopped the Saturday outings, then, as soon as he started?

Poor Gloria! Stretching out beside his daughter again, Vince prepared himself for a night of insomnia. His muscles are aching after all these days on the water. This churn of thought, he sensed, the evening's sounds and images, they wouldn't release him. Suddenly to know you are dying like that! he remembered, to feel your body changing, you're head filling with blood. She had rushed to the phone. She had apologised. I'm so, so sorry, Vince. He listened to the words again and again. The minutes passed. Perhaps she had only meant: I'm sorry I'm dying. He let the thoughts flow on. Let them flow. I won't fight them. She hadn't meant that. I don't feel unhappy, he decided. He had seen the girl's lithe body, her dark sex. It's strange. He didn't feel depressed or guilty at all.

LIKE GODS

I know this will sound a bit weirdy-beardy, Clive said, but I want you all to close your eyes for a minute, okay? Close them Phil. Moment's sheer silence. You're all kitted up, right, you're in your boats, nice and tight, okay? You've got your hands on your paddles. Good. Now, take three or four long slow breaths, in and out. No, really slow. Fill your lungs and empty them. Mark? Slowly. And again. Okay. And while you're doing that, I want you to remember the last time you did something really cool in your kayak, something you're really proud of. Maybe it was the perfect tail squirt. Okay? You went vertical without capsizing. Or maybe you were surfing a busy wave, right on the crest, or you rolled up perfectly in a stopper. Some moment when you and the water seemed to go together like old friends. You were helping each other. The paddle was like a wand. Remember? Picture it. Keep breathing deeply, eyes closed, and picture that moment. Got it? The sheer magic, the well-being, you and the water. It was great. Right, now, on the count of three, I want every-one to say out loud, no, I want you to shout out loud: TODAY I'M GOING TO PADDLE LIKE A GOD! Okay?

Then we'll open our eyes and we're away. Ready? But I want you to really belt it out, okay? Psyche yourselves up. Even Adam who hates this mystical stuff, he's going to say it. Right Adam? Okay, on the count of three. One Two Three . . .

They were lined up on the bank. It had begun to rain, hard. The high plateau was flat here and the river seemed tame enough. I'm going to paddle like a god! they shouted. And again! Go for it! *I'm going to paddle like a god*! Great, now, everybody launch and eddy out river-right below the bend. Did I hear, like a clod? Max asked. Like a sod! Brian giggled. Your buoyancy aid's not buckled, Adam muttered to his son. Buckle it.

Michela didn't shout with the others. She hadn't eaten breakfast. Enjoy yourself, Keith had told Vince by the kitchen tent. Remember, the leader said, the key to survival is to be totally alert and totally relaxed at the same time. The Louts were cooking bacon sandwiches. The Slobs prepared the packed lunches. Food in the boat today, guys! And never fight the water, the leader confided. Which is funny, I know, coming from a guy with his arm in a sling. But the moment you're fighting it, you can guarantee you've lost.

Eat for energy everybody! Mandy shouted. The bacon smell was overpowering. Vince ate, but then felt sick. Shut that hamster up! Adam yelled. The tall chinless man went round with a cardboard box full of wine gums and jelly babies. Instant glucose, he promised. At least six packets in every boat. Believe me, you really don't have to worry, the hamster sang. Mandy came to eat her bacon next to Vince, but now he had to get up for the first of his pre-trip craps. You're going to have a great day, she told him. When they left, Tom still hadn't appeared from his tent.

The minibus led the way pulling the trailer, while Vince drove behind in his car to run the shuttle. Entering the gorge, Adam asked Clive if there weren't any places they should get out and scout on the way up, what with all the rain there'd been. The decision to include his son seemed to have settled the quarrel between the two men. They were both intent on the job. Can't from the road, Clive said. We have to scout as we paddle down. Practise for the four-stars.

In fact, almost immediately above Sand in Taufers the road left the river to climb and wind spectacularly over the valley. Jesus, Mark whispered. Clive drove surprisingly fast beside drops of hundreds of feet. Jesus Christ! It was a landscape both massive and crumbling. From the seat behind, Brian plunged his hand down Amelia's T-shirt to grab Wally. Not funny, she said. The boy couldn't get the string over her head. You're *hurting*! It had tangled in her hair. Her eyes were red. The minibus attacked another hairpin. Belts everybody! Adam shouted. Brian!

I hope I can keep my breakfast down, Vince was saying in the car behind. To his pleased surprise, just as the two vehicles were setting off, Michela had climbed out of the minibus and come over to his car. In case you get lost, she explained. Now she smiled, but without opening her eyes. She had her head back on the headrest. The nerves will go as soon as you are on the water. After a pause, she added: When you speak someone else's language, you are always repeating what someone else has said. Vince was eager to please, but couldn't understand. Her eyes still shut, the girl seemed to be elsewhere. What's repeating on me is the bacon, he said. In front, the minibus had dived down a steep track towards the river.

After the kayaks had been lifted off the trailer, and everybody had changed and put their dry clothes back in the bus, Vince and Clive had to run the shuttle: that is, to drive both vehicles back down to the get-out point, then return in the car, so that minibus and trailer would be waiting at the bottom when the group arrived, tired and perhaps cold, in the late afternoon. So forty minutes later Vince would again be fighting his nausea as he drove up the steep road a second time, now with Clive beside him. The rain had begun to fall. Large sections of the landscape grew grey and insubstantial.

Any demonstrations planned? Vince asked. Talk of the river would only make him more nervous. There was the international heads of government summit on global warming in Berlin next week, Clive said. He drummed his fingers on the dashboard. And you're going? Sure. With Michela? A bunch of people they knew, Clive explained, would be there to picket. We're in touch through the net all the time. The cheap flights make it easier.

Then Vince said that, leaving aside the clash with Adam, he admired Clive for his commitment. Why do I keep telling them this? he wondered. He was thinking of the man lying on the wooden floor of the chalet with his reading glasses and stacks of photocopies while the pretty young woman stretched naked on the bed. He wanted to understand. So often, he started to say, people can see that a cause is right, you know, but it seems impossible actually to do anything about it. They were stuck now behind a tractor pulling a trailer loaded with logs. Like, up on the glacier, you were saying how all together we've managed to destroy it, without even really trying, but individually we feel powerless to reverse the process, our lives are so set. Clive leaned forward and stared into the rain. He wore a peaked cap on his long, tawny hair. This is one hell of a river, he said quietly. Let's enjoy it. About twenty minutes later Vince got into his boat, secured the spray-deck and shouted: *Today I'm going to paddle like a god*! He didn't even notice the nerves had gone.

Four-star assessment! Clive shouted. Rescues. Time out, guys. They had run about two kilometres of hectic river. The plateau ended in a narrow race of water bouncing through stones, eroding its way into the gorge. Vince's right shoulder ached from the wrench it had taken yesterday pulling Mandy's boat off the rock. All in all, though, the old body was holding up surprisingly well. Gloria would be proud, he thought. He'd learned so much so quickly. Up front, Michela paddled mechanically in Clive's wake. The boys darted all over the place, crashing over rocks into stoppers. Wild, but manageable, Adam remarked, banging into Brian's boat when they eddied out. We need volunteers, Clive said. Three swimmers to be rescued by our three four-star candidates. All you have to do is jump into the stream from the bank. Nothing dangerous here. The rescuers will throw you a line from the bank and haul you in. Important technique, kids, because we'll probably need to do it in anger at least once today when things get trickier.

I'm on. Adam volunteered. He obviously enjoyed this registration of measurable achievement, the business of stars and certificates. Mark? he asked. Cold, the boy muttered. He was slouched in his boat. I'll do it, Vince said. He beached and pulled his deck. Michela seemed hardly to notice what was going on. She didn't offer to help. Amelia announced: Since I feel suicidal anyway, I may as bloody well. She climbed out of her boat. Clive picked up the sour catch in her voice. What's the matter? The girl exploded: Don't ask me what the fucking matter is, ask her! Without actually turning, she gestured in Michela's direction. The young woman was arching right back in her cockpit so that her helmet rested on the deck behind her. The rain fell on her smooth cheeks and closed eyes, the boat turned slowly in the eddy.

Ask your *friend*! Amelia repeated. Then she said brutally: Are you bloody blind or what? The girl was on the brink of tears. Michela appeared not to have heard. Phil was watching with a twisted grin. Vince wondered if Clive had understood. He seemed puzzled. Come on, kids, he said determinedly, sheer concentration now. Where do you want me to jump from? Adam asked. Hobbling along the bank downstream, Brian called: I'll rescue you, Melly. Count on me. Under a blue helmet, the boy's round freckled face and chapped lips made him seem no more than ten years old. Don't call me that, she snapped.

They jumped from the spur above the eddy. The rescuers had a good fifty yards to save them before anything serious could happen. It was a question of tossing a nylon throw-bag stuffed with rope, while holding the loose end of the line. Always throw just behind and beyond the swimmer, Clive explained. The rope floats faster than a body and naturally swings round to the bank you're on.

Vince leaped into the swirl. To his surprise his feet hit the bottom hard, jarring his hips – there must be a ledge – then the current took him. Even in full kit, the body felt the shock of the cold. He assumed the textbook position, on his back, feet downstream to meet any obstacles. There was a sudden acceleration as the water rushed round the spur. Now, now, now, his mind sang. He is in it. Now is always the important moment. This water, in this part of the river. Now! Max shouted. The bag fell perfectly, so that the yellow rope unravelled across the water just half a yard behind. Vince had it. Feet braced against a rock, the fifteen-year-old hauled him to the bank. Easiest fishing ever, he joked. His thin arms were strong and sure. Impressive, Vince told him.

Phil then pulled out Adam with similar ease. But Amelia wasn't concentrating. She swirled round the spur, lifted an arm for the line, floundered after it, seemed to have it, then lost it. Brian, who had sat down after throwing, the better to brace his lame foot, now stood to shout instructions. He limped and hopped over the boulders along the bank. The girl was sliding past. When she finally grabbed the rope it was with such a tug that the boy lost his balance and crashed forward into the water. Clive scrambled down the bank and got hold of him.

Who's the fucking wally now! the girl hissed as she got a foothold on the stones. Brian was nursing his ankle. He was in pain. Amelia relented. Not your fault. At the top of the bank, she turned to Michela: I hate you! she screamed. She took off her helmet and shook the water from her black hair. I fucking hate you!

Waiting quietly in her boat beside Mark, the Italian girl looked bewildered. Vince saw it. She doesn't understand. Better than a seat at the opera, Max quipped. Amelia hit the boy hard. Idiot! But now she had hurt her hand on the buckle of his buoyancy aid. Shivering and shouting, she began to cry.

Amelia! Adam said. Kids! His voice took on a pained authority. Enough. Come on now. Putting an arm round the girl's shoulders, he turned her away from the others and spoke quickly and quietly. Vince thought he heard the words, your mother. Clive was still at the water's edge, squatting beside Brian, holding the boy's bad ankle in both hands, gently flexing the joint. Back in your boats, Adam eventually called. Let's hammer on down.

Only days later would Vince have time to reflect that the following hour and a half had been one of the happiest of his life. Never had his mind thought so intensely and lucidly, never had thinking been so dissolved and extended into every part of his body – shoulders, spine, wrists, hips, feet – the way sky and mountainside, as they pushed off from the bank, were dissolving now into driving rain and all the world pouring into the river where the kayakers were no longer eight individuals picking their separate ways through a wide flow, but a closely knit team signalling each other forward along the only line possible, every paddler constantly watching two others, protected by two others watching him.

These are more serious rapids now, Clive warned. He gave orders. Sometimes they leap-frogged from eddy to eddy. Or Clive got out on the bank with Phil or Max to scout ahead, to check there was no debris, to choose a line. Then the four-stars went with him and Clive placed one boy behind a rock at some tricky point to signal the way to the others as they passed and one at the end of the rapid on the bank with a throw-bag ready for possible swimmers.

Rafted together in an eddy upstream of these perils, the others looked for a paddle blade to appear above the horizon line where the river began its plunge. There! Adam saw it. Okay, Amelia, go! Wait. Okay, Mark, go! Even Michela seems to have been drawn in to the urgency of it. She woke up. She made the signals, became part of the group. She poured a pack of candies into her mouth for energy. Now, Vince, go! And stay relaxed!

Vince's eye read the water intensely, the snags, the pull of something beneath the surface, the turbulence of a broken eddy-line, the bright rippling that marks a sudden shallow. And his muscles reacted immediately to what the eye saw and the brain interpreted, planting the paddle left and right, his whole body wired and attentive for those hazards the eye had missed: the pull of a hole, the smack of a wave, a sudden swirling round to the left against a rock wall that is dangerously undercut. Stopper! It was Clive's voice. Paddle! Pad-dle!

Phil was on the bank beyond with a line. A great curve of water arched down before him into the boil. Vince crashed through. How different, his mind was singing as he waited in the calmer water for the others, how different from the knowledge of the financial institution, from discrete units of measure to be added and subtracted, the mind racing but the body only a burden in its frustrated inertia. To everyone's delight, it was Adam who was first to swim. He pulled out, trapped in a hole. Max tossed him a line. The man didn't seem upset. Wipe that grin off your face, he laughed to his son. Shit happens.

Should they stop for lunch? This was the place Clive had chosen, a small clearing on the left bank where a stream plunged in. But Adam was worried that the river had started to rise. And with this rain still teeming down it's getting muddier every minute, he pointed out. Clive reflected. The kids needed a break, he decided. We're tired. Also, there was a waterfall to see here. Something they really shouldn't miss. Stretch our legs. Afterwards they would still have a couple of hours jammed in the boats.

Everybody had replaced one of the two buoyancy bags behind the kayak's seat with a dry-bag full of food and drink. Clive had no buoyancy at all, only every conceivable item of tackle crammed into the stern of the boat. Time for the Kiss You! he announced. I beg your pardon, sir. The what? Unpacking a bag no bigger than a stuffed coat pocket, the instructor produced a large cylinder of some thin nylon fabric perhaps four yards long by two in diameter. K-I-S-U, Adam explained. Don't build up your hopes, kids. Karimore Instructor Survival Unit. As the cylinder flapped open, the wind snatched at the edges and the rain streamed on its waxy surface. Bundle in, Clive ordered. He spread it on the flattest patch he could find. The ground was coarse sand, shale and pine cones. Everybody in!

As soon as you were out of your boat, the body began to chill. Their wetsuits steamed. Mark's teeth are chattering.

My feet are numb, Amelia wailed. But inside this nylon cylinder, they immediately began to warm up. Clive arranged them sitting down in two lines of three, facing each other. At the ends, he and Adam pulled the material closed round their shoulders. Now they were in a strange blue space, breathy and damp, with the fabric held up only by their bent heads as they ate their sandwiches. First to fart gets lynched, Phil threatened. Where's me air-freshener, Max quipped. The neoprene of their kit was rank. Don't you think they could sell wetsuits with more attractive fragrances? But Vince was startled by the sudden intimacy of it. Six faces were less than a foot from each other as they chewed, eyes constantly meeting, knees pressed against and between each other.

A steady breeze nagged at the fabric where it was loose, and where it was tight the rain pattered sharply. Michela had ended up opposite Amelia. All morning her face had been blank. Now, forced into contact, she leaned forward a little so that their foreheads were almost touching. I didn't think, Michela said. Honestly. She spoke softly. I'm so sorry.

Amelia looked down. Sitting beside her, Vince heard and held his breath. I'm so sorry, his mind echoed. Amelia rummaged in her dry-bag, found another sandwich. Guys, she announced suddenly, Wally says someone here has got really foul breath. She shook her hair. Isn't that right Wally? The protecting bear was tied on a loop in her cag. She kissed it on the nose. And he hopes it isn't Adam, since that's who's going to be looking after him tomorrow. Dead right! Mark crowed. Instructor level two fails to roll up in simple hole. What a wally! Max was shaking his head: When boys are men, the men will be boys. All in a day's chaos, Adam smiled. Actually I was just testing the rescuers. There were loud

135

groans. Everyone's doing brilliantly, Clive told them. Sheer genius. Like gods.

Vince chewed his food. Michela had said those same words, but instead of plunging him into misery and isolation, it was as if the phrase had been exorcised on her earnest young lips, dissolved into the warm steamy atmosphere of a new family. So sorry. Amelia hadn't acknowledged or rejected the apology. Vince turned to see if Adam had noticed, but the man was laughing with his son at his own misadventure. They were all curiously one, in the damp, blue air, in the suffocating intimacy of the KISU. Then there was a rude shout, right beside his ear. From outside. A hand grasped the fabric and shook it. A drunken voice.

Adam released the edges he was holding, rolled backwards. Excuse me? In a moment they were all fighting their way out of the flapping cloth. Vince recognised the man he had seen that first day at his shack by the river. He held an old fishing rod, a battered bag, a bottle. He was shouting, shaking his head, turning to point theatrically down the river. He bent down and spread out his arms and moved them outwards as if touching something low and long.

Leave us alone, you're drunk. Adam was abrupt and sharp. Hang on, Clive said. Listen, he asked, speaking slowly to the man. Want some food? Eat? He had his lunchbox in his hand. The man stank of spirits. He started shouting again. His eyes were mad. Max understands German, Vince said. Everybody is shivering. The bloke's drunk, Adam insisted. Come on, then, Max. But the man's voice was slurred, he was shouting and yelling in dialect. The only thing I can get is *gefährlich*; the blonde boy shook his head. Ge-what? Phil asked. We know it's *gefährlich*, Clive said patiently. The man knocked the sandwich out of his hand. He seemed angry. He stared at them all, gesticulating at the sky, along the river.

His movements were jerky and unnatural. He says the river's dangerous today, Michela said. But the visitor had already turned and was picking his way along the bank downstream, his body bowed, jerky but oddly agile.

Clive watched him go. We've got about fifteen minutes to visit the waterfall, then we'd better get moving. You could see from the mud in the water, he said, that the river was coming up fast. Are you sure there's time? Adam worried. This is an important experience, Clive repeated. Quite a find. You'll need your helmets, Michela warned. Brian said he couldn't walk. His foot was hurting. I'll stay with him, Amelia offered. Oh Kiss You! Max shouted as the two pulled the makeshift tent around them. Hope the old pervert doesn't come back, or you're dead meat.

The little group climbed steeply for about two hundred yards among tall trunks, their knuckly roots fastened into the rock. Everything was twisted, crushed, flaking, leaning, broken, sharp. Everything dripped and drizzled. Phil began to throw pine cones. What did that word mean, ge-what-sit? It means absolutely-fucking-terrifying, Max lied in his poshest voice. I wish, Phil sighed. Don't worry, he said the same to me, first day, Vince remembered. I think he has trouble imagining there are people who can't speak his language. Or people mad enough to kayak, Mark muttered. A cone bounced on his helmet. Then they met the stream tumbling down and saw the waterfall about fifty yards ahead where the slope ended abruptly against a wall of rock. I've seen bigger, Adam remarked. The water poured down steadily in a broad sheet. Wait, Clive said.

They had to scramble up in the stream itself now. The rocks are slippery, but they have their wetsuits on and rubber shoes. Use your hands, folks! Clive had to shout over the noise. Can't afford any injuries now. Sometimes a leg sank in up to the thigh. It was definitely colder than the river. Oh my poor bollocks! Phil sang. Look at this! Max had found something jammed between two stones: a sheep's skull. Attractive fellow, Adam said. Friend of Wally's no doubt, Max declared. Pioneer of canyoning! He threw the thing at Phil, who dodged to let it rush off in the stream. Vince offered Michela his hand as she jumped from one boulder to another. She refused it.

At the top, at the foot of the rock wall, the falling water had hollowed out a pool about fifteen feet across. Clive waded round and climbed out on a narrow ledge just to the left of the fall. Instead of the rain, a fierce icy spray blew into their faces here. A strong breeze was rushing down with the water. The roar was so loud they had to put their heads together to talk. Adam – Clive challenged the man – why don't you walk across and see what's behind. Walk under the water? That's what I said. You're joking, Adam told him.

It was difficult to say from close up, with the spray stinging their eyes and the trees dripping gloomily all around, how high the waterfall might be. Forty feet perhaps. That's why I said to bring helmets, Clive explained. There was a deep chill in the air. I thought it was for the pine cones, Max laughed. But how do I know the water's not too deep? Trust me, Clive told him. Glistening with bright drops, his bearded face suggested both prophet and explorer. There was a glint in his eye. He looks older than he is, Vince thought. Mark was watching his father. Go on, Clive yelled. I'll give it a whirl, Phil offered.

Adam immediately stepped into the water. His leg sank to the knee, then the thigh. The water crashed on his helmet. Leaning forward, his hands supported on the rock behind the fall, he edged along with nervous slowness. There was no regulation way of doing things now. The waterfall is perhaps twelve feet across. The man had reached the middle when suddenly he stumbled forward through the curtain of white spray and disappeared. Jesus! Mark breathed. For about thirty seconds there was no sign of him – Don't worry, Clive laughed – then Adam reappeared further along and began to climb out from the water. From the opposite bank he turned and shouted something, held up a thumb. Now you, Clive told Phil, and try to enjoy it more than he did.

One by one the group inched along the ledge, then, with nowhere to stand on the far side, people began scrambling back down the slope to the boats. Vince was second to last with only Michela behind. As he stepped into the falling water, he was astonished by the force of its downward thrust beating on his helmet. His neck tensed to resist. Nobody said I wouldn't be able to breathe. The air was all water. His eyes are blind, ears full of sound, cheeks stinging with cold. His hands advanced, pressing numbly on the slippery rock behind the fall. Then, as he imagined, the resistance suddenly disappeared. There was no wall. He stumbled forward through the heavy water and stood, thigh-deep, in a space that might have been the size of a tall wardrobe. So little light filtered through, it was impossible to make out what was above him. Vince stood there breathing deeply.

Why didn't he just hurry on then, as the others had? Was it guile? Suddenly, it seemed essential that he should have come here, that he should know this cold, roaring place, at the heart of everything, he thought, but dark and hidden. It's important that there are places like this. He couldn't think why. But he knew the Italian girl would be coming. Any moment. He waited, breathing the saturated air. Sure enough, she suddenly blundered forward through the water and against him. He could just make out her pale face as she yelled something inches away. What was it? He couldn't hear. He started to edge out, but she is holding an arm. He turned to her. She pulled him against her. Her hands had fastened tight on his jacket. Their cold wet faces are together now. Still she was yelling something. The water thundered. He shouted: I'm crazy about you. Absolutely crazy! He was shouting at the top of his voice knowing she couldn't hear. I do nothing but watch you. She shook her head. Their eyes had caught each other, gathering a faint brightness from the shadow. Something was quivering there. She put her hands behind his head. Their helmets banged. And for perhaps three or four seconds she pressed her cold lips to his. Then she let go. She pushed him. He turned. Stepping outwards, the weight of the water was again so unexpected he lost his footing on the ledge and fell outwards. The pool was up to his neck and he had to swim. By the time he reached the shallow water, Michela was already ahead, hurrying down after the others.

Mystical experience? Clive asked Adam as they got into their boats again.

Claustrophobic, Adam replied. He had his sardonic smile. Place could use some good garden lighting.

Bit of a toilet, if you ask me, Phil sneered.

Vince?

Can't describe it. He shook his head. What could he say? A great wind was blowing through him. Like a place, he hazarded, I kind of always knew existed but had never been to. Does that make sense? He didn't look at Michela as he spoke, but saw Clive lift an eyebrow in her direction. There was a squint of anxiety in his expression. The Italian girl's voice came very flat and clear: Last place on earth, she said. Terminal.

Did we really miss anything? Amelia was demanding of Max. And has anybody got any lipsalve?

Rapid poke in Mother Earth's old womb, Max said. Core of the universe kind of thing.

Earth's what?

For Christ's sake, Phil, where have you been, where did you come from? The womb!

Cunt to you, Brian explained, checking his spraydeck.

Kids, Adam began.

Not exactly, Amelia protested. She pressed a stick of Vaseline against her lips.

Thereabouts, Brian said. And just as wet by the sounds.

You should be so lucky, Max told him.

Cunt is warm, Phil objected.

Unless you're into necrophilia.

Kids, I said enough!

Then they were on the water again. It was distinctly dirtier now as the rising streams brought down earth from the mountain sides. There were the first bits of debris. A broken branch, a dead bird. Yuck, Amelia said. Bugger off, foul fowl. The creature rolled over softly in the eddy-line, limp feathers outspread. How quiet the valley seemed, Vince thought. The dull roar of rain and river made a strange ferocious hush.

Just before the first rapid, Clive told Phil and Max to go ahead together and scout. First sign of anything really tricky, out of your boats and check it from the bank. This is the definitive four-star test, okay?

The boys paddled off and disappeared over the horizon line. The others chattered. Adam acknowledged that the little cave behind the fall was worth a visit, but didn't see why Clive wanted to insist on the word mystical. Michela stared glassily into the water: because it was where she and Clive had kissed so passionately three weeks before, she thought. Amelia was asking Brian if they would let him have his four-star even if, with his bad foot, he couldn't do this scouting business. Then Mark shouted, Listen up!

It was Max's voice. He was hoarse. Shrieking. Unable to get along the rocky bank, the boy had climbed five or six yards up in thick bushes. Quick! He's drowning. Quick. Oh God! Hurry. Help!

Clive thrust his boat out into the stream. Adam! With me. Everybody else, stay. The two men were out of sight in a matter of seconds. Max was crashing away again through the trees. About halfway through the rapid, the instructors found Phil trapped under a tree that had fallen, uprooted, across the water, its trunk just clear of the flood, the branches beneath forming an impassable sieve. This was a place to die in. But a man was already out there. Straddled on the trunk in a mass of broken twigs, he had got a hand under the boy's shoulder, keeping his face just half out of the water. That crazy bloke was waiting there shouting, Max explained later. The boys had gone down over the pour-over, heard him yelling, seen the obstacle and tried to eddy out. But Phil must have planted his paddle exactly between two rocks as he turned. When he lifted it, the blade had gone. He hadn't even felt it snap. The river had him. The boat was dragged beneath the tree. The water pulled him down into the tangled branches.

With a coolness that was the opposite of his reaction to the violence in Milan, Clive found two half-submerged stones to wedge his boat between, got out and tossed his tackle to Max who had arrived on the bank. In a moment he had brought Adam alongside of him. But for all their competence, with the strength of the current sweeping into the matted branches and the difficulty moving along the bank and then out onto the trunk, it took the men almost fifteen minutes to get the boy free. Meantime, the old tramp held onto his shoulder in the freezing water, shouting incomprehensibly, while the instructors secured ropes to the belt of his buoyancy aid.

Pulled clear, Phil retched and vomited. Never again. He would never get back on the water again. His gormless face was white, lips bloodless, and his whole body shaking. Never, never, never! He shook his head violently. It's my fault, Clive told Adam. He studied the narrow gorge with its steep banks, the fallen tree. We'll have to portage.

The kayaks were dragged out with ropes. They must find a way round. At this point it was clear that the person who really ought to have been excluded from the trip was Brian. Safest in the water, the crippled boy couldn't carry his boat and couldn't even walk unaided except on a fairly flat surface. Ask the guy if there's a path, Clive told Max. *Wie heissen Sie?* Max asked. The man was squatting on a rock with his shoulder bag and rod, filthy khaki trousers soaking below the knees, a sodden raincoat. He had shaved perhaps a week ago. The stubble was white. Roland, he answered. There was a smell to him. He wore boots with no socks. Roland. He grinned now. I'm Max, Max said.

The man began an expansive monologue, gesturing constantly towards the tree. He seemed to be scolding them. *Gibt es ein Weg?* Max asked. *Ein Wanderweg?* The man pointed up. Tell him how grateful we are and ask him if he can help us with the portage, Clive instructed. We have someone who can't walk. Tell him we'll buy him a meal. Anything.

Max interpreted, but Roland didn't seem to understand. Max repeated the offer. The man picked up his rod and opened his bag. It stank of fish. I think he's saying he has to stay by the river. *Cius*, Roland stood up abruptly and without moving began to wave as though to people already in the distance. *Auf wiedersehen, au revoir*. It was clownish. We

143

should have scouted ourselves, Adam said. But if his paddle hadn't snapped . . . Max objected. We'll debrief later, Clive said. We've been lucky.

The slope above the river bank was slippery with rainwater trickling down through roots and pine needles and patches of exposed rock. Having got back to the main group and then found a way up to the path far above, they arranged a pulley with the throw-ropes and hauled the eight boats more than a hundred steep yards through undergrowth and thickets. Clive lifted Brian on his shoulders and staggered zigzagging among the trees. Keep your helmet on, he told him. Good view, the boy said, ducking his head. Then they regrouped along the path. It was narrow but clearly marked, following the contour of the gorge through slim pines a couple of hundred feet above the river.

The rain still fell heavily. They hoisted the kayaks onto their shoulders. How far do we walk? Back to the minibus, Phil said. I'm not getting in the water again. The others were silent. Each boat weighed twelve kilos plus whatever kit they had. Emergency candy supply, Adam announced cheerfully. He still had a dozen packs of wine gums. Clive carried two boats, one on each shoulder. Brian used paddles for crutches. He seems undaunted. How far? Mark repeated. There's a sort of chute here, Clive explained. He had run it twice. Too fast and steep to get back in on. Especially in the state we're in now. About quarter of a mile. Maybe half.

Suddenly they were exhausted, what with the waiting around, the cold, the dragging the boats one by one up the slope. Everyone had a blister, a rash, scratches. Only Vince was still in a strange state of elation. Why had he behaved like that? He hadn't even told himself he was crazy about her. So why had he shouted it? And why had she kissed him, then hurried off? But he wasn't really thinking of

Michela. He wasn't sure at all that she mattered to him. His main thought is: When I wake up tomorrow, will I really have changed? Is it over, the paralysis of these awful months? The canoe bit into his shoulder. He didn't notice. He wanted to speak to Louise, though he couldn't tell her of course. Phil almost died, he chided himself. It didn't seem important. Okay, here, Clive eventually decided. He put down the boats. We'll try here.

Clive and Adam slithered down the slope to scout. They have found an understanding, Michela noticed. She sat apart from the others, her body numb, her mind fixed. I am not going back to the campsite, she decided, not to the chalet. Clutching her knees, she rocked back and forth in the damp pine needles. It was like the moment on the train between Brescia and Milan when she had told herself that she would never see her mother again. That's it. I will never speak to you again. This clarity is a relief. She didn't question the moment with Vince beneath that thunder of water. She didn't see the wooded slope in the rain. Her head is leaden. But she knows: I'm not going back.

Do-able, Clive announced, but only if everyone's feeling positive. While the instructors were away, Phil had been going over and over the accident with the others. When I started to go under the tree, I thought I was dead. There was like, this roar of noise. I was grabbing at the branches, shitting myself. I must have swallowed a bathtub full. From time to time, as he spoke, the boy had fits of shivers. Jesus, Jesus, Jesus, he shook his head fiercely from side to side.

They were sitting on their upturned boats on the path in their uncomfortable waterproof clothes. Now Clive appeared from the woods with his solemn smile, weighing them up. Time for a morale massage, kids, he said. You've got to tell yourselves that essentially nothing has happened and that you're going to go on paddling just the same way you did this morning. Like gods. When no one replied, he said slowly: In the end, it's all here folks, he touched his forehead just above the nose. It's just a question of believing you can do it. It's in your head. Phil, he went on briskly, you take my paddle and I'll use the splits. It was a BCU rule that a trip leader carried a collapsible paddle. But Phil said no. He was shaking his head wildly. No way he was going back on the water. No fucking way. I've got a flask of tea, Adam told him. Warm you up. Come on. Then Mark said: Don't chicken out, Phil. Suddenly Max was on his feet. Shut up! he shrieked. You fucking stupid wimp! How can you talk about chickening out? Phil nearly fucking died. He was choking. It's a miracle that bloke was there. And you, you . . . Max seemed about to explode with frustration. You're useless! You're shitting in your pants the whole time.

Two years older, Mark muttered, I didn't mean anything. I . . . Just stay out of it, Adam told his son quietly. He said nothing to Max. If you really can't, Clive told Phil quietly, then I suppose you can climb up to the road and just wait for as long as it takes for us to come and pick you up. We'll get someone else to volunteer to stay with you. But it can't be me or Adam. There have to be two instructors with the group. Then Amelia said, actually, if she wasn't mistaken, the road must be on the other side of the gorge. And she was right.

The pressure of the group now was to get the boy back on the water. There was some discussion. The leaders couldn't decide how much of an emergency this was. The day hung in the balance. What's the water like, Phil eventually asked. Adam said coolly: More or less the way you've always wanted it, Phil. Worst comes to worst, Clive said, you can ferry over to the other side and climb to the road there. But everybody remembered that the road had been dizzyingly high, right at the top of the gorge. As they set up a rope and sling to lower the boats down, Michela got to her feet and walked over to Vince. At once he was tense with expectation. She put her mouth to his ear: He wants to save the whole world and now someone in his own little kayak group is going to die. Vince was shocked. The girl's face was pale with anger and scorn. Her dark eyes were gleaming. As he was trying to think what to reply, she turned away.

We should abort, Adam announced. Half an hour later they had got the boats lined up in a thicket of young saplings precariously rooted over a drop of perhaps four feet into a roar of muddy water. The river has come up two or three inches, Adam insisted, in the time it's taken us to bring the boats down. I've got my mobile in the dry-bag, he said. We can call Keith and sort something out.

Michela said, Really, it's fine. There's nothing specially difficult from here on. Vince stared at the swollen water. A couple of small planks came tumbling down, part of a broken pallet perhaps. We should abort, Adam said firmly. Your dad's scared you won't be able to make it, Max taunted Mark. Max! Clive said. Shut it! Okay? Enough! Now listen, come round — they were huddled on the mud among the thin trees — listen, if we played it strictly by the rule book, I think Adam would be right. We can rig up a pulley across the river, do a rope-assisted ferry-glide, climb about a thousand feet and spend till midnight and gone getting the boats out.

He paused. The others were watching. Amelia was trying to press the water out of her hair. But I'm for running it, kids. The higher water will make it faster. A lot of the usual obstacles will have gone under, so it's going to be less technical, just a bit wilder if you have to swim. He spoke calmly, but very intensely, turning his bright eyes from one to the other. All the afternoon's poor light seemed to be drawn into his face. Obviously, one or two of us are at the limits of our ability here, but that's when an experience helps you grow, doesn't it? Now who's for it?

Me, Michela said in a flat voice.

Me, Amelia echoed.

There was a powerful charisma emanating from the bearded man. I don't want to put any pressure on anyone, he added. It was a lie.

Well, I'm not for walking, Brian grinned.

That made three, four with Clive. Adam cut in: The rule is, we don't do anything beyond the ability of the weakest member of the group. Especially if there's real risk of serious injury. And that's undeniable. The weakest member of the group was clearly Mark, but Adam didn't say this.

Okay, I'll get back in, Phil said, I'll try it. He grinned, but it still wasn't his old voice. If you think I'm up for it, like.

Vince wavered. The water was frightening. It was only Clive's will that was pulling them round. I'll give it a go, he eventually said.

But Adam seemed extremely agitated. Had he promised something to his wife? I'll stay behind with you, he suddenly announced to Mark. The boy hesitated. The launch looked daunting to a degree. There was no eddy here to hide in. They must push the boats through the bushes, climb in right on the edge, then plunge four or five feet straight into the brown flood with a rock to get pinned on only ten yards downstream.

You can't stay if we go, Clive said calmly: the rules demand two instructors.

So you can't go if we stay, Adam said.

The antagonism had surfaced again. But Clive seemed

more relaxed and authoritative now than when the problem was politics. His face radiated that manly reassurance that had made Michela fall in love with him. I'm the river leader, he said quietly.

It doesn't make sense to go, Adam said, if we think there's a real danger.

There's always a real danger, Michela said quietly. Just being alive.

Vince felt the anxiety of not understanding what was going on. The girl had been silent all day. What was at stake? Why did she insist now? Then, pushing his fringe from his eyes, raising his thin nose in a sort of defiance, Mark said, I wanna do it. He hesitated. Let's hammer on down, he said. Let's do it.

On one condition, Clive cut in quickly. We forget all arguments, okay? Max? Mark? Amelia? All individual niggles. Forgotten. Is that clear?

Alles klar, Max said. He turned and offered a hand to Mark. The boy took it. His narrow eyes were full of anxiety.

Community experience, Amelia said solemnly. She lifted two fingers in a V-sign.

We look out for each other all the time, Clive insisted. With no distinctions, no likes, no dislikes. We're a team.

Right, Vince said. This was the delirium of the real thing, he thought, the highly levered gamble. Adam said nothing. One by one then, Clive ordered. His voice had the assurance of military command. Myself, Max, Brian, Phil, Amelia, Michela, Mark, Vince, Adam. Same procedure as this morning. I scout with Max. Otherwise, we're three boat-lengths apart. And nobody ever out of sight. Okay? Sorted, Phil said. We're going to paddle like gods; at the bottom you'll feel like you've never felt before. You'll have adrenaline coming out of every pore of your body. And tonight we'll go out and get blind drunk, promise. The beers are on me. All of them. What a hero! Max applauded. May Wally protect us, Amelia announced. Adam said calmly: Okay kids, if we're going, let's go.

Somehow Vince's boat got tipped the wrong way as it shot down the bank. At once he was over. The paddle was dragged violently down. His knuckles banged on something hard. They banged again and scraped. Keep calm. He has the experience now. There's time. As the boat reached the speed of the current, the pressure on the paddle eased off. Vince crouched forward into position, swung his arm over his head. Coming up, he found Adam right beside him. All right? Just fine, Vince said. He even smiled.

Ten minutes later, Vince was only a couple of boat-lengths behind Mark when the boy tipped over in a swirl of water piling against a rock wall on the outside of a bend. It seemed the kid made no attempt at all to roll up, because his head was already bobbing in the water as Vince passed. Max had been placed on the bank at the first safe pool and tossed his throw-bag. Amelia and Brian were chasing the runaway boat, while Vince followed the swimmer into the bank. Okay? Max asked. Bash on the knee, Mark grumbled. Then he started to grin: Just one more thing to tell Mum. He's lost his fear, Vince saw. He felt moved.

Half an hour later they had to portage again around a rapid that Clive felt was too much. There are risks and risks, he said. Adam carried Brian this time. From a well-trampled path they were able to see three six-foot drops in quick succession, twisting from left to right and back. Ex-treme, Phil breathed. His confidence is coming back. There was a general feeling that they had cracked it now. Fucking fantastic, Mark kept repeating as he carried his boat. Bet I could do that too, he crowed looking into the boiling water. Fucking fantastic, Dad! Language, Adam said mildly. And don't start celebrating till you're home and dry.

Amelia went down in the next rapid, it was her first swim of the holiday, but again Max was on the bank to pull her out. Am I a safe pair of hands or what? he demanded. As she scrambled ashore a long dark box floated by, banging on the rocks as it passed. Brian shot out into the stream to inspect the thing. Some kind of cupboard, he reported, shaking his head. You wonder how this stuff gets in the river. Clive told them to watch out. A knock from a log coming over a rapid can be fatal. This is the last stretch now, kids, he shouted. Remember, we go under the road bridge and it's two hundred yards on your right. I'll be there ahead of you. There's that orange plastic strip on a tree too. On your right, just before the spur. You can't miss it.

As soon as they launched again, Vince appreciated that the danger was over. The river was wider. The gorge had broadened and flattened before its next plunge into Sand in Taufers. He felt exhilarated, but also slightly disappointed. The tension that had seized the mind entirely was dissolving. Clive no longer went ahead to scout with Max. The line of boats grew more ragged as people chose their own routes through easy rapids. And the rain had eased too. The cloud was lifting, the late afternoon brightening. With the sudden change of temperature, a mist began to steam off the water.

Yee-ha! Phil ran straight up against a smooth flat rock, forcing his boat vertical. Adam shook his head, exchanged knowing glances with Vince. Clive has won, Vince thought. Michela was wrong, thank God. The Italian girl had dropped back a little and was paddling slowly down on her own. They glided under the road bridge. The water was barely turbulent here. I must thank the man, Vince told himself. Clive got it right. He is a man you can follow. Even Adam was radiant. Here was the orange ribbon fluttering from the spruce tree. The rock shielding the eddy was just beyond. Easy! Ahoy, canoeists! Max was already out. He had scrambled up to the vantage point where they had been yesterday. He waved his paddle. Paddlers, ahoy! Vince was just turning to pull out of the current when he saw that Michela was not stopping. She paddled straight by.

His responsibilities over, Clive was kneeling on the bank helping Brian to get out of his boat. The swelling on the boy's ankle had reached the point where he could barely stand. The others were in the eddy or already beaching. A watery sun was brightening the patches of mist. Bringing up the rear, Adam was turning into the slack water right beside the big rock. With almost cartoon merriment he was whistling the hamster song. It was the biggest smile he had smiled all week. He banged his paddle on the water so that it spun up in the air over his head, caught it and held it there, using only his hips to control the turn and deceleration as the kayak crossed the eddy-line. Someone applauded. Epic! he laughed.

Hey! Micky! *Micky*! Apart from Vince, only Max had seen. What are you doing? This is the get-out. It's here! Micky! Come back!

Everyone looked. The girl was still well within striking distance. She could still regain the slack water. And in fact she had swung her boat round to face them now, about ten yards down, but drifting rather than paddling. For Christ's sake, Clive called, get to the bank! Sitting erect, the girl lifted her paddle and tossed it away into the stream.

Vince has never thought of himself as courageous. He is

152

not a man of action. But with no caution now, he veered away from the eddy and set off straight for the girl's boat. A clamour of voices rose behind him. Vince had no idea what warnings were being shouted. He knew what was waiting if he crossed the water's horizon line, shimmering in the mist up ahead. But it seemed to him that since she had no paddle he must catch up with the girl before the drop, he would drag her to the side, somehow. Reach forward, was all the voice in his head was shouting. Reach forward! The kayak surged.

Using her hands in the cold water, Michela was keeping her boat turned upstream towards the others. Now she raised her arms, pulled off her helmet and dropped it in the water. She shook the water from her short hair. Vince was almost there. The girl's drifting kayak began to spin. Grab the sling, he shouted. He released the thing from round his waist. Clip it on! He would tow her. But the girl had put her arms straight down by her sides. Her eyes are closed, Vince saw. It was the concentration of the diver on the high board. She leaned her head away from the approaching rescuer and capsized.

They were only a few yards away from the rapid now. The boom of the rushing water had drowned out any cries behind. Yet to the very brink the river was flat and calm, sliding mud-brown under a bright strip of surface mist. Two ducks flapped up as the red boat tipped over. They raced for the trees. Vince leaned to grab at the upturned hull. There was nothing to hold. He rocked it. She hadn't pulled out. Now the stream was accelerating. There is no time. Leaning on the hull, he reached right under the water, found an arm and tugged. She wasn't helping. Her hands were stiffly at her sides.

Quick! He pushed the boat away. For a few moments he

back-paddled furiously, but only to get his bearings. He knew he was beyond the point of no return. The capsized hull went over. Turning his head a split second before taking the plunge Vince saw another paddler approaching rapidly. It would be Clive. Then he was on the brink looking down into a chaos of spray and stone. There was no time to choose a line. Relax, a voice sang in his brain. Don't fight the water.

He fought. What else can you do? For two or three seconds he held his own. He had come over at a good spot. He planted the paddle way out to the left to drag the kayak away from a rock, tried to force it into an eddy as the water crashed between two boulders, failed, then leaned right out again to brace as the boat was dragged down in a deep hole of foam. Suddenly upside down, he rolled up at once. He was careering backwards now. The sight of the flood of water rushing towards him shook what confidence he might still have had. He thrashed the paddle. He was over again. A rock slammed against his helmet.

It was all frenzy now. His knuckles and wrists are scraping on the bottom. A desperate swinging of arms and hips unexpectedly tossed him upright. The boat was thrown against a wall and he was down again, pinned, head under water, the river piling onto his deck. I've lost it. Blindly, his fingers felt for the tab. Mustn't panic. The spraydeck popped but the sheer pressure of the water had him trapped in the boat. He panicked. Yaaaah! Vince screamed away his last breath and every last ounce of energy to force himself out of the boat. Air. I need air. In the flood his knee took a tremendous knock. Boulders and branches rushed by. There was the log they'd seen. He was falling, then abruptly trapped against another rock, arms and legs outspread, stomach crushed on stone. But he had his head above the water. He could think. He found a hand hold. Clinging and slithering and fighting, he pulled himself up onto the round, rugged top of a boulder.

Vince was in the very midst of the torrent. Had anything been broken? Chunks of flesh were gone from his knuckles. Every muscle was trembling. I'm alive, I'm alive. His wetsuit was in shreds at the knee, the leg completely numb. His teeth chattered. His boat was gone. There's something wrong with my neck. Can I move it. Yes, yes. Just stiff. Then Clive appeared. His yellow kayak shot down the rush from above. The man's big torso and hands were moving rapidly, the shoulders swaying, the paddle flashing left to right, back and forth. But it was perfectly deliberate, even graceful. Vince saw the bearded face beneath the helmet. Clive! he shouted. Clive! Their eyes met. But there was no acknowledgement from the canoeist. The face was in a trance of concentration and as he slewed the boat around the rock Vince was on, leaning hard on his paddle, Vince saw that a sort of grim smile was playing on Clive's lips. He plunged down the rush and was gone. Only then did Vince remember the girl. Clive was going after Michela. She must be dead, he thought.

Vince crouched on all fours. It didn't seem safe to sit. He would have to put his legs in the water. He was afraid it would snatch him away. He was afraid if he stood he might faint and fall. I must wait for the others. How cold it was! He felt sick. How long would they be? I might pass out. They would have to throw him a rope. How will I hold it? Try to stop your body shaking, he ordered himself. Relax. Breathe. Breathe deeply.

The water thundered above and below. Even the foam was brown with mud. What is taking them so long! Then Vince realised that he was happy. He was euphoric. Something has shifted. He smiled. He couldn't worry about the Italian girl. In a strange flood of emotion, he felt grateful to her. He was weeping. Grateful to his wife too. Gloria gave you this, he whispered. She died and I took her place on this trip.

Still crouching, shaking, he looked at his hands. They were bluish-white. The cold had stopped the bleeding. All the skin on the knuckles of the left hand was gone. He could see a bone. It was uncanny. Vince took hold of the ring on his fourth finger. It hardly pained him now to pull it off. The pale gold lay on the dead white palm and in a gesture he couldn't understand, he let it fall into the fast brown water.

Oy! Vince! Wake up. Hey, Vince! It turned out they had been shouting at him for ages. Adam was in the brushwood on the bank, about ten feet above the water. Max was beside him. They had secured a line to a tree and were tying themselves to it in case someone should get pulled in. At the third attempt they managed to land a throw-bag directly in Vince's hands. But his fingers wouldn't move. He couldn't tie it. Yelling over the sound of the water, Adam repeated his instructions. Pass an arm through a loop. Now, hold on tight and jump. Vince hesitated. Wrists and knees and feet and neck were all so stiff and numb. Trust me, Adam shouted. Vince looked across at the man. Trust me, do it.

Vince jumped. His head plunged into the dark water, but already strong arms were dragging him across. His face came up. He felt a surge of energy and when his feet banged into the rocks at the edge he was able to use the rope to climb out and up. Michela? he asked. He went down on his knees. Adam was looking at him curiously. I called the ambulance, he said. On the mobile. Max was opening a space blanket. He draped it over the kneeling figure. Wrap it round you. Come on. And he laughed. You don't know how long I've been waiting to use this. I thought I'd never get my money's worth.

'EL CONDOR PASA'

People had to eat and so they were in a restaurant ordering pizza. Nobody really knew Michela. Had anyone spoken to her, really spoken? Tom had made love to her the night before, but they hadn't talked. He had talked all week to Amelia. Made love is the wrong expression. She had forced it on him. She had been brash and abrupt, acting a part that wasn't hers. He knew he was too young to understand. You thought that was what you wanted, then it wasn't. Now Amelia and Louise both seemed far too young for him. He was eager to confess, but didn't know whom to speak to. He sat silent and shocked. He felt old.

On the other side of the table, it was hard for Mark not to shout his excitement with the day's achievement. He has run a wild river. With his father present. He has overcome fear. In other circumstances there would have been a buzz of euphoria. Now high spirits were forbidden. She was definitely alive when they put her in the ambulance, Mandy insisted. The adults took refuge in the technicalities: that Clive had dragged her out of the boat so quickly was the crucial thing, even if it meant swimming the last part of the rapid himself. He had done everything possible. And her being unconscious would actually have helped, Keith thought. The buoyancy aid is designed to keep your mouth out of the water. The guys at the rafting centre had given her mouth-to-mouth as soon as they pulled her ashore. Impossible to know how long she had been without oxygen. But why did she do it? Amelia demanded guiltily. I hate you, she remembered screaming. She hadn't acknowledged Michela's apology. She's so pretty, she protested. So intelligent. They all had the impression that the Italian girl was very intelligent. Never heard a foreigner that spoke English so well, Caroline gave her opinion. I thought she was a happy person, Amal muttered.

Then Adam and Vince arrived from the hospital. The Waterworld group were sitting round one long table in the Meierhof in Sand in Taufers. They had booked of course. The space was large and noisy. It was Saturday night. On the level beneath them, a burly boy with a ponytail was at work beside the pizza oven, while across the restaurant beneath tall pink curtains an improbably old musician, stiff in suit and tie, stood behind a keyboard cranking out the predictable favourites: 'Santa Lucia', 'Lily Marlene', 'Spanish Eyes'. She's in coma, Adam announced solemnly, but stable. Nobody understood whether this was good news or bad. Clive says we'd better leave tomorrow as planned, he added. Vince had his left hand bandaged. There was a dull pain in his hip. Get your orders in, folks, Keith told the new arrivals, or we'll be here all night. It was ten already. Tomorrow they must drive eight hundred miles.

Vince found a place between Amal and Tom. Can I ask you a question? Adam had asked, driving him back from the hospital. They had taken Vince's car. Adam had waited two hours and more while Vince was X-rayed and medicated.

He had gone back and forth between Casualty and Intensive Care where Clive sat with a sort of furious patience in a busy corridor. As long as it's not about money supply, Vince laughed. He was exhausted and aching. When we came running along the bank and saw you there, on that rock, and started calling you . . . Adam hesitated. And you didn't reply . . . Yes? Maybe I'm wrong, I don't know, I had the impression, well, I thought I saw you doing something with your hands. He stopped. I threw my wedding ring in the river, Vince told him. He stared out of the windscreen. After the day's rain it was a softly transparent evening of deep shadow and brightly lit road signs. Steering the long bends up the valley towards Sand in Taufers, their headlights swept this way and that across the hill to the left, the trees that screened the river to the right. Vince sighed. Anyway, the answer to your question is: I don't know why I did that. Oh. Adam waited. Then he said: I thought perhaps it had caught in a wound or something. Vince didn't reply.

At the table, he ordered a ham and mushroom pizza. Then Mandy appeared at his shoulder. She had left her place beside Keith and walked round the table. She bent to speak in his ear. You risked your life, Vince! she said. Amal was talking across the table to Phil about a stunt kayaker who had shattered his pelvis trying to run a huge waterfall in Kenya, a hundred-foot drop. Vince was obliged to look up at the woman's kindly face. It was criminal of her to put you in danger like that. I'm okay, he told her. An odd feverish quiet had fallen on him. He was impatient for the parenthesis of this holiday to be over, so he could know how he really felt. If Adam hadn't insisted he eat, he would just have gone to lie in his tent and wait for tomorrow.

Now Mandy was bending to push a kiss on his cheek. I'm so glad you're okay, she said. It was disturbing to see the brightness in her small brown eyes, the smile on her weathered cheeks. She was wearing lipstick. A toast to Vince! She stood up and raised her glass. Most improved paddler! Louise shouted: You're a hero, Dad. The whole table yelled, To Vince! Adam's cheers were particularly loud. The admirable Vince! Then Keith was explaining that a coma was normal in these circumstances: a sort of defence mechanism, actually: It only gets dangerous if it lasts more than about forty-eight hours. Vince's pizza appeared. I'll cut it for you, Amal offered. Mandy was taking a photo. The amazing thing is that there were no fractures. Once again Vince met his daughter's warm eyes across the table. Her hand and Mark's were touching. Thank you everybody, he said vaguely.

The others had already finished their first course, and were ordering sweets. As Vince bowed his head to his plate, the noise level rose around him. Under the influence of a couple of beers, the long table was breaking up into a series of conversations shouted across each other. Subdued concern about what had happened to Michela dissolved into a last-evening excitement. When all was said and done, the Italian girl was not one of their group. Nobody was missing her. Yeah, she just chucked away her helmet! Mark was repeating to Louise. And, like, we're all staring, thinking, Wait a minute . . .

Clive always had a negative effect on his women, Mandy was telling Adam. She spoke harshly, almost angrily. Both Adam and Keith seemed uncomfortable. Remember Deborah, she demanded, who used to teach two-star preparation? The group leader muttered something about not being one to throw the first stone. Then in response to a question from Amal, he announced: Ten sharp tomorrow morning, everybody. That means tents and gear all packed and the trailer hooked up and ready to roll. Otherwise we won't make our ferry. So much for Wally protecting us, Caroline was complaining. It's hardly his fault, poor little thing – Amelia pulled the creature from out of her T-shirt – if people go trying to get themselves killed. Is it? The pretty girl was beside Brian, but darting occasional glances at Tom. I feel a bit guilty, she confided.

Slowly chewing his pizza, Vince's mind drifted. He began to notice the restaurant. It was a large room with space for a hundred and more. The walls were a light varnished pine, the upholstery pink and flowery, the tablecloths red with white flowers in white vases, white candles, and everywhere there were ornaments and trophies dangling from the ceiling, hanging on the walls, perched on ledges and along the backs of the long sofa-benches that divided the tables.

How bright the room is! Vince was suddenly aware. On different lengths of wire, scores of plastic lampshades were designed to look like pieces of old-fashioned parchment stitched together. To the right of their group, suspended on three taut pieces of twine, were a dozen carved wooden hearts. There were aluminium tubes in the form of elongated bells, wooden cats and dogs and squirrels and fish, all hanging from the varnished cross-beams and swinging very slowly in the smoky draughts of opening and closing doors. A stuffed owl raised its grey wings on the wall behind Brian's head. An eel was pinned in a coil beside the red and white banner of the Tyrol.

Meanwhile, the ancient musician, dressed, Vince now understood, like an undertaker, was picking out 'El Condor Pasa'. His moustached face, that so much resembled the photos of the old men on the tombs in the little churchyard on the hill, was completely impassive. The computerised keyboard added the accompaniment. I'd rather be a hamma sandwich, Max had begun humming, than an escargot!

Spearing two bread rolls, he made his knife and fork dance together on a dirty plate. A deer with shabby antlers gazed across the bright glassware. The Chicken Song, Caroline cried, let's ask the bloke to play the Chicken Song! The fat girl burst into uncontrollable giggles. A stuffed fox bared his teeth. It is too much, Vince whispered.

Rather be a banana than a . . . a . . . Phil was tone deaf. Oh shut up! Tom told him. Than a what, may I ask? Max wanted to know. A dildo? Brian suggested. Oh do leave off. Tom seemed livid. He turned to Vince and asked in a low voice: Have you any idea why she did it? There was an explosion of laughter from a group of men drinking schnapps. Obviously locals, they sat with their dark-red cheeks and heavy moustaches mirrored in the shiny black slabs of the windows. The curtains hadn't been drawn. Never had Vince been so struck by life's coloured density.

You see, the young man confided, something strange happened last night. He looked around to check that none of the others were listening. Without a flicker of expression, the keyboard player switched to 'Sweet Little Sixteen'. He was seventy if he was a day. A condom than a bog roll, Phil howled. Kids! Adam said sharply. It was really weird, Tom insisted. Vince tried to pay attention. You mean you and Michela, I suppose? he asked. The young man's soft eyes were full of anxiety. Did everybody see? Pretty much, Vince said. I feel bad, came Mandy's voice over the buzz, us going away without even saying goodbye to her! At moments it seemed to Vince he might just fade into all the bright surroundings. Perhaps this is the effect of shock. The earnest Tom was looking hard at him: I mean, it's so strange her doing that with me and then the next day, well . . . You see? He's pleased with himself, Vince realised. He's dying to tell someone. Trying to close the conversation, he said: She must have been going through a crisis, you know, and whatever happened with you was just part of it. But Tom became more intimate and agitated. You don't think it's in any way, I mean, at all, my fault?

Vince drained his beer. A sense of irritation helped him to focus: You certainly ruined Amelia's holiday, he said abruptly, though actually the girl had her head down beside Brian's now over a plate of profiteroles they were sharing. The really strange thing, you see, Tom lowered his voice even further, is that she didn't say a word. You know. Nothing! I felt so stupid. This wasn't in fact quite true. Over and over Michela had kept repeating something in Italian, fierce words that meant nothing to Tom, as if he wasn't really there. I mean, if she'd said she was depressed or something . . .

Kids! Kayakers!

It was Keith's voice. Standing up, the group leader banged a spoon on the table, then lowered the volume a little when other people in the restaurant looked round. A tampon than a loo-brush, someone whispered. Kids! Keith sighed. Bright with emotion, his eager, glassy eyes looked round the table. Tonight was supposed to be a big celebration, of course. And normally, as you know, I'd have asked everyone to sum up what you thought of the holiday and we could have voted the Wally of the Day and so on. Adam! muttered a voice. Keith half smiled. But that doesn't really seem appropriate, does it? With what has happened. Now he got silence. In fact – the speaker bit a lip – the truth is we *all* deserve the Wally award today. Yes. He scratched his beard. The whole point about Wally, when we invented him, was that he goes to someone who's been careless. They have to protect Wally for the day, and that, that protecting, I mean, that not being careless, is what protects us all. We remember we have to look out for each other. I'm sure those of you who did the upper Aurino today will have seen how important that is. Instead, the fact is that we've all been incredibly careless, because nobody realised that one person among us, okay, not really part of our group, but still certainly with us, one person was feeling bad, very bad. To the point that she tried to kill herself, and, doing that, like it or not, she selfishly put the lives of two other members of the group in danger. Clive and above all Vince.

Following the old musician's arbitrary repertoire, the keyboards had launched into 'A Whiter Shade of Pale'. The schnapps drinkers were roaring. Yet it seemed to Vince, as at certain moments on the river, that there was a deafening silence around the table as Keith delivered this layman's sermon, at once inescapably true, but embarrassing too, and somehow pointless.

And when you go home now, Keith continued, and inevitably you talk about this, to your mums or dads, or whoever, obviously I want you to make sure they understand that this wasn't, strictly speaking, a kayaking accident. That's important. In nearly twenty years of activities, Waterworld have never lost anyone in a kayaking accident. We've never even been close. You all know how many precautions we take.

Looking up from an inspection of his bandage, Vince found Adam staring at him diagonally along the table. And his eyes were saying: Today anything could have happened. He has his mobile, Vince saw, lying on the table before him. He's in touch with his crippled wife. But getting it right on the water, Keith finished lamely, doesn't let us off looking out for each other in other areas of life. Dead right, Mandy said. She too looked at Vince. Which is the lesson I'd like you all to take away from this trip. Mark, Vince realised now, had his hand on Louise's leg beneath the table. The boy's face was radiant.

To close on a more cheerful note, though, Keith's voice suddenly reverted to its ordinary authoritative jollity, I want to extend my warmest congratulations to Max, Phil and Brian who've all earned their four-star awards with flying colours. And special congratulations to Max, who, from what I've been told, scored top marks for group awareness and river rescues. Well done, Max! Mandy started to clap. He's a he-man! Brian shouted into the general applause. A jolly good fellow! To everyone's surprise, young Max, with lemon shirt and green cravat, had tears in his eyes.

I'll drive you, Mandy told Vince at the door. You can't hold a steering wheel with your hand like that. In the restaurant's small car park the others were piling into the minibus. Two or three couples had decided on a last romantic walk. In the car, the small woman adjusted the driving seat, ran her hands quickly and practically over the controls, found the headlights. Actually, I was just thinking, you're going to need someone to drive you tomorrow too. It's over eight hundred miles. When Vince began to object, she said. After all, we live so near each other, don't we? At the end, I can drop my stuff off at my place, drive you home and just walk back. Again Vince protested that he thought he would be okay by tomorrow. Most of the journey would be motorway with just one hand on the wheel. Mandy didn't appear to have heard. Louise'll be wanting to travel in the bus with Mark, I bet, she chuckled. We can have some adult conversation at last. You get fed up with all of this group and kiddie stuff after a week.

The car was creeping along the few hundred yards to the campsite. Mandy braked for a rabbit and almost came to a standstill. When Vince said nothing, she asked: Was it really terrifying? I imagine you're still jittery. I keep seeing myself in that pin yesterday, you know, trapped down there and the deck not wanting to pop. Yes, Vince said vaguely, then he asked: You know when I started at Waterworld, what was it, two years ago? Yes? Mandy turned into the dirt track of the campsite. Well, a couple of months later, I mean just after I'd started lessons, you probably won't remember, Gloria stopped. She'd been canoeing about ten years, then she stopped right after persuading me to start. I mean, she really made an effort to persuade me. The exercise would do me good, etc. But then she gave it up. So then it was just me, and Louise too. We were in a beginners' course. Saturday afternoon. So? Mandy asked. So, I just wondered, Vince sighed, I wondered if you knew why she did that. I mean why she stopped right then?

They had turned off the track to park on their pitch behind the kitchen tent. Even towards midnight there were still some small children playing in the fluorescent light by the bathrooms. Is this my starter for a thousand pounds? Mandy asked. They sat a moment in the stillness of the car. In the distance someone was playing an accordion. Oh, it doesn't matter, he said and he made to get out. Mandy put a hand on his arm. Why did she *say* she stopped? To concentrate on her tennis, Vince said. She went to the tennis club. Well, that sounds fair enough. But then, Vince insisted, then she booked herself on this trip, didn't she? And on the Ardèche trip last year. She only stopped as far as the Saturday afternoons in the estuary were concerned. When I went.

Mandy ran a hand through her hair. She turned to him and smiled. The shadowy space was quiet and intimate. Why are you asking me this, Vince? You were on that trip too, weren't you, he said, in France? I always go on the Ardèche trip, she told him. It's my job. And? The woman breathed deeply. Her lips had puckered into a shrewd smile. She leaned across the car, put her hand round his neck and drew the widower towards her. When he neither resisted nor responded, she shifted her mouth to his ear and whispered warmly: Saturday afternoon is just training time, but trips are trips. She pulled back from him, leaving just a hand on his shoulder. *N'est-ce pas*? Her eyes were smiling.

In his tent, Vince let the flood carry on over him. I don't know where they are, he told Adam when the man came to enquire after his son. It was almost one o'clock and the river was still flowing over and over him. Is it really carrying me back to London, he wondered, back to the City, the service flat, the empty fridge? Where else? A man gets tied up to the ground. Was that how the song went? Lying in the dark, he was intensely aware of waiting. He could feel a strange momentum. The thoughts flow by and I am waiting, he told himself. Why should I live in a service flat and keep a house that is empty? I'm not waiting for Louise. There are so many decisions to be taken. Louise wouldn't live with him again. Gloria would be furious, he thought, to know that their daughter was out late at night with a boy, and him, Vince, doing nothing about it. No, it was a different kind of vigil, lying quite still in the fresh evening as the river rushed over him. I tossed away her ring, he muttered. It's just a holiday flirtation, he assured Adam when the man again came to enquire. The more worried the other father was, the more Vince would show he was relaxed. It's the kind of thing people do on a trip, Adam, you know, he said lightly. It's two o'clock, the chinless man grumbled. They're too young for this kind of thing. Apparently not, Vince laughed, and he asked, any sign of Clive getting back? But how amusing, he reflected, that Adam shared this anxious trait with Gloria. I didn't toss it away in anger, he told himself when he was alone again. He tried to hold on to some image of her: of Gloria at breakfast, Gloria humming 'El Condor Pasa', one of her old favourites, Gloria back from tennis, her face flushed. The flood carried him on. Away, I'd rather go away! He remembered her humming that. I was too self conscious, he suddenly thought, the day I scattered the ashes. Too conscious of the ceremony of it, eager for feelings I didn't really have. The grit had clung to his damp fingers and blown in his eyes in the estuary wind. Whereas the ring thing was just the opposite. I did it *naturally*. And now someone in his own little kayak group is going to die! First the Italian girl said, I'm so sorry, almost as if she had *known*, and then she comes to me to announce her death. Why to me? Because Tom wasn't at hand perhaps? Tom hadn't been chosen for the trip. Or because I waited for her under the waterfall. She knew I was waiting. *I* was the careless one who should have understood that message. But I had to concentrate on my paddling. I was terrified. Now he saw Michaela's strange expression again as she sat, beautifully straight-backed, in her boat, arms by her side, eyes shut – she leans that pretty head, the long neck, to the left and begins to keel over into the muddy water.

Vince sat up. What is this vigil for? He must sleep. I have eight hundred miles to drive tomorrow. He must find some way of not being alone in the car with Mandy. And Monday, the City, the fray. Mandy wants a ménage, he thought: the service flat during the week and her house with my kid and her two at the weekend. A man gets tied up to the ground. Stupid song! He shook his head, listened in the dark. There are always people chattering in campsites, distant pleasures and dramas. Quite possibly my daughter is having first sex this evening, Vince thought. She seems so adult. I *asked* not to go, she had said. She didn't need the thrill of fear. She was quite happy with herself without going on a dangerous river expedition. Am I waiting to hear if Michela is okay? he wondered, a young woman I hardly know, with naive political views and a cripplingly dysfunctional background. She had been quite rude two days ago in the hospital waiting room. But this afternoon she put her lips against mine under the waterfall. What long eyelashes she has! And dark eyes. A man, Vince thought, whose invalid wife was always in and out of hospital, could surely be forgiven a little love affair with the diligent nurse who played tennis so well. *El condor pasa*. A bird of prey. Perhaps they never made it to the tennis courts. Mum was the soul of the party, Louise wept. I wouldn't throw the first stone, Keith said. It was as if, all of a sudden, outside the tent, the mountain air was full of whispered conversations. How many photographs there were on all these paths of people who had died in falls and accidents! It would have been Gloria made the move, Vince thought. She was the hawk. It seemed he was overhearing snatches, debris of old conversations carried on the flood. Perhaps one day I will feel I was mad to imagine this. Mandy, he told himself soberly, most likely had an affair with Keith, but then wasn't able to stop him going back to his wife. Keith wasn't a widower. Somebody laughed low in the distance. It sounded like mockery. Monday I'll be at my desk, Vince told himself for the thousandth time. Would his secretary notice the absence of the ring? Will people say, Ay, ay? What is this vigil for then, if I know what the future is; my office, my desk; if my daughter is beyond me, if I missed the moment when I could have been helpful to Michela. Again he saw the elegant neck bend towards the water. A swan. She was a swan. She gave herself to the water. Here and gone. She had turned the boat so she was facing back to Clive, to her man. She was punishing him. Then there was the downward rush of the stream. With extraordinary vividness, Vince was in it again. He was shooting down into the rapid. He felt the acceleration of the plunge. I want to do it again, he realised. If I could. That rapid, those impossible manoeuvres. The speed and wrenching when he dug in his paddle, the icy foam and the slam of the rock on his helmet and the wild slewing and turning to the limit of control and beyond. I want to do that again, Gloria. Gloria. Oh Gloria, I want to do it again!

Vince? This was more than a whisper. A voice called him softly. He was sitting bolt upright, knees drawn towards him. The zip squeaked. Vince, can I talk a bit?

Clive! How is she? What's the news? In the dark light Clive's bearded face showed surprise: I thought you were talking to someone. Waiting for Louise, Vince said. She must be out with Mark. All these youngsters, in love! Clive managed a faint smile. I need to talk a moment. I've got a favour to ask. I'll get up, Vince said. There's no room in here. Come to the chalet, Clive told him. He would put on a coffee.

The fly-sheet was soaked in dew. Vince headed for the bathroom first. The fluorescent light greeted him like an old friend. He wanted to burst out laughing. What a volatile state! If I only could. He was thinking of the rapid. Then, heading for the chalet, it was with a sense of wonder that he remembered taking the same path only yesterday, to spy on their erotic happiness. Perhaps my own marriage wasn't so bad, he thought. He and Gloria had always shared the same bed.

Clive was making coffee on a gas ring. It's a pretty big favour, he warned. He busied himself with the flame and the percolator, then began moving rapidly around the room gathering various bits and pieces. Leaning against the bed was an open backpack.

170

Vince sat on a stool by a counter along the wall. It was odd, he thought, how cluttered and at the same time impersonal the room was. There are no pictures or ornaments. It was all kit and tackle and clothes and papers. Ask away, he said. Clive went back to the coffee, shook out the dregs from two cups, brought a mug to Vince, then stood facing him. I want you to hold the fort here for a few days, while I'm away.

At once Vince felt alert; some animal intuition told him he was in danger. Standing before him, feet squarely planted, steaming mug held in both hands, Clive was searching for his eyes. His own were intense and persuasive, brightly blue. The thick beard and the strong tanned forearms thrusting from rolled-up denim sleeves made such a man of him. He didn't seem tired at all. I have to leave in a couple of hours, he explained. For Berlin. I should be back on Thursday. Meantime, someone will have to stay here to be near Michela and visit her and so on. I thought, with you having your own car, you'd be best placed to do that. I've got to drive down to Bolzano, to the airport.

Immediately Vince said: Really, I'm afraid I must be back at work Monday. I've already been away too long.

Clive ran his tongue over his lips, half smiling, still looking directly into the older man's eyes. He drank from his mug, then set it down on the counter, turned abruptly, crouched beside a small chest of drawers and began pulling out underwear. Vince's mind is racing. How is she? he asked.

Clive pushed the clothing into his backpack. She's going to be okay, I think. The scans suggest she'll be out of the coma any moment. It isn't deep. So they say. He spoke without emotion, then got down on the floor to straighten out the sleeping bag and roll it up. You can stay here in the chalet. It's rented for the whole summer. I'll show you where everything is.

Vince watched the man, his efficiency and hurry. He gave the impression of someone who has heard an urgent flood warning and is moving fast to get out, someone used to flood warnings. Or again of a soldier preparing his kit before action. There was a lithe quality to the man's rapidity, a sureness and presumption that was seductive; and Vince was reminded how, during the walk to the glacier, he had looked up and seen Clive climbing quickly through the stones and the girl doggedly following. Exactly the man I'm not, Vince thought. The man who attracts women. He was half aware now that he had been thinking this all week, since the moment Clive had stood and leaned across the table to slap Adam's face. Clive completely dominated Adam today on the river, he thought. In the end he won him over. Or at least wore him out. He won over the whole group. Only his will brought us safely down. Don't you think, Vince said at last, that you should be beside her when she wakes up.

No. Clive didn't turn to Vince, but had started collecting things and laying them on the table now: keys, a torch, a map. Actually, I'm the last person who should be there.

But . . .

She can tell you about it, Clive said. I'm not going to explain. I said at the hospital that her uncle would be arriving in the morning.

Her uncle?

Clive finally turned and grinned. That's you. Look: these are the essentials for living here. The long key is for the door, the small one for the padlock on the gas cylinder under the window outside.

I imagine you've told her mother.

No.

But that's the first . . .

Next to myself, her mother is the other worst person for Michela at the moment.

Vince tried to be judicious. In so far, he said, as an attempted suicide is always a cry for help, don't you think the person, or people cried to should be the ones to respond? Again he saw the girl turn her boat to look back across the water, to her lover.

Clive pulled the cord tight to close his backpack. In that case people would only have to threaten to kill themselves to get exactly what they want, wouldn't they? There's still some food in the fridge, by the way, milk and cheese and stuff.

Vince drained his coffee. I'll tell Mandy, he said. She can use my car. I'll go back with the minibus.

Clive stopped. As if making a considerable concession, he interrupted his packing and came to sit at the counter on the other stool. He was very close now. He pulled a tin of rolling tobacco from his pocket. Again Vince was aware of the shape and power of the forearms lying on the counter as they rolled the cigarette. The fingers were thick but nimble.

Mandy won't do it, Clive said, nor will Keith, because they are *in loco parentis* as far as the younger kids are concerned. And Adam is the wrong person.

We'll see, Vince replied. I don't know the terms of their contract, but I can't see why one of them couldn't stay. Like I said, I can leave my car. Actually, Adam seems perfectly suitable to me, if he can get the time off work.

Clive lit his cigarette, narrowed his eyes. Listen, I've been thinking about this all evening. Again he was searching for eye contact. I'd rather it was you, Vince.

Vince laughed. Clive, he said softly. He adopted the voice of the older wiser man addressing an over-enthusiastic employee. Clive, listen, I'm a bank director. I have just taken my longest holiday in ten years. I am expected back in the hot seat on Monday morning. There will be hundreds, literally hundreds, of e-mails to answer, reports to consider, a team of accountants awaiting my instructions. I have responsibilities, Clive. The person who has to stay here, with his girlfriend, is you.

Clive smoked. It is towards three in the morning. Around them the camp is quite silent, so that they can almost feel its silence and darkness tugging at them. I pulled her out of the water, he said. And now I'm going to do what she expects me to do. I have my responsibilities too.

Like shouting at a demonstration? I can't imagine in her present state Michela cares too much about that.

I've got something important to do, Clive said evenly. She will tell you. Otherwise I wouldn't be going. They both sat on their stools by the counter with the room's one dim light reflecting in the thin glass of the window beside them. Vince could hear the other man's breathing, then the whine of a mosquito. Both smiled. Vince waved his hand.

That was quite a river today, Clive said after a moment. You enjoyed it.

Vince nodded. But he was not a man people could just push around. All my old professional self is coming out, he realised. Getting to my position in life is not just a question of a way with figures.

Clive was studying him. At the beginning of the week, you'd never have been able to do it.

No, Vince admitted. No, it felt good today.

You've learned a lot.

Vince waited.

And it's not just a question of the proper BCU strokes, is it? In a certain sense, it's not even to do with paddling.

No, Vince agreed. It's not just a question of paddling.

It has to do with the spirit, Clive said, breathing smoke. He hurried on. There's no point in denying that, is there? So why be afraid of the word?

It's to do with the personality, Vince said carefully. That's for sure.

Clive told him: So, you keep an eye on Michela, then you can go out on the river again if you like. Go and ask at the rafting club; they'll give you a guide. There's always someone.

Vince laughed with exasperation. But I told you, I have a job.

Clive again blew out a ring of smoke. I chose you, he said, because the sheer fact is, that you want to stay. Don't you?

No, I don't. I'd be letting people down.

Crap. Clive checked his watch. He stroked his beard. Isn't it a bit ironic, he began again, that a guy who supposedly has so much power and influence and money, a guy at the top of his career, isn't even free to take an extra few days off when he wants? He's in such a straitjacket, serving multi-nationals and the like.

Vince sighed. Clive, listen, to do anything, or become anyone, you have to get involved with a group, don't you? You have to accept a yoke, something that allows you to gear into the world. Otherwise you're just a loose cannon. Even in the kind of politics that you are in, you have to be part of a group. You can't go and demonstrate on your own. You wouldn't achieve anything. I chose the bank ages ago and I'm committed. Then he added: It's like a marriage.

Clive immediately took a deep breath and raised his eyebrows. Vince himself wondered why he had said this. The other man sensed his confusion. It's only four days, he said. At most you lose a week. If you're really so important, they'll wait. If you're not, who cares anyway?

Now Vince thought: that's actually true. Suddenly he wondered why he was resisting so much.

I should be back Thursday, Clive said softly. Towards evening.

What do you mean, should be?

The return flight is Thursday. The next group arrives on the Saturday. He added, If it's really like a marriage, your job, a wife waits, doesn't she? You're not betraying anyone, are you?

Vince stared.

You're not that kind of person, Clive said. Nor am I for that matter. The cigarette was down to a soggy butt drenched in tar. Clive dropped it in his mug and wiped his hands on his jeans. It really is important that I go.

If I'm going to stay, Vince said, you could at least tell me what's going on between you and Michela, why you think she did it, how I'm supposed to behave.

Smiling broadly, Clive jumped to his feet. Thanks, he said. For just a moment, he took Vince's arm and squeezed it. The grip was powerful, but somehow furtive too, an end, not a deepening of intimacy. I was forgetting. I must give you her health card. Any expenses – sometimes they have a charge for scans and things – keep track and I'll pay when I get back.

Clive!

She can tell you, he said. His voice was petulant now.

You're scared, Vince said quietly. If I am going to stay, you can do me the favour of telling me why you think she did it.

I'm not scared. Clive spoke abruptly. And I'm not going to tell you anything.

Why wouldn't you tell me, if you weren't scared?

Because it's none of your business! And believe me if I

was scared I'd tell you right away. Anything I'm scared of I do at once.

If I stay, it becomes my business, Vince said.

All at once, Clive seemed quite beside himself. He turned. Vince was still sitting, quiet and curved, on the stool by the counter. Are you going to hit me now? he asked.

Clive must have seen himself in the window behind Vince's head. He stepped back. Sorry, it's been a hell of a day, he said. I took a few knocks myself. Listen, Vince – he seemed to be thinking quickly, shrewdly – it's been a big shock for me, Micky doing that. You know? It's painful to think about. He pursed his lips, ran his tongue behind them. In the end, what can I say, it's just a banal break-up, men and women, you know, different thoughts about the future. The sheer fact is, we were more together for the politics than anything else. Just a regular break-up.

That's not true, Vince said. Anyone can see you two are in love. Both of you. The way you look at each other, the way you keep touching.

Clive had his lips set. A glazed look has come over his eyes. Think what you like, but I have to go.

Vince sighed. Show me the keys and things, he said.

Outside, the night had finally grown chill. He used the bathroom again, then walked back to his tent. Louise still hasn't returned. Lying down, without even bothering to take jeans and sweater off, Vince tried to decide if he was pleased with this turn of events. Louise would be happy to sit beside Mark in the minibus. I have escaped Mandy, he thought. In the end, he had been lying awake waiting for something to happen, for some improbable transformation. The sparrow rather than the snail. Stupid words. You *want* to stay, Clive said. Do I? As before an exam in the distant past, or the night before his wedding for that matter, he had been keeping himself awake to avoid entering the gorge, the moment when all choice was gone. I'm a chubby chicken waiting for the chop! So now you've delayed it a few days, he told himself, a week. Big deal. I haven't thought about Michela at all, he realised. I certainly didn't jump at staying because of Michela. Unless Clive had guessed something about that moment when he and she had been together under the waterfall. How long was it? Thirty seconds. A minute? Why did I shout those things? You're not betraying anyone, Clive said. He asked me because he senses I like her, perhaps. It was odd how strong and fragile the bearded man was. I chose you! As if he was Jesus after disciples. No, it was hardly, Vince thought, because of that kiss, that brushing of lips, that I threw away my wedding ring. Last place on earth, she had said of the waterfall. Now Vince remembered the photo of the girl who'd died up on the glacier. What was her name? Suddenly the obvious occurred to him. He jumped to his feet, crawled out of the tent, slipped on his sandals. His car was parked beyond the kitchen tent, beneath a tree. Sure enough, there they were. He peeped through a steamy back window. Only for a second. The seats were down and he could just make out their heads poking from beneath the old blanket he kept in the boot. It was pointless to wake them now. They're not in love, he thought. They had wound down a window an inch to breathe. Should he wake Adam? The sound of a Jeep starting over by the chalets was star-tlingly loud. Headlights moved up the track, turning the tents to blue and orange transparencies. Clive escaping. No, I'll pretend I don't know. He waited until the noise had faded and the hushed flow of the river rushed back into the silence from beyond the trees. It was all a pleasure, he decided, going back to his tent. Gloria would have been furious.

TOD

No, I'm not her uncle, Vince said. He wanted that clear at once. It was a scandal, a complete scandal, Mandy had raged when he explained the situation. The mad morning bell-ringer was at work. The valley was full of sound. Vince smiled and kissed her cheek. Seven a.m. You're a disgrace, Adam told his son. Your mother will kill me. You don't tell her everything you do, the boy said. His nose was blocked from the swimming he had done yesterday. Everybody's nose is blocked. Vince packed up the tent to clear their pitch, then set off to the hospital while the others were still having breakfast. Thanks Dad! Almost at once his daughter texted him. He had said nothing to her about her night out. Despite not having used it all week, his phone was down to its last bar. And almost at once she sent a second message. Can't believe you're not hurrying back to the office!

He hurried to the hospital. It had occurred to him Michela would need clothes, pyjamas, toiletries and so on. He unlocked the chalet and searched. Clive hadn't tried to tidy or left any notes. How different from their own home where everything had always been ironed and ordered, where Gloria always left explanatory yellow Post-its on cupboard and fridge. Vince wasn't even sure if the things he found had been washed. The intimacy excited him. There were toiletry products with Italian and German names. A complete scandal, Mandy repeated, running over to say goodbye again. I wish I'd been there to give him a piece of my mind. She was angry. She took both Vince's hands. She is jealous of the girl, Vince knew. It was silly. Of a girl who had tried to kill herself. Our families are indissolubly linked, Adam said wryly. The man offered his hand. Steady on, Vince smiled. He wouldn't open to him. Don't worry, I won't fight the water, he told Keith. The paunchy man had a twinkle in his eye. Wish I was staying, mate. He was enjoying Mandy's rage. Please, Tom whispered, give her my love. This – he handed over a beer-mat with a scribble – is my e-mail address.

And now Vince was repeating to some sort of ward sister that he was not Michela's uncle. He spoke very slowly and clearly. It was important to have that farce out of the way. I-am-not-her-uncle. No. The truth was he had only just learned her surname: Donati. But I would like to see a doctor about her. Yes. She hasn't woken up, the nurse warned. The woman was grim. She shook her head under a green cap. Not voken, she repeated. And not all the staff were here on Sundays. Vince waited more than an hour in a corridor before a doctor took him into a small office to insist that they must inform the girl's next of kin. They couldn't discuss the matter with a stranger. As always, Vince explained the situation truthfully. He had put on the most serious clothes he had with him. Cotton trousers, a battered linen jacket. The doctor didn't agree: On the contrary, I think it is very probable that she really wants her mother to know most. He too spoke with a strong accent. She wants to say, look,

Mutti, I can kill myself too. For some children, this is a way of showing they have become adult.

Vince was polite. I can only tell you the very little I know, he said. His whole career had been built on a habit of complete candour. He didn't trust himself to lie. From the one personal conversation I had with her, he said, I would say that seeing her mother might be counterproductive. She might react very badly. She was very angry with her family. The doctor pursed his lips, played with his pen. He was a small earnest man in his mid thirties. No doubt he knows the regulations. Her boyfriend, Vince repeated, the man she lives with, will be back on Thursday. He had to go to Berlin. The doctor shook his head. I don't think so, Mr, er, Marshall, yes? I don't think the partner of a pretty woman goes away at a time like this. What could be more important?

Vince offered no comment. They looked at each other across a metal table-top. You have hurt yourself too, I see? Just a couple of stitches, Vince admitted. Aren't you a bit old for falling in rivers? This was irritating. I don't think age has much to do with it, doctor. The doctor played with a pen. You have only known her a week, then? Five days, Vince said. And why are you the one to stay now? Her boyfriend asked me to; I was the only person with my own car. So you have no special relationship with her? Vince sighed. A friend, nothing else, a member of the same group. Then he added: People have a strong sense of solidarity, you know, doctor, when they do these things together. I'm sure that is true, Mr Marshall. Now, you will please inform the mother of this accident, or you will find the telephone number so we can inform, okay? Okay, Vince said. He hesitated. Can I see her, though? Should I leave my own phone number? I have a mobile.

To his surprise, he was allowed to sit by the bed. There

was a cabinet to put her clothes and things in, but Vince decided first he would find a laundry. Michela lay as if deeply asleep. Her breathing seemed normal enough; the face, with its high cheeks and tanned skin, was transformed by a huge bruise beneath the eye. She's sweating, he noticed. He wondered if perhaps they had covered her up too much. Gloria always had stories about the incompetence of nurses. I'm on Gloria's territory, he thought. He picked up a hand and said, Michela. Michela? He wouldn't call her Micky. Funny, her hands were quite unscathed. She hadn't grabbed at anything. She hadn't tried to save herself. The skin was cool and soft. Not the heavy cold Gloria's had been.

After twenty minutes he left her and walked into Bruneck, but everything was closed. Church bells were clanging. He couldn't buy a phone charger and he couldn't find a launderette. He bought a coffee, a pastry, and sat out in the same square where he had been with Keith and Michela three days ago. I am waiting again, he thought, waiting to be someone new. But it had been a pleasure to use his old persona on the doctor, the quiet authority he knew he transmitted. When he returned to the campsite the others had gone. How hot it is, Vince realised, when you're not spending the day on the river. The air in the chalet was stifling. He suddenly felt tired, uncomfortable. In Sand in Taufers he bought a *Herald Tribune* and discovered it was the warmest summer ever recorded. In France old people were dying like flies. Clive was vindicated, then. What could be more important at a moment like this than a summit on global warming? The markets seem stable enough, though. Vince didn't study the figures. He glanced, but his mind wouldn't focus. I'm still on holiday, he decided.

He drove to the river where it tumbled into the gorge above the town. This was where Clive had parked the minibus after their walk on the glacier. I can't keep away, he realised. He stepped carefully down the steep path that followed the rapid, trying to remember not to grab at anything with his bad hand. Pushing through tangled branches, he found a place that allowed him to see the fifty yards of wild water he had traversed. There was the rock that had pinned him. Was it? He wasn't sure. It was strange to think he had been upside down in that tumult. Tons of water crashed constantly against a black solid mass. I didn't really take it in. But this was certainly the rock he had climbed out on. Yes. He recognised the dome-like shape, the way the stream swirled round and by. What happens to a ring under water? How far would it travel? Is this, perhaps, it crossed his mind, how the old tramp first started hanging about the river, after some accident? A death even. His wife had drowned. Or a child. Probably not, Vince thought. Probably he had fished on the river as a boy. It's the natural place for him to be. And yesterday he had saved Phil's life. How casual that seemed! The boy had forgotten almost at once. Then Vince realised his phone was ringing. He liked to keep the tones discreet and the water was thundering. Mr Marshall, could you come to the hospital?

It was after three now. I can't believe it! Michela was muttering. Her lips were pale. She was attached to a drip but nothing else. In the only other bed, beneath the window, an older woman was unconscious. Michela! Vince said. Again he was surprised they had left him alone. You're awake! He felt an intense, nervous pleasure, an apprehension. Where's Clive? she asked in a low voice. I thought they meant Clive was coming.

With no air-conditioning the room was stifling. The window was closed. The girl is confused, he realised, and sweating. She tried to sit up but fell back, as though oppressed

183

by some invisible weight. Shouldn't she be sedated, he wondered? Perhaps you're not supposed to sedate coma patients. Why are you here? she whispered. Where's Clive? Vince tried to be natural. He wiped a sleeve on his forehead. I don't really know why, he admitted. Clive said he had to go to Berlin. He asked me to stay.

Vince wondered how much he should say to the girl, what allusions might upset her. The doctors hadn't given him any instructions. I've brought your clothes and bathroom stuff. She stared at him. Actually, I'm not sure if they've been washed. I couldn't find a launderette. Staring, she seemed to find everything he said incomprehensible. Again she tried and failed to sit up. She was pinned to the bed, panting. When's he coming back? she asked. When can I see him?

He said he should be back Thursday.

A look of puzzlement clouded her eyes.

When Thursday, what day is it today?

The flight is due Thursday, that's all I know. In Bolzano. Today is Sunday. He saw her fists clench on the bed. Until then, I mean, if there's anything you need . . . Do you have a mobile, by the way. That might . . .

And that's all he said? Is that all he said?

Vince was unprepared for this. It occurred to him that he had been spared any hospital scenes with Gloria. Only the morgue. Casting about, he told her: Actually he did say something about going because you would have wanted him to.

She managed to turn a little in the bed and pushed the sheets aside. Everything oppressed her. Me? And you believed him?

Vince said, I don't know anything about you two, do I? I'm sure he believed it, though.

Making a huge effort, she dragged her head higher up the pillow. The drip bottle swung on its pole. Crumpled and damp, the white hospital smock they had given her clung to her body. Vince can see her breasts. Apart from the facial bruise, her body appears to have flushed through the rapid without a scratch. You really believed him! Her voice was harsh and dazed. Are you stupid?

It's hardly up to me to believe or disbelieve. Vince kept his voice quiet, adult. I told him I thought it would be much better if he stayed with you, not me. He said he had something very important to do and you would understand. You would want him to go.

Ah, important. Again she grimaced. It was as if she were looking for the energy to express her anger. What could Clive ever do that was important?

Vince watched her. He was annoyed with himself for not having prepared the meeting at all, not having scouted ahead. He doesn't want her to suffer some kind of relapse. Clive saved you, he told her in a matter-of-fact voice. He pulled you out. Without him, you'd have drowned. She thought about this for a moment. I wish I had drowned, and him too, she muttered. I wish we'd both drowned! Now leave me alone! she finished. Leave me alone and don't come back! I don't want to see you.

Vince stood up. You should have thought more before coming, he told himself. He sighed. You rest, he said, I'll come back tomorrow. Don't, she said. I don't want to see you. Go back to your bank and your calculations.

He was at the door when she must have noticed the bandage on his hand. Oh, did you hurt yourself? For the first time, her voice registered curiosity. She was propped on one elbow. I went down after you. I couldn't avoid it. She began shaking her head rather strangely. I didn't ask you to, did I? I didn't say you did, Vince replied. He paused a moment by the door. I'm not complaining. It was quite an experience. As he turned to leave, he heard her repeat. Don't come back. Please.

Vince spent the late afternoon cleaning the chalet. He could have got in his car and driven right back to London if he had wanted to. She's awake now, he thought. She's out of danger. She can give the doctors the phone number of family and friends. She has her clothes, her health card. I forgot to leave any money, he remembers, washing a pile of dishes. But he knows it's a detail. Someone would drive her back here. It was only a few miles. And it's only about sixteen hours to London, he thought. If I drive through the night. I needn't even be late for work. She made it perfectly clear she doesn't want to see me.

He settled down to clean the chalet. To do it seriously. There was this urge in him to get in the car and go. He felt his body straining towards it: the air-conditioning, the long hours at the wheel through the continental night, the autobahns, the tunnel beneath the sea, the early morning on the M2, old friends at the bank, authority. For years now Vince has wielded authority. But the resistance is steady and strong. That was not the way forward.

Sweating and sticky, he heaped a hundred odds and ends onto the big bed and found a broom to sweep the floor. It was one of the witches' variety with yellow bristles that caught between planks of bare wood. He scraped in corners. There are nail parings, the tar-drenched ends of rolled cigarettes, a couple of cotton buds, crumpled receipts, a piece of chewing gum, even a dried-out teabag. They don't keep a clean house, he thought. When was the last time I used a broom? He didn't feel critical, but dogged, trying to establish a geometry, a system. Both Clive and Michela are powerfully present to him. He can hear their voices. Sweep from the walls in, he decided. There was a cleaning firm for the service flat in Vauxhall. Everything is always clean when Vince gets back after a long day, everything in the right place. Then he found a rag, put it under the tap, wrung it out and wiped the floor twice. In this heat, with window and door wide open, it dried at once. At six-thirty the sun dropped behind the glacier. The valley began to cool. It was a relief. Some kids had started kicking a ball where Waterworld's kitchen tent had been.

He tried to sort out the clean clothes from the dirty and put the latter in a bin-bag. Why am I doing this? he wondered. The girl's underclothes in one drawer, sweaters in another. These two people are in grave trouble, he thought. He gathered stray books together on a shelf – *Strategies of Subversion, Carbon War, Stupid White Men*. Why will people never give up anything? someone had scrawled inside a cover. We must give up things! Clive, he thought. He stacked papers, invoices, brochures, printouts of e-mails. Some were signed 'Red Wolves', with an indication of a website. There was an IBM Thinkpad, but he didn't turn it on. Did Michela have a mobile phone? he wondered. If so, where? He opened and closed various drawers. They are asking too little for these holidays, he reflected, considering a paper quoting the price of the canoes. It would take for ever to recover the outlay.

Suddenly, Vince realised he was crying. The tears are flowing as he shifts the bed and sweeps the big dust-balls from under it. He doesn't stop. There are two old Durex foils. I should have done this before wiping the floor, he realises. Nobody has swept here for a month and more. I'm doing what Gloria always did, he mutters: tidying up. He shifted the bed back into position, turned up a photocopied pamphlet: 'The Bomb in the Garage: How To!' He shook his head. It used to infuriate him, having got home late Friday night, that Gloria would then spend Saturday morning cleaning. I never protested. He crouched down with the dustpan, collected up the dust and the foils and tobacco shreds and sweet wrappers. Should I wipe again? These are tears of shame, he decided. He didn't stop. He tipped the mess into a Despar plastic bag, wrung out the cloth again. Could that have been what she meant? He got on his knees. That she was sorry for the Saturday morning cleaning sessions. The wet wood had a musty smell. We could have loved each other better, Vince thought.

He had nearly finished now. Adam was a detail, he decided. He wiped the table and counter and moved the chairs back. In six months, nothing has brought him so close to his dead wife. So close to the edge. He sat on the stool by the counter. There was still the sink to sort out. Deep trouble, he muttered, thinking of Clive and Michela again, their books, their bad investments, their aggressive concern about the world. Was there any bleach about? he wondered. They need an accountant. Then a vibration in his pocket told him a text had arrived. Let us know your news. How is M? Mandy. M awake, he replied. All well. Safe journey.

Vince stood at the open door of the chalet. The campsite was busy with new arrivals organising their gear. The evening was moist and warm and beyond Sand in Taufers the profile of the mountains rose quiet and clear into a pale sky. Did that girl commit suicide? he wondered. Katrin Hofstetter. The name came to him. It hadn't seemed an obvious place to fall from. The path was easy. He gazed up above the castle to the glacier. They hadn't visited the castle. The landscape is patient, he thought, staring at the high slopes. It waits patiently. But perhaps memorials aren't always put exactly in the place where an accident happens. That might be dangerous. Perhaps she had died a hundred yards away, on some tricky bit. I left no memorial for Gloria, he thought. They're not the fashion these days. He imagined a plaque on some boulder up in the mountains, his wife's photograph and a date. Perhaps that way you could restrict remembering to a place, a routine, an anniversary visit. Jingling the car keys in his pocket, Vince walked through the campsite towards the village. Even after shedding the ring, she won't let me go. Unless it was just a question, he thought, dropping the Despar bag in a bin, of not being used to having nothing to do. I arranged a holiday, Vince realised, that would be all action. I did that on purpose so as not to think. I am always so busy. And how strange that through all those years, in the office, in the flat, at home, these mountains had been waiting here. They always will. Even after the glaciers have melted. The world waits for you to be tired of your life. To save himself having to choose, he went to the same restaurant they had eaten in yesterday evening.

As soon as he sat down, Vince knew he was touching bottom. The place was not the same without the group. This is it, he realised. They hurried him to a corner, a small table for two. The waitress spoke no English. She was in a hurry with all the other clients, the holidaymakers. Trying to get a grip, Vince looked around. The room assailed him. Without the others, he has no resistance. This schlock is horrible, he realised, these dangling hearts that aren't hearts, these fake trophies, these dead animals, this awful international music with its sugary electronic rhythms. How could I have loved it so much yesterday? Why did I find it so wonderful?

The same ageing musician presented the same impassive face above his keyboards. A mahogany face. The tune was 'Smoke Gets In Your Eyes'. He must have grown up with the accordion and folk dances, Vince thought, or with the organ in church, with festivities and solemnities. How can he play this stuff? The music suddenly seemed very loud. It's a betrayal, Vince thought. The man was not incompetent. He's betraying his past. And the voices were swelling too. There was a huge buzz of voices. The international clients aren't listening to the entertainment that has been laid on for them. They bring their money, Vince thought, but not their attention. The musician's eyes stared across the heads of the holidaymakers. Into nothingness. He pays attention to nothing. Like a photo on a grave. And knows no one is paying attention to him.

Suddenly, Vince was covering his face with his hands. I miss them. His head was shaking. I miss Brian and Max and Amelia and Tom. People I've only known a few days. Gloria is dead, a voice said. Oh then please, *be dead*! Vince wailed. *Die*! He had spoken aloud. Don't come back please, Michela said. Don't come back.

Entschuldigung? The waitress is at his side. She wants to take his order. I am about to make a scene, Vince thought. He forced back his chair. I'm sorry. The waitress had seen his tears. Her face didn't soften. I'll have to go. He turned and made quickly for the door.

There is no question of thinking now. He walked swiftly along the lamp-lit street. This is a complete impasse. I don't want to see you. What had he expected? How lightly he had scorned Mandy's sensible interest. Abruptly he turned into a bar. Whisky, he said. They would understand that. He pulled out his wallet at once. Behind the counter a young man was moving quickly between the beer-taps and now Vince noticed kids playing at screens around the walls and others sitting at keyboards typing out e-mails. This must be where Louise and the others had come most evenings. It was smoky. I still haven't said anything to the bank, Vince remembered. Where Phil had downloaded pornography. The barman was showing him an ice-bucket, eyebrows raised enquiringly. Vince shook his head. Louise scorned Phil and his dirty pictures, but in the space of a couple of days she had slept with a boy she hardly knew. Why did I let her do that? She's far too young. Vince sipped the whisky. He doesn't like whisky. Then downed it. I should have said something, about relationships, about commitment. I'm nervous about calling the office, he realised, like an adolescent afraid of parental reproach. Yet he only has to inform them of an emergency, a forced absence. For God's sake, I'm one of the most important people in the bank.

The whisky burned outward from his stomach. It was satisfying to do something out of character, something destructive. He feels nauseous. He feels better. I constantly feared Gloria's reproach, he thought. He put the glass down. Why? He had shed her ring, but not the sharp reproachful voice that runs in his head. You never take a holiday. You've given your whole life to that bank. If we moved to London, though, he told her, we'd have more time together. That was always how the conversation went. But she wouldn't give up her job. Gloria was secretly happy I didn't take holidays, he realised now. Without modulating his normal voice at all, he asked: Is there a bottle I can have. *Was*? A bottle. Can I buy a bottle of whisky? To take away. The young man smiles. He can see I'm in trouble. *Haben wir eine Flasche Whisky?* he calls to a sour-looking girl making up sandwiches. That's his wife, Vince thought. He stepped out into the street with a bottle of something called Highland Dew.

Where was he going? He hadn't crossed the bridge that led back to the campsite. He was walking along the road down the valley to Geiss and Bruneck. As soon as he was beyond the village lamps, the pavement disappeared. To the left was a thin strip of woodland between road and river; all around, the quiet mass of the mountains. He was exposed to oncoming headlights, swerving as they saw him. Three, four, five together. The glare is blinding. He had to stop. Then there was a break and the darkness and silence flooded back. He could walk again, until the next car arrived, speeding, glaring. Two worlds that alternated. The landscape, the traffic. We ignored each other, Vince thought. That was the simple truth. That's why it is impossible to be alone now. For years you ignored each other and now she won't leave you alone, now you must pay attention. I am talking to myself, Vince stumbled. I am lost.

But at that very moment he found the path. The bushes opened to the left, down towards the river. He trod slowly in the dark. The old man will have a lamp, he thought. Sure enough, he met the river at exactly the point where they had tackled the wave the first day. Got it right! He stopped a moment at the river bank. The black water was fast but unhurried. The foam of the stopper glowed a little, as though phosphorescent. He looked across. I know the call of it now, he told himself, the water's invitation. He could understand the gesture of the limp arms, the girl's neck bent like a swan's towards the current.

Through the bushes a few yards on, the tramp's shack was in complete darkness. For some reason, Vince moved very quietly, stealthily even. He trod on tip-toe with his whisky bottle in one hand. The dwelling is made of old plywood panels anchored with nylon cord, draped with tarpaulin and corrugated iron. Vince bent to move aside a blanket. *Ist jemand da*? He had prepared the words. He didn't know if they were right. He poked his head in, but saw only three or four small grey chinks where light leaked from outside.

The smell was powerful. *Ist jemand da?* Vince repeated softly. Suddenly the whisky bottle was wrenched from his fingers. Ow! As he turned, a torch shone in his face. He had a vague impression of an arm raised, of the whisky bottle attached to it. No, he yelled. *Für Sie!* He tried to protect his head. *Trinken. Geschenk.* Don't you understand? Roland! Finally he remembered the man's name.

There was an old mattress laid across two loading pallets and an assortment of filthy cushions and blankets, fruit boxes with plates, tools, fishing gear. Roland lit a gas lamp that hung from the sagging roof. He must have some money, then, Vince thought. Some relationship with the world. It was hard to get accustomed to the smell. *Rauchst du?* Unlike Clive, Roland smoked regular cigarettes. I've accepted a cigarette! Vince hates smoking. Roland was talking excitedly all the time. They sat at each end of the mattress. The cigarette trembled in his fingers. Roland drank straight from the bottle and handed it to him. Occasionally the flow of words was interrupted at what seemed to be a question. But this was not the German Vince had learned for O level. *Ja*, he filled a gap at random. He knew it wasn't necessary. *Ja, ja.*

He handed the bottle back. Roland cocked his head to one side. The face was gaunt and in the white light of the gas it was as if the skull were somehow outside the skin, had risen through the broken veins and blemishes, the loose lips, long sparse hair. He's younger than me, Vince realised. Roland's eyes were young and glassily blue in bloodshot rings. The Adam's apple jerked sharply when he drank. *Nein*, Vince said into the next pause. The bottle came back. Then he said. *Ich bin allein.* It wasn't clear whether Roland had understood this. Talking fast in a German that was strangely liquid, sing-song almost, he fumbled in a pile of paper bags, brought out a roll of bread, made to break it. It wouldn't break. He started smiling, then laughing, making a comedy of his failure to break the bread, then at last handed half to Vince.

Meine Frau, Vince said, *ist* . . . He couldn't remember the word. My wife is dead, he said. Roland began to speak again. Drinking from the bottle, Vince was vaguely aware of hot ash falling on his trousers. *Tod*, he remembered. Gloria *ist tod*. Roland shouted something quite raucously, then lowered his voice to a muttered monotone. Vince watched. The man was fumbling in the pile of paper at the head of the mattress again, but this time found nothing. He shook his head theatrically. The air was heavy with smoke. At some point Vince heard the shout, *Draussen! Draussen!* Roland was yelling. His voice was suddenly clear and he was making a throwing gesture towards the blanket across the door. *Ja, Sie ist tod*, Vince repeated. He felt a sharp pain burn into his fingertips.

When he woke it was broad daylight. His bladder was aching. He had been in a board-meeting, pissing under the big polished table. Almost at once the shame was swamped by a pounding head. His hand went between his legs. He hadn't. Hadn't heard the bells either. Roland must have stretched him out on the mattress. Vince stumbled out of the shack and had to lean both hands on a tree while he relieved himself. What time is it? I'm late. Ten-thirty. The phone was still in his pocket. He had slept in all his clothes. He felt suddenly for his wallet, then was ashamed of doubting the man. Why wouldn't the phone turn on? Why was it taking so long? Vince realised he had never turned it off. It was dead. It's Monday. *Tod*, he thought. He shook his head and began to shamble back to Sand in Taufers under a blistering sun. Amazingly, it was getting hotter.

Hello, is that Colin? There was no electricity in the chalet. He had bought a car charger, but there was no shade in the campsite to park in while he phoned. All the places under the trees were taken. When he opened the car doors, the air swirled with heat. The seats and steering wheel were too hot for bare skin.

Vince, old chap! Welcome back. Not before time. Are you coming up for coffee?

No, actually, I'm still here, Col, I'm still in Italy. There's been a bit of an emergency I'm afraid. Accident.

Colin Dyers began the inevitable mix of concern and cautious questioning. Not Louise?

Vince hasn't had a hangover for more than a decade. Explaining the situation, he was aware that he didn't sound his normal self. Thank God for that, Dyers said. Though actually we were rather counting on your being here. The older man's voice was rich with catarrh. He was conventional and astute. That was very kind of you to, er, stay on for the young woman. I was the only one with my own car, Vince said. There was a slight, significant pause. Paul has been collating the figures from the States, Dyers said. There are a couple of urgent questions to be addressed.

Then Vince was aware of how absolutely unlike himself this behaviour must seem from the point of view of his colleague. Not so much the staying behind, but he could easily have phoned Dyers or one of the other directors on Sunday. He had their numbers. He could have warned them at once. He could have presented himself as extremely concerned about this delayed return, about all the many problems one had to deal with at this time of year. I should be asking who is handling what, sounding worried that I'm not personally in charge. Listen, Col, I can make it to an internet point, he said, if you want to send me some stuff to look at. And I'll have the phone on twenty-four hours a day now. I had trouble finding a car charger.

When do you think you'll actually be back, Dyers asked. There were strict rules of course about what could be committed to e-mail and phone conversations. Vince hesitated. He had stretched his sleeping bag on the car seat so as not to have to sit on the scorching material. The charger was plugged in. The heat trembled round his head. A fly was buzzing against the windscreen. Next Monday, he said. At the latest. You are well yourself, though, aren't you? Dyers asked. I've had a wonderful holiday, Colin. Wonderful. Just the break I needed. That's great, Dyers said. He would be sitting at a desk stacked with tasks and reports. At least one other person would be in the room awaiting his attention, one other phone-line is on hold and as he speaks the man's eye will be ranging constantly over the constantly incoming e-mail. Vince said: Listen, Colin, just give me this week. Trust me, okay. I won't let you down. Dyers immediately responded. We'll expect you next Monday, Vince. Back with us.

In the chalet, Vince opened the two windows and lay on the bed. His head aches. There was no way to shade out the light. He had left the phone to charge in the car. Closing his eyes, it suddenly occurred to him that there was an obvious purpose to this empty week. I must think about Gloria. I must give time to it. Real time. Not the few confused minutes before falling asleep. I must go at it as a task, a job.

For seven silent hours then, Vince lay on the bed in the chalet and told himself the story of his marriage. He remembered first meetings, holidays. He tried to list presents, to recall decisions, the cars they had owned, her father's death, the miscarriage after Louise. He remembered Gloria's sporting achievements, her body, her brusque but loving ways. She was loving, he thought, despite the austere, hurried meals, despite the Saturday morning cleaning. He remembered a way she had of dressing too lightly, of insisting they sleep with the window open, he remembered her fortitude when the first company he worked for had failed and there were mortgage payments and her father was ill. She had been solid then. She was never frightened of life. He remembered her laugh, her loud raucous laugh. She was taken from me, he said to himself at last, before there was time to understand, before I could prepare. I didn't sit by her bed. Perhaps it was a love story, he decided. In its own way. He tried to remember Christmases and dinners and discussions about Louise, about schools. He felt better. He stood up and switched on the radio. There was a small digital set on the counter. He brought it back to the bed and lay down again. The problem is not the past, he decided, but what to do next. He was surprised by this sudden clarity. What a strange night last night! He pressed the search button looking for a station in English. Reception wasn't good. The mountains no doubt. I haven't eaten for twenty-four hours, he thought. He remembered Roland trying to break his piece of stale bread. At last a woman's stern voice was talking about Iraq, about an election, an international disagreement, a plot to kill someone. Gloria would listen to two or three news bulletins one right after the other. Vince had always thought there was something disturbing about this attachment to chronicle. To return to the Berlin summit, the woman was saying – her accent was American – the three men who have chained themselves to the railing outside the Reichstag, now claim to have a bomb that they will explode if the police try to remove them. Vince got up, went out to the car, turned on the phone and texted a message to his daughter. Thinking of you, he wrote. It was lovely to be on holiday together.

SELF-RESCUE

Was it possible though? In the same internet café where he had bought the whisky, Vince studied a photo on the Guardian website. He has written to all his closest colleagues apologising for his absence, giving generic instructions, promising that he will be in the office on Saturday morning and will work through the weekend. The three men are wearing masks. Willing to Die to Wake Up the World, is the headline. Their spokesman speaks three languages fluently. No one knows who they are. The police have cleared the area. How can they sleep? Vince wonders. Or piss or shit? The masks are bags of white linen with holes for eyes and mouth. A strategy to prevent the police putting pressure on them through relatives, the article surmises. The temperature is in the mid-thirties. They are in full sunlight. Vince recognises the Reichstag with its pompous monumentality. He has visited the city more than once. But what he is looking at very closely is the exposed wrist of one of the men where it is handcuffed to the railing. This man seems to have a familiar build. Or perhaps not. He presses the 'back' button to return to the Waterworld site where

Mandy has already posted four sets of twenty pictures. The quality is good. Here you are folks! she has written. Our mythical Community Experience! Vince searches for one of Clive and clicks to enlarge. The instructor is photographed face-on in his yellow boat, paddle held across his blue buoyancy aid. It's a fine face, lit up somehow, the eyes glinting, the beard giving an impression of vigour, a secretive smile playing round the lips. Vince tries to find some distinguishing mark on the exposed wrist and forearm, but it's hopeless. A tattoo or a scar would do it. The red boat just poking into the background must be Michela's, he thinks. Or my own perhaps. He glances at one or two of the other pictures. Although there is loud music in the café, it's strange the silence that gathers around these images. Max doffing his straw hat. Caroline balancing the singing hamster on her head. Vince returns to the *Guardian*. He checks all related articles. They have the latest figures on global warming, speed of temperature rise, glacier retreat. There is a map predicting flooding, shaded in different colours to suggest possible dates. Holland gone mid-century. The Po valley gone. World in state of denial, a psychologist writes, like a party on a riverboat drifting towards Niagara. Odd he used that metaphor. Can it really be Clive? Vince goes back to the photo. The three men have small coloured backpacks. Ready to blow themselves up, is the caption.

Vince checks his mail again, then spends the day repeating last Thursday's walk up on the glacier. He takes the chairlift above Sand in Taufers, finds the path, bends his back to it. He has put on his walking shoes. Making the trip alone, he gradually becomes aware, all around him, of the same silence that emanated from those photographs, the silence of voices that are no longer there. All my life has a kind of silence to it, he reflects, these days. He remembers Clive's uncomfortable apology to Adam. It's a noisy silence. I don't think I can get through the whole summer like this, Michela had said. Vince stops to straighten his shoulders and look around. He had imagined she was referring to the heat. I didn't pay attention. Same with Gloria. And it's hot again now on the steep slope. The views are awesome. The peaks rise up one after another, quivering, immense and blue, but mainly bereft of snow. Perhaps we can feel a new tenderness for the landscape, now that we know we are killing it. Further down the valley there are cowbells clanging. Every time an animal moves, tiny, far below, a bell clangs in Vince's mind. It must drive them mad. And across the wide air that separates him from a further slope comes the tinkle of children laughing. Some party or other. Vince listens, he picks out the distant figures. This is the silence of the mountains. Does Michela know what is happening? he wonders. How will she react? There were a hundred thousand, the *Guardian* said, at Sunday's demonstration. It won't be Clive.

Long before he reached the top, Vince was aware of speeding up, of marching more purposefully. He wants to get to Katrin Hofstetter's death marker. On the way, he has seen three or four other memorials. Why didn't I see them last time? Now he comes across a small iron cross driven into a boulder and the name of a young man, Karl Länger. There's no photo, but a plastic rose has been fixed to the cross with a piece of wire. It's the girl's photo that draws me. Vince is aware that he has become hypersensitive to everything, and aware that it won't last. I should enjoy it, this intensity.

The high ridge where the glacier begins is a strange mix of heat and cold. The sun is burning his forehead and the grainy ice freezing his feet. Then he can't find the photo where he thought it must be. It's irritating. He stands aside to let a group of German hikers pass in the opposite direction.

Only four days and I've forgotten. *Grüss Gott*, a stout woman says. *Grüss Gott*. Eventually he finds the memorial twenty yards further on, facing west from a low wall of rock. 1999 she died. The thirty-first of August. How strange. And what a little miracle of technology to seal a photo so well it can survive the winter blizzards, the summer sun! The face is not quite as he remembered it. She's prettier, happier, the hair wavier, brushed forward on one shoulder. Katrin Hofstetter: 19.1.1979–31.8.1999. Vince imagines her eyes staring west into the sunset when the world around is all desert, when hikers no longer pass by, the planet is quite dead, and for the first time it occurs to him that those men chained to the railing in Berlin are not, perhaps, completely mad. Dyers and Hilson and the others will be in some committee meeting now. Much of the money the bank deals with is oil money. Inevitably. Glancing round to check that the path is quiet, Vince takes out his wallet, removes an ID photo of his wife and, without looking at it, lets it drop into the glassy crack between glacial ice and rock wall beneath the little memorial. In company, the dead may visit him less often.

Driving back, below the gorge at the entry to Sand in Taufers, he stopped the car at the sign 'Rafting Center' to the left of the road. In a small closed yard stood rack after rack of wetsuits and life-jackets. A tall, blonde man was loading gear into the back of a van. Do you know of any kayak guides I could contact? Vince spoke clearly and slowly in English. Not for myself, he explained. There was a group who already had their own instructors, but they might need a guide to show them round the local rivers. An expression of caution and recognition crossed the young face. You are with the English people, right? The girl who is nearly . . . He made a comic, choking expression. Right, Vince said. My name is Gerhard. The young man reached out a damp hand. She is okay? I helped to pull her out of the water. Very pretty girl. Vince gave his name. How much would a guide cost? he asked. It occurred to him now that there might be some local resentment of the English canoe group moving in like this on their pitch. We could have to talk about that, Gerhard said. I could have to see who is . . . who can help. Okay. Vince explained that he would only know on Thursday if their own guide could come or not. Then the work would be from Sunday onwards. I'll call you Friday morning. Gerhard gave him the Rafting Center's pamphlet, with a phone number.

The protestors have set a deadline of Wednesday evening at six o'clock, the radio said. Tomorrow. Vince listened stretched on the bed. It was early evening. There is one demand: a commitment to reduce greenhouse-gas emissions in line with Kyoto. Outside the open door of the chalet, the campsite sounds reminded him of the previous week: the singing, the shouts of children playing, radios, the occasional drumming. A diplomat who spoke in some unrecognisable tongue was translated as saying that his country would never be seen to reward terrorism. They were calling it terrorism. You have to keep a clear head, said an American. Vince was struck by the idea that the men at the railing might have very clear heads. As they saw it. Certainly they were keep-ing their nerve, despite the heat. How clearly I saw every-thing as the boat tipped down into the rapid. The image is sharper in his mind than any photo. What does clarity mean exactly? All those years doing the accounts, how clear-headed I was! How blind. Police spokesmen said they were taking the bomb threat very seriously. Vince looked at his watch. I could go and have a drink with Roland again, he thought, and get thoroughly muddled. Instead he fell asleep easily and early and woke in the night to hear the radio crackling voicelessly and feel the cool air drifting in through the open door. I didn't even close the door. Returning from the bathrooms, he was aware that his mind felt peculiarly healthy and purposeful, but without quite knowing what the purpose was. Caught yourself smiling, he muttered.

On the Wednesday morning he drove down to Bruneck, stopping at Geiss to check the bus timetable. He had put a change of dry clothes in the car. If someone like himself, he thought, could paddle the easy section of the lower Aurino on his own, then, in the event, there would be no guide required until the Monday.

Arriving at the hospital, he found the ward sister and asked her if she could tell Fräulein Donati he was here and would she be willing to see him. About five minutes later Michela appeared in the corridor, belting up the towelled robe he had brought her three days before. What are you doing here? she asked. I thought you'd gone. The bruise on her cheek has drained to yellow. She is standing very straight. Vince only shrugged. We can talk in the garden, she said brusquely.

Turning, she walked away so quickly he had to hurry to catch up. Her sandals slapped down two flights of stairs, along a corridor and out into a courtyard with five or six benches. I told you not to bother, she repeated over her shoulder. That's why I sent the nurse to ask if you were willing to see me, Vince answered. Michela went to a bench in the shade and curled herself up right in the corner, arms folded, knees drawn in under them. But Vince could sense she was better now. Her body had a quick feminine lightness as she moved. You look well, he said. Not because I want to, she told him.

He waited. The so-called garden was just a few square yards of lawn and shrubs with a near life-size Madonna, carved in wood, on a pedestal in the middle. Has Clive been in touch? she asked. No. He sat uncomfortably with his hands on his knees. Again it was fearfully hot. He was sweating. Actually, I was wondering if either you or he had mobiles, you know, it might be useful. He hates them, the girl said. What do you need to call us for anyway? Vince let it pass. Also, I thought you might need some money, but I couldn't find a wallet or anything, in the chalet. I don't have one, she told him. Clive left some money for me with the doctor.

Vince was surprised at this level of dependence. Again he waited. He wasn't going to tell her anything, if she didn't know. Eventually she said: They're letting me out tomorrow morning.

So you'll be there when Clive gets back.

Right.

Casually, he asked: You don't know if he had any special plans for while he was in Berlin?

No. At once she was more alert. Why?

Oh, I just wondered what on earth these demonstrators could actually get up to for four whole days.

She relaxed. If it's like other things I've been to, there'll be a kind of alternative conference in some abandoned warehouse or other.

Catching a smile in her voice, Vince turned to look at her. A soft irony was playing round her lips. He raised his eyebrows. Quite unexpectedly, she reached across the bench and took his bandaged hand. Is it bad? Vince couldn't hide from himself a sudden flutter of excitement. Just a couple of stitches. He didn't say he was planning to take out a boat this afternoon. So why haven't you gone back? she repeated. I wasn't very nice when you came last time, was I? Vince bit his lip, cast about. I promised Clive I would stay. Then I thought, you know, I might as well take advantage of the chalet for a couple of days. He wasn't so much lying as speaking at random. You're sad, aren't you? she told him. He hesitated. Not especially. Yes you are. One night I was sitting outside, behind the kitchen tent, and I saw you walking to the bathrooms. Really late. You had your shoulders bent – she sat forward and mimicked, cruelly, her face comically gloomy – like you were carrying something that wasn't there. Something pretty heavy. Oh, that's just old age, Vince said. He had expected to talk about her problems, not his. She laughed. Not true, you're sad. Why not admit it? Your wife died, didn't she? That's right, he acknowledged. The girl was looking at him. Did you love her?

Vince was unprepared for such a direct question. Yes. I did, he said. Of course I loved her. Poor fingers, she muttered. She was still holding his hand. And did she love you?

Yes. Listen . . .

You do know there was a nasty story going round?

Vince turned and looked straight at her. He pulled his hand away. She shrugged her shoulders, pursed her lips. She had done it deliberately. Her eyes are glinting. But he won't rise to it. Speaking very quietly, he asks: So what have you been up to these last couple of days?

Nothing. Lots of neural tests and scans and things.

Results?

Apparently I could be an athlete.

Great.

She didn't reply. She still has a mocking smile in her eyes. I suppose, Vince tried after a moment or two, the hospital must get pretty boring when you're not really ill. I mean, people must end up watching the TV and listening to the news the whole time.

There is a TV room, but I haven't been, she said. I can't bear TV voices. I can't stand the way the world talks. I . . .

but she stopped. She was repeating things Clive said. Oh, and a counsellor came to see me, of course.

Any good? Vince felt more relaxed now; she doesn't know. He told me I'd chosen a dangerous way to cry for help.

Is that all?

Michela sighed. I didn't really talk to him. I've seen counsellors before. They work for money. My mother's seen millions of counsellors.

Did they get in touch with your mother?

I wouldn't give them her number. Michela lifted her face in a wry smile. Can you imagine? Another hysterical loser is the last thing we need.

You're not a loser.

Oh please, the girl said abruptly.

Vince breathed deeply. So what are you going to do when they discharge you?

I'll have to see through this summer. There are the canoes to be paid for. We owe the bank.

Vince said: I've been thinking about that.

What?

I've been thinking about your business. Frankly, you need to do a few sums again.

In what sense?

You're not charging enough for what you're giving, for the investment you've made. I picked up a couple of papers off the floor, in the chalet, and couldn't help but see some of the figures. I hope you don't mind. If you want, I could work out the right price to ask.

Clive did all of that, she said. Talk to him when he gets back.

I will. The fact that she was so convinced that Clive was coming back made his melodramatic suspicions about Berlin seem ridiculous. Again they fell silent. The heat in the little

206

courtyard was oppressive, yet neither of them mentioned it. Finally Vince took a piece of card from his pocket. Tom asked me to give you his e-mail.

Who?

Tom. Tom.

Right! Oh God, she put her face in her hands, shaking her head. He watched her. Was she laughing or crying? I am drawn to this unpredictability. Without looking up, Michela reached out an open hand for him to put the card in, took it and shredded it into little pieces. They sifted down onto the gravel. Tom, she sighed. She was still shaking her head.

Vince said, So why don't you tell me about you and Clive?

After a moment she threw her head back rather dramatically. Took you a while to ask, didn't it?

Vince held steady. She is wishing I would go. She doesn't want me here. Yet for some reason, even if it was only the merest social inertia, Michela began to talk. They had met in London, she said, at a peace rally. She began to tell Vince the story of herself and Clive, how she had liked him at once, how enthusiastic he had been, how full of projects. They went for long walks across the city, talking about everything they saw, kissing, hugging. They liked to walk in the rain, roll cigarettes under bus shelters. Clive really cared about things, about mountains and rivers, got so upset at the state of the world. He looked after me in every possible way, she said. When she glanced up at Vince there were tears in her eyes. They had made love so much. They started living together only a couple of days after they met. Nottingham. Carlisle. I'd never lived with a man before. Clive had been teaching an outdoor survival course. He taught me how to paddle. He's a great teacher. When he wants to be. But sometimes he sort of loses interest. He hates bullshit and hypocrisy so much. He's sort of obsessed by the way people just go on and on consuming. Then we went to the French Alps. He was teaching courses on the Durance. I worked in a restaurant to build up some money. It was wonderful.

So you should be happy, Vince said.

Don't pretend to be stupid! She glared. I hate that!

What I meant—

What you want to ask is why I kissed you under that waterfall, why I went after Tom like that.

Again he felt that flutter of excitement. Actually I was thinking more of your tossing away your paddle at the top of the rapid.

The kiss meant nothing, she said. It was a joke.

Vince watched her. She smiled now. As always there was a sardonic twist to the lips. The fact is I'm not good enough for Clive. That's the truth of the matter.

Rubbish.

Perhaps I know things you don't. She was biting the inside of her lip now.

Tell me.

You wouldn't understand.

Vince waited. Michela had put her feet on the ground and was sitting forward now, her hands on her chin. She turned her face to him rather brashly.

A couple of weeks ago he said he wouldn't fuck me anymore because I was no good in bed.

I don't believe you.

Oh well then, if he doesn't believe me! If the banker doesn't believe me!

Clive doesn't seem to me the kind of man who would talk like that.

She had begun to breathe very deeply. She pushed her head down, between her legs almost, breathing hard. For a moment he thought she might be sick. Instead of leaving be, he asked. Why don't you just tell me the truth? It can't be that bad.

Sounds like you didn't believe your wife was the kind of person who did the stuff she did.

Vince let it pass. I'm sorry, she said. She spoke softly, half laughed. I just can't believe you haven't gone and left me alone. You should have gone. I can be really awful.

Still Vince said nothing. He has ceased to ask himself why he is bothering. Two griefs are calling to each other. Tell me, he says.

What's the point, he'll be back tomorrow.

There was a clatter and a young woman appeared, stepping backwards between the swing doors, pulling a wheelchair. She forced down the handles to turn it on its back wheels and pushed its occupant into the shade against the wall. It was a young man, his head lolling on one side, his tongue pushed out between his teeth at the corner of the mouth. Michela watched. The nurse squatted down and began to do something with the young man's hands. Almost before Vince was aware of it, Michela began speaking very slowly and softly. He told me this world was such shit that it was pointless our being together. Okay? He said it isn't a place for love. This isn't the right world, this isn't the right world. He must have said it a million times. This isn't the right world for love, Michela. For us. She was crying now, Vince saw. Not sobbing, just letting tears run. Her voice was still steady. That's why I can't watch the news, the atrocities, the wars, the elections you know? I can't read the papers, I can't listen to the radio. I'll just hear his voice telling me I can't love him. I mustn't love him. I see a fire, smoke, and it's Clive telling me it's not the right world. I see a truck with filthy exhaust, the same. I see a cripple on a wheelchair and it's Clive saying we mustn't have sex, we mustn't have children in an ugly world. Oh God! She put her face in her hands and sobbed. Vince sat still. He made no move to touch her. Deliberately coarse, she sucked up hard through her nose, then wiped her face on her sleeve. Her lips quivered. The eyes were miserable and defiant. Satisfied?

I believe you now, Vince said.

Oh, well, thank God for that. What a relief!

He hesitated. What I don't understand, though . . . I mean, he didn't leave you. You were still together. And now he's coming back and you'll be together again. I don't understand that.

You don't understand! I wish he had left me. I wish he had done something cruel and left me. He could have kicked me out when I went off with Tom. Everybody must have seen. He should have told me to get lost.

You could always leave him.

She tried to smile. I thought that was what I was doing on the river the other day.

There must be easier ways.

Not that I can think of! Then she was laughing and snuffling. No, don't worry. Don't worry, Mr Banker, I haven't the energy to try again. She shook her head. You can't imagine the energy it took. Actually, come to think of it, I can't believe my mother's tried so often. That must be why she's so wiped out all the time.

Unthinking, he asked. What did it feel like?

What do you mean?

When you did it. When you turned the boat over.

The question has surprised her. She sat back, closed her eyes, smiled. Actually, you know, it felt great. When I finally decided, like, when I said, I'm going to do it, I'm really going to do it, it was great. I didn't feel anything going down. I mean any pain or anything. I just let myself go in a sort of trance. It was the waking up that was shit. She looked up. And you?

What?

Well, you came down after me. How was it?

Absolutely terrifying! From nervousness, Vince burst out laughing. You know how Keith kept saying not to fight the water? Well, I started fighting the moment I dropped into the rush and the water won in about one second flat. The only weird thing is, he hesitated, wondering how to put it, the strange thing is that although it was frightening, I mean I knew I could die, I had the sense I was sort of detached, my mind was clear. And now I keep waking up wishing I could do it again.

I suppose, she said, that Clive came down with no trouble at all? She looked away.

That's right. She's still in love, he thought, watching her face. He made it look easy. As he spoke, Vince remembered the man's bearded face as he passed the rock that he, Vince, was stranded on. Yes, Clive had been smiling! But he didn't want to say this now. Instead he suddenly offered: Look, if you tell me what time they're letting you out, I'll come and get you tomorrow.

Why don't you just leave now? she asked. Aren't you supposed to have a terribly important job? Not to mention a lovely daughter. Why don't you go? You can see I'm all right.

Do you want the lift or not? I'll go home Friday. After Clive is back. As promised.

She looked up and smiled. He was struck by a certain mischief about her fine features, sly eyes, a wayward shrewdness. Okay, she said, taxi-driver.

Vince parked the car at Geiss and had a beer and a sandwich in the Brückehof while waiting for the bus. He feels good. He is almost pleased now to be so lost. Disorientation need not be a problem, he thinks. The bus came on time, full of housewives returning from their morning's shopping in Bruneck. An older man fanned himself with a newspaper. A couple of young hikers were consulting maps. Nobody spoke to Vince. He got off at the stop before Sand in Taufers and crossed the bridge to the campsite. The canoes were stacked on the trailer beside the chalet. Clive had told him where the keys were hidden. The boat he had been using was the third from the top. He dragged the others off, put them back, locked the chain again. My hand feels okay, he decides. It was two o'clock. Four hours to the deadline in Berlin. He has stopped imagining that it could be Clive now, yet feels attracted to those men. Suddenly all kinds of behaviour seem explicable. They are gambling their lives.

It felt strange putting his kit on alone. He took the bandage off his hand, clenched his fist, thrust it carefully through the tight rubber cuffs of his cag. Then the spraydeck, the buoyancy aid. Again he was struck by the noisy silence of doing things without others. He heard Louise's voice now: Dad, where are my thermals, I've lost my thermals. There was always something she couldn't find. And Brian's. I'm Brian, the boy had said, Max is the fairy. Vince smiled. Car keys, he thought. Where? He threaded the leather loop into the ties that held the boat's backrest. Perhaps I should have been a scout leader.

With the kayak perched on the bank where Keith and Clive had deliberately capsized them all the first day, he checked and double-checked the spraydeck, running his fingers round the rim of the cockpit. The tab was out. I won't drown. His buoyancy aid is tight, his helmet tight. I'm afraid, he thought. Just being nearer the water made the world cooler, even shivery. Now, paddle like a god. Vince tipped forward and the boat slid in.

At once, he was surprised by the pull of the current, even where the water was calm. He had barely thought of this when he was with the others. Perhaps because they always moved along together. He was already twenty yards downstream. He broke in and out of a couple of eddies to build up confidence. It was worrying how awkward he felt, how loud and inhibiting his mind seemed to be. I should be back in the City with my figures and phones and papers. Then he remembered the beep of a reversing truck coming through the trees, remembered the mist on the water, the ducks flying low. It was the quiet stretch before the first rapid.

There is no mist now. Midges rise off the shallows in small clouds. Where had they entered the rush? I was following Mark. But where? He back-paddled, ferrying a little this way and that. This is why people need guides. To choose the line. River-left, he decided. He put in three or four strong, determined strokes and met the chute perfectly. This was the place. He steered through the rush, saw the terminal stopper racing to meet him and began to paddle hard. But the river seemed to be higher today, the stopper more powerful. As he ploughed through the soft foam, the tail of the boat began to sink. The canoe was pulled down. Vince stayed absolutely calm. The icy water gripped his face. The noise was furious and muffled. Wait, wait till it flushes you out. Five seconds later he rolled up in calm water. Everything is in order. Hand okay? More or less. He is laughing. Paddle hard now to warm up again.

Two hours later, just moments from the get-out point, the bridge at Geiss where his car is parked, Vince made the inexplicable error. Moving out of an eddy into the stream, he tried that clever flick of the hips the boys made that sunk the stern into the oncoming stream and lifted the bow vertical. He was feeling that confident. It worked perfectly. The front of the boat reared up. Vince experienced an entirely childish thrill. He was on his back on the swift water looking up at the sky beyond the nose of his kayak. The boat came down on top of him. No problem. Under water, he was happy. He set up the roll carefully and swung the paddle. Basic self-rescue. Been here before. He didn't come up. Or rather, he came half up and sunk back. Still, no problem. He had got a gulp of air. He set up again. He repeated the roll stroke confidently.

The same thing happened. The boat hung a moment on its side, then sank back. Now his mind began to cloud. He can't remember how far it is to the next hazard. There are rocks in the water. There is a small drop, the rush beneath the bridge. Any second now something will crash into my helmet. Try once more. But his knee was slipping from its brace position now. His body was cooling fast. This time he didn't even come half up. He didn't get a breath. Now he is afraid. His right hand felt for the tab on the spraydeck and pulled. Exactly as he broke surface, his back slammed into the central pillar of the bridge.

The river split in two for a few yards here, rushing under dark arches. Vince had had the wind knocked out of him. The boat had gone the other side. He was sucked under a moment. The paddle caught on something. Then he was up again the other side of the bridge. All okay. But the boat was yards away. Vince swam for the bank. There were stones and roots. He stumbled, floundered, sat in the shallow water. Get your breath back. The car keys, he remembered then. The car keys were tied into the boat.

Recovering his energy, he was struck by the inexplicable nature of this reversal. Losing the boat, the keys, if he did eventually lose them, was not the kind of disaster that changed your life. An irritation, an expenditure. But why had it happened? I must get going, Vince decided. I must get them back. He was on his feet. I didn't try anything beyond my capabilities. The path, he saw now, was not on the road side, where he had climbed out, but the other. I did five miles of river with no real trouble. He hurried back to the bridge and crossed. The kayak was already out of sight. Five miles! He tried to trot, but his breath was short, the wetsuit rubbed behind his knees. Then less than a hundred yards from the end, I fail to do something I can do perfectly well.

There was no sign of the boat. He would have to scramble through a thicket now. Already he was seriously overheated in this powerful sunshine. For a moment he thought of taking off the heavy rubber cag, the helmet. But what if I need them to retrieve the boat? He pushed through the trees. The path has gone. I felt so confident, so sure, so close to taking a decision that would have changed everything. Then the river had rejected him, reminded him he was the merest novice. Or I screwed up myself, on unconscious purpose as it were.

The thicket ended, but there was still no sign of a path. A meadow of deep grass sloped down towards the river. On the opposite bank was a timber business of some kind. He had trotted almost half a mile through long dry grass before he saw it. The river took a sharp bend to the left, and immediately after that he noticed something odd, something red in the water. The canoe was almost completely submerged, pinned against a boulder in the middle of the flood.

Vince gazed. The boulder was the first of a small rapid. Nothing dangerous, a fall of only a yard or so spread over five or six little steps, but the pressure of the water that was holding the boat must be huge. The glassy surface curled upward to pour into and over the red hull. It was about twenty feet from the bank, and Vince has no rope with him. Or rather, he has a rope, in a throw-bag, but it is attached inside the boat. The cockpit is facing upstream, the river pouring into it. So he might be able to get at the rope. Or even the keys, though they were hidden away behind the seat. On the other hand, the water might have carried the throw-bag away.

Vince squatted on the bank and stared, lips pursed. Then, amid the anxiety, he began to feel the pleasure of it. The water swirled round the bend, piling on the further bank. There is a scattering of stones, some breaking the surface, some below; trees on the far side, meadow on this; the boat right in the middle, the water piling and nagging against it. High above, the mountains shimmer gently in the heat rising from the valley. Against the dark green of the forests, a hang-glider is spiralling with rainbow wings. Nearer at hand, a dragonfly darts over the muddy bank. Without the boat, no car keys. No ride back to the chalet. The river is challenging me. I accept.

Vince tried to measure the force of the stream. What if I allow my future to be decided by whether I retrieve the boat or not? He felt excited. He walked about thirty yards up from the boat to the apex of the bend. The water was sweeping round and away from the near bank across the river. You won't even have to swim hard. He plunged in. In his overheated state, the cold was even more of a shock. But it was too easy. The current was taking him exactly there. He steered himself round a rock. He mustn't be swept past. You're going too quickly! He grabbed at the submerged cockpit, missed, just got a hand on the handle at the bow. It was his bad hand. He saw the black stitches sunk in inflamed knuckles as he pulled himself along the top of the boat. The stream was holding him against the hull now. He grabbed the rim of the cockpit and felt inside. The rope was there, in place under a stretch of elastic cord.

With some difficulty, Vince had tied the leading end of the rope to the bow-handle and was planning to toss the rest, in its bag, to the bank, when the folly of this occurred to him. Without anyone to catch it, the stream would pull at the rope floating in the water and carry it away. I need someone on the bank. Pressed against the kayak, his shoulders just above water, he untied the rope with fingers that had already lost their sensibility. Can I throw it unattached? It must reach the bank with the trees. No. Feeling under water, he loosened the waist of his cag, thrust the rope between the two rubber layers and tightened the waist again. Then he pushed off sideways into the rapid.

It wasn't so much a question of swimming, but holding his body in such a way as to reduce the blows to a minimum. This isn't serious stuff, he thought, letting the water flush him through. As he was swept round the end of the bend into calmer water, he remembered the boys' four-star test. Clive prepared us well. It isn't him in Berlin. As soon as he had passed the rapid he began to swim to the shallows.

On the wooded bank, he scrambled back upstream through thick undergrowth till he was opposite the boat. He unravelled all the yellow rope from its bag, tied one end around a slim tree-trunk and the other to the belt of his buoyancy aid. Just before plunging in again, he suddenly thought: Stop, think. Nothing more dangerous than momentum.

He sat on the edge of a four-foot drop into the water. He was on the other side of the river now. The bank was undercut by the current swirling against it. Instead of taking him towards the boat, it will pull him back in to the bank. Vince stared. If I swim diagonally into the current, as if ferrying, how far will I get? He had no idea. I must psyche myself up, he decided. I'm tired. Fleetingly, he was thinking of the memorials on the mountain. People who no doubt thought they could overcome some obstacle, or didn't even realise they were in danger. We know catastrophe is awaiting us, wrote the psychologist on the *Guardian*'s web-pages, yet we choose not to see it. The hell with that, Vince grinned. He started to walk upstream. Twenty yards from the tree where the rope was tied, he chose his spot. For perhaps a minute he took long deep breaths, filling his lungs. Now, plunge and swim.

Keith called it power swimming. Head well out of the water in case of rocks, arms crawling like crazy, feet paddling hard. I'm being swept away. Pointing upstream and across, fighting like mad, he can't see the boat. Something banged his left knee. Then his helmet. I've overshot. No, it was the boat's stern. He grabbed it. Suddenly, his body is dragged under. The rope has snagged on something on the river bed. It's tight. The current is pulling him below the stern of the boat. Calm. Vince tugged. It won't come loose. Don't wait to be short of breath. He released the buckle of the life-jacket, let the rope go and was swirling through the rapid again. This time, before he could get into position, feet first on his back, he took a fierce knock on his shoulder. For a second his mind clouded. Then he was through to the calmer water, swimming for the shore.

He needed more time to rest now. Sitting against a tree-trunk, eyes closed, his thoughts have lost any structure. The river, the boat, Gloria, the men chained to the railings in Berlin, the girl's lips approaching his, the torch coming through the undergrowth, his daughter's perfume bottle, Dyer's voice: We were expecting you back . . . everything is present to his mind. Everything is muddled, as if dissolved in the blood flooding his head. Slowly, he began to focus again. There's no real danger, he thought. I'm just tired.

He fought his way along through the undergrowth, found the rope, pulled it in. One tug in this direction and it came easily. This time he packed the rope back in its bag and clipped the bag itself to the life-jacket belt. It would unravel as he swam, rather than being loose from the beginning. That way it shouldn't snag. He walked back to where he had dived in. A fish flipped up from the water. A trout presumably. This must be the last attempt, though, he told himself. He feared for the moment when his strength would just go. Adam had warned them of that moment. The cold finally gets to you. Now dive.

Vince tried to keep the strokes fast and determined. Suddenly he had a sense that he was both fighting the water and not fighting it. Perhaps this was what Keith meant. He was fighting, but not *against* the water. Use the thrust to force your way across. Then he was sweeping past the boat on the far side. Almost a yard further than last time. The rope wrapped around the boat, under it probably, and held. At once, he grabbed the rope tight and pulled himself, like a climber, into the small boiling eddy behind the boulder. He could stand here.

Now he was behind the rock with the boat on the other side. Without the pressure of the water against him, he could move. He had time. He tied the rope to the bow-handle. Now all he had to do was dislodge the canoe. He kicked and pushed and shoved. It won't budge. It needs to be pulled away sideways, he realised, slipped between the opposing pressures of current and rock. Whereas I am behind it.

Vince is almost screaming with frustration now. Then he understood. Once again, he launched into the flood, let himself be flushed through the rapid, swam to the bank, climbed back, very slowly, to the tree, the rope. He sat on the bank a while, just gazing at the yellow rope sinking into the white water, attached to the red hull. Then he began to pull. The rope came taut. At the third tug he felt the boat shift, it definitely shifted, and with a couple more yanks it was free. It went tumbling away through the rapid. Vince lifted the rope as high as he could to keep it clear of the rocks. Good. Inevitably rope and boat were swinging in to the near bank. Vince scrambled back downstream. When he arrived, the canoe was already there, banging against the bank, the yellow rope taut.

He pulled the canoe ashore, felt inside with shaking hands, found and released the buckle, retrieved the keys. Then leaving canoe and kit in the trees, he began the long walk back. There was no way along the bank this side. He had to strike away from the river till he reached the road. Then it was a good half mile. He kept stopping to sit. Have I ever been so tired? But his mind was full of pride. I did it! I screwed up, then I put things right. This is infantile, he thought. He felt wonderful. Towards Geiss he was aware that the sun had fallen behind the peaks. Already! The wetsuit was chafing him, under the arms, behind the knees. How late is it? he wondered. The boat will have to wait till tomorrow.

When he reached the car, he didn't even have the energy to undress and change clothes. Seven o'clock. He turned on the radio. I should have put some food in here. I need sugar. Checking his mobile for messages, he was vaguely aware that the German newscaster he was listening to had used the word *Mord* in the headlines. *Selbstmord*. When are you coming back, Dad? Louise had written. Miss you. Things to talk about. An hour later, in bed in the chalet, he thought again, it won't be Clive. The American Forces radio station said that the protestors were as yet nameless. They had blown themselves up before the deadline when an armoured car had approached them.

PASSWORDS

Vince already had the boat loaded in the back of the car when he reached the hospital. His left shoulder and right knee were aching. When Clive returns, he can tell her about it, he thought. But if Clive didn't return? Surely if Clive were one of the three, the police would know, they would already have come to the chalet. Vince had thought of hiding the laptop; but then someone might imagine I was stealing. Michela was already waiting for him on the steps at the main entrance, wearing dark glasses. Suddenly she looks like some kind of celebrity. She has a bright blue mini-dress. They let me go into town yesterday afternoon, she smiled. She seemed cheerful. I spent Clive's money. Then she added: I've decided to live, by the way. Her tone was deliberately casual. Glad to hear it, Vince told her. He was awed by her easy elegance, a sort of natural disdain she has.

Throwing her bag in the back, Michela asked, how come the canoe? He had had to lower the back seats. I went out on my own. This morning? She raised her eyebrows. The bruise on her cheek was almost gone. He explained. He had had to drag the thing through brambles. You're mad, she told him. You could have drowned. Against all his plans, this prompted Vince to say: Did you hear what happened in Germany? She was opening the passenger door. They were in the hospital car park. The pause she left was so long, settling herself now in the seat, wriggling a little to be out of the way of the nose of the kayak propped between the headrests, that he wondered if she had heard. This afternoon, she said firmly, I must check through all the kit. There's some administrative stuff to do as well. And tomorrow morning I'll have to shop, because the deal is that we have to provide the food for the first meal. They're supposed to arrive after lunch. She turned and looked straight at him, smiling falsely. I'm not to mention it, he understood. She knows. As soon as Clive gets back, he said, I'll hit the road.

When she opened the chalet door, she hardly seemed to notice the transformation that had taken place, the clean floor, clean sink, tidy table. She put her bag down. To work! Vince drove her to the post office, the bank, the internet café. She and Clive had a business e-mail. She made notes of one or two messages. At the post office there were brochures from equipment manufacturers. Invoices and cheques. Heads turned as she stepped out into the street. The blue of the dress was dazzling in the sunshine. She is conscious of those looks, Vince saw. She is enjoying them. But there is still something brittle about her. She is tensed for Clive's return. Take me to lunch, taxi-man, she told him. She is warm and mocking. The Schloss Café is good, she said.

This was at the end of a dirt road two or three hairpins above the castle that dominates the village. An ample terrace was packed with tables. What time did he say he'd be back? she asked. To Vince's surprise she has ordered steak and wine. They are sitting under a red and white sunshade looking down over pine trees into the warm green hum of the valley. Yesterday's river is a harmless brown ribbon flecked with white. Early evening, I think, Vince said. He didn't give a specific time. Vince has never bothered with sunglasses, but feels the need for them now. The slopes and mountains are pulsing with light. The very air is too bright. I should be back Thursday. He remembered Clive's voice. The man hadn't said when.

Good! She was rubbing her hands. Just a few hours, then.

He is struck by her cheerfulness. Her hair is glossy from a morning wash. Perhaps she's had it trimmed. She's eating and ordering without any concern for the price, as though this were some special celebration.

I was wondering . . . he began.

Ye-e-e-es? she laughed, raised her sunglasses for a moment. Her eyes are playful.

Wouldn't it be better, maybe, to come to some agreement with Clive, about the, er, money side of things, then for you to go and live elsewhere, perhaps, with friends. I mean, with the situation as it is, you risk getting upset. Or getting more attached, without solving anything.

She put down her knife and fork, patted her breast. I was wondering, she mimicked, head cocked on one side, voice pompous. Wouldn't it be better if Mr Banker minded his own business? She burst out laughing.

Please call me Vince, he said.

Anyhow, I don't have any friends, she said.

Vince found this hard to believe.

Not in Italy. And anyway I don't want to speak Italian. But we've been through that. I don't even want to think it.

Go to England.

Are you inviting me? she asked.

Vince was taken aback. Actually, I wasn't.

She smiled brilliantly. Please, Mr Ba— No, sorry, Vince, please, stop worrying about me. Okay? Come to think of it, after lunch, you might want to get going right away. If Clive is late you risk falling asleep at the wheel.

Vince told her he enjoyed starting a long drive in the evening, then stopping at a hotel as soon as he felt drowsy. She refilled her glass. She is drinking steadily. Behind her sunglasses he senses the eyes are searching him. She said: You think he might not come back, am I right?

Vince was caught out. Not at all, I just promised I'd stay till he did.

The waitress arrived, hovered, went off.

Why wouldn't he come back?

Oh I'm sure he will, Vince said. His voice sounded wrong. And then, I'll get moving, obviously.

They ate. The fare was standard but good. The day was too hot again, though they were pleasantly shaded, lightly dressed. Vince's body ached in various places from yesterday's adventure, but when sitting down to meat and wine these are not unpleasant aches, more reminders of being alive. Perhaps Michela feels the same way about the bruise fading from her cheek. There comes a point when a wound makes you more aware of the healing process than the damage. Even the tension between them is something to savour.

Tell me what you will do when you get back home, she asked. He explained that strictly speaking he wouldn't be going home. He must drive straight to the office. There would be at least ten days, non-stop, of sixteen-hour work stints, sandwiches grabbed in the canteen, a few hours' sleep in his service flat.

What's so important?

It was a question, he says, of deadlines for filing accounts, mainly for the bank's American operations. Things can often be accounted for in various ways.

You mean you have to look for loopholes, to avoid taxes.

Vince shook his head. Not at all. He smiled. Everybody thinks that. Actually, it's a question of choosing the form of accounting for every transaction that most nearly and clearly represents reality, so that everybody is in a position to understand what's going on, the directors, the institutional investors, the shareholders. If they don't understand the situation, it's hard for them to know how to behave.

So, at least with money, you know how to behave. She was smiling. She enjoys making fun of me, he thought. My job is more to do with defining what has happened, he said, not making the investment decisions.

And after those two weeks, you can go back to your house and daughter?

He explained that Louise lived with her uncle's family.

Why?

I spend the week in the city and her school is a hundred miles away.

You put your work before her, Michela said.

Vince has understood that these provocations do not necessarily indicate hostility. When Gloria died, I didn't know what to do. I was thrown. I thought the best thing was to keep working as before.

Giving your whole life to money.

Vince poured himself more wine. You let me off the hook with that kind of crude attack, he told her. Mouth full, she raised an eyebrow. Money, he spoke quickly, is that invention which makes all resources measurable in common terms and hence transferable, so that people don't have to swap a cow for a field. Yes? Or a goat for a kayak. The bank is that place where the units of wealth can be stored so that resources can be exchanged when and where it is most convenient. Or alternatively they can be used by someone else while the real owner is deciding what to do with them, so that wealth is not just left lying around in heaps of gold. A banker is not serving money, he's at the centre of a complicated network of exchanges that makes life possible.

Yes, Professor. Of course. But the way it actually works stinks, doesn't it? No one is thinking where the resources should go. Only where money is most likely to multiply. There's no morality in it, let alone compassion.

In my case, Vince said, the morality is in the honesty of representation.

She had finished. She wiped her mouth with a paper napkin, pushed her chair back, crossed her long legs. What do you do in the evening, then?

Vince shrugged. Nothing. I get back to the flat late. Bit of TV. Bed.

And at the weekend?

Maybe I take the canoe out on the estuary. Which is going to seem pretty dull after last week.

Or you could visit Mandy.

I could, yes.

You must have lots of friends, she said.

Not really.

Oh, I find that hard to believe. Again she is mimicking. She is almost too good at it. He smiles. Acquaintances, I suppose. Business friends. Gloria's friends.

You don't really want to go back to your job, do you, Mr Banker?

Vince remembers that Clive had suggested the same thing. Perhaps they had talked together about him. He decided to be honest. You know, I don't quite understand what I want. Actually, I don't know how I can understand.

It would mean knowing the future, knowing myself. I've changed.

You see, Michela said, I was right, you don't want to go back. The young woman seemed very pleased with herself. She lifted her glass to her lips again.

Vince looked down the valley. Clouds were gathering over the peaks now. Perhaps there was the first smell of a storm in the air. There seemed to be a lot of birds on the move. I feel I would like to take a risk, he said. That's all.

Like you did yesterday on the river.

I suppose so. I had a good time. I mean, even when it was bad.

You know what Clive says?

What?

A fragile candour crept into her voice. You know he liked to run rivers that he really shouldn't? Like on the last day of the trip. We should really have got off the river at lunchtime, you know.

Looking back on it, yes.

Well, Clive always says, the trouble is, after the high of getting away with it on the river, nothing has really changed. It isn't a real risk. That's what he said. Not a real risk.

Vince watched her. Behind the enigma of the sunglasses there was a sudden vibrancy. So, he asked, what would a real risk be, as far as Clive is concerned?

She was shaking her head slowly. He waited. You don't want him to come back, she said, do you?

Vince hesitated.

Tell the truth! She was trying to laugh, but her voice faltered. Give an honest account.

I've been worried he might not, Vince admitted now. Actually, well, I contacted a possible alternative guide, you know. Just in case. So you wouldn't be in trouble with this group that's coming, I mean contractually, if he doesn't turn up.

You did what?

Vince feels ridiculous. He explained his conversation with the people at the rafting centre.

But why should you care? It's nothing to do with you.

I . . . it seemed a way to help. Vince began to search in his wallet for the card he had been given. Shuffling through three or four, he heard her say:

So, you think Clive blew himself up.

Vince shut his wallet. He looked up. Her face wore a strange expression of triumph, pained and exulting. He shook his head. He didn't know what to say.

If he doesn't come back, you want to stay and have sex with me, right?

God! Vince was appalled. No. For heaven's sake, Michela!

Why else say you're staying till he comes back when you don't think he is coming back. I don't mind if you want to have sex with me. Most men do.

It's not what I want, and certainly not something I've been planning.

Don't be so upset! She leaned forward across the small table and put her hand gently on his. Vince can see the tops of her breasts. There's a sort of . . . she smiled, but slyly. Yearning is the word, isn't it. There's a yearning in you.

Vince said firmly. I'm sure Clive wasn't one of the people who blew themselves up. He's not that crazy. And I assure you that I'm not trying to get into your bed.

She withdrew her hand abruptly. Let's get the bill and go. She stood up, pulled the dress down a little on her thighs. But climbing into the front of his car, she asked, When was the last time you made love?

I beg your pardon.

Come on, Mr Proper, don't pretend you didn't understand.

But why do you ask me a question like that? She has him riled now.

Why not? I just wonder if you're, er, giving the best possible representation of all your various transactions. Laying it on, she said: I'm concerned for you of course. It was crazy of you to stay here when you should be back in London accounting for all that money. Oh, and by the way, I don't think those men who blew themselves up were crazy at all.

Despite his age, Vince has no experience of conversations like this. Perhaps this is why he can't leave be. Michela has a strange glow on her face.

Let's talk about Clive, Vince says. You didn't seriously imagine I thought he might be one of the three. Watching the road as they began to drive, Michela told him: The last time Clive and I made love was four days before your group arrived, and one day before two people were killed in a demonstration in Milan. I don't know if you heard. The police charged some demonstrators and two protestors fell under the wheels of a tram. We were right close by. That night Clive was mad. He smoked a lot of dope. Then the day you arrived, that night, he told me that we weren't going to make love anymore. He was obsessed that he should be doing more about everything that was wrong.

Maybe, Vince said, negotiating the unsurfaced road, to go back, that is, to what we were saying before – maybe the real risk, for Clive, would have been to settle down with you.

Don't be sentimental, she snapped.

Vince was remembering Clive's peculiar charisma. It had to do with a sort of sovereign aloneness. He turned the car onto the main road through Sand in Taufers. After a moment's silence, Michela picked up: Anyway, I told him, if he really couldn't live because of how things are in the world, he should do something important, not just go chucking himself down dangerous rivers. Again an odd ring to her voice made Vince glance sideways. Michela was sitting on her hands, back straight, lips pressed tightly together. He wondered then if she had bought her new dress and sunglasses before or after hearing that news from Germany. Seat-belt, he said. You haven't done up your seat-belt.

They spent the afternoon checking out the equipment. Michela changed into some old denim shorts. Vince pulled all the boats off the trailer and Michela got into them and checked what size of person they were padded out for, more or less, and put a sticker on the boat – small, medium, large. There were twenty people in this group, she said. From Birmingham. I hope I can understand their accents. But at least five would have their own kayaks. There was no one under seventeen. It should be a question of removing padding rather than adding, she said. Towards four, the first thunder rumbled far away up the valley. Clive will have to drive in the rain, she said. It would take him an hour from Bolzano.

They had all the boats out on the baked ground between the chalet and the pitches and Vince moved quickly to stack all of them on the trailer again and cover the top with a sheet of heavy plastic. Shit, we're two paddles down, Michela discovered then. The one Phil had broken. The one she had lost. If necessary somebody could use the splits, but that still left one short. I'll go to ask at the rafting centre, Vince offered. They'll have paddles. The first big raindrops were falling. A wind rose. All around people were hurrying to zip up their tents and tighten the guys. Stay here, she said. We can ask tomorrow. If necessary there's a place in Brixen we can buy from.

They hurried to the chalet. The rain began to fall in slapping waves. The wind gusted violently. Hang on, Michela said. Let's freshen up. She stopped just outside the porch, on the steps, and let herself be soaked. Vince was already in. The doors and windows were banging. He turned and saw her shoulders shiver as the yellow T-shirt darkened. Then she came in, drenched, laughing. But the moment everything was shut, it was hot again. How tense we are, Vince realised. He had thought they were relaxing, sorting out the boats. Instead it seemed they were more on edge than before.

It was past five o'clock. Her T-shirt was clinging to her body. Vince looked away. Bending forward, Michela peeled the shirt off, towelled herself quickly, put on another. Then took off her shorts. Her pants are white. He couldn't understand if she was doing this on purpose. She seems so natural, opening and closing a couple of cupboard doors. Where did you put my jeans? she asked. I can't believe you sorted our stuff out like this. Second drawer from the top, he said, I think. You're weird, she told him. He gazed determinedly out of the window where somebody was trying to ride a bicycle under an umbrella across a field of mud. There! She was dressed. Let's be English and make tea.

The rain beat on the wooden roof. They sat quietly over their tea. There was too much at stake to say anything now. Outside, plastic bags, bits of polystyrene, a sheet of newspaper, are being chased about in the wind. Michela's face is crossed by sudden spasms. Vince watches. A moment of misery is transformed into elation. She gets up and walks back and forth between sink and table. She throws herself on the bed. Oh shit! Suddenly Vince is aware she is smiling at him. A warm smile. Then she is gathering up an armful of clothes, kicking the wall. She wants it to have been Clive who killed himself, Vince thinks. And she is terrified he has done it for her. The news, the girl suddenly said. Where's the radio. Damn! It was a couple of minutes past six.

She found an Italian station. Vince can't understand. Her face is concentrated. She's sitting on the bed, chin on hand. Then, with a grimace, she turns it off. So? Oh various groups have claimed responsibility. Police think they may have identified the one who spoke to them, matching the recordings they made of his voice. They didn't say who though. Then she was furious. Can you believe they had some prick expert comparing them with the Islamic suicide bombers. I can't believe it. They're not terrorists. They didn't hurt anyone else. Then not a single word about what the conference decided! Vince watched her. Nothing, most probably! The girl was full of pent-up energy. Their world is burning up and all they can do is criminalise the people who care. She stretched forward and grabbed her ankles. For a moment her arms seemed to be straining to pull her legs towards her, while her knees thrust down against them. Ow! She sat up. In a hundred years from now, those men will be heroes, saints.

Vince's phone was ringing. He saw from the display it was his colleague, Dyers. Vince? Listen, I won't be in the office tomorrow when you get back. His wife's father, the director said, had just passed away. He was going to Edinburgh for the funeral. I just wanted to tell you what you'll find on your desk when you get back.

Vince listened and asked pertinent questions. At the same time his gaze met Michela's. Their eyes held each other's as they never did when they were talking. It was close in the room with the rain outside and the accumulated heat of the morning in the wood. Vince was sweating. I'll give precedence to the stuff from V.A. then, he said. I presume we can rely on their assessment. As he spoke, her bright eyes were intent and enquiring. There was just a hint of a smile on her lips. Vince imagined her passing judgement on the work he did every day. She wants to see into my world and dismiss it. Is everything okay there now? Dyers was asking. Ready for the drive back? I should be leaving in a hour or so, Vince said. Michela raised a mocking eyebrow. When he closed the call she was still watching him. Should be? she asked. Then she said, Look, call the airport. We can find out what time he landed.

Vince gave her his phone and she called directory enquiries. The rain still clattered on the roof. He said it was a charter flight, Vince remembered. Michela spoke in Italian. Her voice seemed sharper, more nasal. They were sitting together now on the stools by the counter beneath the window. The earth outside was black and splashing with puddles. The trees screening the river were waving darkly, but above the peaks, to the right, Vince could see a break in the clouds. It is easing off. Michela suddenly smiled. Waiting to be connected, she ran a fingertip round the wound on his left hand. Then she saw the white mark on his ring finger. She looked at him, lips pursed, head cocked.

Pronto? Sì. Volevo sapere . . . Vince didn't understand. The conversation went on longer than seemed necessary. Apparently Michela was objecting, insisting. He understood the words *Germania, Berlino, Dusseldorf.* She closed the call. There is no charter flight, she said. She shook her head. It's a small airport. There was a flight from Vienna this morning, Frankfurt early afternoon, Dusseldorf at seven. But it seems crazy to go from Berlin to Bolzano via Dusseldorf.

She stood and paced the room. He was bullshitting you. Oh fuck! She flung open the door. The cool air rushed in with a sprinkle of rain. Fuck and shit! Don't say anything, Vince warned himself. He was trying to understand. Perhaps the flight was cancelled, he eventually said. What reason would he have had to lie to me? Charters often get cancelled.

233

Perhaps he's called the campsite, to leave a message. At once, Michela was pulling on her sandals. She hurried off. Vince stood at the door watching. It was pushing seven now. A beam of sunshine lay horizontally across the glacier high over the village. I am afraid even of thinking of the next few hours, he realised.

Nothing. Michela came back. But she seemed pleased. She was smiling. We'll just have to be patient. Why don't we take a look at his laptop, Vince said. Perhaps there'll be some letter or something. The girl was wary. Clearly she is nervous that they will indeed find something. But as Vince expected, the screen demands a password. Any ideas? As he asks, he taps in, 'Michela'. Error! Incorrect password. Then 'No global'. And 'No-Global'. Error! He tried zeros instead of 'o's. Stopper, she said. He likes those river words. Eddy-out. Vince typed in one after another. She was standing at his shoulder watching. Error!

I give up, she suddenly said. What do I know about Clive in the end? Nothing. Vince kept typing. I mean, I know him, but I don't know anything about him. He never said much about his family, old girlfriends, anything. Vince stared at the small luminous rectangle. Come on, he said. Try, think. But how can you ever know the word another person will choose? After all, Vince had never found the password Gloria used for her e-mail. Kyoto, Michela said. Destiny, Vince tried. No doubt there would have been some way of accessing the program, with expert help, but he hadn't bothered. He had packed her computer away and forgotten about it.

Rabiaux, Michela said. That's the name of this mad wave he loved to play on in France. They do rodeo competitions there. R-a-b-i-a-u-x. It's on the Durance. Error! Incorrect password. Rebel then. The girl began to laugh. She is relieved when the error sign comes up. Paddle. Puddle. Ferry-glide.

234

Break-in. Break-out. The sheer fact. She was giggling. He always says that. The sheer fact is . . . It drives me crazy. Free-style. Rodeo. Vince gave up. She had put a hand on his shoulder. He turned to look at her. Maybe we might go out and grab a pizza, he said. He'll already be here when we get back and I can set out on a full stomach.

They sat in the same pizzeria with the ancient keyboard player and the clutter of kitsch. Vince explained that they had come here after that last trip, when she was in hospital. I booked the bloody place, she told him. And for next week too. They should kiss my feet the business I'm giving them. Then she asked: I hope everybody was properly concerned about me, by the way.

Waiting for their order, Vince ran through people's attitudes, mimicking. He isn't a very good mimic. But suddenly they were laughing together. It's as if we were happy, he thought. Amelia and Tom, he remembered, were both being terribly solemn and self-important, as if they were involved. He described the conversation with Tom. Michela did her characteristic head-shake. I should never have bothered them like that, poor things. At last the girl seemed completely relaxed. I thought she was a happy person! Vince did Amal's high-pitched voice. I really liked Amal, Michela said. She frowned. You don't think he was castrated or anything? Sorry, not funny.

The keyboard guy, Vince resumed – isn't he fantastic, by the way? – was playing 'El Condor Pasa'. You know? I'd rather be a sparrow than a snail. Gloria used to like Paul Simon, he said. My wife. Tell me about her, Michela asked. Having cut up her pizza into slices, she folded each one in long fingers, eating elegantly, with appetite.

Vince talked. He feels strangely at ease, speaking without pain or embarrassment about his wife, about the music she listened to, the sports she did, her rather brusque, efficient ways. We will drive back to the chalet now, he thought, and Clive will be there. I will shake hands with him, say a word or two about the prices they should be asking for their courses, then set off for England, the City. My desk is piled with papers. For a moment it crossed his mind to worry whether his passport was still in the glove compartment.

And your ring, she asked. She still had food in her mouth. Smiling an apology, touching her lips with a napkin, she looked very young, fresh, at ease. Vince explained how he had dropped it into the rapid. The moment seemed far away. It's the strangest thing I ever did in my life. She is attentive again, reflective. Perhaps you should do more things like that, Mr Banker.

Don't call me that, Vince said.

Their eyes met.

But you are, she said. I'll give precedence to the stuff from what's-its-name, she mimicked his phone voice.

If I was just a banker, I would have gone back a week ago.

That's true. Looking away, she said: I'm glad you didn't.

The chalet was as they had left it. Clive isn't back. Again the young woman was on edge. They spread a bin-bag on the damp steps outside the door and sat there together as darkness fell. The evening was fresh and mild. There was still thunder somewhere far away. Lights high up on the mountainside seemed nearer in the clear air, as if the night were blacker and softer than usual. After a while she slipped a hand under his arm. At what point will you decide to go anyway? Vince sighed. Good question. He felt anxious. Then he said: Help me put up my tent somewhere. I'll still be in time to leave in the morning. She didn't move. It's horrible putting up a tent in the wet. You can stay in the chalet.

Vince isn't happy with this. Michela, he said firmly, I am not, repeat not trying . . . Clive slept on the floor, she said, in his sleeping bag. If you've got an inflatable mattress, you can use that.

Every time headlights turned into the campsite, there was a moment of tension and expectancy. But the cars never came this far. Towards midnight she asked: Assuming it was him, I mean, you know what I mean, do you think he would have done it to prove something to me. Am I responsible? Or would he have done it even if he had never met me?

What kind of answer is she after? There are a hundred and one reasons, Vince said, why a guy comes back late from a trip, or doesn't come back at all for that matter. The car, he suddenly thought, their Jeep! The thing to do would be to find out where the Jeep was, whether it had been abandoned. Though even that wouldn't actually prove anything. Out loud, he said: Whoever blew themselves up like that, it was their decision and no one else's. He paused. Like it was your decision to go down the rapid the way you did. You can't blame Clive for that. On the contrary, you put his life and mine at risk. That's true, Michela said. Keith and Mandy, Vince went on, kept talking about a community experience, and it was, I suppose, but that doesn't mean people aren't responsible for themselves, does it? This car, he thought, as headlights swept into the site, this will be the one. Here he is. The headlights were in fact coming their way. They were passing the bathrooms. He felt her hand tense under his arm. The lights stopped abruptly and went out two chalets away. She sighed. She is shaking her head. It's so weird, not knowing if he's alive or dead. And no one to phone. There's no one I can ask.

When Vince went to the car for the inflatable mattress, she called, Vince! He already had it under his arm. You may as well sleep with me.

I told you—Vince began.

It's not an invitation to have sex. She was giggling. It's a big bed. Keep your clothes on if you like.

I'll be waking you up. I always go to the loo a couple of times a night. He was pleased with himself for having admitted this.

I don't think I'll sleep anyway, she said.

And when Clive arrives . . .

He won't. She seemed quite certain now.

But if he does.

You're not doing anything wrong. You slept in the same tent as your daughter last week. Anyway, he doesn't own me. He wasn't even sleeping with me.

There were still cars pulling into the campsite from time to time. Headlights swung across the curtainless windows. The wooden walls whiten and spin. Vince had lain down on the bed fully clothed, his hands behind his head, his legs crossed. She had changed into pyjama shorts and top. She didn't hide when she took off her clothes as his daughter did, and even his wife in her way, but she was quick and discreet. She got under the bedclothes. He glimpsed the long legs, the lithe stomach. She too turned on her back and lay still, listening to the last of the campsite noises, a tinkle of low music, a drunken voice. Vince's mind had just begun to drift, when she said: I'm afraid. At once he was awake.

What of?

Afraid he'll come back, afraid he won't come back. She sighed. Afraid he's dead. Afraid he just left me without even the courage to say so. She sighed again, turned and found Vince's hand. Afraid in general. What will I do now? I was so sure of him, she whispered, so sure. It was like, everything was decided. Then first he cuts me off. He won't sleep with me. Now he disappears, right when this group is arriving. I don't even know if he has disappeared.

Again there came the sound of a distant car. They waited. Then a door slammed, there were low voices. She laughed softly. Her fingers squeezed his unresponding hand. When I heard you on the phone earlier, talking about your job – this, that, give precedence, we can rely on so and so – I felt so jealous, the way you know who you are. You have a place. Her voice was a thread now. I'm not even the romantic girl who killed herself. After all, if I'd really wanted to die, I wouldn't have done something so useless as trying to drown myself within a hundred yards of a guy who's spent his whole life teaching white-water rescues. She laughed. She is on the brink of tears.

Vince opened his hand and let hers slip into it.

I'm afraid of everything really. The dark and the intimacy had freed her to speak. I'm always afraid something won't happen, you know, and at the same time I'm afraid it will. I was afraid Clive would want children right away, and afraid he would never want children. I'm afraid the planet will burn up and afraid they will prove us wrong, it won't burn up, and we've wasted all our lives protesting for no reason. She paused. I'm afraid of being weak, and terrified what it would mean to be strong, to take the lead. Clive always said, Be strong. Be strong. But I was always following. I think that frightened him. When we were paddling he would invent little tricks to make me go up front and take a rapid first.

Again headlights crossed the room. This time they didn't even listen carefully.

Maybe, in the end, we weren't really that different. Again she laughed softly. She lifted her head from the pillow. You're being very quiet, Mr Banker.

I'm listening, Vince said.

You're dirtying my sheets with those jeans, she said. Take them off. What are you afraid of? It's the woman's supposed to be afraid. I know you're not going to rape me.

I'm afraid of giving the wrong idea.

Take them off, she told him. Don't be uncomfortable.

Vince let go of her hand, climbed out of bed, removed his jeans. She was curled towards him. It was disturbing. He climbed back in.

I think, she resumed, so many of these people who do dangerous things on rivers and mountains are afraid. It's funny, but I'm pretty sure. Afraid of dying, afraid of settling down. Afraid of life beginning really, and afraid it will never begin. These sports are something you do instead of life. Suddenly, she propped herself up on an elbow. Do you see what I'm trying to say, Mr Banker? They're things people do instead of living. Really, you should tell your bank to invest in all these high-risk sports because it's what everyone really wants. Hang-gliding, deep-sea diving. To feel they're really living, when they're not in danger of living at all. She lay back on her pillow. Clive's problem was, he had seen through it. It didn't work anymore. That's why he was so sad. But you should invest your money in these kinds of things, she finished. You could get rich. Now she was running a finger softly back and forth in the hair of his forearm.

Vince said: How would you like to run the upper Aurino with me. Just us two.

The finger stopped. You what?

Tomorrow. We could run the upper Aurino again. You do the shopping early. I sort out the paddle and the guide at the rafting centre. We should have about four hours before the party arrives. If we don't take any breaks, we can do it.

After a thunderstorm?

It can't be any worse than it was last time.

She was intrigued. You have to drive to England, she reminded him.

If I drive through the night, tomorrow, I'll still be back Saturday morning.

In fine condition for a sixteen-hour working day.

Right, Vince laughed. Let's do it.

Suddenly, she threw an arm across his chest and snuggled towards him, her cheek was on his shoulder, her lips only inches away. My old banker wants to kill himself.

I want to run that river. With you. You lead.

You really don't want to go back at all, do you?

Vince was silent.

At that point, we may as well just make love, she said. Her arm tightened round him.

No, Vince said.

Why not? It's not so dangerous as running the upper Aurino, and it'll eat up less of your precious time. You can leave as soon as we've finished.

I can't.

She laughed. I know you've grown old counting all that money, but not that old.

I'm terrified, Vince said.

The girl's grip softened a little, but the arm stayed where it was. After a minute or two, he said quietly, I would like to run that river again.

You can count me out, she whispered. I've chosen to live.

The minutes ticked by. The air coming through the window was chill now. Soon someone would have to close it.

Listen, Vince eventually said. Are you listening?

Ye-e-e-es.

If Clive doesn't turn up, tonight, before lunch tomorrow . . .

Which he won't.

I think he probably will.

Let's say he might.

Well, if he doesn't, what about . . .

Ye-e-e-es.

Vince hesitated.

Mr Banker will try to make love to me?

No. No. What about . . . if I stay. He stopped.

What do you mean?

I stay and run these summer courses with you. I phone the bank, tomorrow, and tell them I'm resigning.

Again she lifted herself on an elbow. She was looking down on him. You're not serious.

I wouldn't say it if I wasn't. He smiled. I'm always serious.

Well, you're mad then. You're more suicidal than I am.

The only thing I want to know, he said, is whether you would like me to stay, or not.

Don't make me responsible, she objected quickly.

It would always be my decision. You haven't forced me to do anything. You haven't even invited me.

Where would you stay? she asked.

I have my tent, Vince said. My airbed.

You can't spend the whole summer in a tent.

Why not?

Not at your age.

Go to hell. Now, would you like me to stay or not?

And afterwards? When summer's over?

I don't know. I haven't thought. I want to do something different. I've got enough money in the end. I don't need money. I've decided I want to do something different. Work for a cause even. I don't know.

Not because of me?

Vince hesitated. Maybe partly because of you. Does it

242

matter? I know there can't be anything serious between us.

Why not?

You're in love with Clive. He'll be back in the end. You just said how old I am. And there are thousands of nice young men.

Michela sank back on the bed. She shook her head, then giggled. Funny if he arrived now.

So? Vince asked.

I won't say, she said. It's your decision, regardless of me.

But you won't stop me.

I'll tell you after you've phoned the bank and resigned.

Vince thought about this. Fair enough, he says. I'll call as soon as someone's in.

They lay in silence for perhaps five minutes, then Vince got up to go to the loo. He closed the window and let himself out. The night was bright with stars and the gleam of a crescent moon. The glow of the sky made the mountains loom darker. Vince stopped and gazed. Was it that all life until now had been a tired spell, from which he was suddenly released? Or was it this situation that was snatching him from reality? The lights of the bathroom came on as he approached. He emptied his nervous bladder. Or each state was a form of enchantment, worth as much or as little as the other. Every place is its own spell, Vince thought. Walking back, something again forced him to stop and look around. The sheer bulk of the mountains imposes a sense of awe, he thought, looking away to the jagged silhouette of the peaks. I'm impressionable, he decided.

Entering the chalet, he found to his surprise that Michela had fallen asleep. She has invaded his side of the bed. He climbed in and lay beside her. He is cramped. I'll never sleep. What if Clive had killed himself. It must be so horrible for

243

her. Very lightly, he allowed his fingers to push her short fringe across her forehead. We haven't really taken this in yet. The skin round the eyes tensed, wrinkled, relaxed again. Michela, he whispered, not to wake her. It is impossible to imagine the girl will ever be his lover. She is playing with me. She likes to mock. To lose such a woman would be terrifying, he thought. Yet, Clive had thrown her away. Clive, Clive, Clive. His mind drifted. You were always awed by men like Clive . . .

Then, towards dawn, there was a sudden explosive clatter and the door banged open. A hot wind rushed in. Vince is sitting up, rigid, staring. Clive! The man seems appallingly dishevelled, grizzled. Wally is swinging from his neck. Vince, what the hell are you doing here? Vince looks down. The girl is still asleep. Vince can't open his mouth. He shook his head. We haven't. It's not . . . Clive swung off his backpack and banged it on the floor. He was laughing, a loud, booming laugh. Well, you should have, mate. While you had the chance. And he began stripping off his clothes. He is going to get in the bed too. There is a strange smell in the room, Vince noticed. Rather boldly, he said: So you didn't blow yourself up, then? Clive stopped. Yes, I did. Of course, I did. Vince stared. What do you think that smell is? It was burning. Clive's hair is smoking. Wally too. The air is full of ash. *Gefährlich!* he shouts. *Draussen!* His clothes are black. His legs slipping out of his jeans are charred stumps. There is ash on the floor, ash on the bed. You throw a handful of ash in the river and it comes back in clouds. Vince can taste it on his lips. Do you think, Clive laughs, I'd be afraid of blowing myself up? Thrust close to him now, the face is blackened bone around gum-less, grinning teeth.

Vince! For Christ's sake. His waking eyes met Michela's. She's leaning over him. God, I thought you were having a heart attack. Vince breathed deeply. Stupid nightmare, he told her. What about? He collected himself. Nothing. The usual angst. She is on her elbow, smiling. Without thinking, he said, You're beautiful. I beg your pardon? Beautiful. She laughed: No sooner do you show a man you trust him than the flattery begins! Vince shook his head. I'm sorry, if I woke you. No problem. She resumed a sleeping position, turned her back to him. Then she said softly: I do know you're only after a nurse for your decrepitude. Yes, I'm ancient, he told her. Like the planet. Well, she was still teasing, I can't look after both of you.

Vince lay still. Outside the light was brightening. What time was it, five, six? Soon the bells would ring. In just a few hours he would have to make that call. The fact is, she went on, an old guy like you could pop off any minute. I could wake up with a corpse in the bed. He found this too cruel. Don't worry, I'll be in the tent tomorrow. Oh I don't mind, she laughed. Better than a man who sleeps on the floor. After a moment's silence, thinking of his dream, Vince said: He probably just had a problem with the car or something. I don't know, a flat tyre. Please, she said. Please. Let's sleep.

Vince knew he wouldn't sleep now. Again he found himself looking at her. Above all, the long neck, the soft V of glossy hair growing on the nape. How careful, it suddenly occurs to him, how careful I've always been! With what caution his life had been planned, his career. How they had gone back and forth, back and forth over the business of Louise's school, the possibility of a move to London. Then Gloria was taken. She was there one minute and gone the next. Just the one phone-call. Those thirty seconds of intimacy. I'm so, so sorry, she said. They had blocked out everything that came before. Vince gazed at this white neck, the wonderful pattern of that cropped hair. It is a miracle. Do you think, he asked then in a low voice – do you think it would be crazy of me if I asked if I could hug you? She didn't reply. She must be sleeping. Michela? he whispered. After thirty seconds or so there came a low chuckle. Sorry, I thought you must be talking to someone else. Well? Hmm. On reflection, yes, I think it would be crazy. The light was growing steadily now, sharpening the angle of her shoulder, colouring her hair. Yes, it would definitely be crazy, Mr Banker. You promised to stop calling me that. Only when I see you've phoned the office and resigned. I'm a sceptical modern girl. Hug me, he said then. She lay still. Oh, did you say something? Hug me. Sorry, what was that? *Hug me!* Just a hug, mind, he added. She turned and all at once her arms are round him, her cheek pressed against his. Vince held the girl quite tightly and waited.